MAPPING
the
RAILWAYS

Collins

MAPPING THE RAILWAYS

Collins
An imprint of HarperCollins Publishers
Westerhill Road, Bishopbriggs, Glasgow G64 2QT

First published as The Times Mapping the Railways 2011

Paperback Edition 2013
Reprinted 2014

ISBN 978 0 00 750649 1
Imp 002

British Library Cataloguing in Publication Data
A catalogue record for this book is available from the British Library

Printed in China

If you would like to comment on any aspect of this publication, please write to:
Collins Maps, HarperCollins Publishers, Westerhill Road, Bishopbriggs, Glasgow G64 2QT
e-mail: collinsmaps@harpercollins.co.uk
or visit our website at: www.harpercollins.co.uk

Search Facebook for 'Collins Maps'

 Follow us @collinsmaps

Historical maps available to view and buy at
www.mapseeker.co.uk

MAPPING
the
RAILWAYS

Julian Holland *and* **David Spaven**

With special thanks to

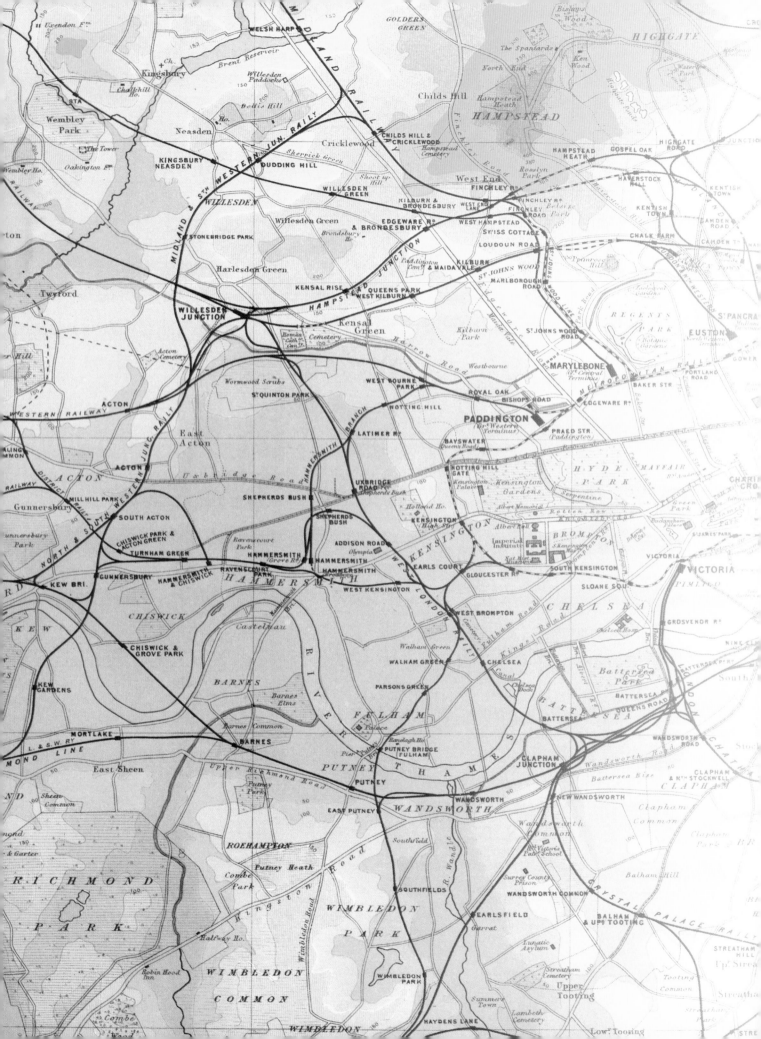

CONTENTS

INTRODUCTION

Britain invented railways, and can also lay claim to being the best-mapped country in the world. Put the two together and you have a recipe for adventure and discovery. *Mapping the Railways* illustrates the history of Britain's railways through a carefully chosen selection of maps – from a wide variety of sources – that have never before appeared in a single publication. While maps are, of course, primarily functional, guiding us across the face of Britain, they can also be a visual feast – works of art with a very practical purpose – as this selection demonstrates.

The inherent characteristics of rail operation – steel wheel on steel rail, on a guided track, within a segregated and signalled right of way – give railways a particular strength, in that the great reduction in friction between wheel and land surface allows heavy loads to be moved at high speeds with a small power input. However, this lack of friction prevents railway locomotives from negotiating the steepness

of gradients which road vehicles can readily tackle.

To minimize gradients, the construction of railways therefore demands careful choice of routes, and major engineering works on embankments, cuttings, bridges and tunnels – and this has had a distinctive impact on the landscape. The other major impact of topography on railways is through route curvature – in areas of more difficult terrain, the railway builders often faced choosing between sharper curves which would reduce the cost of earthworks (but would also limit train speeds), and gentler curves which would increase construction costs but allow faster speeds. The story of how railways overcame these challenges is well illustrated by maps, particularly those of larger scale.

Railways and maps have been closely linked since the first days of the 'iron road'. From 1803 – by which time the wooden 'waggonways' which preceded railways as we know

them were being replaced with iron rails – Parliament required the sponsors of new railways to submit detailed surveyed plans or large-scale maps of the intended routes. Once the successful schemes had received Parliamentary approval, and had been built and opened to traffic, the presence of these major new lines of communication in the landscape were inevitably marked on the various general topographic maps covering the country. In the era of early railways, lines would typically be marked on the privately produced 'county map' series, but from the mid-19th century onwards the publicly owned Ordnance Survey came to dominate the market for general maps – and the level of detail of railway features increased to reflect their central importance to Victorian economy and society.

The widespread, publicly available archive of general maps depicting railways and specialist railway maps allows us to trace the development of the rail network across Britain –

from waggonways, through the pioneering public railways of the late 1820s and the subsequent railway mania, to the zenith of the system in the early 20th century. The mid-20th century saw great changes on the railways, with maps graphically illustrating the drastic reduction in the network following Dr Beeching's infamous report of 1963. More recently, maps now record the growing patchwork of lines re-opened in response to population changes, road congestion and environmental concerns, while two entirely new rail routes have been built – the Doncaster to York coalfield diversion of the East Coast Main Line in 1983 and the Channel Tunnel Rail Link (or HS1) completed in 2007.

Mapping the Railways charts the history of Britain's railways through a unique collection of 121 maps, with different origins, purposes, design features and content. General maps, such as the Ordnance Survey and the Bartholomew's series produced until the late 1980s, depict railways in the wider topographical scene, and have always been in the public domain. The very first specialist maps of railways were those showing planned alignments of proposed routes as part of Parliamentary depositions – but many of these either did not succeed or were amended to follow different alignments when actually built. Railway companies also produced maps and plans to guide the construction of their new lines, and after 1853 were obliged to produce formal 'demolition statements' – illustrated by large-scale plans – if they wished to demolish more than 30 houses in any one parish in the process of construction.

Once new lines had opened, the railway companies were soon producing network maps – together with timetables – for existing passengers and prospective customers. Other specialist maps were produced privately within the railway industry as working plans for legal, estate, regulatory, system development, commercial and operational purposes – and in the latter category detailed plans and diagrams of rail routes were eventually published more widely in response to public interest. Last but not least, there is now a long tradition of maps produced retrospectively to illustrate the history of railways, such as the Jowett atlases, excerpts from which appear in this volume. *Mapping the Railways* also features three maps specially created for the book: the first showing lines which were reprieved from the 'Beeching Axe' as well as those which later succumbed despite *not* being on the

A triumph of Victorian railway engineering through the West Yorkshire landscape. An 'A4' Pacific-hauled charter train crosses Milnsbridge Viaduct in 1984, on the steep trans-Pennine climb from Huddersfield to Marsden.

Beeching blacklist; the second and third setting out railways re-opened and new railways built since 1969.

One of the key characteristics of the history of maps depicting railways is *change* – both in the rail network as it grew, contracted and eventually revived in modern times, and in the surrounding developments which were stimulated by the arrival of railways, and in turn subsequently influenced the extent and complexity of railway infrastructure in the landscape. During the boom years of rail growth there was a massive demand for maps showing railways – it was a time of unprecedented urban and industrial change, and, as succinctly explained by Catherine Delano-Smith and Roger Kain in *English Maps: A History* (1999):

> *Railway companies required maps for planning new ventures, and the fast-developing railway network was itself transforming the pattern of economic activity and the way land was being used. Regional specialisation in agriculture was intensifying. Urban-based industry was developing in conjunction with the railways as the latter provided a means for the assembly of raw materials and the distribution of manufactured products. All these processes brought a demand for printed maps on the largest possible scale.*

Luckily, a large number of maps have survived to help us follow the development of our railway system over a period of nearly 200 years. In *Mapping the Railways* you will find various examples of 'before' and 'after' maps, showing just how much the pattern of railways changed in specific locales; while comparison of the national maps demonstrates the radical differences in the rail network from one era to another – notably the rapid expansion of the mid-19th century and the drastic reduction of the 1960s.

Mapping the Railways has been designed to appeal to both the general reader and those with a special interest in railways, history, geography or cartography. The maps are presented in chronological order within eight broad eras of railway development, except where different period snapshots of a particular locale are compared in a single map feature. While half of our map features are devoted to the first century of Britain's railways, ending in the 'Grouping' of 1923, we have not neglected the modern period – from the last years of private ownership, through nationalization and modernization, the Beeching era and subsequent passenger rail recovery, to the new world of late 20th-century privatization.

Each map feature covers two or four pages. Many of the maps are shown three times – in their entirety, but reduced in scale to fit the page; in an enlarged extract; and in a 100 per cent scale extract over two pages – allowing the fullest appreciation of particular areas of interest. The maps are

The old and the new – Eurostar international passenger trains at rest below WH Barlow's vast trainshed at St Pancras International, terminus of the Channel Tunnel Rail Link (or HS1) since 2007.

interspersed and linked with 24 thematic 'mileposts' – illustrated with archive drawings, photographs, and railway ephemera; these explore in some detail a range of pivotal events, personalities and topics in Britain's railway history from the early railways through to the present day.

Every map feature is supported by a well-researched commentary, drawing out key aspects of railway history and geography, as well as any notable features of mapping design. While each nation and region of Britain is explored in the maps, we have deliberately increased the focus on those which particularly illustrate key aspects of the development of our railways – such as the role of the north of England in early railway building, Scotland in the development of railways for tourist travel through scenic areas, and London and the South East as the focus for one of the world's great commuter rail networks.

Of the 121 maps in this unique collection, some 20 are partially or fully 'diagrammatic', rather than topographically accurate 'geographic' representations – that is to say, lines of route are straightened and simplified on the map in order to ease understanding of the railway and its stations, or in some cases to fit into a particular format such as a brochure. A classic example is Harry Beck's London Underground map of 1933,

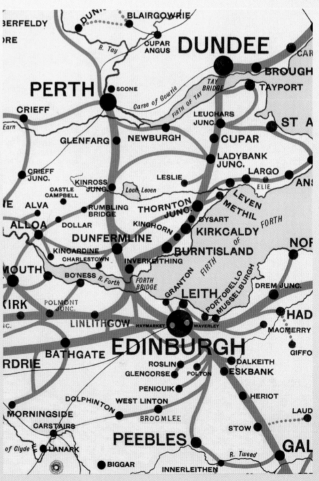

Right: an extract from the North British Railway's striking network map of 1896 (see pages 120–123)

which eliminates virtually all geographical detail other than the rail network – but this is not just a 20th and 21st century phenomenon, the earliest of our selection of simplified maps dating back to 1849. Towards the end of the book, in a feature on Britain's railways today, we compare the relative success of fully diagrammatic, partially diagrammatic and geographic maps in representing the national rail network in the modern era.

In *Mapping the Railways* you will discover, or rediscover, that fascinating combination of railways and maps, helping you to understand better the development of the British railway system over two centuries, or simply to appreciate a collection of maps which for the most part appeal to that most basic of pleasures – they are pleasing to the eye. We hope this selection of railway maps will encourage you to explore further our modern rail system with maps. *Mapping the Railways* includes 15 Ordnance Survey maps dating from 1851 to the present day, and in one of our later map features we examine the way in which Ordnance Survey representation of railways has changed in the last 40 years, as an aid to interpreting railways in the landscape in the current 1:50,000 Landranger series. But now it is time to begin our journey with maps through the history of Britain's railways!

THE RAILWAY REVOLUTION

From origins as wooden waggonways conveying coal, railways as we know them swiftly developed into a nationwide network of steam-hauled train services carrying both passengers and goods. The railways transformed the Victorian economy and made their mark on landscapes the length and breadth of Britain.

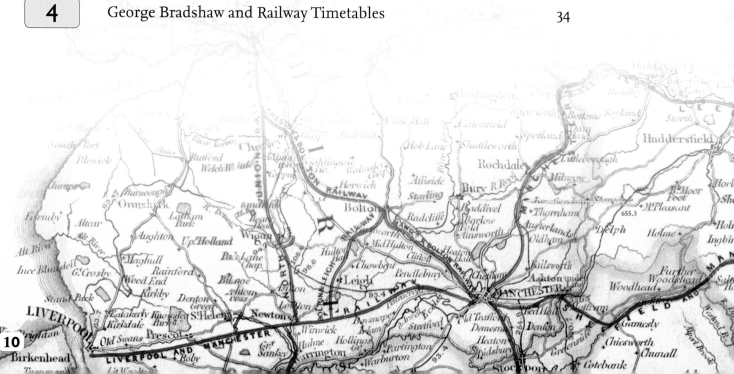

The use of ruts in rocks for guiding carts and wagons along goes back into the mists of time. Certainly the Ancient Greeks exploited them and at various sites around the Mediterranean quite sophisticated layouts still exist where the early engineers carved out contour-hugging rutways, sidings and passing loops.

However, railways as we know them began in the infancy of the Industrial Revolution in Europe and by the mid-17th century horse-drawn wagons with wooden flanged wheels were running along oak rails laid on wooden ties between collieries and the River Tyne in the Newcastle area. It was a dangerous operation with loaded coal wagons running downhill by gravity, their progress slowed by a brakeman operating an extremely primitive brake. After the coal was loaded onto a sailing boat the wagons were returned empty to the colliery by horse power. The problem with this early railway technology was that the wooden wheels quickly wore out and cast iron wheels, introduced around 1760, soon wore out the wooden rails.

The first recorded use of iron rails in Britain came in 1767 when Richard Reynolds of Coalbrookdale in Shropshire cast rails for use on his ironworks waggonway (note the traditional spelling). These proved an immediate success with the reduced friction between wheel and rail allowing much heavier loads to be horse-drawn.

While the latter part of the 18th century saw the dawn of the short-lived canal age, the evolution of the railway continued with various developments, such as Benjamin Outram's L-shaped plate rail which found favour in the South Wales valleys and Lord Penrhyn's double-flanged wheels running on oval rails in his North Wales' slate quarries. Neither of these progressed much further, the latter being particularly over-complicated at crossings and points.

Meanwhile down in Cornwall, stationary steam engines had been in use to pump water out of mines since the early 18th century. Further developed by James Watt, an additional impetus came when the first crude steam-powered road vehicles appeared in the latter part of the century. The most successful of these was built by Richard Trevithick at Coalbrookdale in 1802 and he was soon commissioned to build a steam locomotive for the nine-mile 4 ft 2 in. gauge Penydarren plateway which served ironworks at Dowlais in South Wales. Despite the locomotive's successful maiden voyage with a loaded train in 1804, the cast iron plate rails broke under its weight and the experiment ended. However, the viability of steam haulage was proved beyond a shadow of doubt, although it was to be some years before it superseded traditional horse power.

With the Napoleonic Wars seeing ever-increasing prices for horse fodder, the next 10 years saw major strides forward in the development of the steam locomotive. The public's appetite was whetted by Trevithick when he ran his 'Catch-Me-Who-Can' circular demonstration steam-hauled train in Euston Square (London) in 1808. In Yorkshire, John Blenkinsop designed two steam locomotives that operated with cogs and rail-mounted racks ('rack and pinion') for use on the privately owned Middleton colliery railway near Leeds. These first ran in 1812 and continued in use for 30 years on the world's first commercially successful steam railway.

The horse-drawn Parkmore Waggonway can be seen in the foreground of this 1783 view of Newcastle.

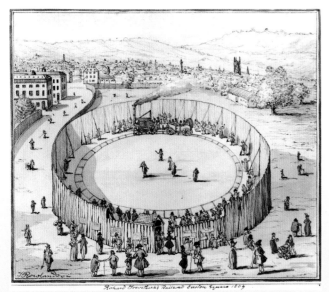

Richard Trevithick's 'Catch-Me-Who-Can' circular steam railway was exhibited at Euston Square, London, in 1808.

Near Newcastle, the Wylam colliery railway had already been operating as a wooden waggonway for nearly 200 years. The colliery's chief engineer, William Hedley, had the line converted to a 5 ft gauge plateway and successfully introduced his new steam locomotive, 'Puffing Billy', in 1813. Building on Trevithick's proven design of an efficient boiler with a single straight flue, his locomotive initially proved too heavy for the plate rails. To overcome this problem Hedley successfully rebuilt it as an articulated locomotive with two four-wheel bogies driven by gears.

At the same time as Hedley's success at Wylam a local self-taught engineer was about to launch himself onto the unsuspecting world. Born in Wylam in 1781, George Stephenson was soon to be known as the 'Father of Railways', the first great engineer of the Railway Age.

Built in 1813, William Hedley's 'Puffing Billy' was used at Wylam Colliery near Newcastle until 1862. The earliest surviving steam locomotive in the world, it was acquired by the Science Museum in London in 1862.

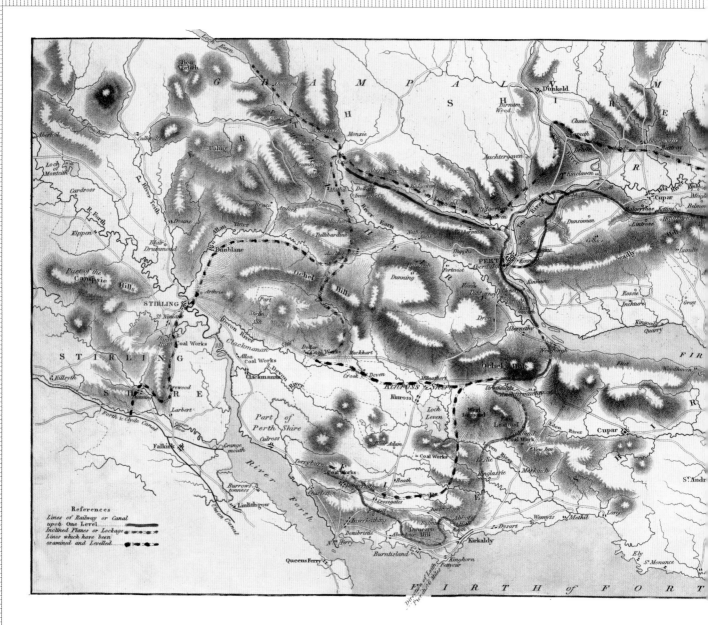

Title	Sketch of the Country from Stirling to Aberdeen. Referring to a Memorial regarding a communication by Canal or Railway through the Great Vallies of Strathearn and Strathmore.
By	Robert Stevenson, Civil Engineer
Date	1819

For a brief period before railways achieved their ascendancy as the most efficient form of inland transport, railways and canals could be planned almost interchangeably, as shown in this map setting out 1819 proposals for a new form of communication through Fife, Strathearn and Strathmore. Some 19 years earlier Dr James Thomson, minister of Markinch in his *General View of the Agriculture of the County*

of Fife: with Observations on the Means of its Improvement had commented that:

> *There are no canals in Fife. The situation of the county, between two large navigable rivers, furnished with numerous convenient harbours, from which the greater part of the county is removed not more than three or four miles, and no part above eight or nine miles, renders this public accommodation less necessary here, than in many other parts of the kingdom.*

However, Robert Stevenson (better known for building lighthouses, and, of course, no relation to George Stephenson) here explored a number of possible routes for canals or railways over a large swathe of eastern Scotland, including the coastal town of 'Aberbrothock', better known

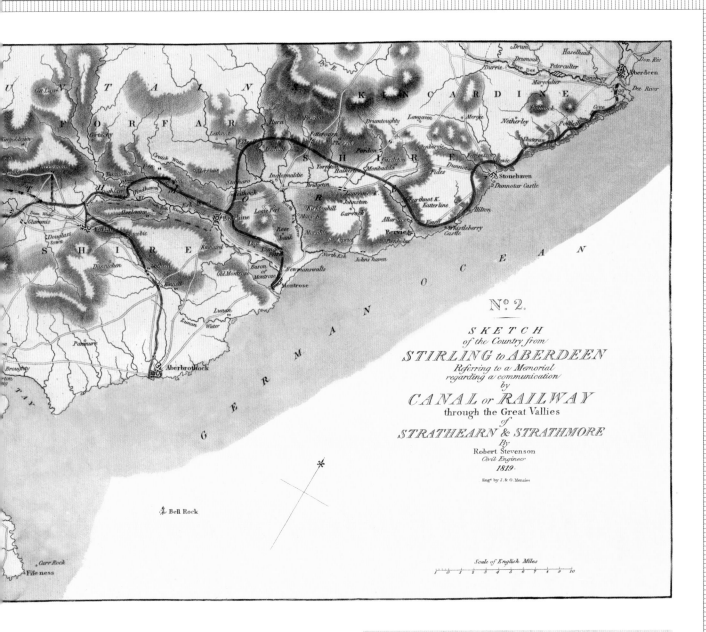

No. 2.

SKETCH
of the Country from
STIRLING to ABERDEEN
Referring to a Memorial
regarding a communication
by
CANAL or RAILWAY
through the Great Vallies
of
STRATHEARN & STRATHMORE
By
Robert Stevenson
Civil Engineer
1819

Engd by J. & G. Menzies

now as Arbroath. To avoid steeply graded ground, some circuitous routes following the contours were surveyed. The routes shown by red dashed lines were alternatives based on 'inclined planes' (cable haulage) or a series of locks, enabling railway or canal respectively to overcome steep gradients without meandering diversions. Interestingly the direct line that was eventually built between Perth and Dunfermline via Glenfarg (not planned by Stevenson on this map) required a six-mile climb at a gradient of 1 in 75 out of Strathearn. Very few stretches of the lines mooted on the map were built as railways on the alignments shown, not least because inclined planes or the alternative of meandering routes soon fell out of fashion.

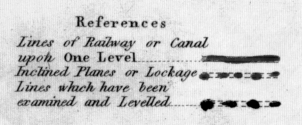

References
Lines of Railway or Canal
upon One Level
Inclined Planes or Lockage
Lines which have been
examined and Levelled

Several railways in Britain were built along earlier canal alignments, including parts of those from Glasgow to Paisley, Carlisle to Port Carlisle and the isolated narrow-gauge railway from Campbeltown to Machrihanish.

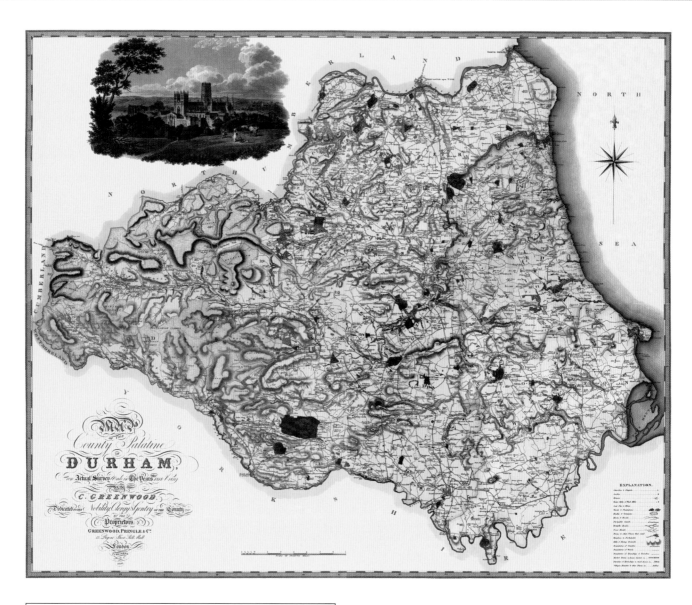

Title	Map of the County Palatine of Durham
Publisher	Greenwood, Pringle & Co.
Date	1820

The origins of the railway revolution lie in the waggonways of northeast England, linking collieries with the coast and with rivers. The Northumberland and Durham coalfield lay close to the coast, facilitating bulk sea shipments to London and other key markets, and wooden (later iron) waggonways evolved over a period of almost 200 years as an efficient overland alternative to poor roads.

The role of waggonways is shown in this map produced by Christopher Greenwood's long-established private mapmaking business, shortly before the Ordnance Survey secured its pre-eminence as *the* nationwide mapmaker.

'County maps' were funded by subscriptions, allowing the mapmakers to undertake physical survey on the ground, rather than simply copying earlier maps – and this map is hence specifically 'dedicated to the Nobility & Gentry of the County'. The word 'palatine' is derived from 'palace' and refers to historic royal privileges that were not finally abolished until 1836.

No waggonways or railways are actually shown in the map's key, but double-pecked lines trace the alignment of several rail routes. As shown overleaf, on the north bank of the Wear some miles inland from the coast, three (untitled) separate routes converged on Washington Staithe, where coal was dropped into keel boats which sailed down to Sunderland, with the coal then being loaded into larger sailing ships (colliers) for the journey to the London market.

The waggonway from the colliery at Bunker Hill or Philadelphia, near West Herrington, to Sunderland (marked as 'Railway' below) is the Newbottle Waggonway, which was a major iron-railed route opened in 1812. For 10 years it was the only line direct to the collier staithes at Sunderland, so avoiding the expensive use of keel boats and the transhipment they involved.

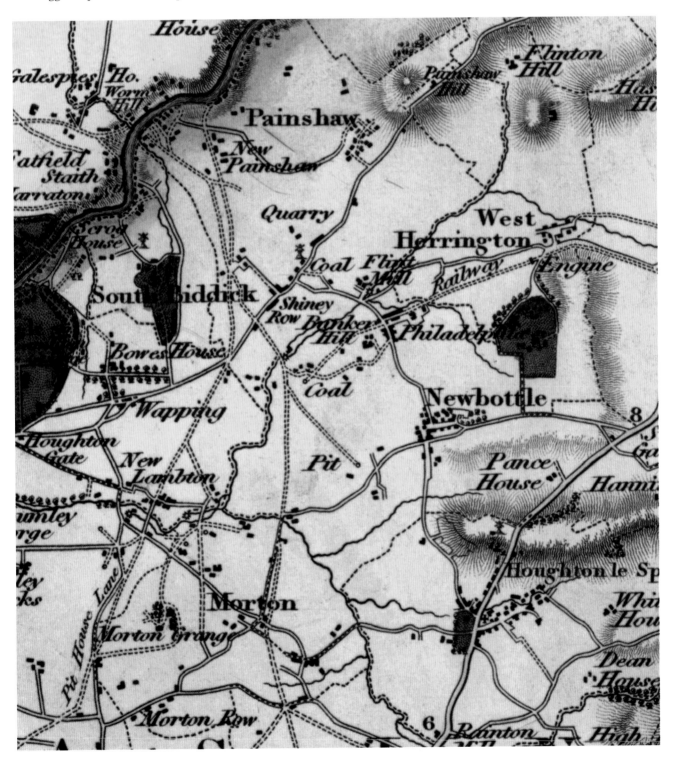

The horse-drawn Surrey Iron Railway was the world's first publicly subscribed railway. It opened for goods traffic between Croydon and Wandsworth in 1803.

Prior to George Stephenson's dramatic impact on the Railway Age, the world's first publicly subscribed railway had already opened in 1803. The nine-mile Surrey Iron Railway was a horse-drawn 4 ft 2 in. gauge cast-iron goods plateway that ran between Croydon and Wandsworth. Built instead of a planned canal, the railway charged tolls to private users in much the same way as our modern railways are run.

The world's first passenger-carrying public railway was also a horse-drawn affair. Opened in 1806 as a 4 ft gauge horsedrawn line, the Swansea & Mumbles Railway started carrying passengers a year later. Slightly ahead of its time, passenger services ceased when a new turnpike road was opened in the 1820s! The railway did however re-open as a standard gauge (4 ft 8½ in.) horse-drawn line in 1855, subsequently converted to steam then electric haulage, prior to closure in 1960.

Cheered on by a large crowd, the opening ceremony of the Stockton & Darlington Railway on 27 September 1825 is depicted in this modern painting by Terence Cuneo.

Back in Newcastle the up-and-coming engineer George Stephenson had been appointed engineer of the Killingworth colliery railway in 1813. His first steam locomotive, the 'Blücher', ran a year later – in most respects it was similar to Blenkinsop's machines on the Middleton Railway but, importantly, it ran on normal rails without the use of rack-and-pinion. Stephenson further developed his steam locomotives but their use on passenger-carrying public railways had to wait until he was appointed Chief Engineer of the Stockton & Darlington Railway. Appointed in 1821, Stephenson planned a 4 ft 8 in. (later widened by ½ inch to reduce friction) gauge railway to run from inland collieries at Witton Park to the River Tees at Stockton via Darlington. While the western end of the line was operated by inclines with stationary steam engines, the 20 miles from Shildon to Stockton Quay were to be operated by steam locomotives. The 1821 Act of Parliament authorizing the building of the railway also included provision for the use of 'moveable engines' and the carrying of passengers – the latter a unique aspect for a steam railway of that period.

The opening day of the Stockton & Darlington Railway on 27 September 1825 was as important a date in world history as 20 July 1969, when man first walked on the Moon. On this day and watched by thousands of people, George Stephenson's 'Locomotion' hauled a passenger-carrying steam train on a public railway for the first time in the world. Around 600 passengers on this first train were carried in the railway's only passenger coach ('The Experiment') and in numerous converted coal wagons. 'Locomotion' was built at Stephenson's new locomotive works in Newcastle and featured, for the first time, driving wheels connected by coupling rods instead of gears. T-section wrought iron rails, connected by 'fishplates' at 15 ft intervals, were laid on heavy stone blocks designed to take the weight of heavily loaded coal trains.

The world's first steam-hauled passenger train arrived at Stockton Quay to be greeted by a crowd of 40,000 and a 21 gun salute! The Railway Age had arrived.

GEORGE STEPHENSON

George Stephenson was born of illiterate parents in Wylam, Northumberland in 1781. His father worked as a fireman for the Wylam colliery stationary pumping engine. At a young age George went to work as a brakesman, controlling the steam-powered winding gear at several collieries in the area. At the same time he attended night classes to learn to read and write and to study mathematics. After marrying in 1802, his son, Robert (who became an important railway engineer in his own right), was born a year later. Stephenson's knowledge of steam engines was greatly enhanced when he was appointed engineer for Killingworth collieries in 1813. His first steam locomotive, the 'Blücher' (named after the Prussian general at the battle of Waterloo) was built in a colliery workshop behind his house in 1814. In 1820 he built the Hetton Colliery Railway, a combination of rope-hauled inclines and loco-hauled sections, the first railway to be built not to use horse power.

Appointed Chief Engineer of the Stockton & Darlington Railway in 1821 and opening his locomotive works in Newcastle in 1823, Stephenson went on to engineer the world's first inter-city railway, the Liverpool & Manchester Railway, which opened in 1830. His locomotive, 'Rocket', won the Rainhill Trial in the previous year, setting a world speed record for steam haulage of 29.1 m.p.h.

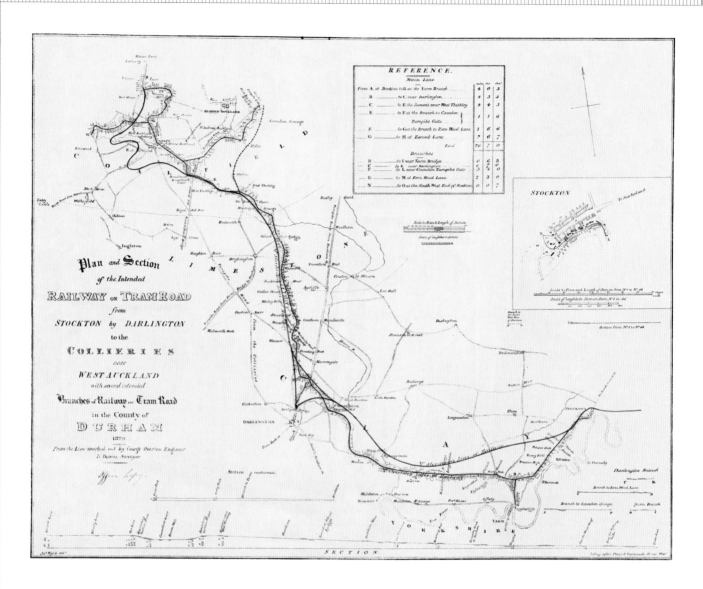

Title	Plan and Section of the Intended Railway or Tram Road from Stockton by Darlington to the Collieries near West Auckland
Engineer	George Overton
Surveyor	D Davies
Date	1820

From 1803 railways of all types required Parliamentary approval, and the provision of maps and plans of the surveyed route was a critical component of the legislative process. Inspired by wealthy local woollen manufacturer Edward Pease, this railway was originally intended to be a conventional horse-drawn waggonway or 'plateway' for the movement of coal. However, George Stephenson had been developing his steam engines at Killingworth for some years, and persuaded Pease that he should resurvey the route and work it by steam.

It seems likely this 1 inch to the mile map represents the first Stockton & Darlington Railway scheme, which was defeated in Parliament. A further Bill was placed before Parliament and received the Royal Assent in 1823, incorporating changes recommended by George Stephenson, consequent on his survey carried out between July 1821 and January 1822 – these included alterations to the route, and a clause added to permit the use of 'loco-motive or movable engines', setting the scene for the opening of the world's first steam-powered passenger-carrying public railway.

The history of the design of this railway is complex, not least because both George Stephenson and Robert Stevenson (no relation) were involved. As shown overleaf, the key features of this map (dated 1820) are the two different alignments shown – 'Mr Overton's Line of Railway' and 'Mr Stevenson's Line of Railway', the former designed in 1818 for horse haulage and the latter designed in 1819 for steam haulage.

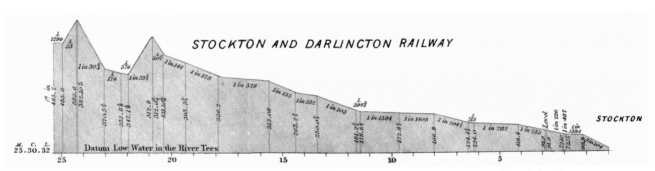

Taken from Bradshaw's map of Great Britain (pages 36–39), this gradient profile illustrates the virtually uninterrupted downhill gradient from the West Auckland collieries to Stockton.

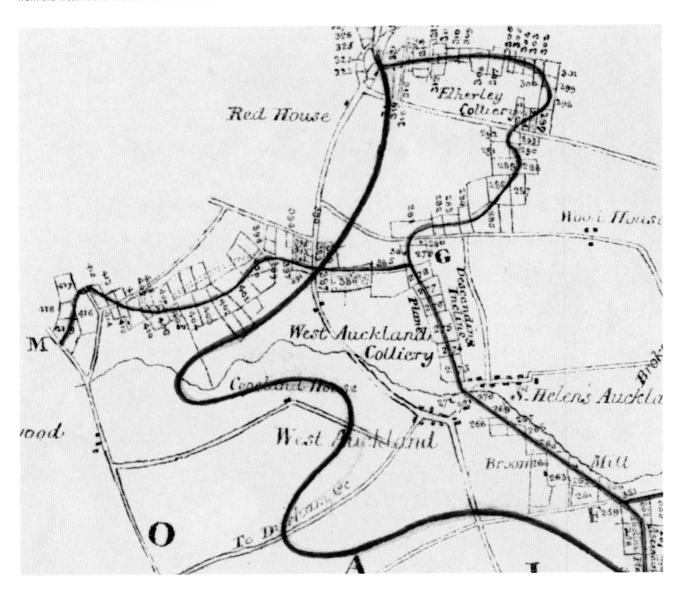

Overton's alignment shows sharper curvature, presumably following the lie of the land (and certainly running immediately adjacent to public roads in places), while Stevenson's is characterized by more sweeping curves.

Numbered plots of land for purchase are marked throughout the length of the proposed waggonway, but not in the case of the railway – suggesting that the development of the railway project was less advanced when the map was completed.

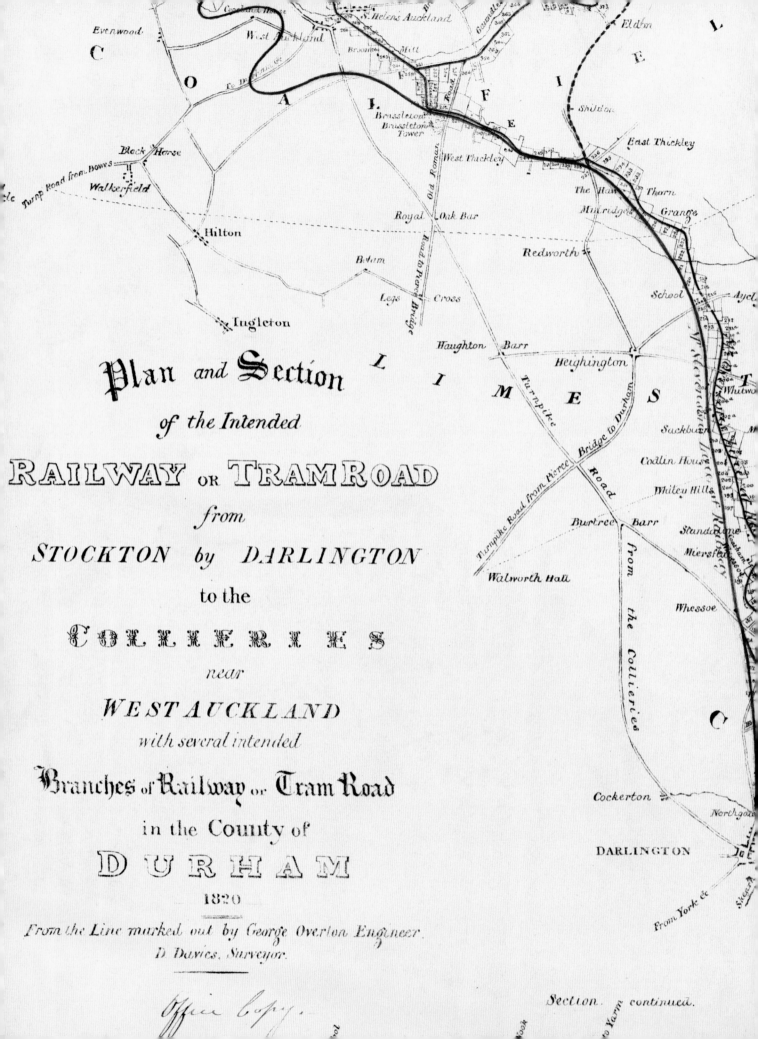

Plan and Section

of the Intended

RAILWAY OR TRAMROAD

from

STOCKTON by DARLINGTON

to the

COLLIERIES

near

WEST AUCKLAND

with several intended

Branches of Railway or Tram Road

in the County of

DURHAM

1820

From the Line marked out by George Overton Engineer.

D. Davies, Surveyor.

Office Copy.

Section continued.

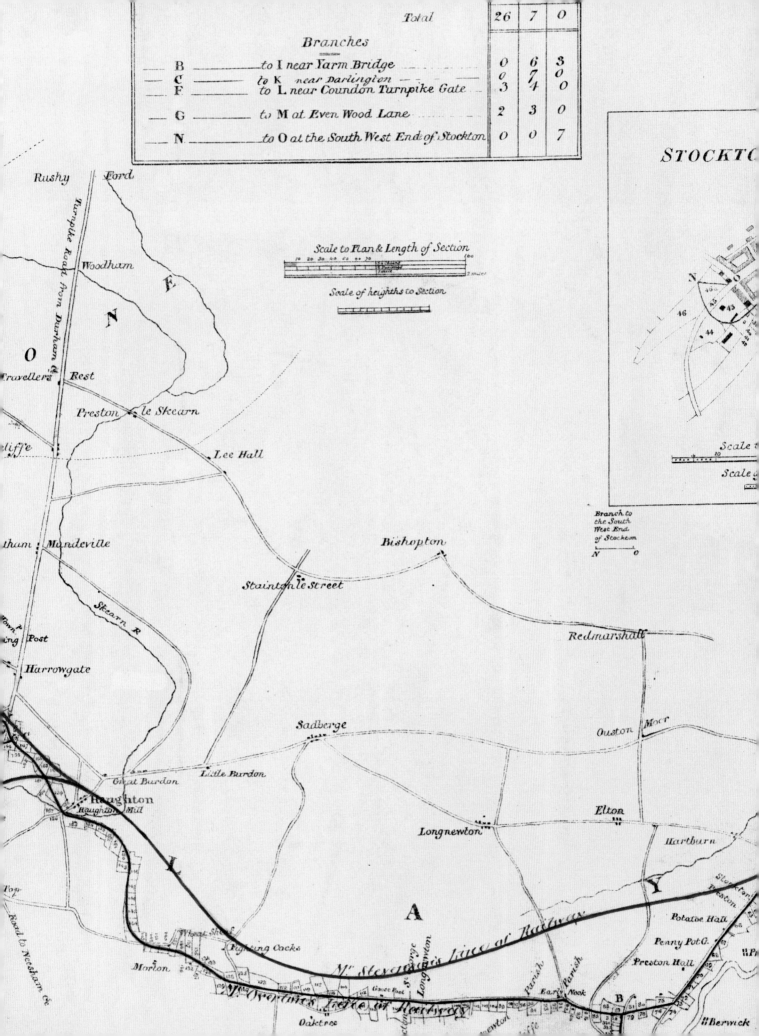

	Total		26	7	0
	Branches				
B	to I near Yarm Bridge		0	6	3
C	to K near Darlington		0	7	3
F	to L near Coundon Turnpike Gate		3	4	0
G	to M at Even Wood Lane		2	3	0
N	to O at the South West End of Stockton		0	0	7

STOCKTO

N
O
E
F

Rushy   Ford

Woodham

Travellers   Rest

Preston   le Skearn

cliffe

Lee Hall

Scale to Plan & Length of Section

2 miles

Scale of heights to Section

ham Mandeville

Bishopton

Branch to
the South
West End
of Stockton

N   O

Stainton le Street

Redmarshall

Skearn R.

ng Post

Harrowgate

Sadberge

Ouston Moor

Little Burdon

Great Burdon

Houghton
Houghton Mill

Elton

Longnewton

Hartburn

L

Top

Y

A

Road to Neasham &c

Wheat Sheaf

Fighting Cocks

Morton

Potatoe Hall

Peany Pot G.

Preston Hall

Mr Stevenson's Line of Railway

Mr Overton's Line of Railway

Oaktree

B

Berwick

The ROCKET of Mr Robt Stephenson of Newcastle.

George and Robert Stephenson's 'Rocket' won the Rainhill Trials on the Liverpool & Manchester Railway in 1829.

Even before the Stockton & Darlington Railway had opened, a group of wealthy Lancashire businessmen had founded the Liverpool & Manchester Railway Company (LMR). Designed to provide cheap transport for raw materials and finished goods between the port of Liverpool and the textile mills of east Lancashire, the railway was surveyed by George Stephenson in 1824. As his son, Robert, was in South America, George relied too much on his subordinates to check his calculations and the survey's inaccuracies led to the first Bill being rejected by Parliament in 1825. Stephenson was sacked and replaced by George and John Rennie as engineers and Charles Vignoles as surveyor. This time they got it right and the second Bill received Royal Assent in 1826.

When the Rennies proved too expensive, George Stephenson was reappointed as engineer with Joseph Locke as his second-in-command. Built to a gauge of 4 ft 8½ in., the 35-mile line was heavily engineered with 64 bridges and viaducts, a 1 mile 490 yd tunnel under Liverpool, the two-mile Olive Mount Cutting and the crossing of Chat Moss on a raft of wood and heather hurdles. It was a triumph of engineering.

While construction of the line was proceeding, Stephenson was also developing his steam locomotive, the 'Rocket', in preparation for a competition that was to be held at Rainhill in October 1829. Competing against three other steam locomotives and a horse-powered version, Stephenson's 'Rocket' won hands down, scooping the £500 prize and setting a speed record of 29.1 m.p.h. Stephenson was also given the contract to produce locomotives for the railway.

The LMR opened to great celebrations on 15 September 1830. Attended by the Duke of Wellington, then Prime Minister, and other political and business celebrities, the festivities were somewhat spoilt when a local MP, William Huskisson, was killed when the 'Rocket' ran over him. However, the LMR, the world's first inter-city railway, was an instant success, particularly with the travelling public.

The success of the LMR soon saw proposals for a host of new railways throughout the land. Of these, the 82-mile Grand Junction Railway (GJR), from Birmingham to a junction with the LMR at Newton, and the 112-mile London & Birmingham Railway were by far the most important. The former, engineered by George Stephenson and Robert Locke, was authorized by Parliament in 1833 and opened on 4 July 1837. The latter, engineered by Robert Stephenson, was also authorized in 1833 but its opening on 17 September 1838 had been delayed by extensive engineering works such as at Tring Cutting (through the Chilterns) and Kilsby Tunnel (southeast of Rugby). At the London end trains were cable-hauled between Euston and Camden until 1844.

The LMR merged with the Grand Junction in 1845. A year later the GJR merged with the London & Birmingham to form the London & North Western Railway – the West Coast Main Line, as we know it today, was already taking shape.

North of the border the Scots were not far behind – the Kilmarnock & Troon Railway, a coal-carrying line, had already opened in 1808 and in 1817 became the first railway in Scotland to use steam locomotive haulage. The first inter-city line in Scotland was the Edinburgh & Glasgow Railway which was authorized in 1838 and opened on 21 February 1842. The original Edinburgh terminus at Haymarket remains in use today.

The Liverpool & Manchester Railway became the world's first inter-city railway in 1830. Here a train is seen passing through the formidable Olive Mount Cutting near Liverpool – blasted out of sandstone rock, the cutting is two miles long and 80 ft deep.

Engineered by Robert Stephenson, the London & Birmingham Railway opened in 1838. Here a train is seen emerging from Primrose Hill Tunnel in North London.

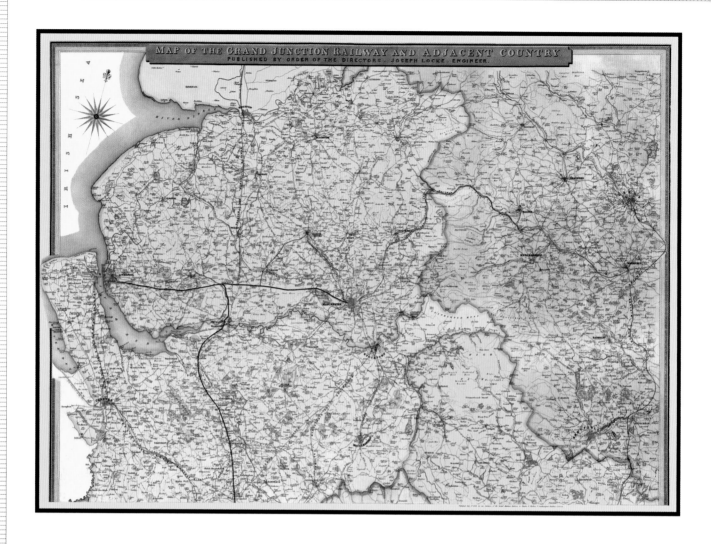

Title	Map of the Grand Junction Railway and Adjacent Country
Publisher	Charles F Cheffins
Date	1836

Following the success of the Liverpool & Manchester Railway (LMR), which opened on 15 September 1830, many schemes were proposed for the building of further railways. Birmingham businessmen were planning a link to London, and the group of financiers involved with the LMR saw Birmingham as an ideal goal for expansion. In 1831 the Warrington & Newton Railway opened; it ran about five miles southwards from Newton Junction (Earlestown) at the centre of the LMR, to Warrington and the River Mersey. This was considered to be an ideal starting point for a route to Birmingham, and after much surveying a route was found that was practical and avoided conflicts with landowners.

The eventual triangular junction at Earlestown was to play an important part in the history of the London & North Western Railway (LNWR), because it was on these very tight curves that the engines then in use frequently broke their axles. This led to the design of the outside-cylinder 'Crewe Type' engines with no crank axles to break, and eventually to the LNWR building its engines in-house. These tight curves remain in use to this day.

The map extract opposite shows the gap in what would become the West Coast Main Line, between Warrington and the railway heading north towards Wigan from Parkside Junction, east of Newton Junction on the LMR. In due course this missing link was completed by crossing under the LMR west of Parkside Junction. Also shown overleaf are a number of routes in planning, including what would become the main line from Crewe Junction via Sandbach to Manchester.

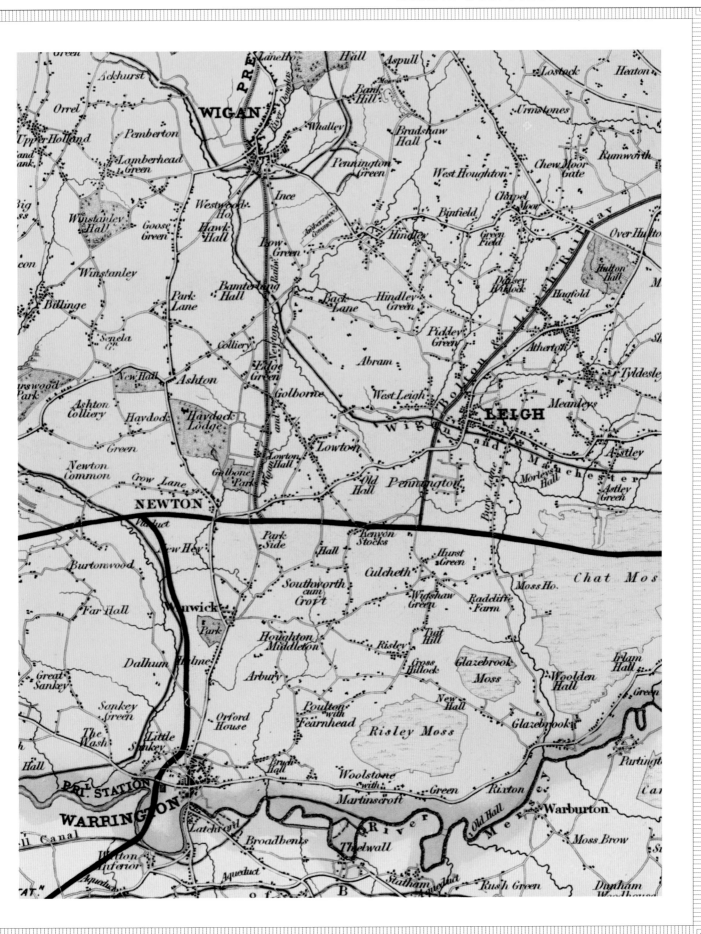

Title	Map of the Newcastle & Carlisle Railway, Shewing its Junction with the Carlisle and Maryport Railway, and thus Uniting the German Ocean with the Irish Sea.
From	*Scott's Railway Companion*
Publisher	H Scott
Date	1837

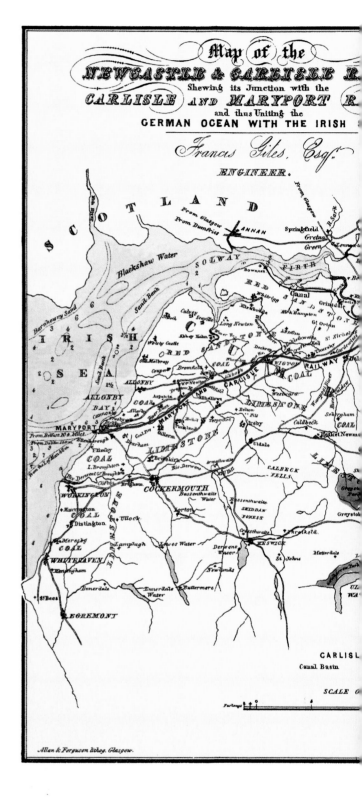

As Victorians increasingly took to exploring hitherto unknown countryside opened up by the rail network, so the rail companies sought to further expand this market with maps and guides. The Newcastle–Carlisle railway crosses attractive landscape, running close to Hadrian's Wall over its western half – and the railway company was clearly well aware of tourism opportunities, as this Railway Companion was published a year before the line was fully opened.

The first suggestion for a new link between the two towns, made in 1794, had been for a broad canal to Hexham on the south bank of the Tyne. Parliamentary opposition and the Napoleonic Wars delayed progress, and it was not until 1825 that a prospectus for the Newcastle & Carlisle Railway (NCR) was issued. The NCR was, however, a true pioneer, being incorporated in May 1829, five months before the famous Rainhill Trials for the Liverpool & Manchester Railway. The Act authorizing the railway had one serious flaw, namely that it forbade the use of locomotives, and an objecting landowner brought a temporary halt to proceedings – but this was soon overcome by an amendment to the original Act.

The map is part of a 105-page booklet which gives not just a route description and short guides to Carlisle and Newcastle,

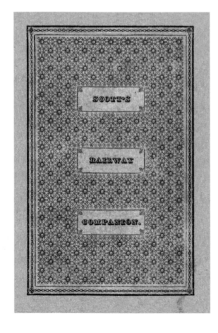

but also fares, mileages and even details of inns near the intermediate stations – and informs the reader that the estimated total cost of the line was £496,731. Unusually, the geology of the area is identified on the map – notably coal, limestone and red sandstone.

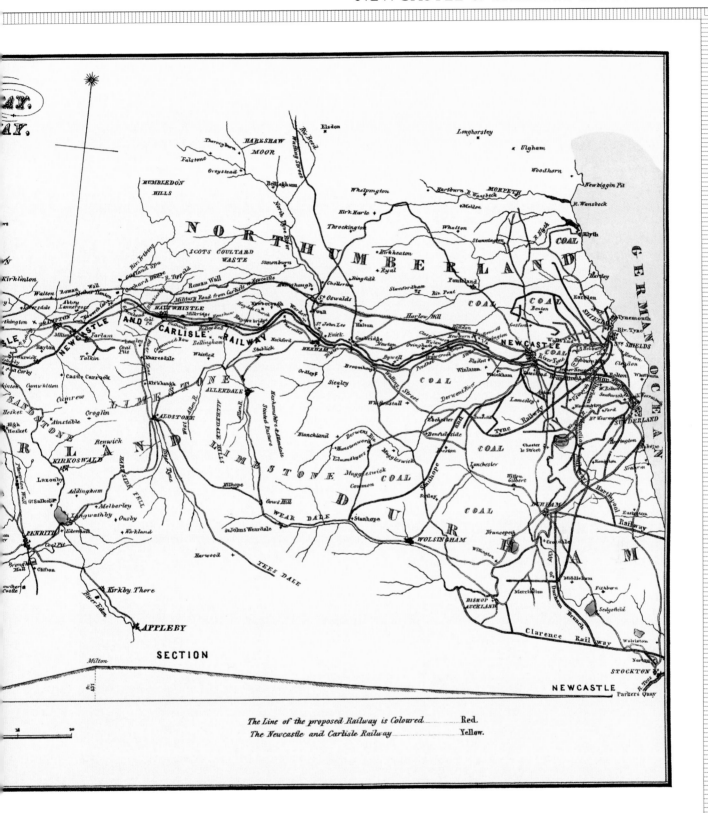

The Line of the proposed Railway is Coloured............Red.
The Newcastle and Carlisle Railway ....Yellow.

Demonstrating that the Victorians had pride in all kinds of development beyond the stereotypical tourist interest, the lineside description starting out from Carlisle comments: 'The first object which will be presented to the notice of the traveller as the trains begin to start, is the cotton factory of Messrs Rothwell & Co. ...' A passenger train operating company today would be most unlikely to draw attention in its 'windowgazer' brochure to, say, an aluminium smelter or paper mill, even if they were still major customers of the railway.

In partnership with his London agent, William Adams, Lancashire cartographer and Quaker George Bradshaw published the world's first railway timetable in 1839. Sold with a cloth cover, *Bradshaw's Railway Time Tables and Assistant to Railway Travelling* (the title was shortened to *Bradshaw's Railway Companion* in 1840) was initially a fairly small publication of eight pages, costing 6d, but as new railways quickly opened it grew in size until it had reached a staggering 1,000 pages by the end of the century. From 1841 it was published monthly under the new title *Bradshaw's Monthly Railway Guide*, compiled from information supplied by the plethora of railway companies, along with a map of Britain's rail system. Each line on the map was cross-referenced with the number of the page on which its timetable appeared. It was soon putting some order into the chaotic railway system, and started to include information on places to visit, hotels and shipping services. It was not an easy guide to use – there were so many companies that it was difficult to standardize the information, and the multiplicity of footnotes and miniscule type that accompanied each

timetable added more confusion. However, despite being the butt of Victorian cartoonists and music hall jokes, it became a unique national institution and was often referred to in famous works of fiction such as *The Adventures of Sherlock Holmes* and *Around the World in Eighty Days*. For over a hundred years it was an invaluable tool for the travelling public.

Bradshaw – his name already synonymous with railway timetables – quickly expanded his railway publishing empire by introducing the *Continental Railway Guide* in 1847 (discontinued in 1939) and, later, the *Railway Manual* and the *Railway Shareholders' Guide*, both of which stayed in print until the early 1920s. Way ahead of its time, *Bradshaw's Air Guide* was also published in 1934–9.

Bradshaw did not face any real competition until the 1930s, when the Big Four railway companies started issuing their own timetables – apart from the Great Western Railway's, even these were produced by the publisher of *Bradshaw*

4

NOTE.

LONDON TIME *is kept at all the Stations on the Railway, which is 4 minutes earlier than* READING *time; 7¼ minutes before* CIRENCESTER *time; 11 minutes before* BATH *and* BRISTOL *time; and 18 minutes before* EXETER *time.*

BATH TO BOX.

7 25 Morn.	2 57 After.
11 28	6 25 Even.
1 25	

SUNDAYS.

2 57 After.	7 0 Even.

BOX TO BATH.

9 48 Morn.	5 55 Even.
11 52	8 47

SUNDAYS.

9 43 Morn.	6 2 Even.

Fares.
1st Class, 1s. 2nd Class, 6d.

5

BATH TO CHIPPENHAM.

7 25 Morn.	2 57 After.
9 5	6 25 Even.
11 28	1 20 Night
1 25 After.	

SUNDAYS.

9 5 Morn.	7 0 Even.
2 57 After.	1 20 Night

CHIPPENHAM TO BATH.

9 28 Morn.	3 45 After.
11 30	5 35
1 40 After.	8 28
	12 15

SUNDAYS.

9 22 Morn.	5 40 After.
1 40 After.	12 15 Night

Fares.
1st Class. 3s. 2nd Class, 2s.

BATH TO CORSHAM.

9 5 Morn.	2 57 After.
11 28	6 25
1 25	

The problem in running trains to a standardized time is noted in this early timetable for Brunel's Great Western Railway.

until 1939. Despite this competition, and then the availability of regional timetables issued by the nationalized British Railways after 1948, *Bradshaw* was the only all-line timetable and continued to be available until 1961 when the final edition, No. 1521, was published.

It took until 1974 before British Railways first published their own all-line timetable and this was last published (by Network Rail) in 2007. Rail users now access timetables online, or can collect printed leaflets on a company-by-company or route-by-route basis – almost taking us back to the pre-Bradshaw situation.

GEORGE BRADSHAW

Born in Pendleton, near Salford, in Lancashire, on 29 July 1801, George Bradshaw began his career working for J Beale, a Manchester engraver. After a short spell in Belfast, Bradshaw had become an accomplished cartographer and his first work, a map of his native county, was published in 1827. In 1830 he published a series of map of the canals of Yorkshire and Lancashire known as *Bradshaw's Maps of Inland Navigation*. His *Bradshaw's Monthly Railway Guide* was published in 1841 and he soon became a household name throughout the land. His printing house, Bradshaw & Blacklock, became internationally renowned for its maps, guides, books and the *Manchester Journal*.

In his private life Bradshaw was a Quaker, a fervent peace activist and philanthropist in his native Manchester. While on a visit to Norway in 1853 he contracted cholera and died. He is buried in the grounds of Oslo cathedral.

Complete with map, the first edition of Bradshaw's *Railway Companion* was published in 1840.

Title	Map & Sections of the Railways of Great Britain
Publisher	George Bradshaw
Date	1839

This classic Bradshaw map was produced in very large format (62 in. by 40 in.) to enable the whole country to be shown, as well as considerable detail of settlements, roads and the relatively few railways which had been built or were under construction by 1839. Even proposed railways were incorporated in the map, including the yellow-marked line from Cambridge north to Lincoln (shown overleaf), which was never built on this alignment. Across the northern half of the map an unknown scribe has roughly sketched by hand (in red) possible additional railways – some of which were built and some which were not. The map is edged by numerous 'sections' or gradient profiles of the principal railways – a form of information which was later deemed not to be of interest to the average passenger, as opposed to railway professionals and enthusiasts.

The Kent, Surrey and Sussex extract below illustrates the very early stages of the development of the dense rail network across what was to become archetypal commuter territory. Just two principal lines south of the Thames are shown – from London to Brighton, and from a junction at Redhill (between London and Brighton) to Folkestone.

By the 1830s Brighton was the most popular seaside resort in Britain, with over 2,000 people a week visiting the town, and the London & Brighton Railway Company was set up to tap this market, with Robert Stephenson advising on the best possible route. The ultimate choice was a direct alignment which involved building four long tunnels and a viaduct across the Ouse valley. In July 1837, Parliament gave permission for the proposed railway; construction started in July 1838, and the first train arrived at Brighton Station on 21 September 1841.

The first railway to the ports of Folkestone and Dover from London was the circuitous route via Redhill (on the London–Brighton line), Tonbridge and Ashford, with Dover finally being reached in 1844. Subsequently, a more direct route for the 'South East Main Line' was built between London and Tonbridge via Sevenoaks, leaving the Tonbridge–Redhill section as a minor but useful cross-country line, which survives to this day.

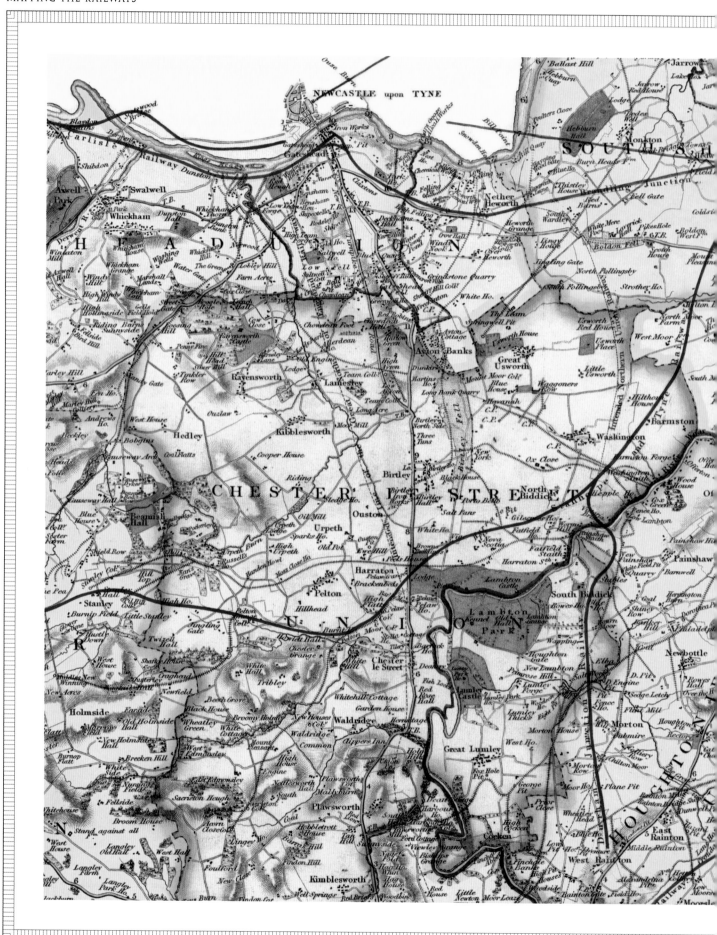

Title	Map of the County Palatine of Durham
Publisher	William Colling Hobson
Date	1840

After the year of this map's production, 1840, there is no record of any new county survey maps, only revisions of earlier maps. With public funding and mass production, the Ordnance Survey had become pre-eminent, so Hobson's map of County Durham represents one of the last of the era. The publisher may have seen the writing on the wall, as the language of the full title is profusely ingratiating to his funding base:

> This Map of the County Palatine of Durham is most respectfully dedicated to the Nobility, Clergy, Gentry, &c. &c. By their most obliged and very humble Servant, the Proprietor, William Colling Hobson

Unlike Greenwood's 1820 map of County Durham (see pages 16-19), rail routes are marked distinctly, with conventional railways in red and waggonways in ticked grey lines. The Washington and Newbottle waggonways shown in 1820 are identified, together with others not previously evident, linking collieries with the rivers Tyne and Wear and direct to the North Sea coast at Seaham Harbour.

The burgeoning railway network has spread in a different pattern from the waggonways – new economic forces were encouraging links between cities, towns and ports, although coal was still very much a driving force.

"Can you tell me how to make £10,000 HONESTLY in Railways?"

This satirical sketch attacks the speculative investment fever of the 'Railway Mania' that reached its peak in 1846.

Following the financial ruin that had befallen speculating investors in the South Sea Company, otherwise known as the 'South Sea Bubble', the British Government introduced the Royal Exchange and London Assurance Corporation Act (commonly known as the 'Bubble Act') in 1719. The Act was designed to prevent similar speculation and fraudulent trading in worthless business ventures, limiting their formation and requiring all new joint-stock companies to be incorporated by Act of Parliament. In its wisdom Parliament repealed the 'Bubble Act' in 1825.

The opening of the Liverpool & Manchester Railway in 1830 and its subsequent success in transporting goods and people between the two cities soon led to proposals for other such railways around Britain. To start with, progress was slow. A combination of banks not lending money due to political and social unrest, coupled with a sluggish British economy,

PANORAMA OF THE CITY OF YORK.

Opened in 1839, York's first railway station was deliberately sited within the city walls by George Hudson, the chief promoter of the York & North Midland Railway (see page 52).

where the high interest rates offered by Government bonds sucked in the majority of investments, put the brakes on railway development.

By the early 1840s the British economy was bouncing back, interest rates were cut and manufacturing industry was experiencing boom times – the period of the Victorian entrepreneur had dawned. The consequent success of the few railways that had already been built, such as the Grand Junction, the Great Western and the London & Birmingham, soon attracted investors who had previously put their money into Government bonds.

Rapidly rising railway share prices soon saw a speculative frenzy in a plethora of overambitious and sometimes fraudulent proposals for new railways across Britain. Known as 'Railway Mania' this period reached its peak in 1846 when 272 Acts of Parliament were passed, authorizing the building of 9,500 miles of new railway. This level of authorization was hardly surprising as many MPs, such as the 'Railway King' George Hudson, were also directors of these fledgling railways. Seeing the chance of a quick profit, the general public were also sucked in, purchasing shares for only a 10 per cent deposit, with the railway company having the right to call in the remainder when they pleased. Sadly, many of these prospective schemes soon collapsed, leaving the investors having to stump up the balance for an already worthless investment – the bubble had burst and, not for the last time, the British middle classes had become the victims. By the late 1840s and early 1850s new railway construction was mainly limited to the established railway companies who had profited by buying failed companies for a fraction of their original value.

GEORGE HUDSON, THE 'RAILWAY KING'

The son of a Yorkshire farmer George Hudson was born in 1800 and by the age of 27 had become a director in a firm of drapers in York. He had the good luck to inherit a fortune from his great uncle in 1827 and went on to establish the York Union Banking Company.

Hudson was elected to York City Council in 1835, becoming Lord Mayor two years later.

Forming a business relationship with George Stephenson, Hudson promoted the York & North Midland Railway which was authorized in 1837. He was also a major shareholder in three other railways – the Midland Counties Railway, the North Midland Railway and the Birmingham & Derby Junction Railway – that were to form the mighty Midland Railway, also led by Hudson, in 1844. To the north of York, Hudson's York & Newcastle Railway was also nearing completion and by 1846, the peak of 'Railway Mania', he controlled a 1,000-mile railway empire and became known throughout the land as the 'Railway King'. By now a personal friend of the Duke of Wellington and not content with his railway empire-building, Hudson was also elected MP for Sunderland in 1845, a position he held, despite his eventual fall from power, until 1859.

However, behind all of this success was a world of fraud and corruption on a big scale. Hudson's world started to fall apart after the bursting of the 'Railway Mania' bubble at the end of 1847 when he was forced to retire as chairman of the railway companies he owned. A committee of investigation then found that the unscrupulous Hudson had bribed MPs to vote for his railway projects, manipulated share prices by using insider information, sold land he did not own and paid dividends out of capital. Admitting his guilt Hudson was eventually imprisoned for debt in York Castle in 1865 but was soon released after friends raised the necessary funds. He died a broken man in 1871.

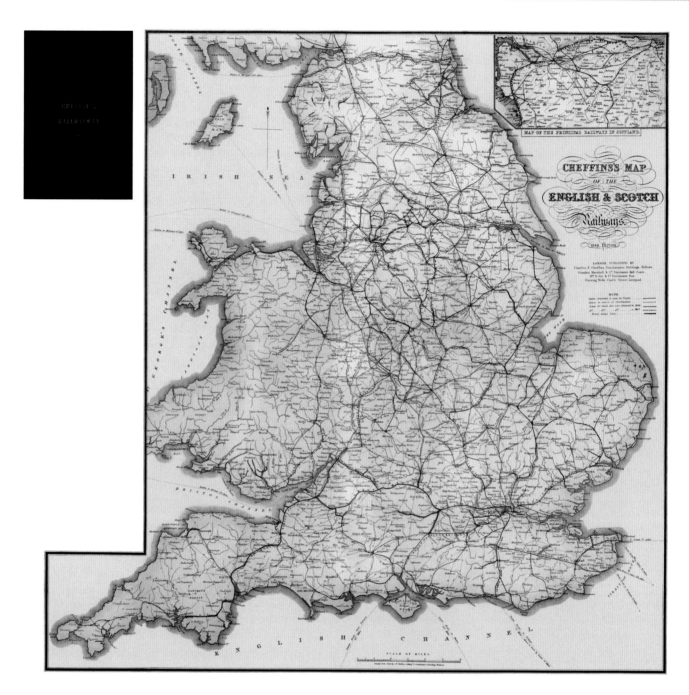

Title	Cheffins's Map of the English & Scotch Railways
Publisher	Charles F Cheffins
Date	1848

The geographical extent of the railway mania is graphically illustrated in Cheffins's 14 miles to 1 in. map dating from 1848. Other than south of the Great Western Railway main line to Bristol, and in Devon and Cornwall, there were as many lines planned (in red) as there were actually in operation or under construction (in black). The linkage between Victorian railways, coal and industry is demonstrated by the dense network of lines all the way from the South Midlands to Lancashire and Yorkshire – in contrast, the swathe of southeast England, long regarded as classic rail commuter territory, had a relatively sparse network at that time. A notable feature, shown overleaf, is the distinctively marked Great Western broad gauge network radiating from London (Paddington) to Basingstoke, Hungerford, Oxford, Cirencester, Gloucester, Westbury, Bath, Bristol and Plymouth.

This map extract of North Yorkshire particularly illustrates the fact that many lines which secured Parliamentary approval, in this case during 1846 or 1847, were never actually built. Thirsk on the Great North of England Railway – presumably an inspiration for the GNER of the 1990s' privatized railway – would have become a more important junction on the East Coast Main Line had the lines to Leyburn and Malton ever been constructed. Equally, Richmond to Barnard Castle, York to Wetherby, and

Lockington to Hornsea were all railways which never saw the light of day. The small coastal town of Whitby, however, was eventually to be served by three lines, although at this stage only the Whitby & Pickering Railway (whose construction had begun from the coastal terminus, in complete isolation from the rest of the network) provided a through connection to the rest of the country. Much of this line is preserved to this day as the steam and heritage North Yorkshire Moors Railway.

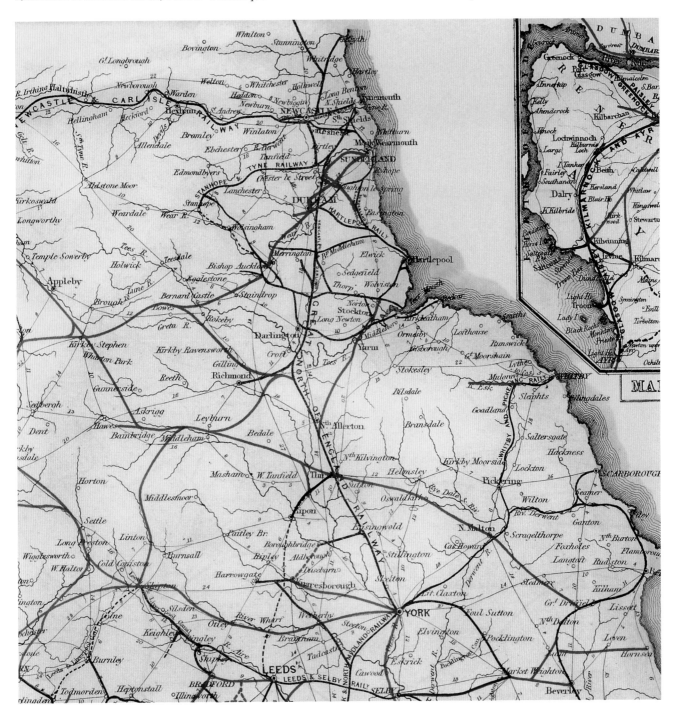

NOTE.

Lines completed & open for Traffic
Lines in course of Construction
Lines for which Acts were obtained in 1846
D.°   D.°   D.°   in 1847
Broad Guage Lines

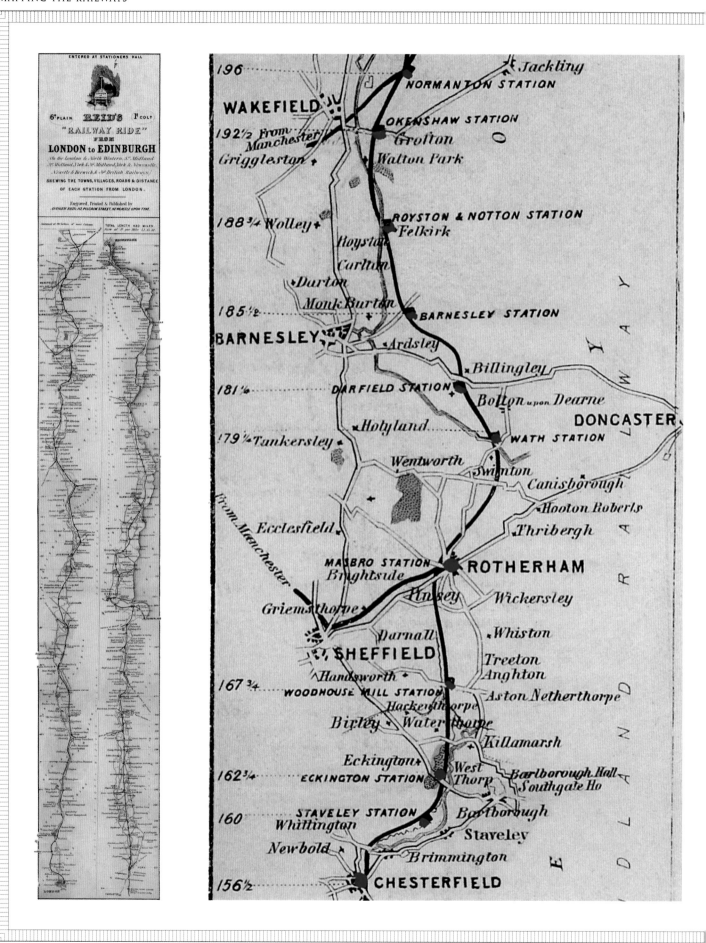

Title	Reid's 'Railway Ride' from London to Edinburgh
Publisher	Andrew Reid
Date	c.1848–9

As the longer-distance main lines spread across the country, Victorian mapmakers introduced 'strip maps' which transformed the representation of rail routes into straighter lines – facilitating reproduction in booklet form for the rail traveller interested in observing and understanding better the scenes through the carriage window.

When this map was produced in 1848–9, there was as yet no direct route between London and York, so an 'East Coast' journey from London to Scotland involved a departure from the London & North Western Railway's Euston terminus to Rugby, then by Leicester, Derby, Chesterfield, Rotherham, Swinton and Normanton to York, where the present East Coast Main Line was joined. While vastly quicker than its predecessor, the stagecoach, the relatively circuitous route followed by the train (430 miles) meant journeys of 16 to 18 hours between the two capitals.

The excerpt opposite from Chesterfield to Normanton is particularly interesting in that it features parts of the route which can no longer be followed in the 21st century. The first section, to Rotherham, which bypassed Sheffield, was superseded in 1870 by a line directly serving the city. The original line remained open as an important freight artery, a function it still fulfils today (see page 265), and as a diversionary route for passenger trains when engineering works are being undertaken on the main line. The section from Swinton to Normanton has now been lost completely as a through route, although short lengths remain open for freight.

This strip map features one of the first known representations of railway stations by solid red circles – a practice that continues to this day, notably in the Ordnance Survey 1:50,000 'Landranger' series.

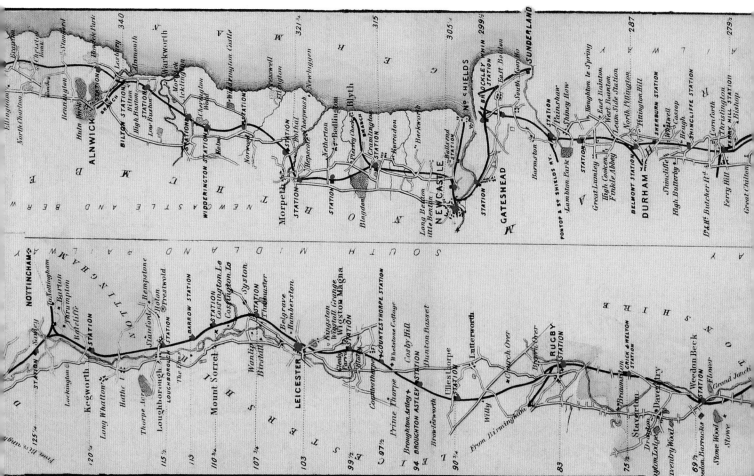

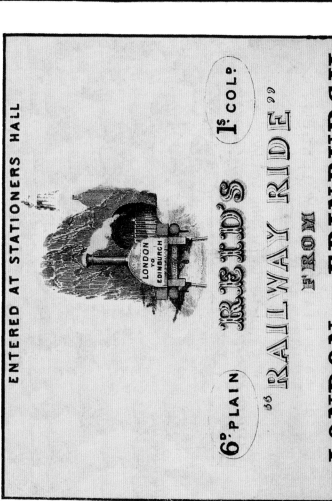

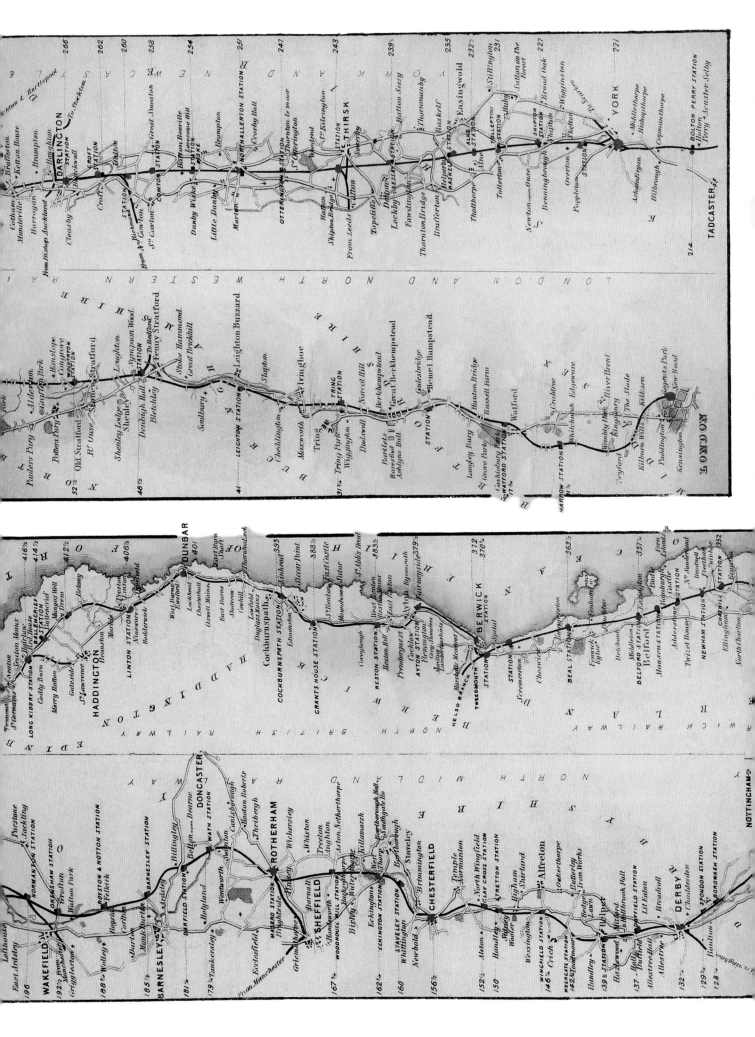

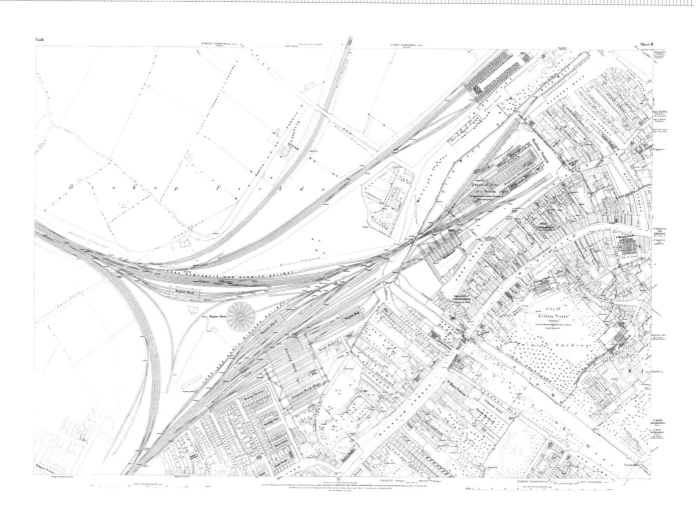

Series	Ordnance Survey 60 in. to 1 Mile
Sheet	York Sheet II
Date	1851

York – which was to become one of Britain's great railway centres – first joined the railway network with the opening of the York & North Midland Railway (YNM) in 1839, the first of the many companies to be chaired by George Hudson, the 'Railway King.' Initially trains terminated at a temporary wooden structure in Queen Street, just outside York's medieval city wall, but the latter was soon breached by a Gothic arch which took the railway into a new permanent station, opened in 1841, on a site previously occupied by the city's House of Correction. Traffic growth led to the enlargement of the station in 1845–6 and the construction of a second arch through the walls.

This early Ordnance Survey map of 60 in. to 1 mile scale shows in fascinating detail the layout of the station and associated railway infrastructure – note in particular the separate Arrival and Departure platforms, and the small turntables used to turn goods wagons through 90 degrees to be positioned in short unloading sidings straddled by warehouses southwest of the passenger station. As shown above, two coal depots stand on the site of the future permanent station just outside the city wall.

The combination of operational inconvenience – trains from London to Newcastle had to reverse out of the station in order to continue their journeys – and restricted space for expansion, led to the construction of the present York station outside the wall, opened in 1877. Railway offices remained within the old station, and carriages were stored on its tracks until 1965 when the station was largely demolished to make way for a new office block for British Rail. The old station frontage can, however, still be seen from Tanner Row, and some ironwork and platform remains have survived to the rear of the building.

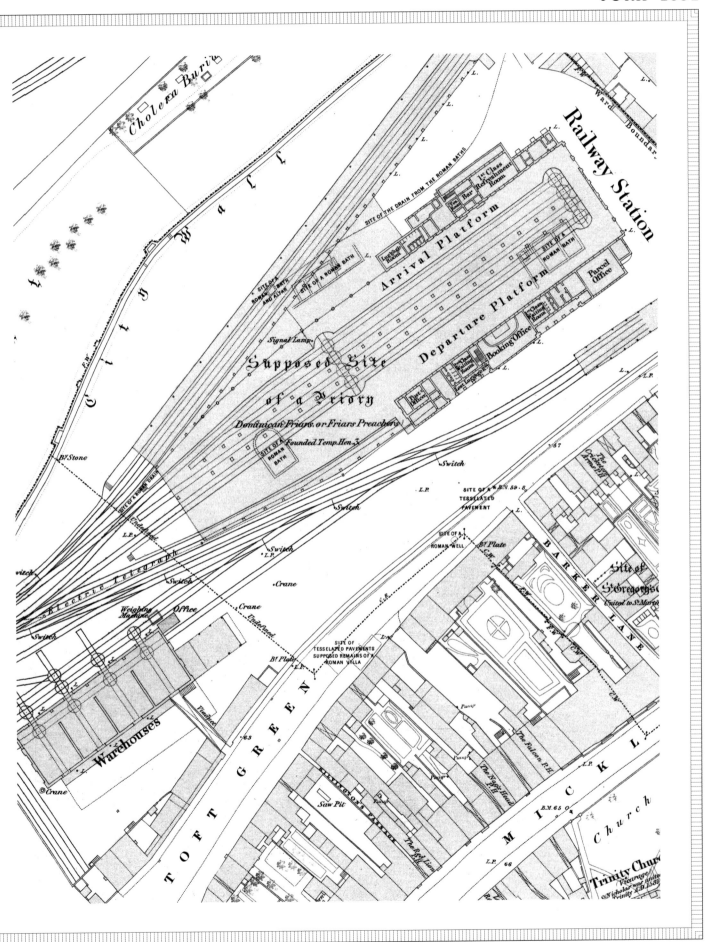

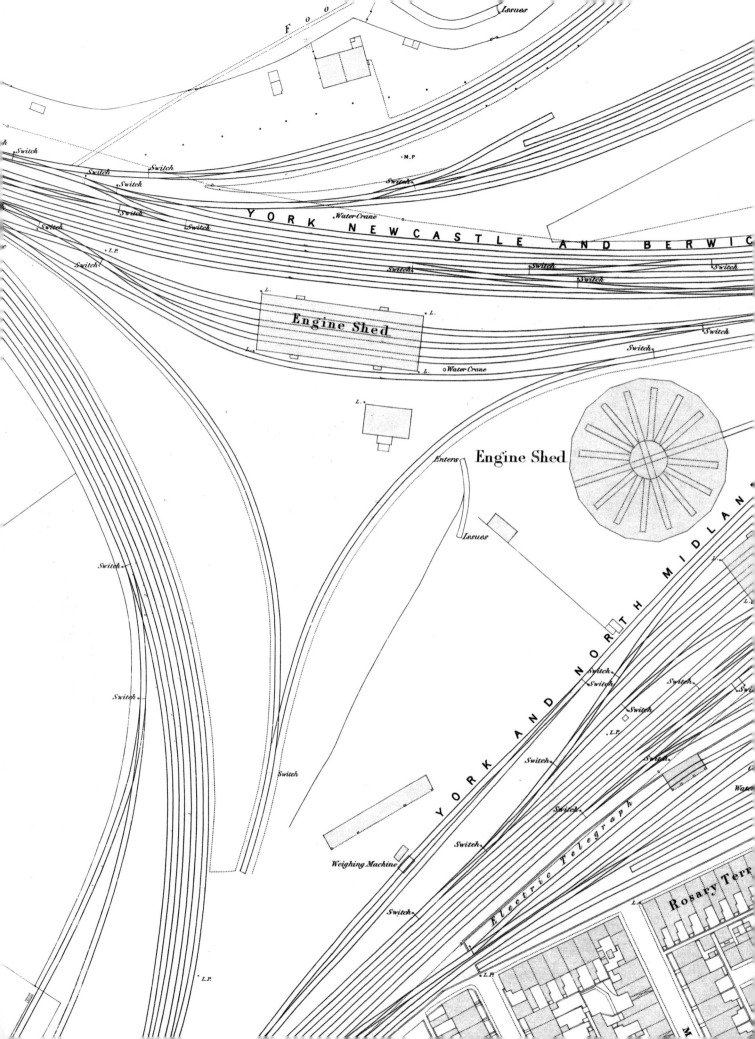

Foo

Issues

Switch

Switch

Switch

M.P

Switch

Switch

Switch

Water Crane

Switch

YORK NEWCASTLE AND BERWIC

Switch

L.P.

Switch

Switch

Switch

Switch

L.

Engine Shed

L.

Water Crane

L.

L.

Enters

Engine Shed

Issues

Switch

YORK AND NORTH MIDLAN

Switch

Switch

Switch

L.P.

Switch

Switch

Switch

Switch

Switch

Electric Telegraph

Switch

Switch

Weighing Machine

Wat

Switch

Rosary Terr

L.

Switch

L.P.

M

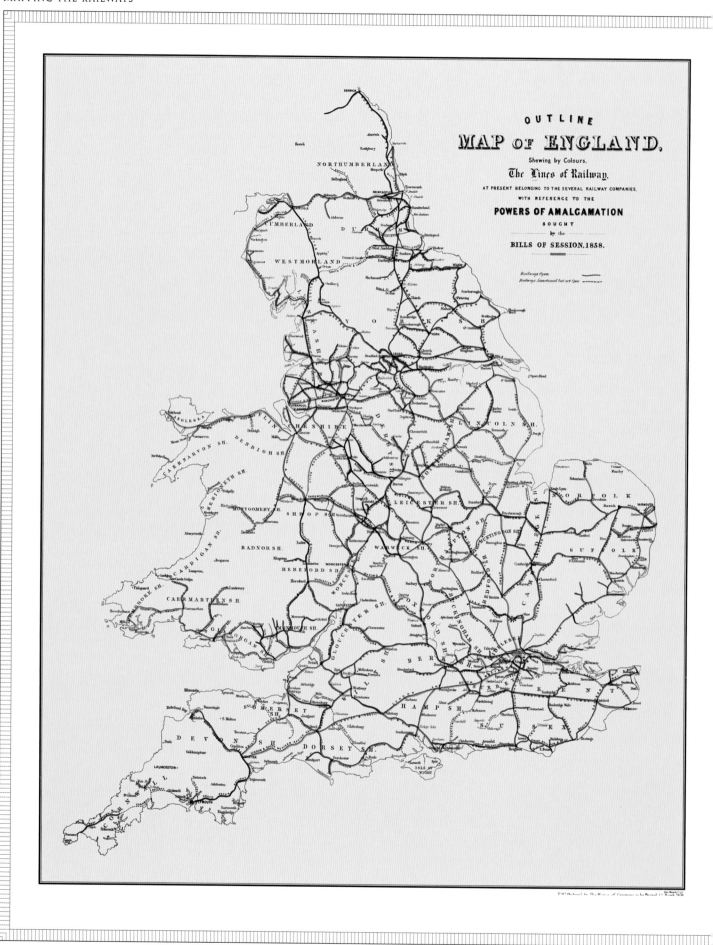

Title	Outline Map of England, Shewing by Colours, The Lines of Railway, at present belonging to the several railway companies, with reference to the Powers of Amalgamation sought by the Bills of Session, 1858
Printer	Henry Hansard
Date	1858

The British railway system developed over the second quarter of the 19th century in a piecemeal (if not chaotic) manner, comprising railways with a strategic intent and those which were much more local in their scope. This plethora of different companies may have been in tune with the Victorian preference for competition, but it became apparent that it was not the most effective way to run what was by then a near-comprehensive national rail system.

The way forward would be further consolidation, but this was not something that could be done at the mere whim of the different railway companies, with Parliament requiring that a Bill be placed before them for authorization before any mergers could take place. This map produced for the House of Commons to assist in its deliberations is not, however, specific on what exactly was being proposed in 1858 and it is not clear whether all the Bills covered even made it to Parliament.

The map extract below features the northern end of one particular line, the Oxford, Worcester & Wolverhampton Railway (OWWR), which certainly did not form part of any amalgamation in 1858. However, the inevitable rationalization could not be put off for long, and it would disappear under an 1860 Act of Parliament into the West Midland Railway (WMR), formed by absorption of the Newport, Abergavenny & Hereford and Worcester & Hereford railways. Even this would turn out to be a short-lived halfway house, because the WMR was leased by the Great Western Railway in 1861, and taken over by it just two years after that. Having earned for itself the less than flattering soubriquet of the 'Old Worse and Worse', it can be safely assumed that the passing of the OWWR was not mourned by any of its erstwhile users.

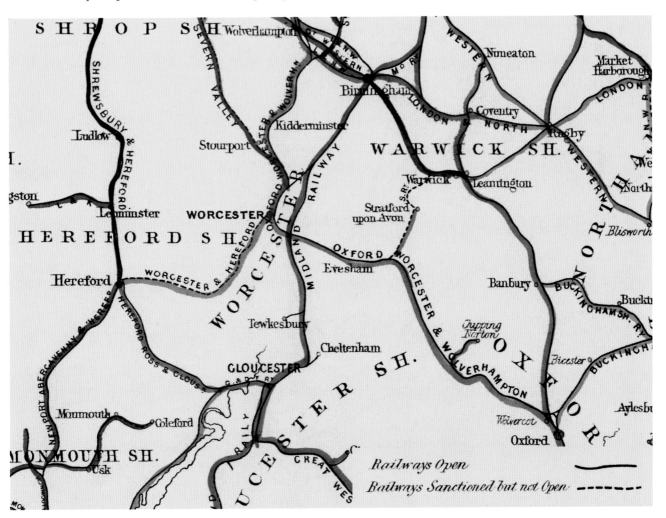

OUTLINE

MAP of ENGLAND,

Shewing by Colours,

The Lines of Railway,

AT PRESENT BELONGING TO THE SEVERAL RAILWAY COMPANIES,

WITH REFERENCE TO THE

POWERS OF AMALGAMATION

SOUGHT

by the

BILLS OF SESSION, 1858.

Railways Open ——————

Railways Sanctioned but not Open ----------

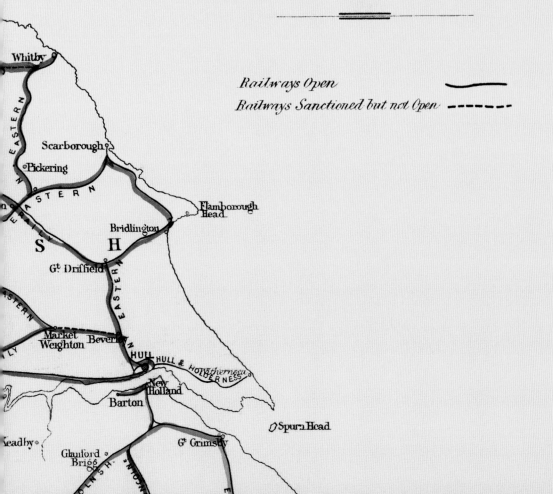

Series	Ordnance Survey of Scotland 1 in. Map
Sheet	32
Date	Originally published 1858. Printed from an Electrotype taken in 1877.

Before the Forth Bridge was opened in 1890, both sides of the estuary were only served by relatively minor railway lines. On the south side, a branch left the Edinburgh–Glasgow main line of the North British Railway (NBR) at Ratho, running via Kirkliston and Dalmeny to South Queensferry pier, where a passenger ferry operated across the Forth to North Queensferry. Passengers could then continue their journey by NBR train on the branch line to Inverkeithing and onwards through Fife to Kirkcaldy and beyond.

At that time, express trains from both Edinburgh and Glasgow to Perth, Inverness and Aberdeen ran inland via Stirling, and the rail network on the north shores of the Firth comprised modestly engineered routes serving an essentially local market. The legacy of these humble origins is felt to this day, as London–Aberdeen trains capable of running at 125 m.p.h. are forced to drop their speed to 50 m.p.h. or less through tight curves at Aberdour, Burntisland and Kinghorn. The North Queensferry branch closed to passengers when the Forth Bridge opened, but the South Queensferry line carried passenger traffic until 1929, and survived for freight into the 1960s (its mainstay loco latterly being J36 No. 65243 'Maude', now preserved at the nearby Bo'ness & Kinneil Railway).

As shown overleaf, by 1858 Edinburgh's suburban rail network was substantially complete, the main exception being the South Suburban Line loop through Morningside. The lack of built-up development in northwest Edinburgh – despite the presence of a number of railways – is striking. This points towards the importance of goods traffic; and fast passenger trains to the city centre were soon to stimulate widespread housing development in these new suburbs.

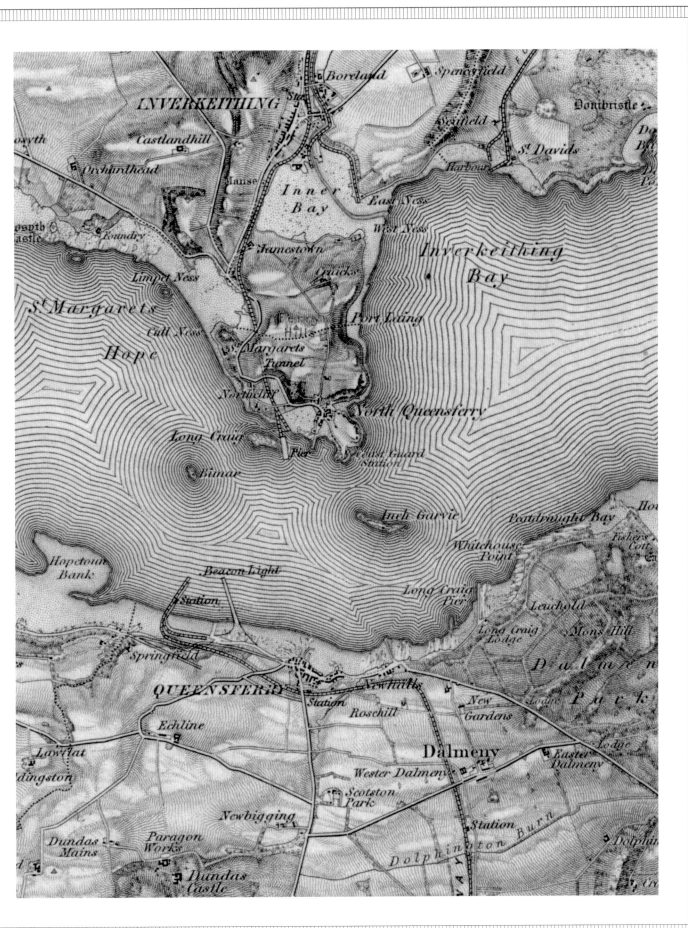

THE RAILWAYS PRE-EMINENT

The railways became by far the most important mode of transport, and the network filled out in every part of the country. In an era of fierce inter-company rivalry, the Great Central became the last main line to reach London, and the Midland pushed across the Pennines from Settle to Carlisle.

From the days of John Cabot's expedition to the New World in the 15th century, the port of Bristol grew to become one of the most important in Britain, the city prospering from its links with the Caribbean and with the slave trade. However, communication with London was slow and even by the late 18th century, when the first mail coach was introduced, the uncomfortable stagecoach journey along turnpike roads could take at least a day.

By 1833 several schemes to link Bristol and London by railway had already fallen by the wayside. In March of that year, a group of wealthy Bristol businessmen appointed a young engineer by the name of Isambard Kingdom Brunel to survey a route to the capital. Less than six months later a near-level route via Bath and the Thames valley through Reading and Maidenhead had been surveyed, a board of directors had been appointed at each end of the proposed railway, and the Great Western Railway (GWR) had been founded.

Although the GWR received Parliamentary authorization on 31 August 1835, there was surprisingly no stipulation about the gauge of the line (the width between the rails) – nearly all British railways were by then adopting the standard gauge of 4 ft 8½ in. Seizing upon this glaring omission, Brunel, who had been appointed chief engineer of the GWR, successfully advocated a broad gauge of 7 ft 0¼ in. Offering journeys between the two cities at unheard-of speeds and in sumptuous comfort, Brunel's broad gauge looked like a world-beater and, for a while, it was.

Built by thousands of navvies using only basic implements, construction of the level, high-speed route was fairly rapid with the first section from a temporary station at Paddington to Maidenhead opening on 4 June 1838. Completion of the entire route was held up by the construction of the 1 mile 1,452 yd Box Tunnel near Bath, then the longest railway tunnel in the world. Opening day came on 30 June 1841, the same date as the broad gauge Bristol & Exeter Railway, soon to be part of the GWR's route to the southwest, opened its northern section.

In its early years the broad gauge GWR was a great success and heralded a new age of high-speed inter-city rail travel. Indeed, by 1867 the GWR's tentacles, with the help of its neighbouring broad-gauge supporters, had reached Penzance with unheard of journey times of nine hours from London – today it takes just over five hours. Unfortunately the rest of the country's railways were being built to the narrower, standard gauge of 4 ft 8½ in. and where these railways came into contact with the GWR, the scenes of confusion were recorded for posterity by Victorian cartoonists.

Following Brunel's death on 15 September 1859, the individualistic GWR soon came to the inevitable conclusion that the broad gauge dream was incompatible with the rest of the nation's railways. Starting in 1864, broad gauge track was converted to standard gauge and in places mixed gauge track was common for some years. By 1892 all that remained of the broad gauge was the main line from Paddington to Penzance and this was converted by an army of workmen over one weekend in May of that year.

Plenty of physical evidence of broad gauge remains to this day – Brunel's original timber-roofed Temple Meads station at Bristol has been preserved and is now in use as a car park for rail users. Tunnels, such as Box Tunnel, have generous broad gauge proportions, while Sonning Cutting, east of Reading – which was excavated by navvies using just picks, shovels and wheelbarrows – is over a mile long and up to 60 ft deep.

The last Great Western Railway broad gauge train leaves Paddington for the West Country on 20 May 1892.

This 1846 illustration depicts the chaos caused by passengers and luggage being transferred from broad gauge to standard gauge carriages at Gloucester station while on their way to Birmingham.

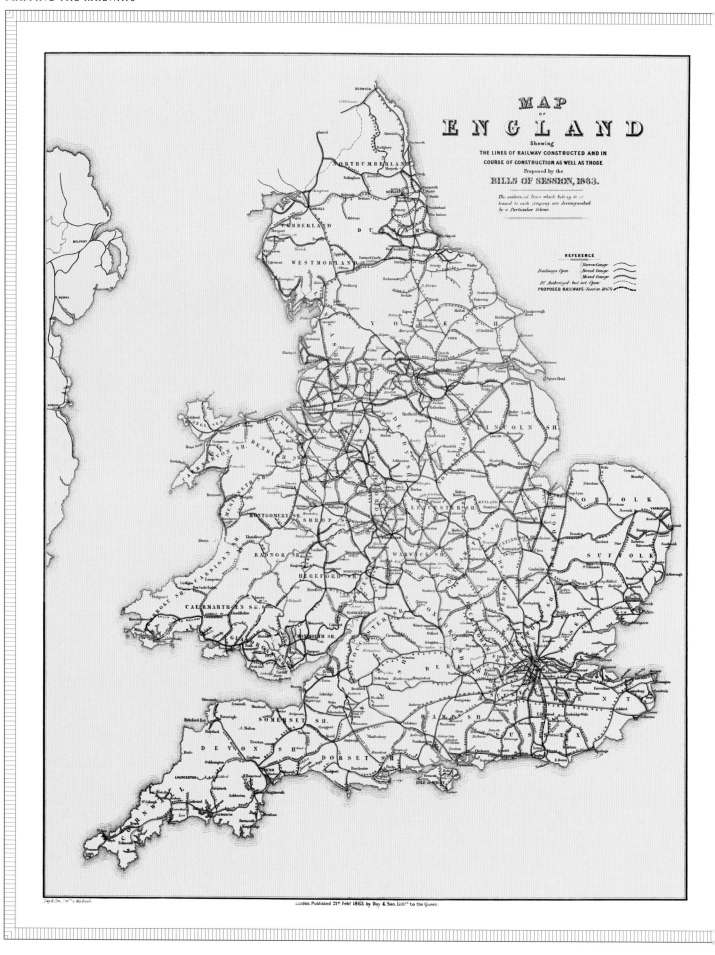

Title	Map of England shewing the lines of railway constructed and in course of construction as well as those proposed by the Bills of Session, 1863
By	Day & Son, London
Date	1863

Comparing this map produced for Parliament in 1863 with the equivalent for 1858 (see pages 56–59) one can see countrywide evidence of significant extension to the rail network. The southeast of England had begun to catch up with the early pace of development in the Midlands and North of England, with the shape of the future commuter network becoming more recognizable.

The map extract overleaf reveals a second route to Dover, the first railway on the Isle of Wight, the Great Western Railway extended westwards beyond Hungerford, and significant infill in counties such as Kent, Sussex, Hampshire and north Essex. Unlike the 1858 map, the 1863 version distinguishes between 'narrow gauge' (standard gauge), 'broad gauge' and 'mixed gauge', which was the technical solution permitting trains of both gauges to use the same route corridor. 1860 (the year after Brunel's death) was the last year in which any broad gauge was laid; the broad gauge between London and Oxford was converted to mixed in 1861, thereby allowing through running of standard gauge trains between London and Birkenhead by the time this map was produced.

Broad gauge was progressively converted to standard gauge from 1864, the Hungerford parish magazine recording in 1874 that:

> Hundreds of labourers have been engaged for the last fortnight in effecting the change from broad to narrow gauge on the Hungerford Branch of the Great Western Railway, the Berks and Hants, and Wilts and Somerset Railways. For five days the traffic was entirely suspended between Hungerford and Marlborough and Devizes; and on Sunday, June 28, the line was entirely closed. It is hoped that the ordinary service of trains will be resumed on Saturday, July 4.

The writer's expectations were met, as the line did indeed reopen on time.

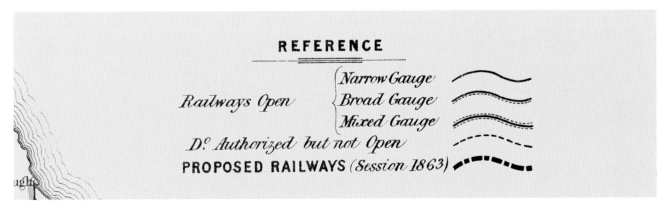

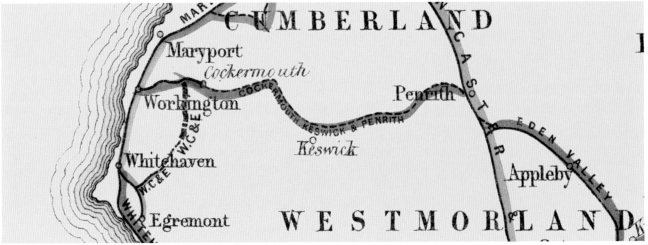

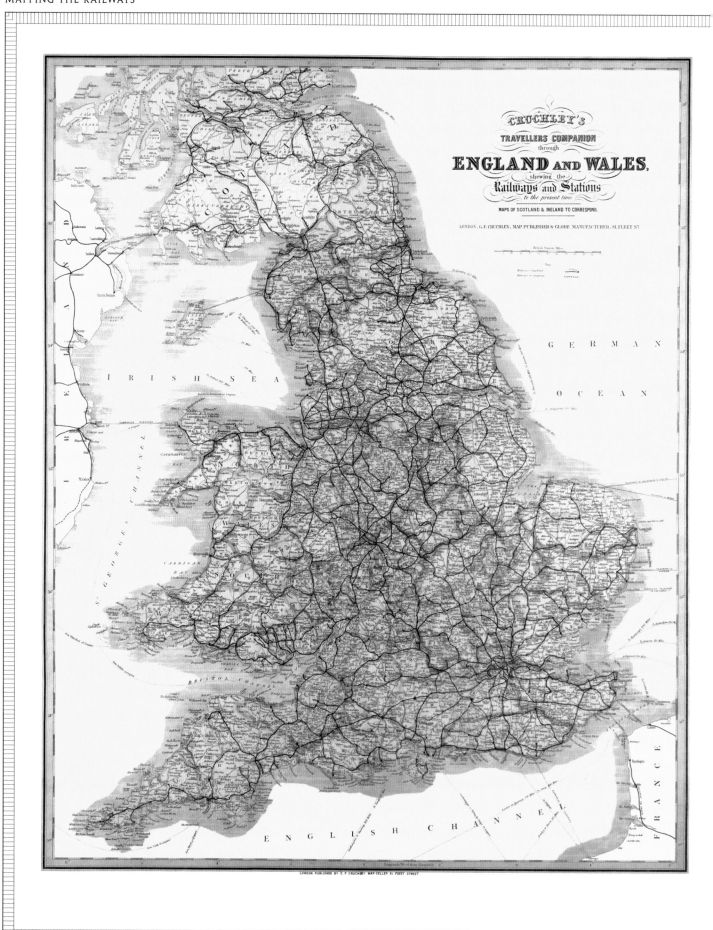

Title	Cruchley's Travellers Companion through England and Wales shewing the Railways and Stations to the present time
Publisher	G F Cruchley
Date	1863

The very substantial expansion of the rail network between the late 1840s (see pages 44–47) and 1863 is well illustrated by this map produced by the renowned map publisher George Cruchley – although it is not immediately obvious how convenient a 'companion' this sheet, measuring 50 in. by 40 in., would have been for the average rail traveller!

Most main lines had been built by 1863, notable exceptions being the Great Western between Pewsey and Taunton, the Great Central Railway into London, the Hull & Barnsley, and the Settle & Carlisle line across the Pennines. The latter

decades of the 19th century also saw further infill of cross-country and branch lines nationwide, not least in 'peripheral' North Devon and North Cornwall. The map extracts below and overleaf show the gaps yet to be filled before the tentacles of the network finally reached five coastal towns which were to play a key part in the boom in train travel to holiday destinations – St Ives, Newquay, Padstow, lfracombe and Minehead.

The very large size of the map allowed considerable detail to be shown of settlements and roads, as well as county boundaries – but a word of caution should be given. In *Maps for Local History* (1988), Brian Hindle notes that:

> *Publishers like Cruchley . . . simply added railways to existing plates or, worse, just overprinted the lines onto existing maps. Cruchley, for example, was still using Cary's county maps of 1801 as base maps in the 1870s!*

Title	A New Map of Metropolitan Railways, Tramways and Miscellaneous Improvements. Deposited at the Private Bill Office Nov. 30, 1871, for Session 1872
Publishers	Edward Stanford, Vacher & Sons, Letts & Co.
Date	1872

After the early development of public railways in the north of England, London soon became a primary focus of the expansion of the rail network. As Brian Hindle notes in *Maps for Local History* (1988):

> In the larger towns [the railways] were unable to reach the centres because of the high land values and the unwillingness of landowners to sell land with good property on it. Areas of lower-class housing proved less of a barrier, and landowners of such areas positively welcomed the railway. Thus it was that the main lines entering London from the north all terminated over a mile and a half from Charing Cross.

By 1871 routes leading to 10 major passenger termini were already in place, but further significant developments were planned and were lodged in Parliament, as shown in this map published on 1 January 1872. Amongst the publishers was Edward Stanford, whose name survives to this day in the world-famous map shop on Long Acre.

Charles Dickens likened the advent of the railways to an 'earthquake' as 'houses were knocked down; streets broken through and stopped; deep pits and trenches dug in the ground; enormous heaps of earth and clay thrown up; buildings that were undermined and shaking, propped by great beams of wood'. By the time the Great Central Railway was advancing towards London in the 1890s (over tracks built and leased by the Metropolitan Railway), the Marylebone area shown in the map extract here was already heavily built-up, and Lord's Cricket Ground also lay potentially in the path of the new railway and its planned Marylebone terminus.

The solution was a largely below-ground route swinging sharply southeastwards from its west–east alignment near Finchley Road, where it parted company from the parallel Midland Railway main line to St Pancras. Over a distance of less than two miles, Hampstead Tunnel, St John's Wood Tunnel (1,606 yd) and Lords Tunnel ensured that citizens and cricketers alike were little disturbed by the last main line to reach London.

Railways in Operation	———————	Railways Sanctioned	— — — — —	Railways Proposed	———————
Tramways „	++++++++++++	Tramways „	– – – – – –	Tramways „	———————

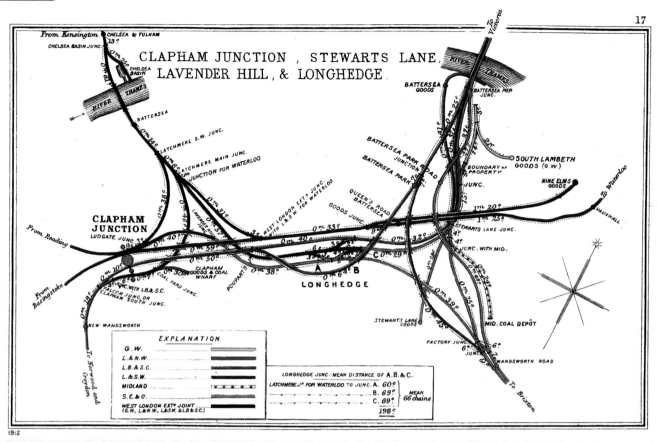

John Airey's Junction Diagram depicting the network of lines around Clapham Junction was published by the Railway Clearing House in 1912.

By the early 1840s railways were spreading like tentacles across the map of Britain and at first sight it appeared that they were all linked, offering the opportunity of through passenger and goods traffic for the first time. This was far from the truth, however, as there was virtually no commonality between them. Despite most companies opting for the standard gauge of 4 ft 8½ in. – the Great Western Railway and its later constituent companies were different as they chose Brunel's 7 ft 0¼ in. broad gauge – that is where the commonality usually ended.

In many cases through carriages from one company to another were not allowed and some companies refused to carry third-class passengers from other lines. There being no standardization of tickets, the through booking of a journey that involved using several railways was not possible either. There was no standardization of goods vehicles, no common classification of goods and there were constant disputes over the allocation of receipts from goods traffic as there were no agreed distances between stations for calculation of chargeable mileage rates. Even station clocks and consequently timekeeping were not synchronized to a common time.

On the safety side, signalling was a very hit and miss affair with some companies using red discs to indicate 'clear road ahead' while others used red discs to indicate the opposite. Goods wagons, whether privately owned or railway owned, had different braking systems and even buffers that did not align.

All of the above caused enormous confusion and was certainly a stumbling block to the continuing successful development of the railways. Painfully aware that some form of organization and standardization needed to be introduced, the Chairman of the London & Birmingham Railway invited representatives of nine other railway companies to a meeting

A selection of confusing early railway signals, 1837–46.

at Euston in 1842. Thus was the Railway Clearing House (RCH) formed, although some companies, notably the Great Western Railway, took another 20 years before they joined.

The agreed objectives of the RCH were to organize the through booking of passengers, carriages and horses between different companies and to divide receipts based on mileage. For goods traffic the RCH also organized a classification of goods, and tried to encourage a rate for these on a per mile basis. Of course they could not set these rates as each company charged differently, but it was a start. Member companies paid the RCH a fixed rate based on their number of stations and also a small percentage of their receipts.

Before long the RCH had standardized railway timekeeping using Greenwich Mean Time, published distance tables, encouraged the use of Edmondson ticket-printing and date-stamping machines and had produced a general classification of goods. Inter-company debts were also settled at the RCH.

The RCH also published many railway maps, the first one being produced by Zachary Macauley in 1851. His work was continued by John Airey who first published his Junction Diagrams in 1867. By the end of the 19th century his hand-coloured maps of the entire rail system, with distances shown between stations and junctions in miles and chains, were an important tool for every railway company when calculating rates.

By the outbreak of the First World War the RCH had a staff of over 3,000, many of them employed in the painstaking task of number-taking to check the numbers and contents of goods wagons travelling over the system. In fact, by the time of the 'Grouping' of the railways into just four companies in 1923, there were around 4,000 private owners using 650,000 goods wagons, and a sheet of paper had to be produced recording each journey made by each wagon – an enormous task.

Despite the Grouping, the RCH remained an important statistic-gathering organization until nationalization in 1948. However, the writing was now on the wall for the RCH, although its much-reduced staff were still called upon by British Railways to provide statistics until 1963, when it finally closed.

The journeys of all private-owner wagons, such as these seen at Birkenhead docks in 1924, were painstakingly recorded by the Railway Clearing House.

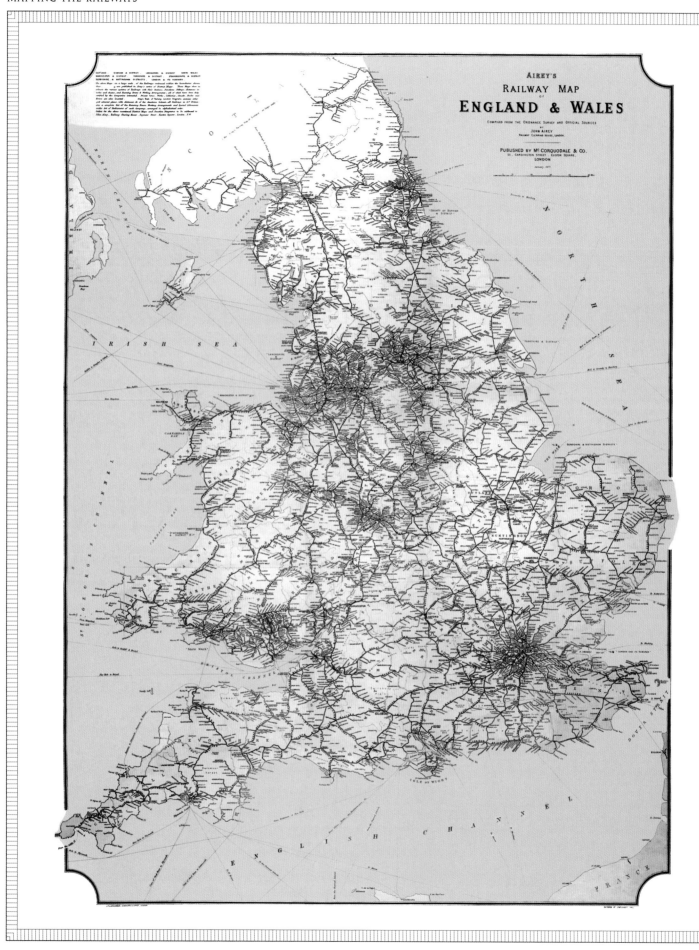

Title	Airey's Railway Map of England & Wales compiled from the Ordnance Survey and Official Sources by John Airey
By	Railway Clearing House
Date	1877

Maps were a key tool of the Railway Clearing House set up in 1842 to handle inter-company dealings across the multiple ownerships of the rail network. A Clearing House employee, John Airey, prepared what were essentially working maps for railwaymen, comprising regional sheets showing ownership, junctions and distances, as well as more detailed 'junction diagrams' dealing with the key interfaces between companies.

The Clearing House maps increasingly came into the public domain, and this large (47 in. by 35 in.) 1877 sheet by John Airey clearly had a wider purpose, covering as it did all of England and Wales plus the Borders and southwest Scotland.

The map extract below illustrates the intricate network of railways that developed in County Durham, Tyneside and Teesside, building on the inheritance of nearly two centuries of waggonways linking collieries to the coast. Branch lines penetrated westwards far into the Pennines to tap mineral resources for the burgeoning industries along the coast from Blyth in the north through Tynemouth, Sunderland and Hartlepool to Middlesbrough, while around Newcastle a dense network of commuter lines served and stimulated the massive housing development of the late 19th century.

In response to competition from new electric street trams, much of the Tyneside passenger network was electrified by the North Eastern Railway in 1904, using a 'third rail' system similar to that so familiar in commuter country south of London. In response to employment and population changes, the system was de-electrified by British Railways between 1963 and 1967 – and replaced by diesel trains – but the key routes were re-electrified (with overhead wires) and new links built, as the Tyne and Wear Metro, the first section of which opened in 1980.

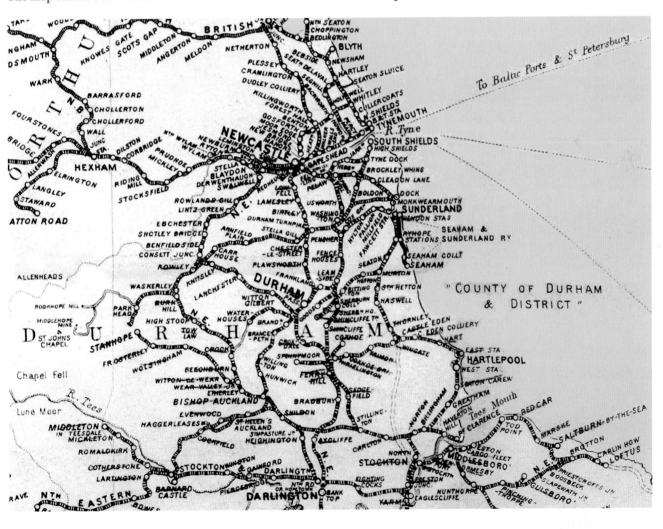

MALVERN LINK
GRT. MALVERN
MALVERN WELLS
COLWALL
STOKE EDITH
WITHINGTON
MORETON ON-LUGG
BARTON JN
BARRS COURT
ASHPERTON
LEDBURY
HOLM LACY
FAWLEY
ROSS
MITCHELDEAN ROAD
LONGHOPE
KERNE BRIDGE
LYDBROOK JN
SYMOND'S YAT
COLEFORD
MILKWALL
PARKEND
WHITECROFT
LYDNEY
WOOLASTON
TIDENHAM JUNC.
NEWENT
GRANGE COURT
NEWNHAM
BULLO PILL
GLOUCESTER
CHURCHDOWN JUNC.
CHELTENHAM
HIGH STR.
LANSDOWN
CLEEVE
ASHCHURCH
TEWKESBURY
RIPPLE
UPTON
DEFFORD
FLADBURY
EVESHAM
BENGEWORTH
HINTON
ASHTON-UNDER-HILL
BECKFORD
BREDON
HONEYBOURNE
CAMPDEN
BLOCKLEY
MORETON-IN-THE-MARSH
ADDLESTROP
STOW-ON-THE-WOLD
BOURTON-ON-THE-WATER
CHIPPING NORTON
SHIPTON
ASCOT
CHARLBURY
HANDBORO
YARNTON
WOODSTOCK ROAD
KIRKLINGTON
HEYFORD
SOMERTON
AYNHO
DEDDINGTON
KINGS SUTTON
BANBURY
CROPREDY
OXFORD ROAD JUNC.
OXFORD
ISLIP
KENNINGTON JUNC.
RADLEY
ABINGDON
CULHAM
DIDCOT
STEVENTON
WANTAGE ROAD
WANTAGE
CHALLOW
UFFINGTON
SHRIVENHAM
FARINGDON
FAIRFORD
LECHLADE
ALVESCOT
BAMPTON
WITNEY
EYNSHAM
BURFORD
NORTHLEACH
CIRENCESTER
TETBURY RD.
KEMBLE JUNC.
TETBURY
BRIMSCOMB
STROUD
STONEHOUSE
STANDISH JUNC.
HARESFIELD
NAILSWORTH
DURSLEY
COALEY JUNC.
SHARPNESS
BERKELEY
CHARFIELD
WICKWAR
THORNBURY
YATE
MANGOTSFIELD
WARMLEY
BITTON
MARSHFIELD
BRISTOL
CLIFTON BRIDGE
BEDMINSTER
BRISLINGTON
PATCHWAY
PILNING
NEW PASSAGE
SEVERN TUNNEL
SHIREHAMPTON
MALMESBURY
MINETY
CRICKLADE
PURTON
HIGHWORTH
SWINDON
WOOTTON BASSETT
DAUNTSEY
CHIPPENHAM
CALNE
CORSHAM
BOX
BATHAMPTON
BATH
TWERTON
SALTFORD
KEYNSHAM
MELKSHAM
BRADFORD
HOLT
TROWBRIDGE
SEMINGTON
DEVIZES
WOODBOROUGH
PEWSEY
SAVERNAKE
BEDWIN
HUNGERFORD
KINTBURY
NEWBURY
THATCHAM
MARLBOROUGH
LAMBOURN
EAST ILSLEY
MOULSFORD
LUDGERSHALL
WHITCHURCH
OAKLEY
OVERTON
ANDOVER
CLATFORD
FULLERTON
STOCKBRIDGE
HORSEBRIDGE
MOTTISFONT
KIMBRIDGE JUNC.
DUNBRIDGE
ROMSEY
CHANDLERS FORD
BISHOPSTOKE
WINCHESTER
MICHELDEVER
ITCHEN ABBAS
SOUTHAMPTON
REDBRIDGE
TOTTON
LYNDHURST ROAD
NETLEY
BOTLEY
BROCKHURST
GOSPORT
BROKENHURST JUNCTION STA.
HOLMSLEY
RINGWOOD
VERWOOD
DAGGON'S ROAD
FORDINGBRIDGE
BREAMORE
DOWNTON
ALDERBURY JUNCTION
DEAN
SALISBURY
PORTON
GRATELEY
AMESBURY
WILTON
WISHFORD
LANGFORD
WILEY
CODFORD
HEYTESBURY
WARMINSTER
WESTBURY
FROME
WITHAM
WANSTROW
CRANMORE
DOULTING
SHEPTON MALLET
RADSTOCK
WELTON
MIDSOMER NORTON
CHILCOMPTON
BINEGAR
MASBURY
WELLS
WOOKEY
HALLATROW
CLUTTON
PENSFORD
MIDFORD
WELLOW
EVERCREECH
EVERCREECH JN
PYLLE
PENNARD
CASTLE CARY
BRUTON
COLE
WINCANTON
SPARKFORD
TEMPLECOMBE
MARSTON
YEOVIL
YEOVIL JUNC.
SHERBORNE
MILBORNE PORT
HENSTRIDGE
STALBRIDGE
STURMINSTER NEWTON
SHILLINGSTONE
BLANDFORD
SPETISBURY
BAILEY GATE
YETMINSTER
EVERSHOT
MAIDEN
CERNE ABBAS
SUTTON BINGHAM
GILLINGHAM
SHAFTESBURY
SEMLEY
TISBURY
DINTON
MERE
HINDON
CRANBORNE
Stonehenge
Salisbury Plain
New Forest
Inkpen Beacon
Ilsley Downs
Marlborough Downs
Cotswold Hills
Mendip Hills
R. Severn
R. Thames
R. Avon
R. Wye
GREAT WESTERN
LONDON & SOUTH WESTERN
MIDLAND
SOMERSET & DORSET
SOUTH WESTERN MIDLAND JOINT
GLOUCESTER
WILTSHIRE
BERKS
OXFORD
HAMPSHIRE
SOMERSET
DORSET
WORCESTER

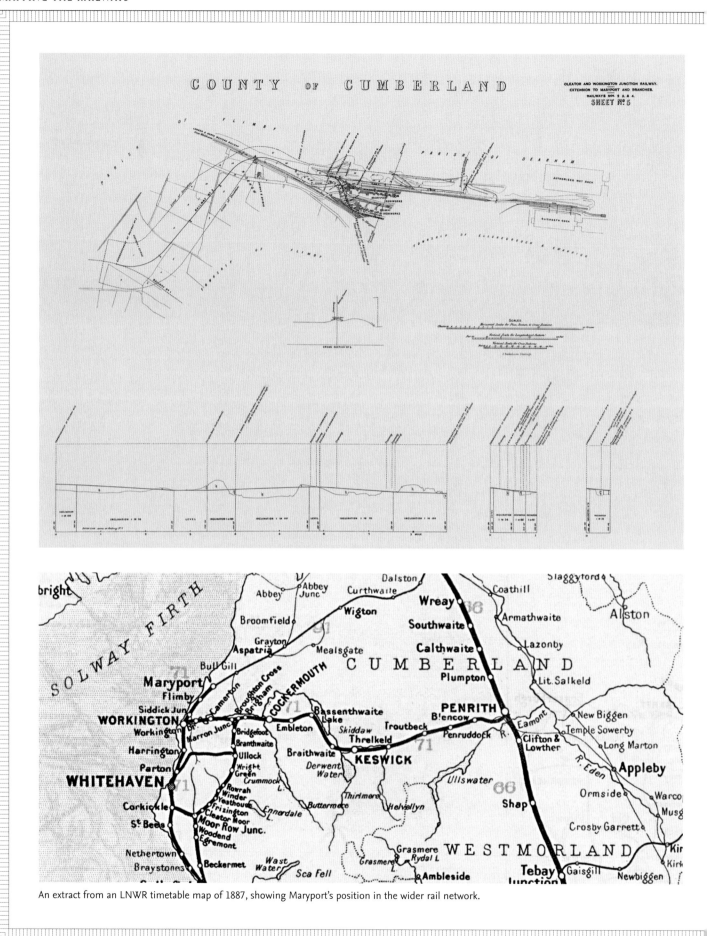

An extract from an LNWR timetable map of 1887, showing Maryport's position in the wider rail network.

Title	Sheet No. 5 – Cleator & Workington Junction Railway. Extension to Maryport and branches. Plans and sections. Session 1880–81
Engineers	John Wood, A H Strongitharm
Publisher	J Bartholomew, Edinburgh
Date	c.1880

The map opposite and overleaf, originally printed at a scale of 1 in. to 5 chains (110 yd), illustrates the level of detail which had to be submitted to Parliament when railway companies proposed to build new lines. The wider network context is shown by the extract opposite from a London and North Western Railway (LNWR) timetable map.

The Cleator & Workington Junction Railway (CWJR) was an independent concern promoted by iron and coal interests in west Cumberland. The original goal had been to completely avoid the coastal route and high charges of the LNWR by constructing an inland line from Cleator Moor to Maryport, where connection would have been made with the Maryport & Carlisle Railway (MCR) for onward access to Scotland and the Newcastle area.

Initially, only the section from Cleator Moor to Siddick, on the north side of Workington, was built, opening in 1879. At Siddick connection was made with the LNWR and it would be some years before an independent extension to join up with the MCR could be realised.

The proposed junction just south of Maryport shown on this map was actually part of the second attempt at effecting this extension – the original intention had been to join the MCR just east of Maryport – but this would also be dropped in its turn in favour of a more ambitious scheme to make a direct connection with the Solway Junction Railway (and hence into Scotland) at Brayton Junction between Aspatria and Wigton. Foreseeing a loss of income, the MCR objected to this proposal.

The CWJR eventually got its independent northern outlet in 1887 by making a junction with the MCR's Bullgill to Brigham branch at Linefoot some three miles southeast of

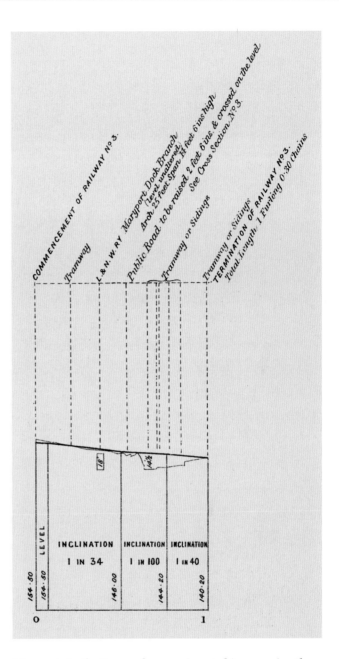

Maryport. So the time and money invested in surveying the route shown on the map, and in producing the map and associated documentation, were all wasted – except in terms of the interest for subsequent map readers.

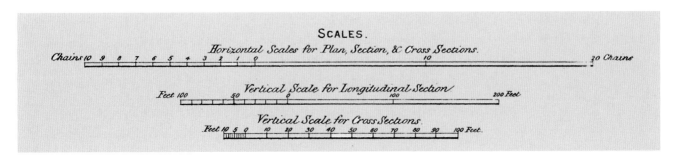

87

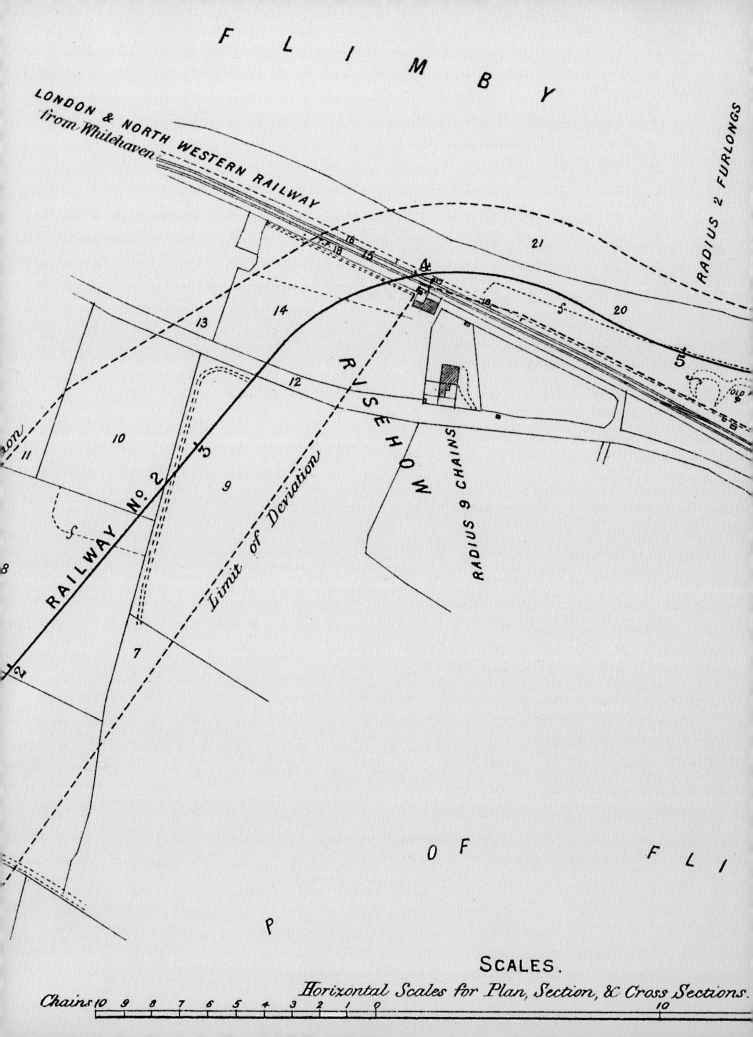

F L I M B Y

LONDON & NORTH WESTERN RAILWAY
from Whitehaven

RADIUS 2 FURLONGS

21

16 18 15

14

13

4

12

11

10 3

RAILWAY N.º 2

9

Limit of Deviation

7

8

R.SEHOW

RADIUS 9 CHAINS

20 18

5

O F F L I

P

SCALES.

Horizontal Scales for Plan, Section, & Cross Sections.

Chains 10 9 8 7 6 5 4 3 2 1 0 10

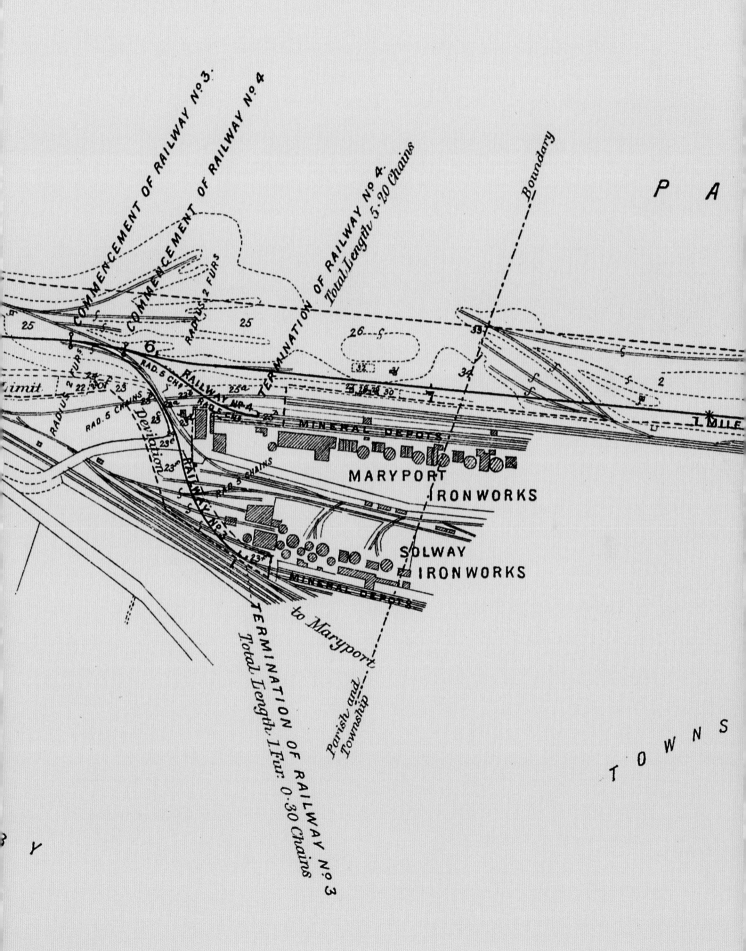

COMMENCEMENT OF RAILWAY No. 3.

COMMENCEMENT OF RAILWAY No. 4

TERMINATION OF RAILWAY No. 4.
Total Length 5·30 Chains

Boundary

P A

25

RADIUS 2 FURS

25

26

33

34

2

Limit

RADIUS 2 FURS

RAD. 5 CHS

6

RAILWAY No 4

25

Deviation

RAD. 5 CHAINS

23°

23°

23°

23°

23°

RAD. 5 CHS

23°

RAILWAY No 3

23°

23°

RAD. 5 CHAINS

23°

1 MILE

MINERAL DEPOTS

MARYPORT
IRONWORKS

SOLWAY
IRONWORKS

MINERAL DEPOTS

to Maryport

Parish and
Township

TERMINATION OF RAILWAY No 3
Total Length 1 Fur 0·30 Chains

T O W N S

B Y

20 Chains

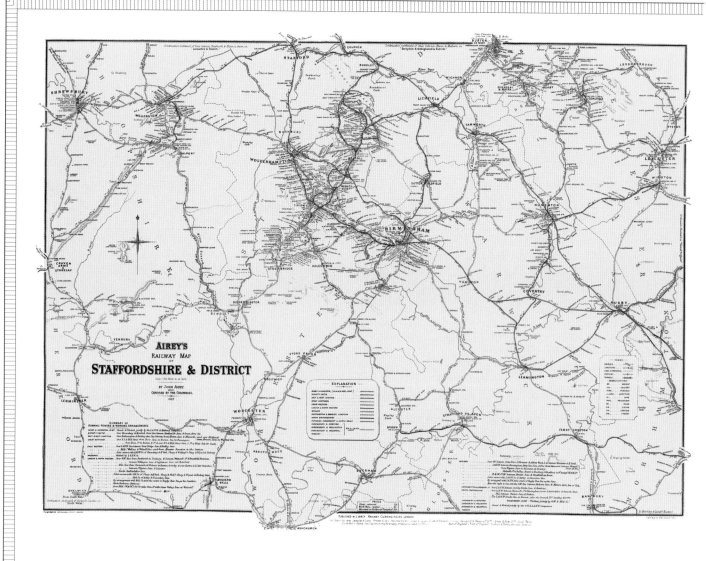

Title	Airey's Railway Map of Staffordshire & District
By	Railway Clearing House
Date	1887

This sheet, at a scale of 2 miles to 1 in., was one of a series of 13 regional maps available at the time from the Clearing House. In addition to railways, county boundaries are marked, together with some topographical detail of hills, rivers and canals. The map key contains not just the usual features such as bridges, roads and streets, but also 'FURN' for furnace, illustrating a widespread manifestation of the Industrial Revolution during that period.

To the west of the map and in the extract opposite is the Severn Valley Railway, whose north–south alignment and lack of direct connection to Birmingham made it an inevitable casualty in the modern era. It was already going through the closure procedure when the Beeching Report was published in 1963, but fortunately was later revived, as far north as Bridgnorth, as one of the longest preserved steam railways in Britain. Nearby Wellington was a major junction – partly through inter-company competition – where routes converged from six different directions, but is nowadays just an intermediate stop on the surviving Wolverhampton–Shrewsbury line.

This map provides some evidence for David Smith's comment in *Maps and Plans for the Local Historian and Collector* (1988) that, 'Despite Airey's high reputation, many of his maps are difficult to date and some were certainly prepared by careless and inexpert staff.' A Bridgnorth to Wolverhampton line is shown as 'in progress', but in fact it was never built.

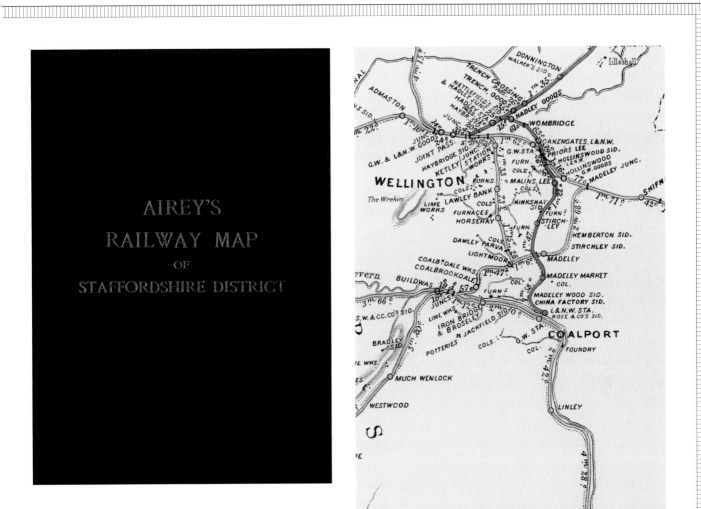

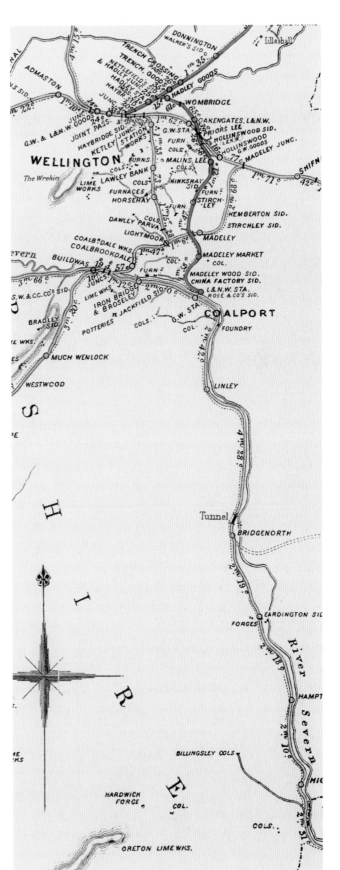

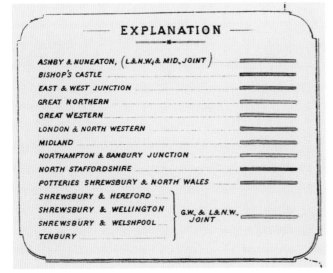

EXPLANATION

ASHBY & NUNEATON, (L&N.W.& MID. JOINT)	
BISHOP'S CASTLE	
EAST & WEST JUNCTION	
GREAT NORTHERN	
GREAT WESTERN	
LONDON & NORTH WESTERN	
MIDLAND	
NORTHAMPTON & BANBURY JUNCTION	
NORTH STAFFORDSHIRE	
POTTERIES SHREWSBURY & NORTH WALES	
SHREWSBURY & HEREFORD	
SHREWSBURY & WELLINGTON	G.W. & L&N.W. JOINT
SHREWSBURY & WELSHPOOL	
TENBURY	

STAFFORD

CANAL

GNOSAL

NEWPORT

LIME PITS

WORKS

Church Eaton

BIRMINGHAM & LIVERPOOL JUNCTION CANAL

Wheaton Aston

BREWOOD

GAILEY

FOUR ASHES

BREWOOD FORGE

Shareshill

BOSCOBEL OAK

White Ladies

Chillington Hall

Chillington Hall

SHIFNAL

LAWTON SID.

RUCKLEY SID.

HOLYOAKES QUARRY

ALBRIGHTON

CODSALL

BILL BROOK SID.

Wrottesley Park

PENKRIDGE GOODS PASS.

STAFFORD & WORCESTER CANAL

CHURCH BRIDGE CANAL

TEDDESLEY Park

RUGELEY

RUGELEY TOWN

BRERETON COL. SID.

FAIR OAKS COL. SID.

Beaudesert Park

CANNOCK CHASE

HEDNESFORD

BALLAST PITS

WEST CANNOCK COL. SID.

EAST CANNOCK COL.

CANNOCK

CANAL DOCK

LITTLEWORTH TRAM EXTENSN. JUNC.

CANNOCK & LEACROFT COL. SID.

NORTON GREEN COL.

JONES'S SID.

GILPIN & CO'S SID.

CHURCH BRIDGE

WYRLEY

GREAT WYRLEY COL. SID.

END OF BRANCH

HARRISON'S SID.

BROWNHILLS

CONDUIT COL. CO'S SID.

BROWNHILLS COL. SID.

OWEN'S SID.

CANAL

NORTON CANNOCK COL. SID.

RHYDER HAYES COL. SID.

ESSINGTON WOOD COL. SID.

GOSCOT IRON WKS.

PELSALL IRON WKS.

PELSALL

LEIGHS WOOD BRANCH

WALSALL WOOD

NORTON BOX SID.

NEWLANDS SID.

ALDRIDGE PASS. & JUNC.

BUSHBURY

BUSHBURY STA. & JUNC.

JUNC.

OXLEY SID.

STAFFORD RD. JUNC.

VICTORIA BASIN

HERBERT STR. GOODS

LOW LEVEL STA.

L. & N.W. STA.

CRANE STR. JUNC.

MID. GOODS

WEDNESFIELD HTH.

HEATH TOWN

WEDNESFIELD

WILLENHALL MARKET PLACE

MONMORE COL.

SHORT HEATH

BIRCHILLS HALL IRON CO'S SID.

THOMAS'S SID.

COLS.

BLOXWICH

BIRCHILLS

RUSHALL

WOLVERHAMPTON

WALSALL STR. W.M. GOODS

MONMORE GREEN

CHILLINGTON SID.

W'HAMPT'N. FURN.

BENTLEY

NORTH WALSALL

RYECROFT JUNC.

COZEN'S SID.

WALSALL

L. & N.W. GOODS

MID. GOODS

JUNC. (MEAN)

EAST JUNC.

PLECK JUNC.

STOW HEATH SID.

JUNC. — COLS.

PRIESTFIELD

ROOFING CO'S SID.

HORTON'S SID.

DARLASTON STEEL & IRON CO.

DARLASTN. PASS.

VERNON'S SID. (OLD BESCOT)

ROSES & LLOYD'S SIDS.

SOUTH JUNC.

BESCOT STA.

ELWELL'S SID.

ETTINGSHALL RD. & BILSTON

PARK'S FURN.

PARKFIELD SID.

BILSTON

SPRING VALE SID. (HICKMAN'S)

BILST'N. W.M.

COL.

BILSTON MAIN LINE

FURN.

G.W. PASS.

WOOD GREEN

CRANKHALL WATERWKS. SID.

WEDNESBURY

L. N.W. PASS.

BEACON HILL QUARRY

COSELEY NEW FURN.

DEEPFIELDS

SPRINGF'L. COL.

COLS.

Sedgley

QUARRY

BLOOMFIELD BASIN

COLS.

DAISEY BANK & MOXLEY

BRADL'Y.

PRINCE'S END

G.W.

L. N.W.

WILLMS.

G.W. GOODS

OCKER HILL

TIBBINGTON SID.

BARROW & HALLS

L. & N.W.

COL.

GREAT BRIDGE

COPPICE COL.

HALL END COL.

SWAN VILLAGE JUNC.

NEWTON ROAD

HAMSTEAD COL. SID.

Wombourne

TIPTON

G.W. STA.

WATERY

LANESIDE

DUDLEY PORT JUNC.

HIGH L. STA.

HORSLEYFIELD

SWAN BASIN

WEST BROMWICH

IRON MINES

DIPDALE FURN.

CASTLE MILL WKS.

IRON MINES

L. & N.W. GOODS

G.W. STA.

SEDGELEY SID.

CEDGREE SID.

IRON WKS.

ALBION PASS.

L. & N.W. STA.

SPON LANE

SANDWELL PARK COL. SID.

HANDSWORTH JUNC.

STH. SIDE & NETHERTON

BRETTELL & CARTWRIGHT'S SID.

DUDLEY

L. & N.W. PASS.

JUNC.

G.W. GOODS

MID. GOODS

BUFFERY IRON WKS.

OLDBURY

G.W. GOODS

G.W. PASS.

SMETHWICK JUNC. STA.

HANDSWORTH

SMETHWICK

FURNACE

SHUTEND

TANSEY GREEN COLS.

WOODHALL & CO'S SID.

BRADLEY & CO'S SID.

KINGSWINFORD & CORBYN'S HALL

MATHEW'S SID.

BROMLEY

BROWN & FREEN'S SID.

KINGSWINFORD GLASS WKS.

BRETTELL LANE IRON WKS.

GLASS WKS.

GOTHERSLEY IRON WORKS

GREEN'S FORGE

FLOTHERIDGE BASIN

ROUND OAK

LEVEL SID.

BRIERLEY HILL COLS.

HIPKINS SID.

MOOR LANE SID.

WITHYMOOR BASIN

WINDMILL END

COCHRANE SID.

WOODSIDE IR. WKS.

COL. SID.

GAYFIELD CLAY WORKS

NEW BRITISH IRON CO.

OLD HILL SID.

LANGLEY GREEN

SALTON JR.

MUNTZ METAL CO.

PATENT NUT & BOLT CO.

WATT'S & SID.

ROWLEY

BLACKHEATH COL.

OLD HILL

STATION & JUNC.

WINSON GREEN

ICKNIELD PORT RD.

ROTTEN PARK RD.

HAGLEY ROAD

HARBORNE

CHURCH RD.

SOMERSET RD.

SOHO

HOCKLEY

STOURBRIDGE

GOODS & BASIN

TOWN PASS.

GLASS WKS.

JUNC. STA.

LYE STA.

MOOR COL.

KING BRO'S SID.

HARPER & MOORE'S SID.

FISHER BRO'S SID.

CRADLEY PARK COL. CO.

EVERS & CO'S SID.

CRADLEY

STOURGREAVES SID.

G.W. IRON WKS.

HALESOWEN

COL.

DUDLEY CANAL

Lappal Tunnel

WEOLEY QUARRY

SELLY OAK

STIRCHLEY STR. & BOURNVILLE

RIVER SEVERN

ARELY

COLS.

CLAY WORKS

DOWLES WORKS

HIGHLEY

COLS.

Kinver

IRON WORKS

IRON WORKS

COOKLEY FORGES

WIRE MILL

BROADWATERS FORGES

CLAY WORKS

HAMPTON LOADE

HAGLEY

CHURCHILL Viaduct

SPRINGBROOK FORGES

BELBROUGHTON FORGE

CLENT HILLS

HILLPOOL FORGES

WEYBRIDGE FORGE

KIDDERMINSTER

FACTORY

STATION

JUNCTION

HUNNINGTON

LIME WKS.

FRANKLEY

RUBERY JNT.

NORTHFIELD STA.

NORTHFIELD JUNC.

Tunnel

ROLLING

BROMSGROVE LICKEY

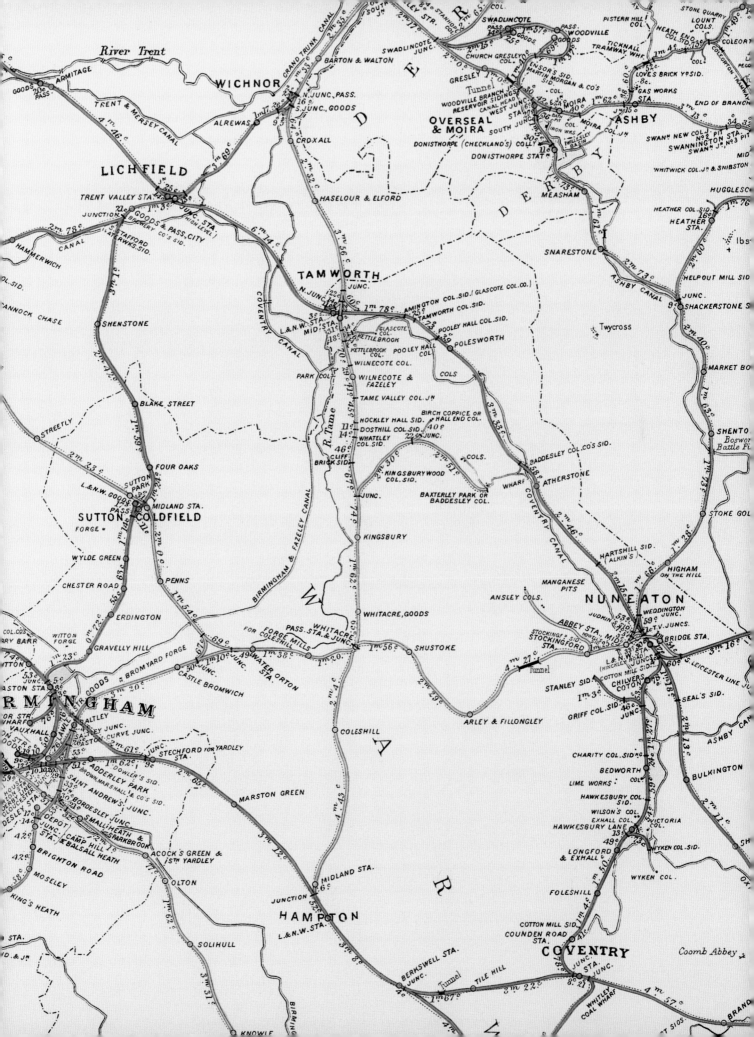

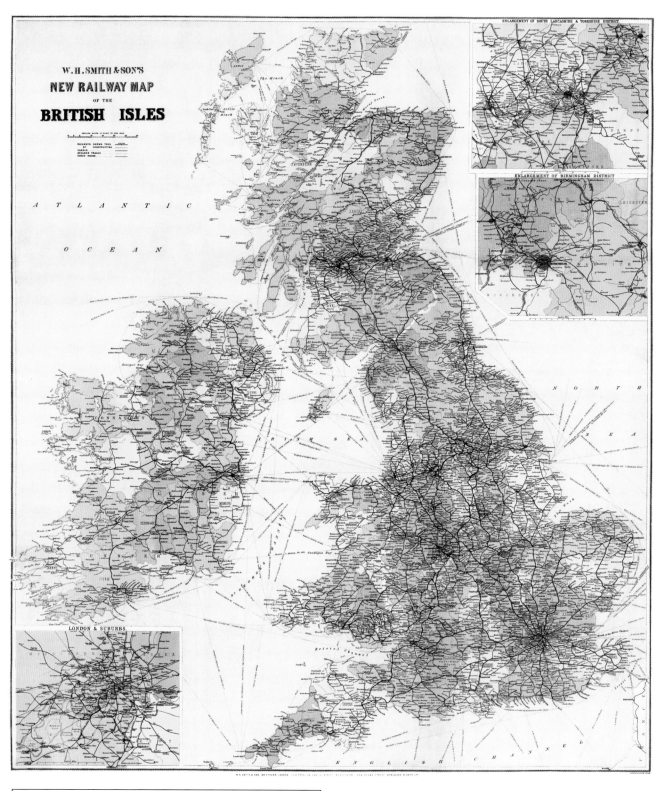

Title	W H Smith & Son's New Railway Map of the British Isles
By	J Bartholomew, Edinburgh
Date	1887

The long-established High Street name of W H Smith (whose origins lie in 18th-century London) took advantage of the Victorian railway boom by developing a network of news-stands at stations throughout England and Wales (in Scotland, John Menzies dominated the market until their takeover by Smith's in the late 20th century).

It was only natural that Smith's would want to commission rail network maps, in this case from the famous Edinburgh mapmaker, John Bartholomew. The original is a fold-up map, allowing different sections of the country to be viewed without spreading the entire large sheet out. As the map and extracts show, a very large proportion of the rail network was complete by 1887.

The extract below focuses on the counties of Devon, Dorset, Somerset and Wiltshire, within which by far the most notable absence is the completed main lines of the Great Western Railway (GWR). A further two decades were to elapse

before the GWR had opened all its important 'cut-offs' which shortened the distance between Paddington station in London and Temple Meads in Bristol (by means of the Swindon–Badminton–Bristol section in 1903), and between Paddington and Exeter (Stert to Westbury in 1900, and Castle Cary to Taunton in 1906).

Amongst the relatively few other lines still to be built were the Blagdon branch in Somerset, the Lyme Regis branch on the Devon/Dorset border, the meandering cross-country route from Halwill Junction in north Devon via Launceston to Padstow in north Cornwall, and one of the very last railways to be constructed in the pre-modern era – the Halwill Junction to Torrington link which was opened as a standard gauge light railway as late as 1925. Across the Bristol Channel in south Wales, the Vale of Glamorgan Railway from Cardiff to Bridgend via Barry had also yet to open.

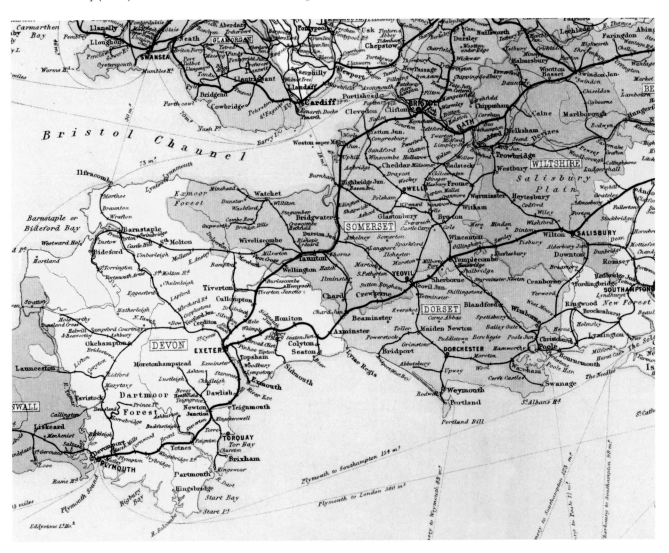

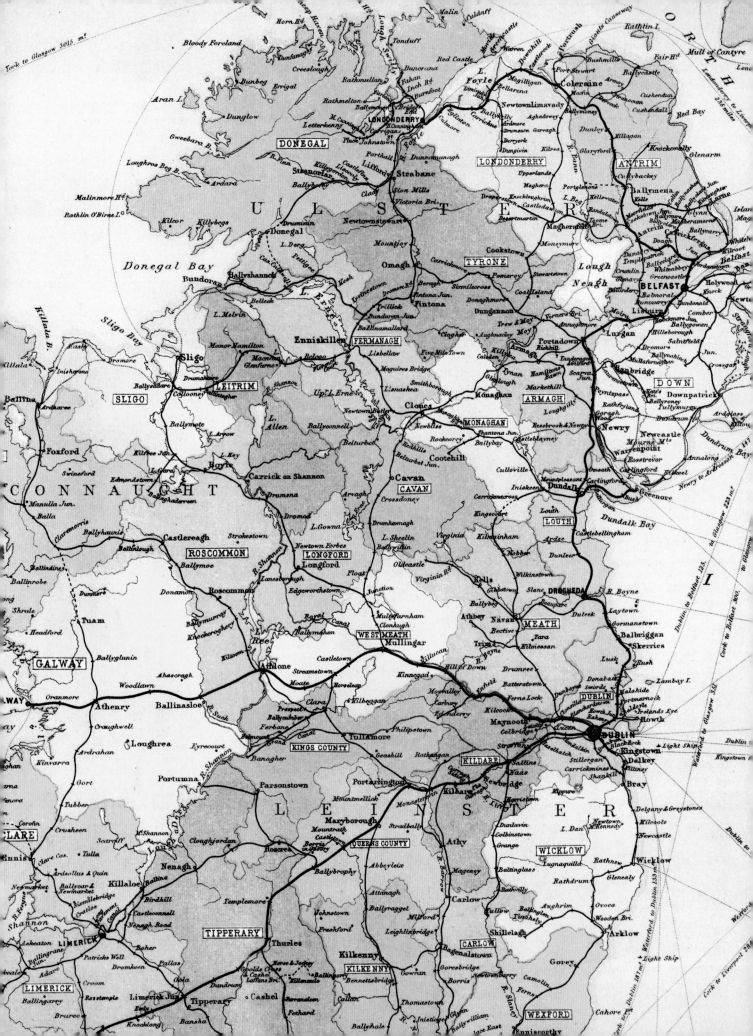

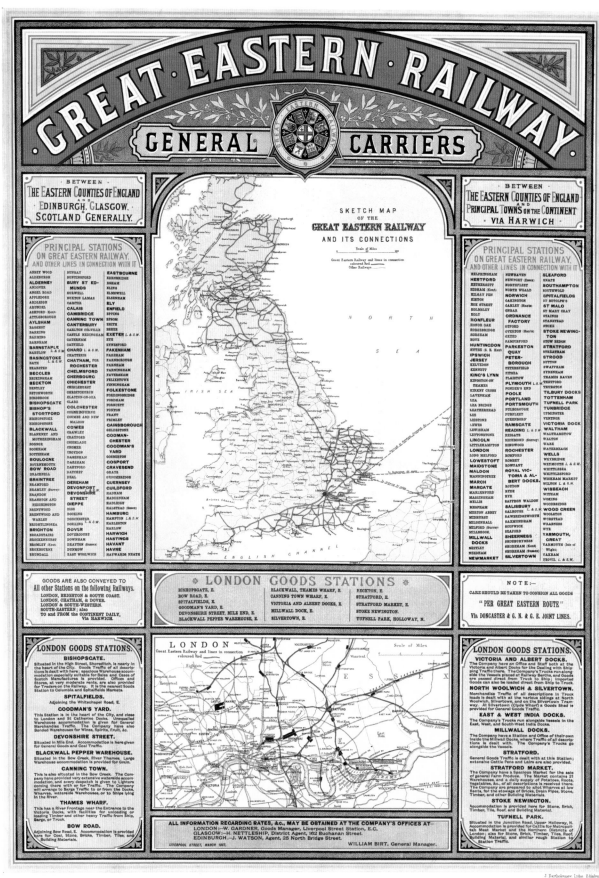

Title	Great Eastern Railway. General carriers
By	J Bartholomew, Edinburgh
Date	1887

This map poster illustrates the major role of the railways in serving the merchandise needs of the nation in the late 19th century. Interestingly, in the main map, the Great Eastern Railway (GER) gives the impression of serving two quite distinct and discrete territories – southeast England and Scotland – with just one railway, the East Coast Main Line, linking the two. In practice the GER would offer through goods services to locations the length and breadth of the country, with the Railway Clearing House sorting out the complex business of financial allocations between those companies over whose rails the goods wagons travelled.

The detailed map of London identifies no less than 16 goods stations operated by the GER in its main zone of influence in the centre and east end of the city. Just about anything would be carried on the railways at that time, and the depot descriptions demonstrate the sheer variety of commodities handled by thousands of railway staff on a daily basis. Within the sprawling expanse of the Bishopsgate depot, which survived until the 1970s:

> Goods traffic of all descriptions is dealt with here; spacious warehouse accommodation especially suitable for Bales and Cases of Scotch Manufactures is provided.

A couple of miles east at the Bow Road depot, 'Accommodation is provided here for Coal, Stone, Bricks, Timber, Tiles and Building Materials'. Today, there is still a rail freight depot in Bow, albeit relocated to the main line, less than a mile away from the original site. Here, stone from the Mendips and East Midlands, and concrete blocks from Yorkshire, arrive by rail for distribution round London by road; while East London's waste is sent by train to landfill in Oxfordshire.

At Stratford Market, yet further east, the poster announces that:

> The Company have a Spacious Market for the sale of general Farm Produce. The Market contains 21 warehouses, and a daily supply of Potatoes, Roots, Vegetable, &c., of all descriptions is received there.

The railways also worked very closely with shipping services at London's many docks on the River Thames. At the Victoria & Albert Docks:

> The Company's Trucks run alongside the vessels placed at Railway Berths, and Goods are passed direct from Truck to Ship.

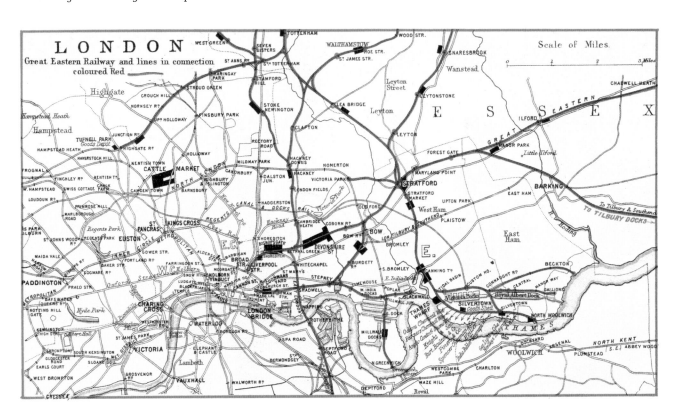

Demolished in 1962, Philip Hardwick's Doric Arch was built at the entrance to London & Birmingham Railway's Euston station in 1836.

During the 19th century the map of London changed beyond all recognition. In less than a century the villages and green fields that once surrounded the city were replaced by the sprawl of Victorian development, all made possible by the coming of the railways and the consequent birth of a modern, mobile society.

By the 1840s the railways were approaching London from all points of the compass – the first true inter-city line to reach the capital was the London & Birmingham Railway (LBR) which opened to Euston in 1838. It took another 11 years before Philip Hardwick's famous Doric Arch and his son's Great Hall at Euston were completed. Sadly these were both demolished by British Railways in the early 1960s and replaced by the current bland modern building.

Although Euston was the earliest terminus of an inter-city railway in London, the first terminus to be built in the capital was at London Bridge which was opened by the London & Greenwich Railway in 1836. This was later developed as two stations, becoming the terminus of the London, Brighton & South Coast Railway and a through station for South Eastern & Chatham Railway trains to Charing Cross and Cannon Street.

Next on the scene was the Eastern Counties Railway (ECR) which opened its Bishopsgate terminus in 1840. By numerous takeovers of other railways the ECR became the main constituent company of the newly formed Great Eastern Railway (GER) in 1862. Outgrowing its cramped Bishopsgate terminus the GER built a grand new station on the site of Bethlem Hospital – Liverpool Street, as it was known, was opened in 1874.

By the time that the LBR had reached Euston in 1838, Brunel's broad gauge Great Western Railway was nearing completion. With its terminus at Paddington, the line to Bristol opened throughout on 30 June 1841 and it soon became a byword for speed and comfort, although the Paddington station we know today was not completed until 1854.

Many other railways were soon reaching London, all of them desperate to take a share in the burgeoning business of rail travel. The London & South Western Railway opened its terminus at Waterloo in 1848 – it was subsequently enlarged on several occasions and is now the busiest station in Britain; the Great Northern Railway opened King's Cross in 1852; the London, Brighton & South Coast Railway opened the west side of Victoria station in 1860 and the London, Chatham & Dover Railway opened the east side in 1862. Built on the site of Hungerford Market, Charing Cross station was opened by the South Eastern Railway in 1864; and the North London Railway's suburban line terminus at Broad Street opened in 1865 – it closed in 1986 and was subsequently demolished. Cannon Street was opened by the South Eastern Railway in 1866; built on the site of slums, a church and a graveyard, George Gilbert Scott's splendid gothic-revival

St Pancras was opened by the Midland Railway in 1868 - at the time its train shed had the largest single-span roof in the world. Escaping demolition in the 1960s, it has since become the terminus of High Speed trains to the Continent via the Channel Tunnel; Holborn Viaduct was opened by the London, Chatham & Dover Railway in 1874, and it closed in 1990.

Last, but by no means least, the Great Central Railway opened its London Extension to Marylebone station, one of the smallest and most charming of the London termini, in 1899. Although it lost its main line services to Nottingham in 1966, Marylebone has since seen major growth in traffic on the Chiltern Lines to Aylesbury, Bicester and Birmingham, with its four platforms increased to six in recent years.

A busy scene on Platform 1 at Paddington station in 1931.

Painted by Fred Taylor, this Midland Railway poster shows the interior of St Pancras station in 1910.

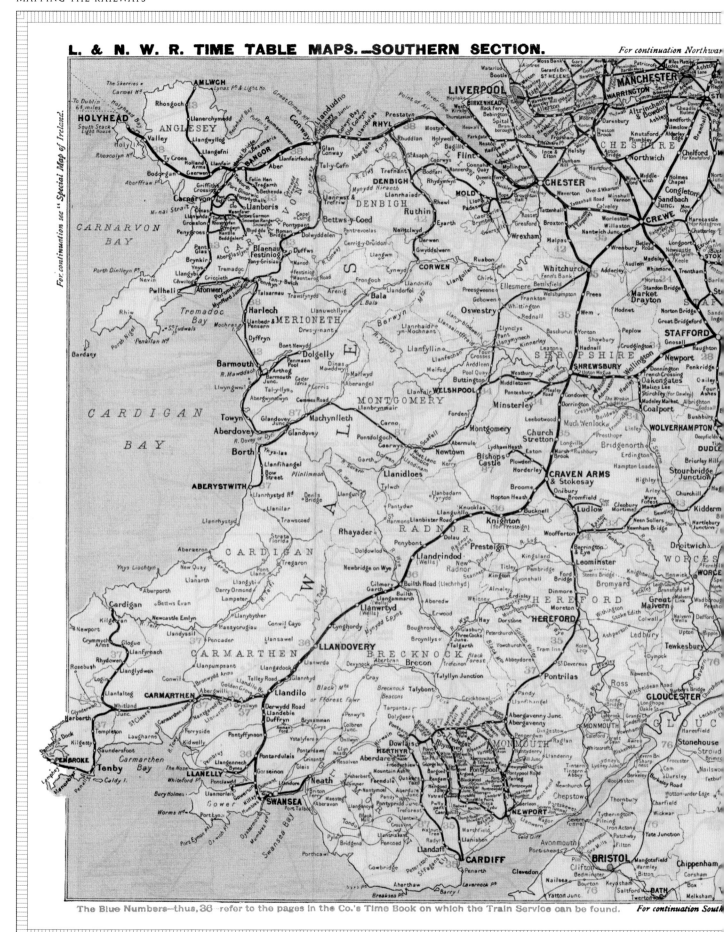

L. & N. W. R. TIME TABLE MAPS.—SOUTHERN SECTION.

For continuation Northwar...

For continuation see "Special Map of Ireland."

The Blue Numbers—thus, 36—refer to the pages in the Co.'s Time Book on which the Train Service can be found.

For continuation South...

Title	L. & N.W.R. Time Table Maps – Southern Section
By	London & North Western Railway
Date	1887

The railway companies issued detailed maps with their public timetables, and the maps would typically, as in this example from the London & North Western Railway (LNWR), show the appropriate train service table number against each line on the map. Companies would often downplay the importance of their rivals, and the LNWR was no exception – relegating Great Western Railway (GWR) routes to the narrowest of lines on the map, yet elevating northwest Wales narrow-gauge lines which connected with the LNWR to the same stature as the latter.

By 1887 there were just a few rural rail routes yet to be built in Wales – including the line to the small town of Aberaeron (on the coast south of Aberystwyth), whose station did not open until 1911, and closed to passengers just 40 years later.

The LNWR managed to penetrate well beyond its core territory – deep into the South Wales Valleys at Merthyr, Ebbw Vale, Tredegar and Nine Mile Point, via the Shrewsbury–Abergavenny line, and far into the Pembrokeshire countryside via the largely single-track Central Wales Line which terminated at Swansea Victoria station – a miraculous survivor, as far south as Llanelli, to this day. This penetration was achieved by joint ownership (with the GWR) in the case of the sections of line between Llandeilo and Llandovery, and Shrewsbury and Hereford, and by 'running powers' over the GWR between Hereford and Abergavenny.

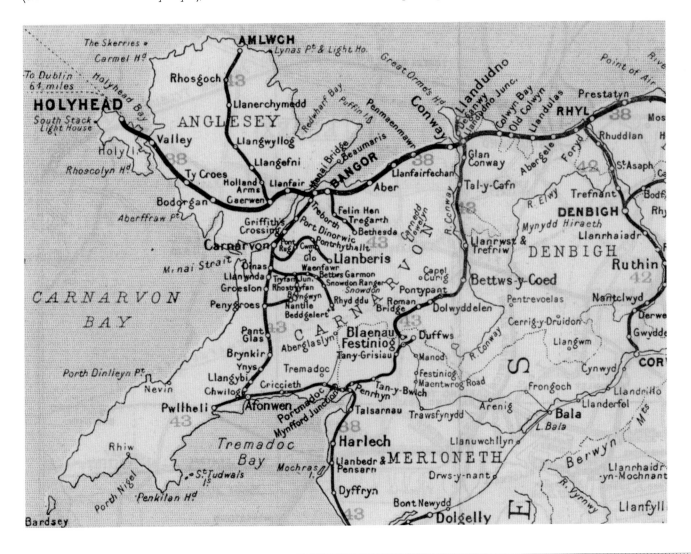

Title	General Sketch Map of the L & N.W.R. and its communications
Publisher	London & North Western Railway
Mapmaker	J Bartholomew, Edinburgh
Date	1887

Railway companies played a key part in developing the concept of the Victorian 'grand hotel', opening large and prestigious establishments the length and breadth of the country, from the 1830s through to the 1930s. The London & North Western Railway (LNWR) and its predecessor company played a pioneering role, as noted by the *Oxford Companion to British Railway History* (1997):

> *The first hotel for rail travellers was built alongside Crewe station by Lord Crewe, opened in 1837, leased by the London & North Western Railway in 1864, and bought outright in 1877. The first to be built by a railway were the twin hotels at Euston, opened in 1839 by the London & Birmingham Railway.*

A note handwritten in the margin of this LNWR 'hotel show bill' (or small poster – possibly also for use inside railway carriages) indicates that 10,025 copies were produced. It features 10 grand hotels served by the LNWR or connecting rail and shipping services, representing the apotheosis of comfort and style in the Victorian era. Fashions changed in due course, and the railway-owned hotels had varying fortunes. In June 1963 *Modern Railways* magazine recorded that:

> *The latest casualty amongst the historic buildings at the old station is Euston Hotel, which shut down on May 13 in readiness for demolition. It was the world's first railway hotel. Designed by P. Hardwick and opened about the year*

1840, it was originally called 'Victoria Hotel and Dormitories' and consisted of two separate buildings with some 40 bedrooms, a large coffee room and a lounge. In 1881 the two wings were connected by a large central block, bringing the total number of bedrooms to 141, and the whole building was renamed Euston Hotel, with separate entrances to the east and west wings.

The remaining hotels in British Rail ownership were privatized in 1981, and only a few of those shown in this brochure still exist – notably the Central Hotel in Glasgow which has recently been restored to its former grandeur.

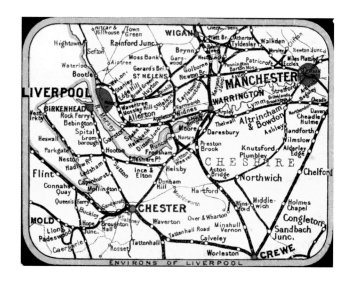

LONDON & NORTH WESTERN RAILWAY COMPANY'S HOTELS

GREENORE

BIRMINGHAM

LONDON & N.W. HOTEL, LIVERPOOL

HOLYHEAD

CREWE

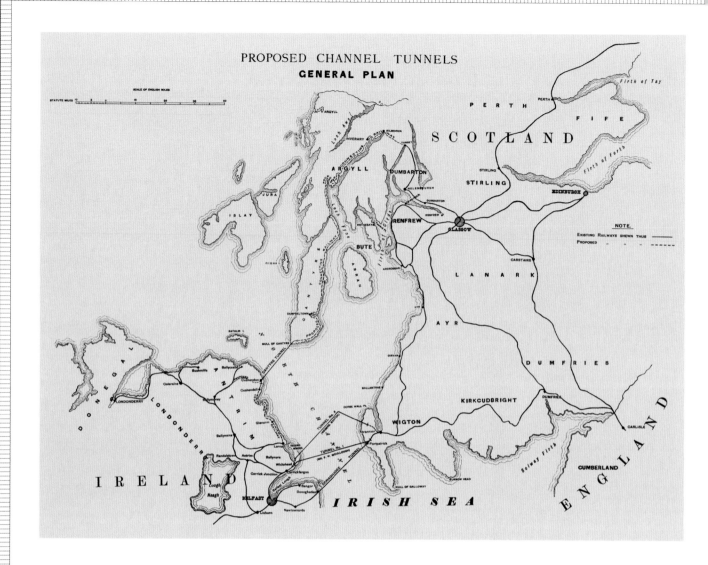

Title	The Proposed Channel Tunnel to Northern Ireland and through trains between Edinburgh, Glasgow, Manchester, Belfast, and Londonderry
By	L Livingston Macassey
Date	1890

This map comes from a fascinating prospectus setting out a variety of options for a little-known Victorian proposal to take trains under or across the North Channel of the Irish Sea between Scotland and Northern Ireland. Increased demand for travel at faster speeds is cited as a key justification for the scheme, but there were also more prosaic reasons:

There is, however, one thing in which time has made no change in the public mind, and that is the dread of sea sickness . . . . They would undergo the fatigue of a hundred miles trip by rail rather than risk the horrors of twenty miles in a rough sea.

No less than seven options are reviewed, perhaps the most fantastic being a submerged tubular bridge, comprising a steel and cement outer shell and an 'inner tube' containing the railway, with the whole structure 'to be kept in position by means of chains and anchors'. Prospective passengers would perhaps not have been wholly reassured about their safety in transit:

At intervals of 500 feet were water-tight doors so arranged as to close in cases of emergency. The rere [sic] of trains to be so designed as to act as a piston in order that in case of an inrush of water the train might be forced out of the tube.

At an estimated cost of £5.25 million, this would have been a bargain compared to the projected £70 million for a 'solid causeway' between the Mull of Cantyre [sic] and Northern Ireland. A Channel Bridge at £30 million is also rejected, and the map focuses on four tunnel options ranging in cost from £7.6 million to £16 million. The overall impact

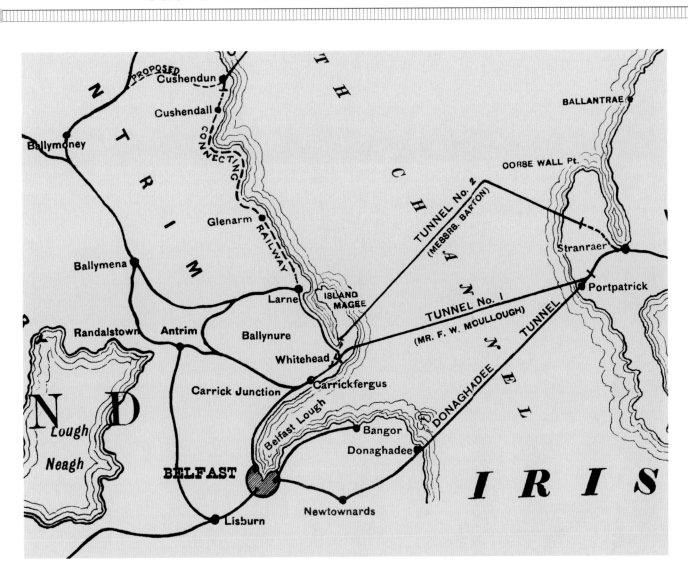

of the prospectus is, however, undermined by its concluding comments to the effect that:

> . . . no amount of traffic likely to arise would make the tunnel a dividend-paying concern . . . the channel tunnel must be constructed at the expense of the state. No railway company or body of speculators would ever venture upon an undertaking of so doubtful a character.

Unsurprisingly, no tunnel, bridge or causeway was ever built. If it had been, there would have been the additional difficulty of Britain's 4 ft 8½ in. track gauge trains meeting Ireland's distinctive 5 ft 3 in. gauge – however, to this day there are plenty of places on mainland Europe where broad gauge meets standard gauge, notably at the Spanish–French border, and suitable technical solutions have been developed. Possibly the Victorians would have provided 'mixed gauge' track from the tunnel mouth to Belfast, but we shall never know.

THE PROPOSED CHANNEL TUNNEL
AND THROUGH TRAINS BETWEEN
EDINBURGH, GLASGOW, MANCHESTER, BELFAST, AND LONDONDERRY.
BY
L. LIVINGSTON MACASSEY,

GLASGOW:
ROBERT FORRESTER, 1 ROYAL EXCHANGE SQUARE.
BELFAST:
WILLIAM MULLAN & SON, 4 DONEGALL PLACE.
1890.
PRICE SIXPENCE.

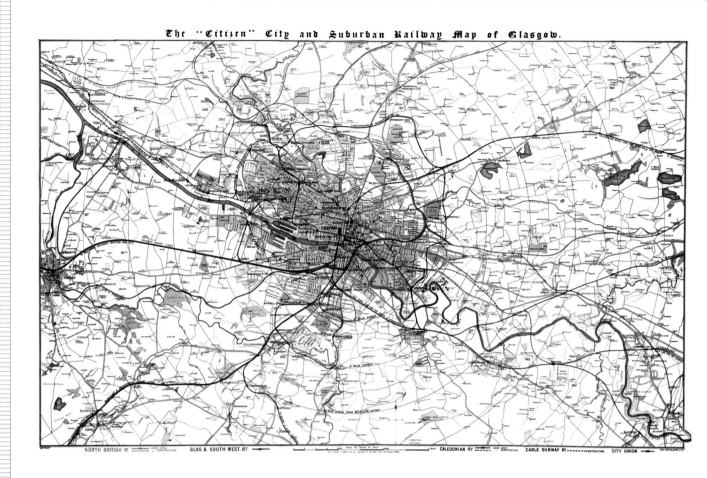

The "Citizen" City and Suburban Railway Map of Glasgow.

Title	The 'Citizen' City and Suburban Railway Map of Glasgow
By	J Bartholomew, Edinburgh
Date	c.1890–96

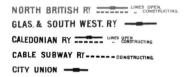

The famous Edinburgh mapmaking company of Bartholomew produced this clear and colourful map of Glasgow's developing rail network for the *Evening Citizen*, one of three evening newspapers in the then 'Second City' of the British Empire. The map's date is not shown, but reference to the 'Cable Subway Ry' (the Glasgow Underground) being under construction narrows the period down to 1890–96.

Bartholomew's map illustrates strikingly the competition between the two large Scottish railway companies battling for traffic in the more developed area of the city north of the River Clyde. This was the North British Railway's heartland in the city, with routes fanning out below ground and above ground from the jewel in the crown, Queen Street station – terminus of Scotland's first inter-city railway, from Edinburgh. The Caledonian Railway worked hard to extend its influence beyond its core territory south

of Glasgow Central, with the Lanarkshire & Dumbarton Railway striking west, close to the north bank of the River Clyde and the big markets for freight and passenger traffic in its dense concentration of dockyards and shipyards. Two offshoot lines converged at Maryhill and then meandered around the northern and eastern edges of the city through Springburn Park and Parkhead to Bridgeton. All the latter system has now disappeared, but the 'Argyle Line' linking Bridgeton, Central Low Level, Stobcross (now Exhibition Centre) and the new Partick interchange station, is a key link in the modern Strathclyde rail system.

Suburban housing development stimulated by new rail routes was still in its infancy south of the Clyde at the time of this map's publication, with two key lines yet to be opened from Cathcart – southwest to Neilston and Ayrshire (1903) and east through Kirkhill to the Caledonian main line junction at Newton (1904).

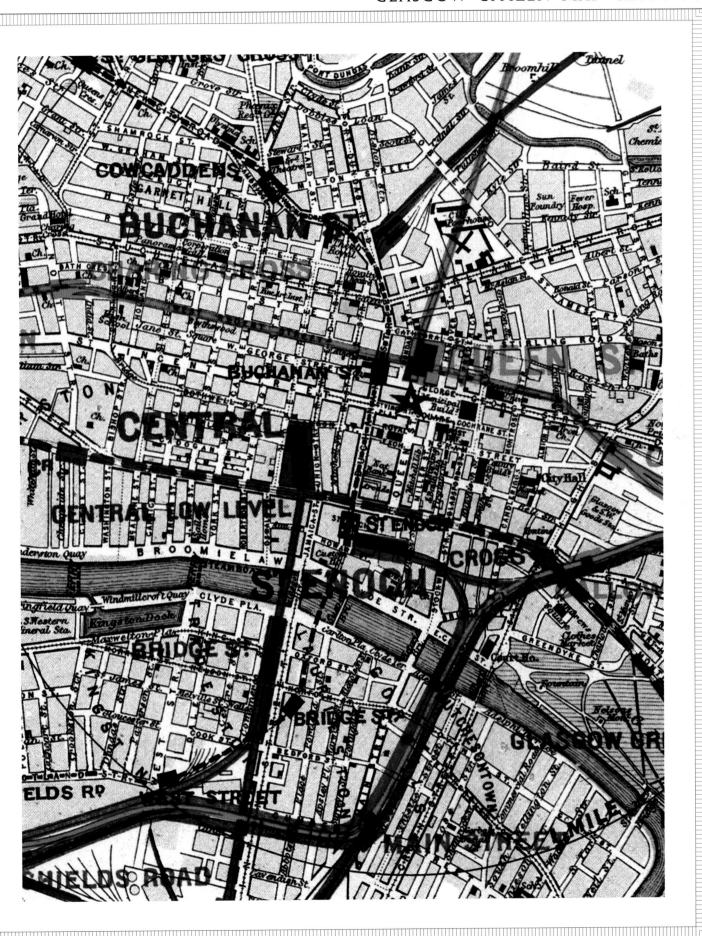

Title	Mountain, Moor and Loch, Illustrated by Pen and Pencil, on the Route of the West Highland Railway
Publisher	Sir Joseph Causton & Sons, London, for the North British Railway
Date	1895

As the railway historian John Thomas writes in his introduction to the 1972 reprint, the North British Railway (NBR) had several motives for producing *Mountain, Moor and Loch* to celebrate the opening of the West Highland Railway from Glasgow to Fort William in 1894:

> With its wealth of delightful pen sketches and accurately observed descriptive material it was one of the most distinctive and best-loved railway guides ever produced. The primary function of the book was to publicize the railway, but the North British used it quite ruthlessly as a political weapon to further the promotion of the westward extension of the railway. Less than two weeks before the opening of the railway the West Highland had obtained an Act for the extension of the railway to Mallaig. However, work on the extension could not begin until the company had a second Act authorizing a Government subsidy for the construction of the line . . . . The North British hoped that the opening of the West Highland would focus on attention on the need for railways in those remote parts and help to break down opposition to the public subsidizing of the Mallaig Extension.

Thomas notes that the 1894 edition of *Mountain, Moor and Loch* ran to 14,000 copies and that a second edition of 10,000 copies was printed in 1895. The overview map and five 'strip maps' of the railway in this book are reprinted from the latter edition. The text of the route guide ('A Bird's Eye View') begins:

> If you look at the map of Scotland you will see that the country on the West, is simply torn to tatters by lochs, either inland sheets of fresh water or far-reaching arms of the Atlantic . . . . Such a wild and picturesque district is a very Paradise for the tourist, but hitherto this 'Land of Mountain, Moor and Loch' has been remarkably difficult of access . . . . The West Highland Railway breaks fresh ground from start to finish of its hundred-mile run; carrying the traveller through what is, perhaps, the most sublime and characteristic portion of Scotland.

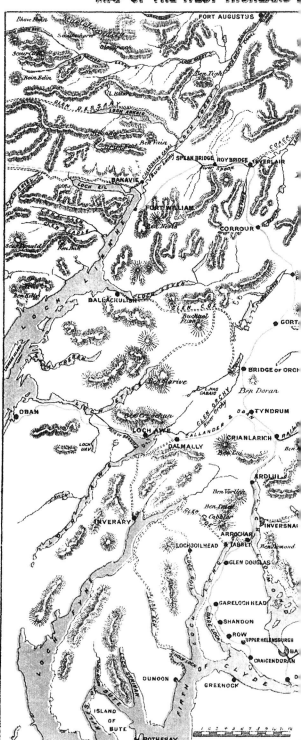

MAP OF THE WEST HIGHLAND

West Highland Railway & connection. Projected Railway, Banavie to Malla

ITINERARY.

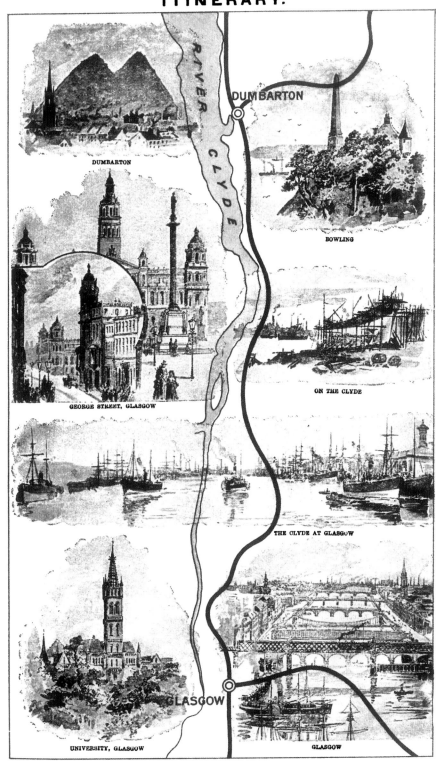

GLASGOW (QUEEN STREET) TO CRAIGENDORAN, 22¼ MILES.

DUMBARTON

BOWLING

GEORGE STREET, GLASGOW

ON THE CLYDE

THE CLYDE AT GLASGOW

UNIVERSITY, GLASGOW

GLASGOW

GLASGOW TO CRAIGENDORAN.
SECTION 1.

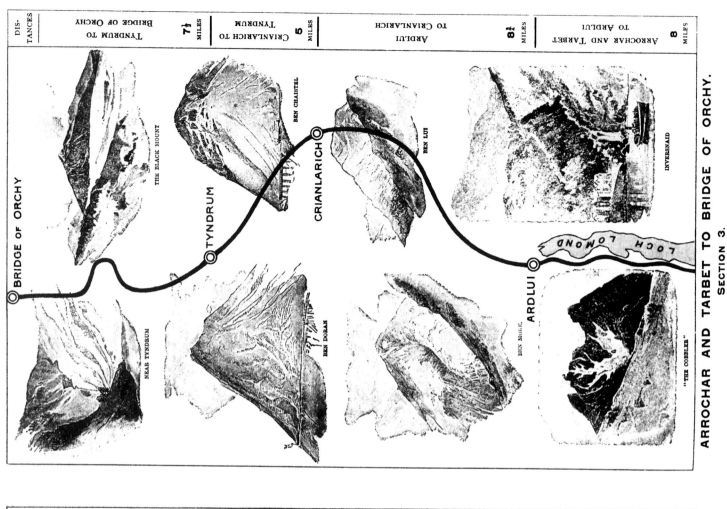

BRIDGE OF ORCHY

THE BLACK MOUNT

BEN CHAISTEL

TYNDRUM

CRIANLARICH

BEN LUI

INVERSNAID

LOCH LOMOND

NEAR TYNDRUM

BEN DORAN

BEN MORE

ARDLUI

"THE COBBLER"

ARROCHAR AND TARBET TO BRIDGE OF ORCHY.
SECTION 3.

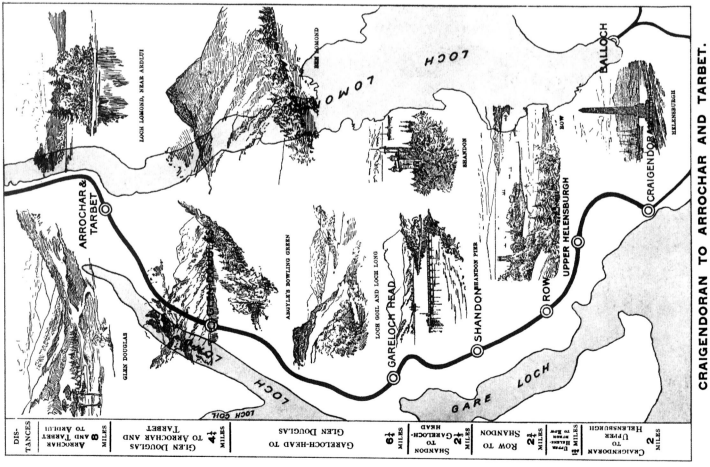

LOCH LOMOND, NEAR ARDLUI

LOMOND

LOCH LOMOND

BALLOCH

ARROCHAR & TARBET

SHANDON

HELENSBURGH

ARGYLE'S BOWLING GREEN

ROW

UPPER HELENSBURGH

CRAIGENDORAN

GLEN DOUGLAS

LOCH GOIL AND LOCH LONG

GARELOCH HEAD

SHANDON—SHANDON PIER

LOCH GOIL

LOCH

GARE LOCH

CRAIGENDORAN TO ARROCHAR AND TARBET.
SECTION 2.

DIS-TANCES		
ARROCHAR AND TARBET TO ARDLUI	8 MILES	
GLEN DOUGLAS TO ARROCHAR AND TARBET	4¼ MILES	
GARELOCH-HEAD TO GLEN DOUGLAS	6¾ MILES	
SHANDON TO GARELOCH-HEAD	2¼ MILES	
ROW TO SHANDON	2¼ MILES	
UPPER HELENSBURGH TO ROW	1¾ MILES	
CRAIGENDORAN TO UPPER HELENSBURGH	2 MILES	

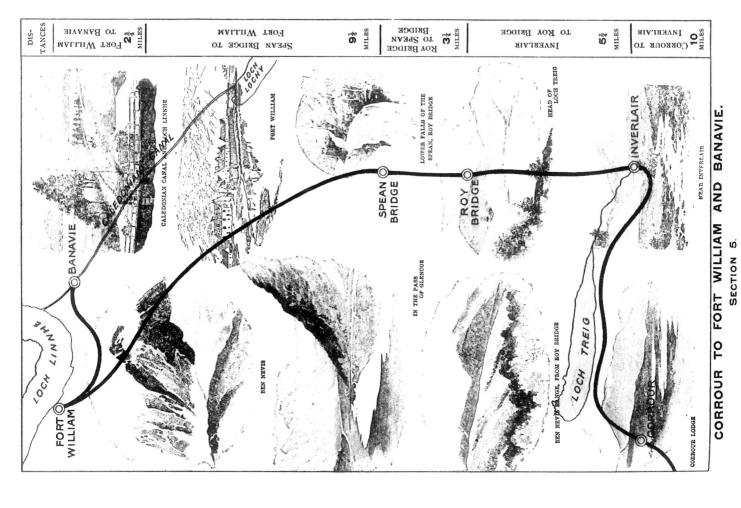

DIS-TANCES	FORT WILLIAM TO BANAVIE	2¾ MILES	SPEAN BRIDGE TO FORT WILLIAM	9½ MILES	ROY BRIDGE TO SPEAN BRIDGE	3¼ MILES	INVERLAIR TO ROY BRIDGE	5¾ MILES	CORROUR TO INVERLAIR	10 MILES

CALEDONIAN CANAL

LOCH LOCHY

FORT WILLIAM

CALEDONIAN CANAL, LOCH LINNHE

SPEAN BRIDGE

LOWER FALLS OF THE SPEAN, ROY BRIDGE

ROY BRIDGE

HEAD OF LOCH TREIG

INVERLAIR

NEAR INVERLAIR

BEN NEVIS

IN THE PASS OF GLENCOE

LOCH LINNHE

FORT WILLIAM

BANAVIE

BEN NEVIS RANGE, FROM ROY BRIDGE

LOCH TREIG

CORROUR

CORROUR LODGE

CORROUR TO FORT WILLIAM AND BANAVIE.

SECTION 5.

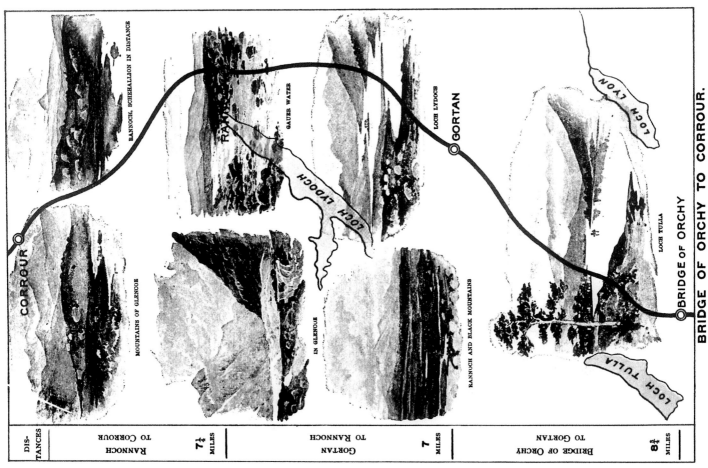

RANNOCH, SCHEHALLION IN DISTANCE

RANNOCH

GAUER WATER

LOCH LYDOCH

GORTAN

LOCH LYON

CORROUR

MOUNTAINS OF GLENCOE

LOCH LYDOCH

IN GLENCOE

RANNOCH AND BLACK MOUNTAINS

LOCH TULLA

BRIDGE OF ORCHY

LOCH TULLA

BRIDGE OF ORCHY TO CORROUR.

SECTION 4.

DIS-TANCES	RANNOCH TO CORROUR	7¼ MILES	GORTAN TO RANNOCH	7 MILES	BRIDGE OF ORCHY TO GORTAN	8¾ MILES

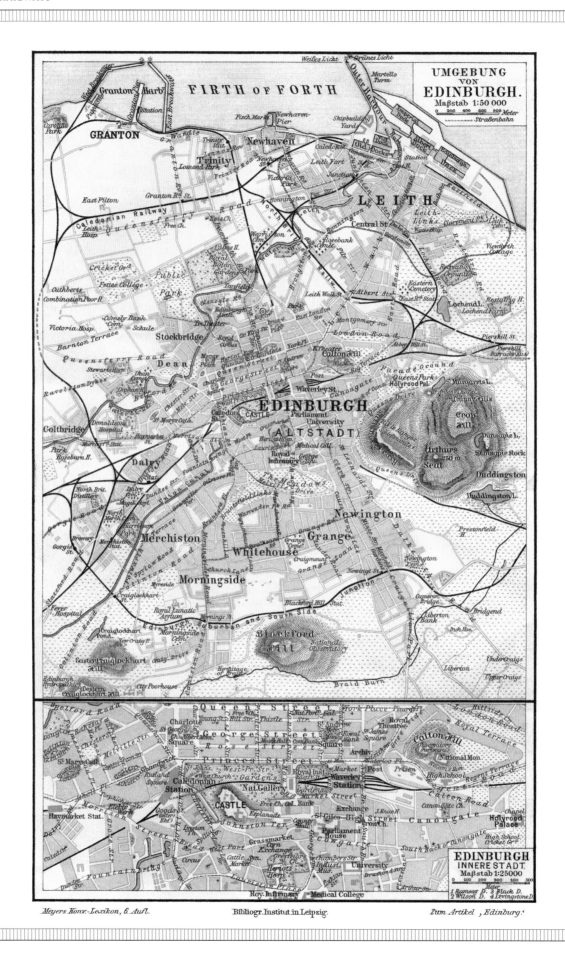

Title	*Umgebung von Edinburgh* (Surroundings of Edinburgh) and *Edinburgh Innere Stadt* (Inner City)
Publisher	Meyers Konversations-Lexikon
Date	1896

Meyers Lexikon was a major German encyclopedia published between 1839 and 1984. This attractive map was probably made in Britain, as the district and street names and topographical features are overwhelmingly in English – although there are some exceptions, such as *Altstadt* (old town), *Güter Bhf.* (goods station) and, intriguingly, *Weisses Licht* (white light) and *Grünes Licht* (green light) at the sea entrance to Leith Docks.

Edinburgh's relatively extensive suburban rail network is clearly delineated in black, while its well-developed tram system (*Strassenbahn*) is shown by hatched lines, including the long stretch linking Edinburgh and Leith (formerly two separate burghs) down Leith Walk, recently scheduled to be re-opened as part of a new Edinburgh tram route.

The routes of trains heading for the train ferries across the Firth of Forth (prior to the opening of the Forth Bridge in 1890) can be readily traced. The original route north from Canal Street station (at right angles to Waverley station) ran underground on a steep gradient down to Scotland Street station (by Royal Crescent) where the line emerged above ground and continued north through Trinity to Granton Harbour. The first section of this route, opened in 1847, had to be operated with cable haulage; the first train ferry in the world – from Granton to Burntisland – began operation in 1850; and by 1868 an eastern diversionary route was opened via Abbeyhill and Leith Walk stations, enabling standard locomotive haulage to replace the cable-operated incline.

The Scotland Street tunnel was then closed to passengers, but was used for some time to store freight wagons, and subsequently for growing mushrooms! Coal traffic, however, continued to arrive by train at Scotland Street goods yard (at the tunnel mouth) from the Granton direction until as late as 1967. The tunnel entrances are now sealed up, but the tunnel itself remains *in situ*, perhaps awaiting a new use in future times.

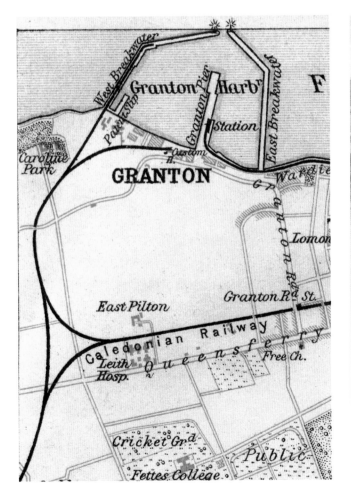

Coal wagons at Scotland Street goods yard, Edinburgh, in 1966, a year before its closure. From 1850 to 1868, passenger trains from Edinburgh Canal Street to the train ferry at Granton passed through the tunnel mouth in the background. A cycle track now follows the old rail route northwards from here to Granton.

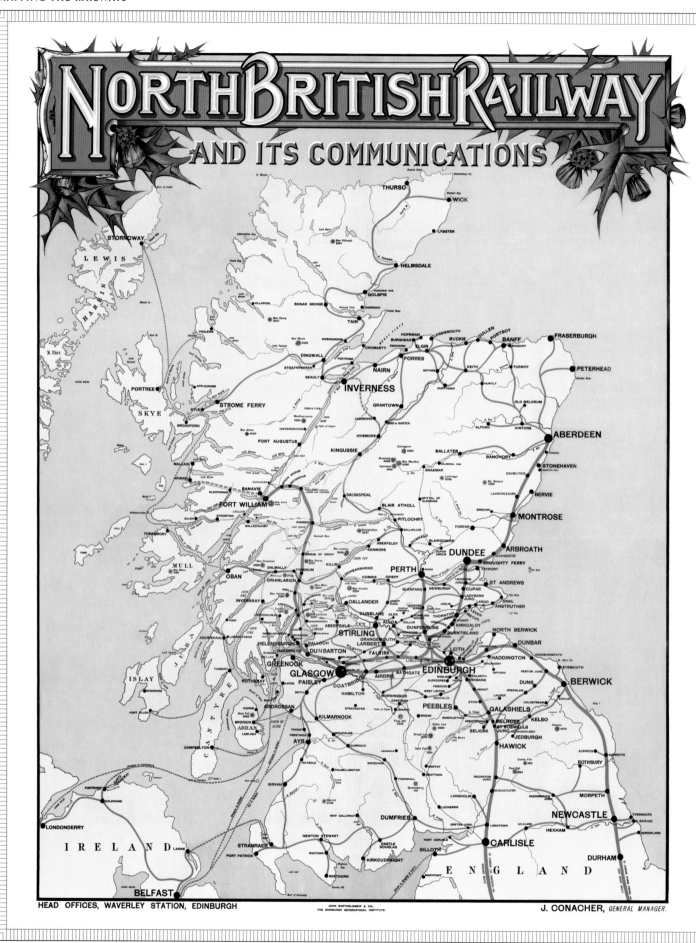

NorthBritishRailway
AND ITS COMMUNICATIONS

HEAD OFFICES, WAVERLEY STATION, EDINBURGH

JOHN BARTHOLOMEW & CO.
THE EDINBURGH GEOGRAPHICAL INSTITUTE.

J. CONACHER, GENERAL MANAGER.

Title	North British Railway and its communications
Mapmaker	J Bartholomew, Edinburgh
Date	1896

The North British Railway (NBR) was one of the two big railway companies which dominated Central Scotland up to the 1923 'Grouping'. As noted in the *Oxford Companion to British Railway History* (1997), competition with the Caledonian Railway (CR) was:

> *a key feature of the railway's existence, the two companies fighting each other over control of Fife and its coal; services from the south to Aberdeen, culminating in the races of 1895; suburban services in the Glasgow area – the CR's home territory; and the provision of great hotels, a contest which the NBR won hands down with its impressive building next to Waverley station, Edinburgh.*

The depth of rivalry between the two companies is aptly illustrated by aspects of this NBR map poster, which uses a simplified geographic style with a distinctly modern feel. The NBR was clearly keen to show all its potential future routes,

and those of companies with which it collaborated – the map represents with a pecked line the Highland Railway's direct Aviemore–Carrbridge–Inverness line (not opened until late 1898) and its own planned Mallaig Extension, which did not come into service until 1901.

The map extract of southern Scotland overleaf demonstrates that the lines of companies with whom the NBR had working agreements – in this case the Glasgow & South Western to Stranraer and Dumfries – were shown just as prominently on the map as its own routes. You have to look very carefully, however, to identify the Glasgow/Edinburgh–Carlisle main line of its great rival, arguably the premier Anglo-Scottish railway. Elsewhere on the map, key connecting horse-bus services are shown prominently, in some cases far from NBR territory – such as the link from the Great North of Scotland Railway's Ballater terminus to nearby Braemar.

The extent of railway-owned and rail-connected shipping services on the Clyde Estuary is also well represented – with routes to the islands of Bute and Arran, to the Kintyre peninsula and across the North Channel to Northern Ireland.

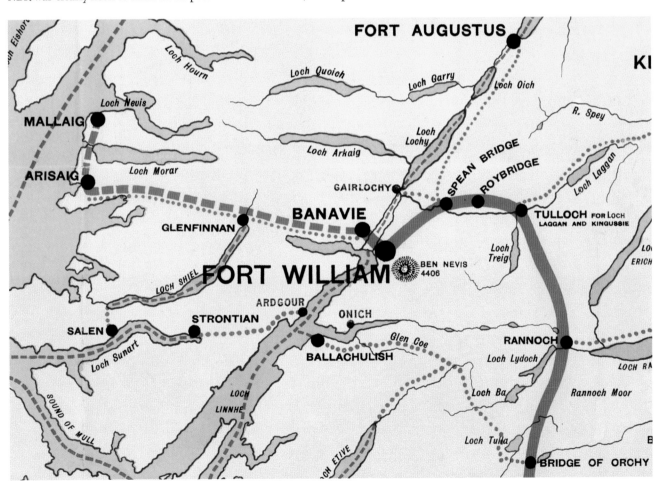

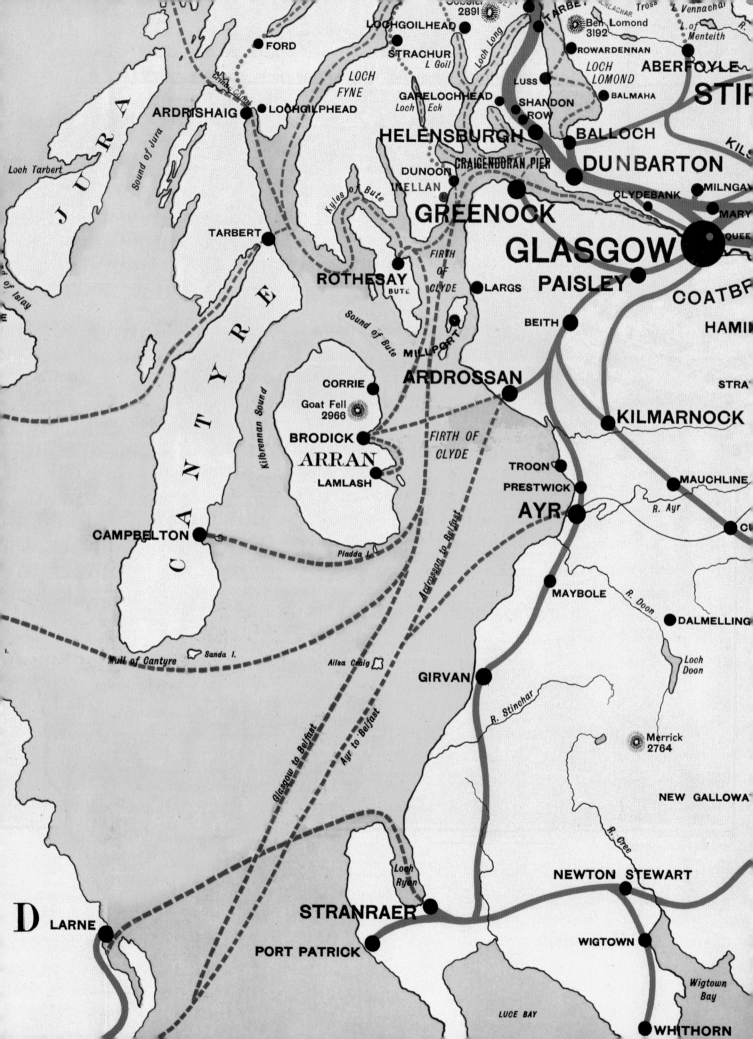

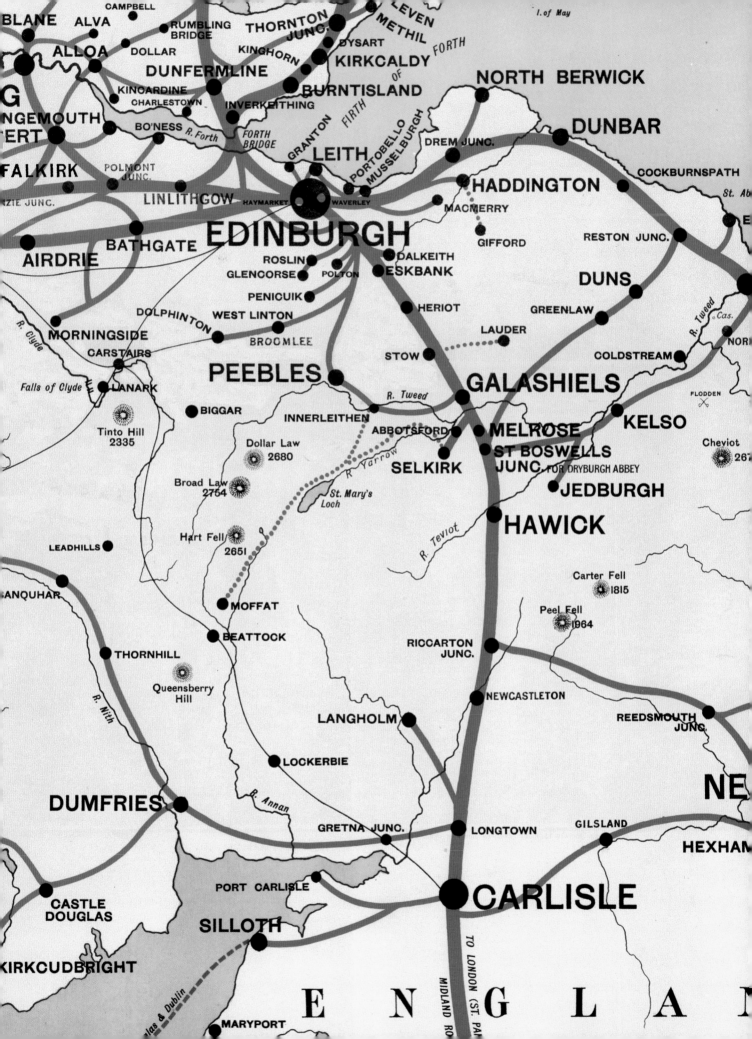

Ribblehead Viaduct is the longest and one of 23 viaducts built on the Settle & Carlisle line in the 1870s.

The Victorian railway builders certainly left their mark on the map of Britain. Standing the test of time, their graceful bridges and viaducts stride majestically across our landscape while their long, dark tunnels burrow deep beneath. The majority are still in use today.

Faced with natural obstacles such as rivers and ranges of hills, the early railway builders' achievements were spectacular. In particular the three trans-Pennine rail routes between Yorkshire and Lancashire merit special mention as they were built not only before the introduction of mechanical excavators but also before the invention of dynamite. The first of these railways was the Manchester & Leeds Railway which opened in 1841 and included the 1 mile 1,109 yd Summit Tunnel, at that time the longest in the world. This was soon followed by the Sheffield, Ashton-under-Lyne & Manchester Railway's 3 mile 13 yd Woodhead Tunnel, which opened in 1845, and the London & North Western Railway's 3 mile 57 yd Standedge Tunnel, which opened in 1848. (To the south the Midland Railway's 3 mile 950 yd Totley Tunnel was not completed until 1893.)

Without doubt the most amazing Victorian overland railway achievement was the building of the Midland Railway's Settle & Carlisle line which opened in 1876. Benefiting from the then recent invention of dynamite, a workforce of 6,000 navvies blasted their way up the bleak Pennine hills, building 13 tunnels and 23 viaducts. Of the former, Blea Moor is the longest at 1 mile 869 yd while of the latter, Ribblehead is the longest at 440 yd.

Down south the Great Western Railway, nicknamed 'Great Way Round' because of its circuitous route from London to South Wales via Gloucester, eventually bit the bullet and built, under the River Severn, what was then the longest underwater tunnel in the world. Beset by problems from flooding during construction, the 4 mile 624 yd Severn Tunnel opened in 1886 and was the longest rail tunnel in Britain until the opening of the High Speed 1 tunnel under London in 2007.

Meanwhile, in Scotland, the rail crossings of the Firth of Tay and Firth of Forth linking Edinburgh with Dundee and Aberdeen had run into problems. Officially opened by Queen Victoria in 1878, Thomas Bouch's 2¼ mile single-track Tay Bridge was then the longest bridge in the world and significantly cut journey times between Edinburgh and Dundee – although passengers still had to cross the Firth of Forth by ferry. However, Bouch's design was flawed and there were weaknesses in the cast ironwork used in its construction – only 18 months after it had been opened, a gale force wind swept away the centre section of its 85 spans while a passenger train was crossing. All 75 passengers along with the crew perished in the icy waters of the Tay. Thomas Bouch was disgraced and died a broken man, his design for a suspension bridge across the Firth of Forth being consigned to the wastepaper bin.

Aided by new developments in the use of steel, John Fowler and Benjamin Baker were able to design a cantilever bridge to carry a double-track railway across the Forth – when completed in 1890 it was the wonder of the Victorian world. Around 65,000 tons of steel were used in the construction of the 1½-mile bridge, then the largest cantilever bridge in the world. The Forth Bridge was built by William Arrol, a prolific contractor at that time as he had also built the replacement double-track Tay Bridge and London's Tower Bridge. These three structures have all stood the test of time and are fitting memorials to Britain's innovative Victorian engineers.

Rescuers search in vain in the windswept waters of the Firth of Tay for survivors from the 1879 Tay Bridge disaster.

Containing around 65,000 tons of steel, the Forth Railway Bridge was the largest cantilever bridge in the world when it opened in 1890.

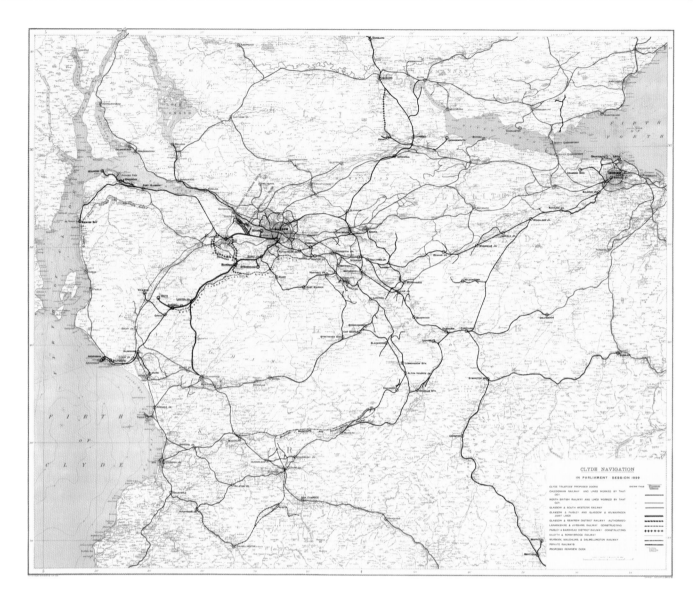

Title	Clyde Navigation
	In Parliament – Session 1899
Publisher	The Edinburgh Geographical Institute
Mapmaker	J Bartholomew, Edinburgh
Date	1899

Shipping-related dock schemes were presumably the primary motivation for production of this map, but in so doing Bartholomew's also created a clear and colourful snapshot of the largely completed expansion of the three big railway companies serving Central Scotland.

The Caledonian Railway had made a major incursion into Glasgow & South Western Railway (GSW) territory with its long isolated branch from the Glasgow suburbs to the key port of Ardrossan, while on the East Coast the 'Caley' pushed

through North British Railway (NBR) country to reach the prized port destinations of Granton and Leith.

The NBR was more modest in its territorial expansion, with only a few notable outreach lines, such as that to Hamilton in Lanarkshire. The smaller GSW remained largely self-contained, but it is interesting to note on the map the proposed railway from Largs to Wemyss Bay and onwards to Kilmacolm and Port Glasgow – this line was never built, and the absence of rails between Largs and Wemyss Bay has always been one of the more striking gaps in the Scottish rail network.

The map extract opposite illustrates how the opening of the Forth Bridge in 1890 had transformed the network immediately south of the Forth Estuary. A well-engineered main line had been built southeast towards Edinburgh,

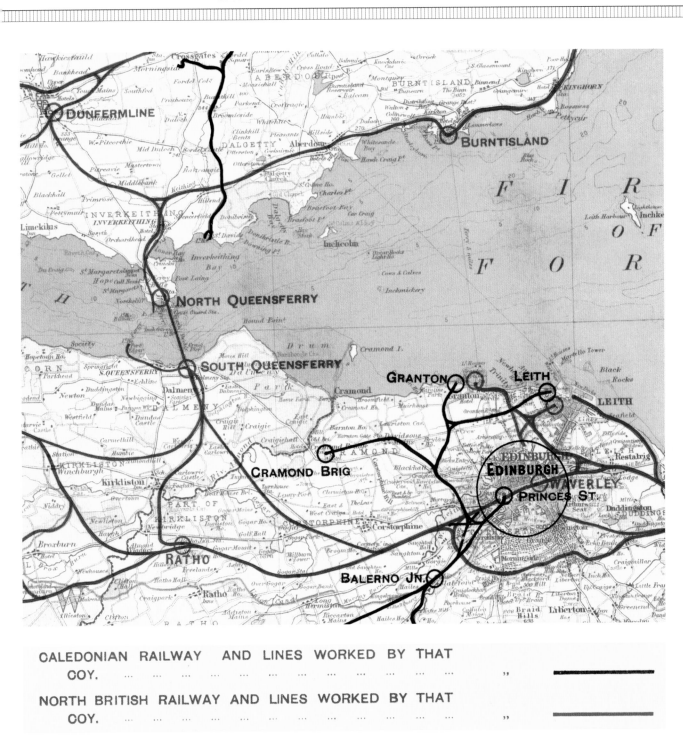

CALEDONIAN RAILWAY AND LINES WORKED BY THAT COY. ... ... ,,

NORTH BRITISH RAILWAY AND LINES WORKED BY THAT COY. ... ... ,,

carrying express trains from Aberdeen, Perth and Inverness, while the important chord line southwest to Winchburgh Junction, on the Edinburgh–Glasgow main line, allowed fast direct connection from Fife to Scotland's biggest city.

A number of smaller independent railways are shown, typically built for coal transport, as in the case of the Fordell Railway in Fife, a former waggonway which had been converted to steam haulage and linked by means of

interchange sidings to the standard gauge network by 1868. The line – which remained at the unusual 4 ft gauge throughout its life – ran from collieries in the Cowdenbeath and Crossgates areas down to St David's Harbour on Inverkeithing Bay. The southern end of the line, and the harbour, were last used for coal exports in 1946, and the remaining section of the line closed in 1966 when the last of the mines it served also closed.

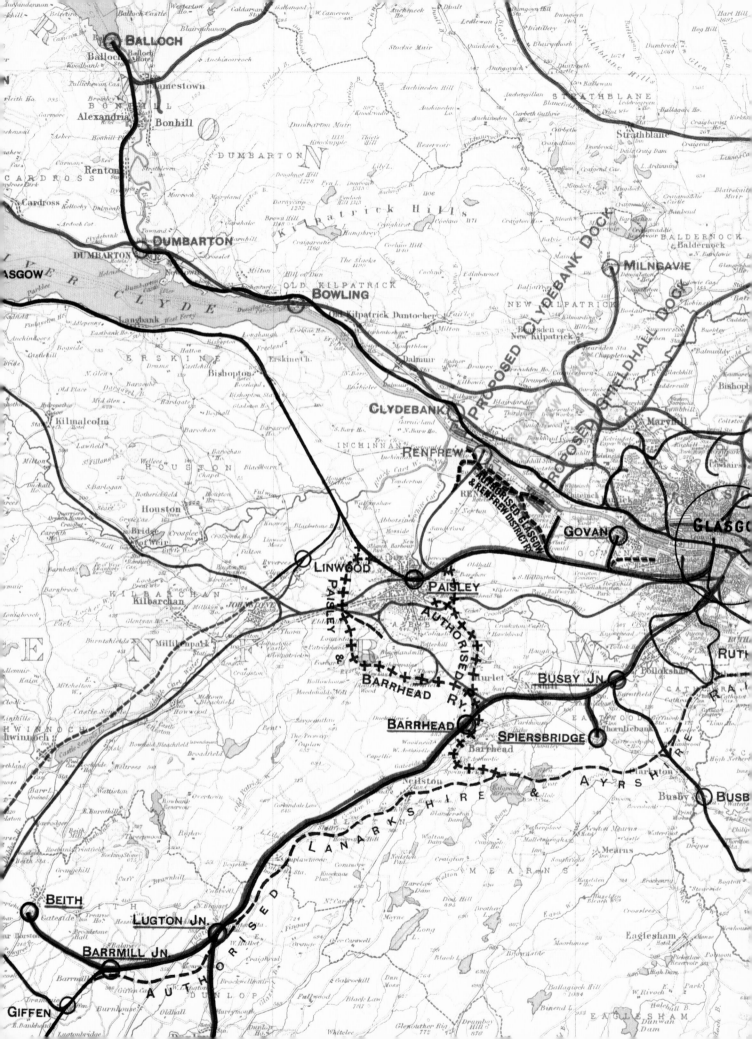

CLYDE NAVIGATION

IN PARLIAMENT — SESSION 1899

CLYDE TRUSTEES' PROPOSED DOCKS	SHEWN THUS	
CALEDONIAN RAILWAY AND LINES WORKED BY THAT COY.	,,	
NORTH BRITISH RAILWAY AND LINES WORKED BY THAT COY.	,,	
GLASGOW & SOUTH WESTERN RAILWAY ...	,,	
GLASGOW & PAISLEY AND GLASGOW & KILMARNOCK JOINT LINES	,,	
GLASGOW & RENFREW DISTRICT RAILWAY (AUTHORISED)	,,	
LANARKSHIRE & AYRSHIRE RAILWAY (CONSTRUCTING) ...	,,	
PAISLEY & BARRHEAD DISTRICT RAILWAY (CONSTRUCTING)	,,	
KILSYTH & BONNYBRIDGE RAILWAY...	,,	
MUIRKIRK, MAUCHLINE, & DALMELLINGTON RAILWAY ...	,,	
PRIVATE RAILWAYS	,,	
PROPOSED RENFREW DOCK	,,	

SCALE 1 : 126,720 — 2 MILES TO AN INCH

THE ZENITH OF THE NETWORK

The national network reached its maximum extent, with the last new rural branch lines and important extensions of the Great Western main line. However, after the railways had made their immense contribution to the First World War effort, early signs of road competition appeared.

· MIDLAND RAILWAY · HEYSHAM HARBOUR ·

DEPTH OF WATER in the harbour 17 ft., and 40 ft. outside entrance, at low water ordinary Spring tides.
LANDING FACILITIES at all states of the tide.
QUAY LENGTH 3000 ft.
ELECTRIC LIFTS & TRAVELLING CRANES and electric light in the Passenger Station, Goods Sheds and Harbour.
HORSES, CATTLE & OTHER LIVE STOCK are landed on sloping ways & without slings. Extensive accommodation for resting & grazing.
LARGE AREA FOR STORAGE of timber, pig iron, slates & other traffic not requiring cover.
FISH STAGE for unloading fish from trawlers or smacks with covered accommodation for packing, sorting, &c. Facilities for storing ice, coaling or ballasting vessels, etc.
TRAINS ARRIVE & DEPART ALONGSIDE STEAMERS.
ENQUIRIES for berths & all information may be addressed to:— Captain Beasley, Harbour Master & Traffic Agent, Heysham. Messrs. Little & Co., Heysham, Barrow & Albert Sq., Belfast, or the Chief Goods Manager or General Superintendent, Derby.

W. Guy Granet, General Manager.   M. Secretan.

An aerial view of the Midland Railway's harbour facilities at Heysham, Lancashire, in 1910.

Britain has always depended on seaborne traffic for trade and communications with the rest of the world. By the mid-19th century the burgeoning industrial strength of Britain had become totally dependent on railway operations – imported raw materials and exported finished goods were all carried between docksides and factories by rail. The days of slow canal transport were largely over.

In the very early years of the railways, companies were not allowed to operate their own ships but by 1863 they were given powers to operate their own passenger ships on specific routes. Although cargo shipping was subject to separate arrangements, the passenger shipping provisions stayed unaltered until 1967 when route impositions were finally swept away.

The first railway shipping service came in 1846 when the Great Grimsby & Sheffield Junction Railway started operating a ferry across the Humber Estuary between Hull and New Holland. Two years later the Chester & Holyhead Railway started operating the all-important Holyhead to Kingstown (now Dún Laoghaire) 'packet' service – packet boats being small vessels designed to carry mail, scheduled cargo and passengers. The South Eastern Railway began the first packet service to the Continent in 1853 with their Folkestone to Boulogne service. By the end of the century railway passenger shipping services had become so successful that there were routes across the North Sea to Scandinavia and the Low Countries, across the English Channel to France and the Channel Islands, across the Solent to the Isle of Wight and across the Irish Sea to Ireland and the Isle of Man; over river estuaries such as the Severn and Clyde; along English lakes and Scottish lochs; and over the sea to the Scottish islands. Special boat trains also ran in connection with these services along with ocean liner expresses to and from Plymouth, Southampton, Liverpool and Greenock. Car ferries using cranes were first introduced (between Stranraer and Larne) in 1939, while the first roll on-roll off vehicle ferry (Dover to Boulogne) came into service in 1952.

Freight traffic was even more important and to handle the vast quantities of raw materials and finished goods many of the larger railway companies had built their own dock complexes by the early 20th century. Principal among these

ENGLAND'S LATEST PORT

IMMINGHAM *(Grimsby)*
DEEP WATER DOCK

For information apply to G.C. Goods Agents or Port Master, Immingham Dock, Grimsby. SAM FAY Gen. Manager

COALING JETTY
WITH INDEPENDENT HOIST
FOR BUNKERING VESSELS
AT ANY STATE OF THE TIDE

A Great Central Railway poster showing the deep-water dock at Immingham, near Grimsby, in the 1930s.

were the London & South Western Railway's modern docks at Southampton which later proved to be of vital strategic importance during both World Wars, and the Great Central Railway's vast freight handling facilities at Grimsby and Immingham. In the early 20th century Britain was also a major exporter of coal, with companies like the North Eastern Railway leading the way in the northeast and the Barry Railway in South Wales – the former company's docks at Tyne Dock were exporting seven million tons of coal a year while the latter's facility at Barry Docks was exporting nine million tons each year.

Following nationalization of the railways in 1948, the newly formed British Railways took over the running of all railway shipping services. From 1970 until 1984, when they were sold off, these services were known as Sealink, with an interesting offshoot in the Seaspeed hovercraft operation across the English Channel. Nowadays international rail passengers speed through the Channel Tunnel.

The British Railways Sealink ferry *Cambridge* leaves Harwich carrying railway wagons and lorries bound for Zeebrugge in Belgium, 1966.

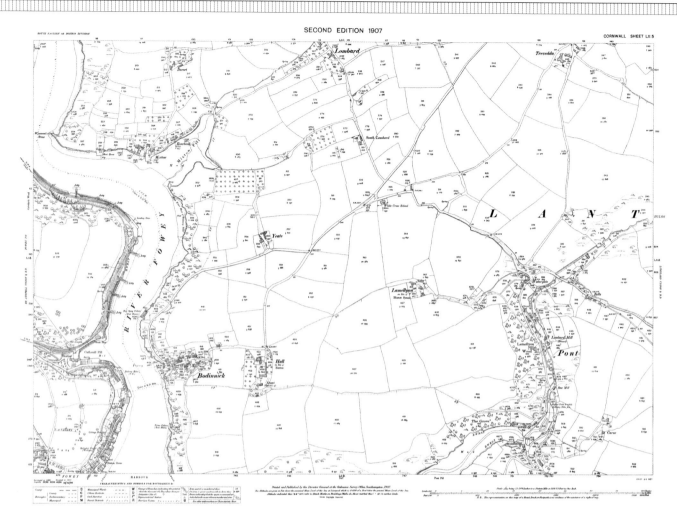

Series	Ordnance Survey Second Edition 1907. 25 in. to 1 mile
Sheet	Cornwall LII.5
Date	Surveyed 1880, revised 1906, published 1907

Although Cornwall had seen the development of an isolated network of tramways and railways serving tin and copper mines since the early 19th century, it took the arrival of the 'main line' railway from the east in 1859 to intensify the exploitation of the county's mineral resources, not least its china clay. The deep water harbour at Fowey on the south coast, and the opening in 1869 of a broad gauge (but independently owned) branch line south from the Cornwall Railway (later Great Western Railway) main line at Lostwithiel, gave the village of Fowey strategic advantage as a point of export for china clay which it enjoys to this day. The rail route ran (and still runs) along the western shore of the River Fowey, hugging steep hills and waterside woodland – a scenic trip normally the preserve of freight train drivers only.

In 1873 the tracks of a rival company, the standard-gauge Cornwall Minerals Railway (CMR), reached jetties around Carne Point north of Fowey, from Newquay and Par to the west. After six years of intense competition between the two railways, the broad gauge line closed in 1879 – but was reopened in 1895 by the CMR as a single-track standard gauge line. The two branches were connected at Fowey, and passenger trains were also introduced.

This Ordnance Survey map shows seven rail-served jetties, while Fowey station – at the edge of the village, due to the steep topography – had its own signal box ('SB' on the map) and goods shed, as well as platforms for passenger trains. The line from Par saw a very early withdrawal of passenger services, in 1934, but clung on for freight traffic until 1968, after which it was converted into a private 'haul road' for lorry movement of china clay from 'the dries' at Par to the docks at Fowey.

Passenger trains from Fowey to Lostwithiel were a Beeching casualty in 1965, and the terminus of the remaining freight branch line was pulled back to the north of Carne Point (west of all the jetties shown), where it now handles trainloads of export china clay several times daily from pits a dozen miles to the west.

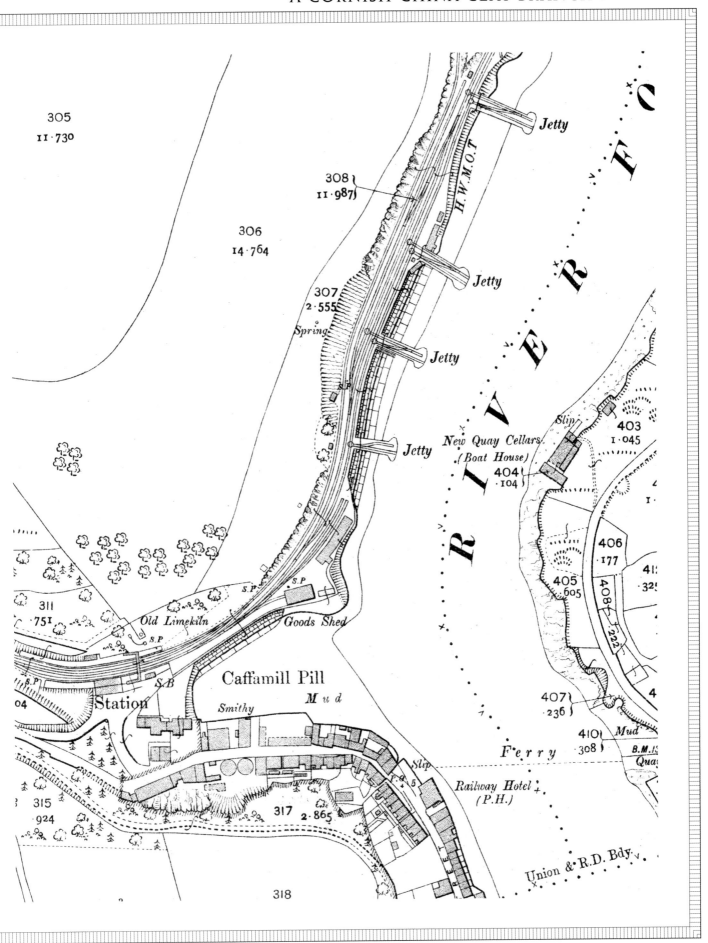

305
11·730

308
11·987

306
14·764

307
2·555

Spring

Jetty

Jetty

Jetty

Jetty

H.W.M.O.T.

New Quay Cellars
(Boat House)

Slip

403
1·045

404
·104

406
·177

405
·605

408
·222

311
·751

Old Limekiln

S.P.

S.P.

S.P.

S.P.

Goods Shed

S.P.

Caffamill Pill

Mud

S.B.

Station

Smithy

315
·924

317 2·865

318

407
·236

410
·308

Ferry

Slip

Railway Hotel
(P.H.)

Mud

B.M.
Qua

Union & R.D. Bdy.

R I V E R   F C

RAILWAY MAP OF LONDON AND SUBURBS, WITH POSTAL DISTRICTS - 1908

Title	Railway Map of London and Suburbs, with Postal Districts – 1908
Mapmaker	J Bartholomew, Edinburgh
Date	1908

By the early 20th century London's inner suburban rail network was largely complete, both in terms of main lines and local routes with a primarily commuter role. The railways were at the core of the daily life of the metropolis, as demonstrated by this map and the following map, both from the *Pocket Guide and Atlas of London* (1908) produced by the Edinburgh publisher and mapmaker, J Bartholomew.

This is a particularly clear and attractive map, which avoids the temptation to overload the sheet with details of built-up areas, roads and other topographical information not essential for a pocket rail guide. Railways are represented in black – which had become a virtually standard treatment in general mapping – and station names are produced in clear black fonts. Wider topographical context – and some colour variety – is provided by representation of the bigger parks (in green), the River Thames (in blue) and postal district boundaries (in red).

The crucial role of mass commuting by rail into and around the capital has ensured that the London rail network has survived more unscathed than in any other British city, and the pattern of routes on this map is still overwhelmingly recognizable today. However, there have been some changes. A number of freight branches have disappeared, notably as a result of closure of most of the commercial docks on the upper stretch of the Thames, while local factors led to the demise by 1963 of a few passenger branch lines – such as those to Alexandra Palace, Crystal Palace (High Level), Greenwich Park and Palace Gates (Wood Green).

London's passenger rail network survived the Beeching threat almost untouched, with reprieves for the Richmond–Camden arm of the North London Line, the Gospel Oak–Barking route, and the Clapham Junction–Kensington Olympia link – all of which now play a key part in the London commuter system. The only significant loss has been the 1986 closure of the line from Dalston Junction to the Broad Street terminus, just west of Liverpool Street station, with North London Line trains then diverted to run east to North Woolwich.

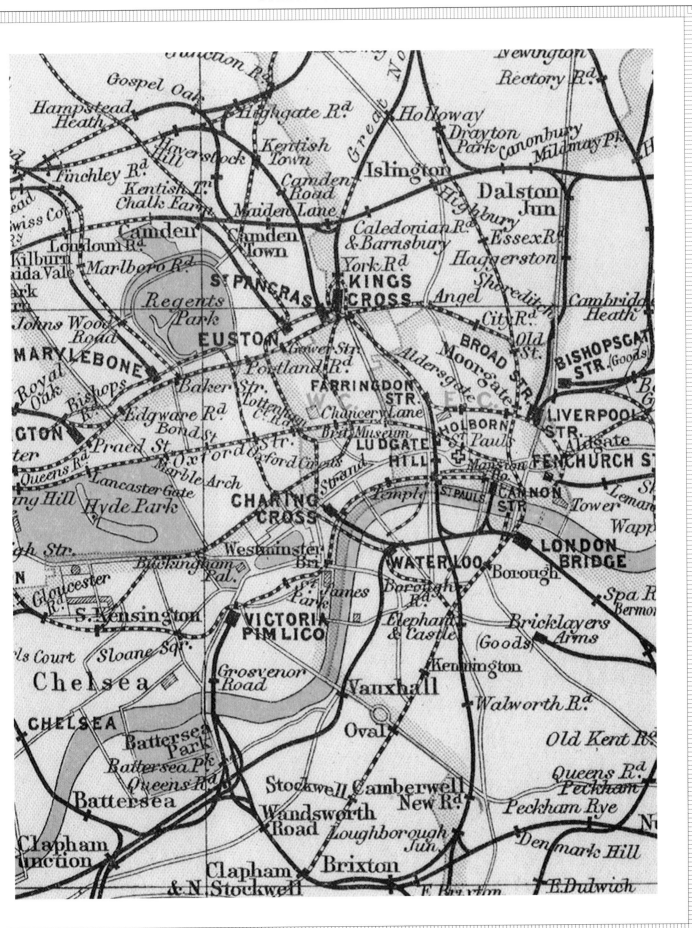

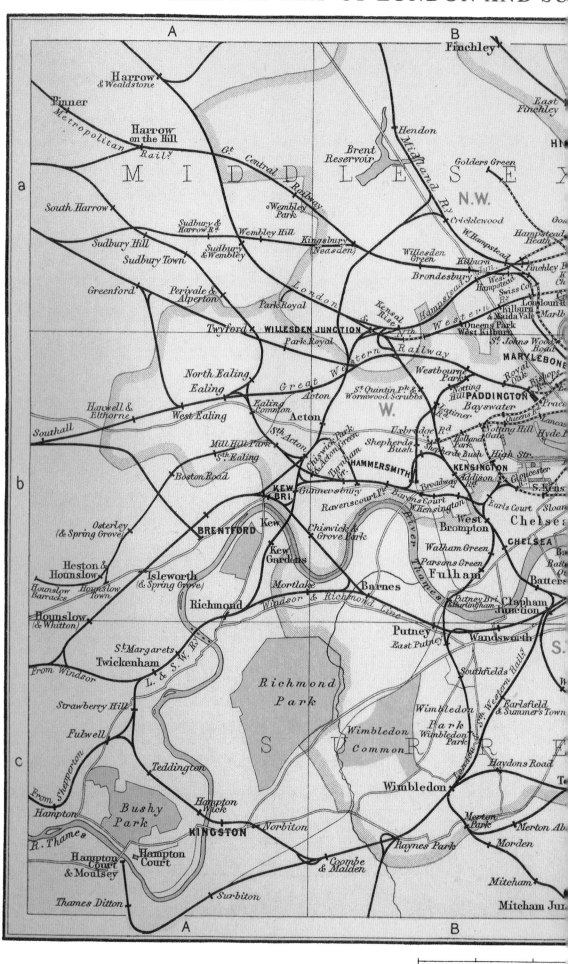

A   B Finchley

Pinner

Harrow
& Wealdstone

Metropolitan Rail.

Harrow
on the Hill

Gt Central Railway

East
Finchley

H

M I D D L E S E X

Hendon

Brent
Reservoir

Golders Green

N.W.

Cricklewood

South Harrow

Sudbury &
Harrow Rd

Wembley
Park

Kingsbury
(Neasden)

Willesden
Green

W. Hampstead

Hampstead
Heath

Goss

Sudbury Hill

Sudbury Town

Sudbury
& Wembley

Wembley Hill

London

Kilburn

Brondesbury

West
Hampstead

Swiss Co

Finchley

Greenford

Perivale &
Alperton

Park Royal

Kensal
Rise

Hampstead

Queens Park
West Kilburn

Kilburn
& Maida Vale

London R

St Johns Wood
Road

Marlb

Twyford

WILLESDEN JUNCTION

Park Royal

Western Railway

Westbourne
Park

Queens Park
West Kilburn

Royal
Oak

Bishops

MARYLEBONE

North Ealing
Ealing

Great

Acton

St Quintin Pk &
Wormwood Scrubbs

W.

Notting
Hill

Westbourne
Park

PADDINGTON

Bayswater

Latimer

Pratt

Hanwell &
Elthorne

West Ealing

Ealing
Common

Acton

Uxbridge Rd

Shepherds
Bush

Holland
Park

Notting Hill
Gate

Queens Rd

Lancas

Notting Hill
High Str.

Hyde P

Southall

Mill Hill Park

Sth Ealing

Sth Acton

Chiswick Park
& Acton Green

Turnham
Gr.

HAMMERSMITH

Shepherds Bush

KENSINGTON

Addison
Rd

Gloucester

S. Kens

Boston Road

KEW
BRI.

Gunnersbury

Ravenscourt Pk

Broadway

Barons Court

W. Kensington

Earls Court

Sloan

Osterley
(& Spring Grove)

BRENTFORD

Kew

Chiswick &
Grove Park

West
Brompton

Chelsea

CHELSEA

Heston &
Hounslow

Isleworth
(& Spring Grove)

Kew
Gardens

Walham Green

Parsons Green

Ba

Batt

Hounslow
Barracks

Hounslow
Town

Richmond

Mortlake

Barnes

Windsor & Richmond Line

Fulham

Putney Bri
& Hurlingham

Batters

Clapham
Junction

Hounslow
(& Whitton)

Putney
East Putney

Wandsworth

S.

St Margarets

Twickenham

From Windsor

L. & S. W. Ry.

Southfields

Sth Western Raily

Strawberry Hill

Richmond
Park

Wimbledon
Park

Earlsfield
& Summer's Town

Fulwell

From Shepperton

Wimbledon
Common

Wimbledon
Park

Teddington

S U R R E

Haydons Road

Hampton
Wick

Hampton

R. Thames

Bushy
Park

KINGSTON

Norbiton

Wimbledon

Merton
Park

Merton Ab

Te

Hampton
Court
& Moulsey

Hampton
Court

Coombe
& Malden

Raynes Park

Morden

Mitcham

Thames Ditton

Surbiton

Mitcham Jur

A   B

0   1   2

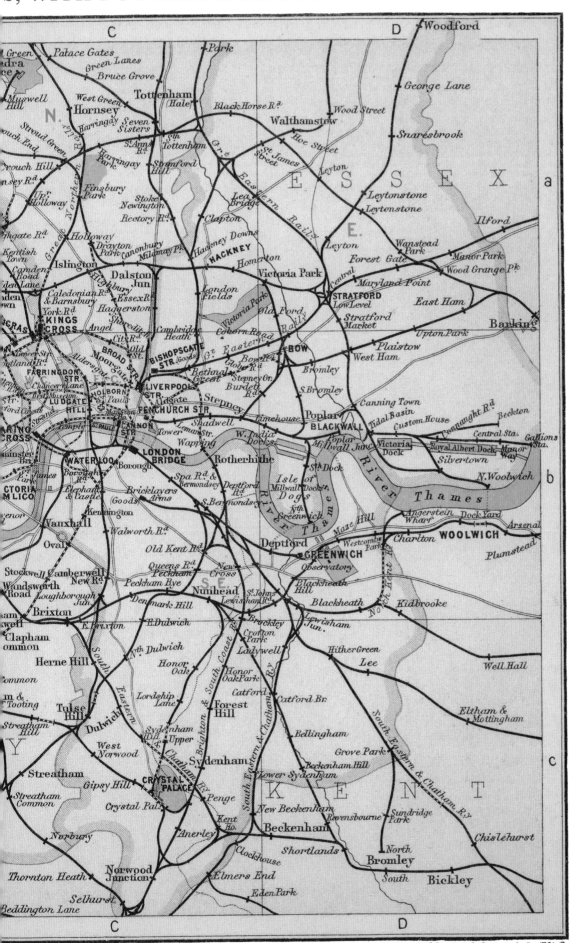

John Bartholomew & Co., Edin?

4   5   6 Miles

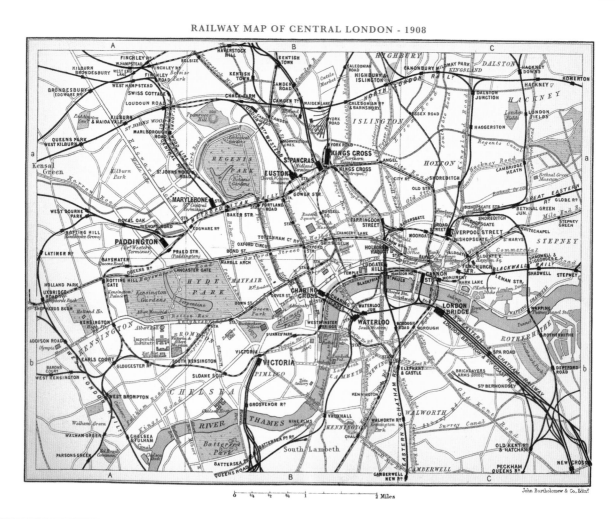

RAILWAY MAP OF CENTRAL LONDON - 1908

John Bartholomew & Co., Edin.

Title	Railway Map of Central London – 1908
Mapmaker	J Bartholomew, Edinburgh
Date	1908

By the time of publication of this map, all of London's main line rail termini had been completed, and mass commuting over an extensive inner and outer suburban rail network was an established part of daily life – the *Oxford Companion to British Railway History* (1997) recording that 'in 1904 passenger arrivals at London main-line terminals before 10.30 a.m. were 318,000', and also noting that:

The period from 1900 to 1914 was crucial for London railway and traffic development. Electrification of the Metropolitan and the District, its beginning on the LBSCR [London, Brighton & South Coast Railway] South London line, and the building of the new tubes, together with a growing interest in London suburban possibilities shown by the LNWR [London & North Western Railway] and the GWR [Great Western Railway] . . . led to a surge of local traffic that the railways both encouraged and found hard to cope with.

Given the larger scale of the map (just over 2 in. to 1 mile) compared to the previous map, much more detail has been shown – but again carefully selected to avoid visual clutter. Principal roads and street names are included – as are the new electric tram routes which were to play a largely complementary role to the railways rather than competitive, except in parts of the inner suburbs.

The tube and above-ground lines of the Underground are shown in full (in hatched black and red) despite being below-ground in most of Central London. This allows us to see the extent to which key routes followed the alignment of the main roads, helping to keep construction costs down.

Major public buildings are also shown, as are additional topographical details within the principal public parks. The map may have been produced with the passenger railway in mind, but the big goods stations, which played a crucial role in the inner London economy, are also clearly marked – note in particular Bricklayers Arms and Nine Elms south of the Thames, and Bishopsgate, Camden and King's Cross north of the river.

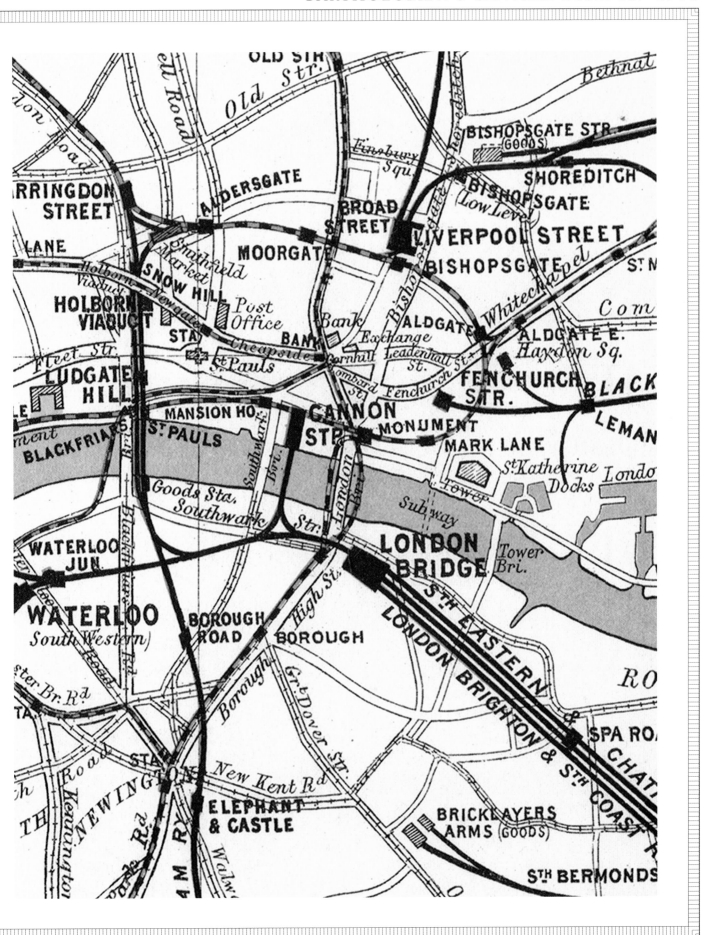

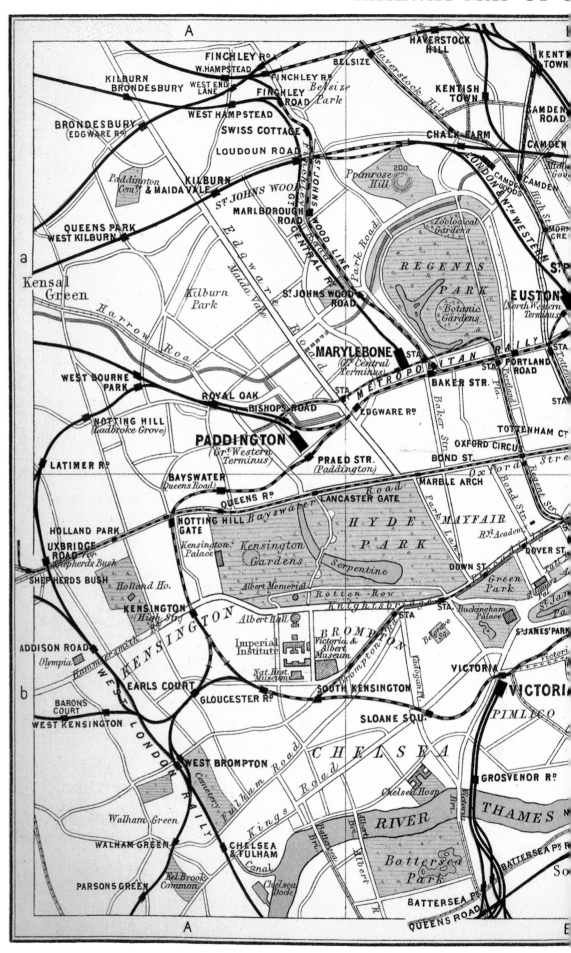

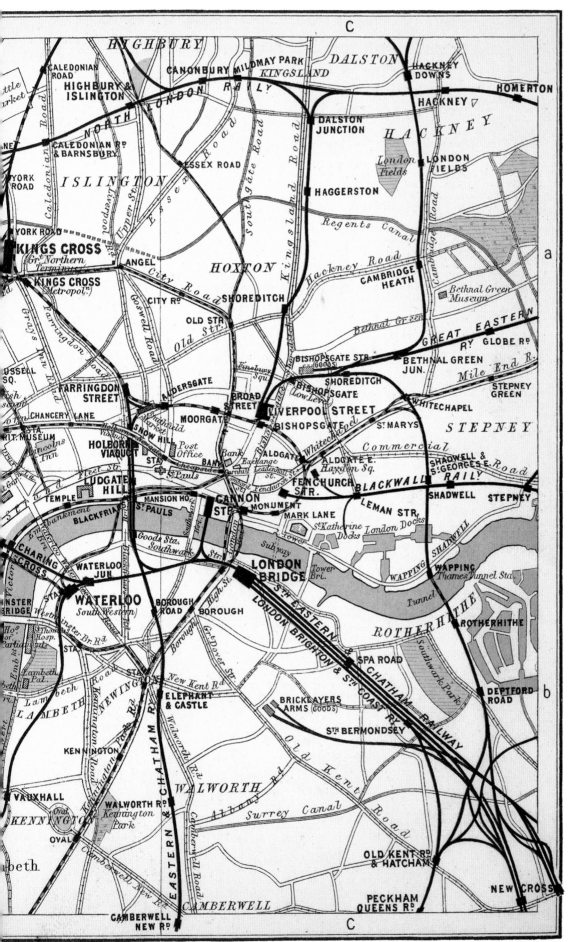

2 Miles

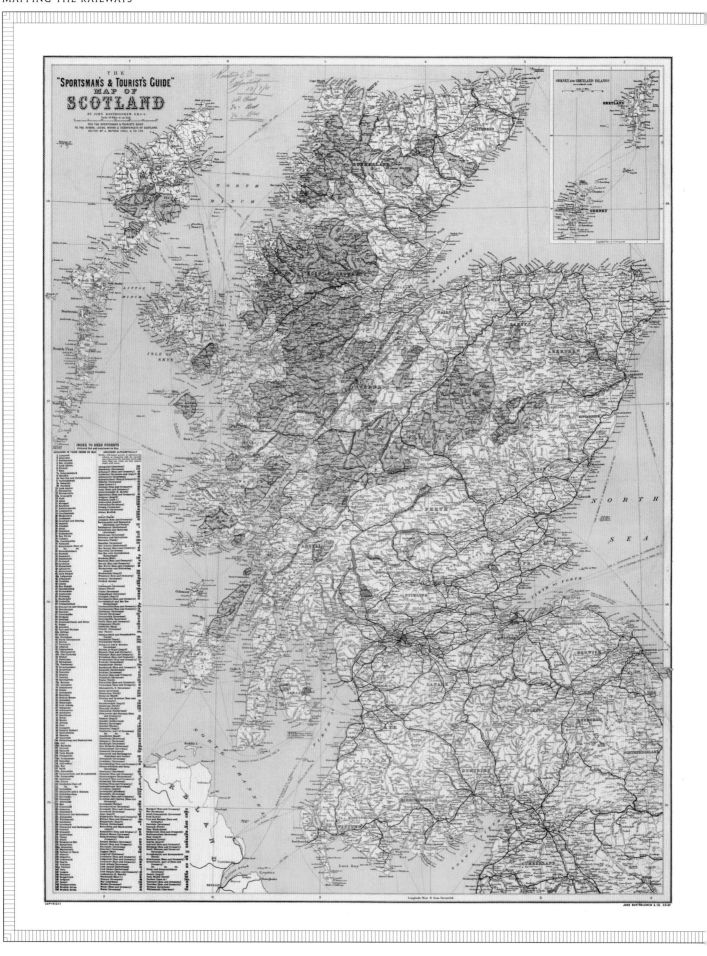

Title	The "Sportsman's and Tourist's Guide" Map of Scotland
By	J Bartholomew, Edinburgh
Date	1911

The expansion of the rail network deep into the Highlands by the late 19th century opened up an enormous market for tourists and 'sportsmen' keen to indulge their passion for hunting, shooting and fishing in hitherto inaccessible country. In *The Highland Railway* (1963), H A Vallance reports a contemporary 1888 account of a train which had become the apotheosis of this traffic – the early morning service from Perth to Inverness over the Highland Main Line during the summer 'season':

In July and August this 7.50 train is the unique railway phenomenon. Passenger carriages, saloons, horseboxes and vans, concentrated at Perth from all parts of England, and intermixed to make an irregular caravan. Engines are attached fore and aft, and the procession toils pluckily over the Grampians.

On 7th August, this train comprised rolling stock from ten companies – 37 carriages and two locomotives at the front, with a 'banker' loco attached to the rear at Blair Atholl for the stiff 17½ -mile climb at gradients of up to 1 in 70 to Britain's then highest railway summit at Druimuachdar, 1,484 ft above sea level.

As shown in the map extract below, with stations at Blair Atholl, Struan, Dalnaspidal, Dalwhinnie, Newtonmore, Kingussie, Kincraig and Aviemore, the Highland Main Line was well placed to serve this lucrative market. Together with the Kyle line, the Far North line to Caithness, the West Highland line from Glasgow to Fort William, its branch to Fort Augustus and the 'Mallaig Extension', the Highland and North British railway companies could legitimately claim to serve the overwhelming majority of the 150 'deer forests' identified on this 1911 map.

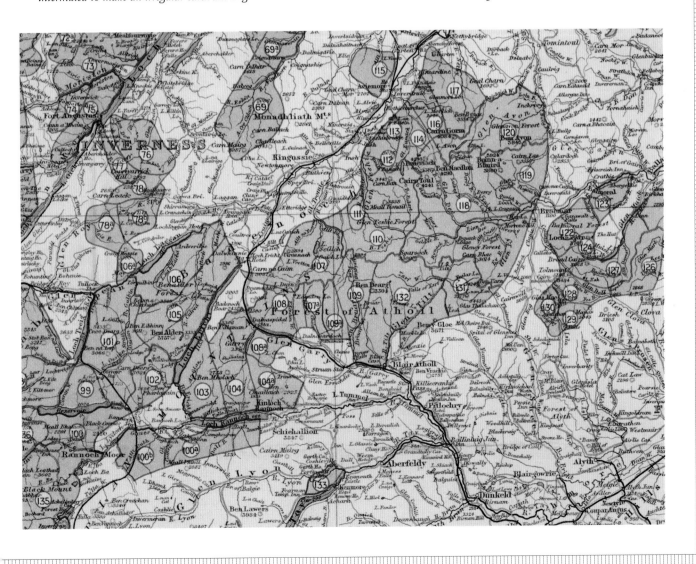

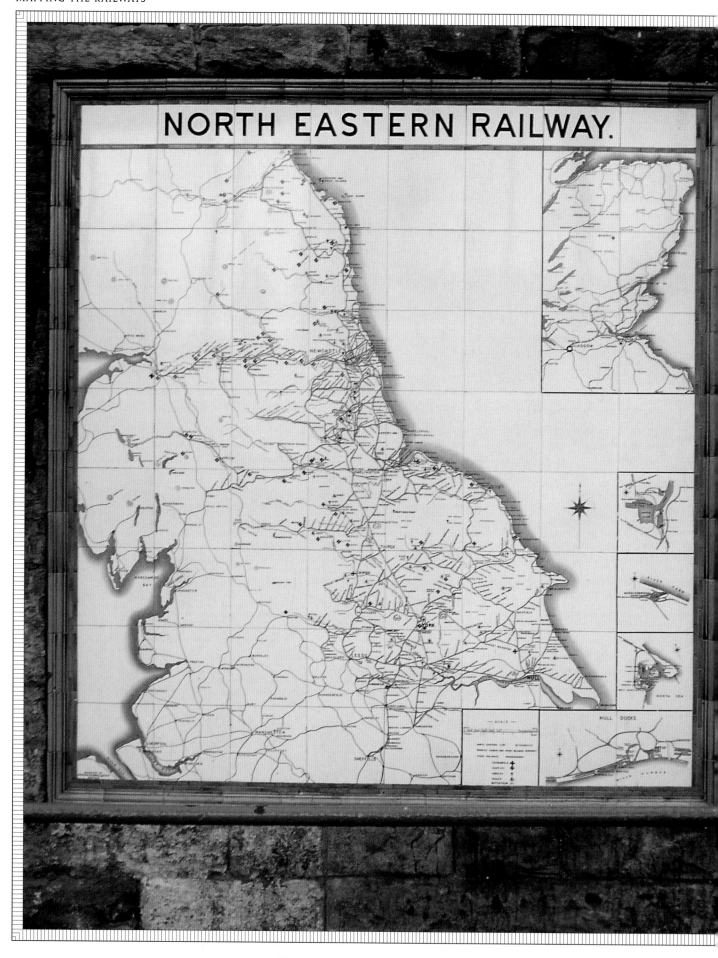

Title	North Eastern Railway
By	Craven Dunnill & Co. Ltd, Jackfield (Shropshire)
Location	Morpeth railway station
Date	*c.*1900–10

In 1900 the North Eastern Railway (NER) began the commissioning of large glazed tile maps for display at a number of its stations, depicting the whole of the NER network, from Berwick and Carlisle in the north to southern outposts at Swinton, near Doncaster, and Withernsea on the North Sea coast.

It is thought that at least 25 maps – measuring 5 ft 8 in. by 5 ft 4 in. – were erected at stations, the last by 1910. A contemporary author, G W J Potter, wrote that the idea had 'attracted considerable attention, and its adoption has much to recommend it – being easily cleaned, very legible, practically everlasting'. The maps were indeed built to last, and 12 still exist, nine of them at their original stations – Beverley, Hartlepool, Middlesbrough, Morpeth, Saltburn, Scarborough, Tynemouth, York and Whitby. The map from King's Cross station – far from NER territory – is now preserved at the National Railway Museum in York. The example photographed here is from Morpeth station, beside the 'Up' (London-bound) platform.

After cheaper foreign tiles eliminated the domestic industry in Britain, the original factory in Shropshire which produced the NER tile maps was abandoned – but the building survived, and was eventually re-opened by the Ironbridge Gorge Museum Trust as a tile museum. By 1989 a demonstration tile works was established there, and in 2007 the wheel turned full circle when the North Eastern Tile Company commissioned Craven Dunnill to restart production of NER tiled maps, using original methods and in their original factory.

Intriguingly, as shown in the extract to the right, the tile map includes representation of a line that was never built – from Beverley to North Frodingham in East Yorkshire. This was a mistake which could not easily be corrected!

The tile map tucked away on Morpeth's 'Up' platform.

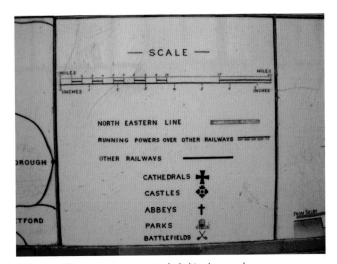

Buildings of historic interest are included in the map key.

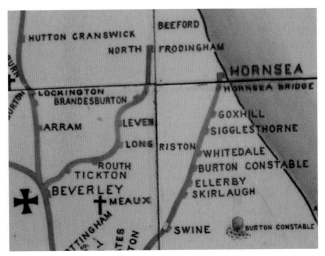

The line that never was – from Beverley to North Frodingham.

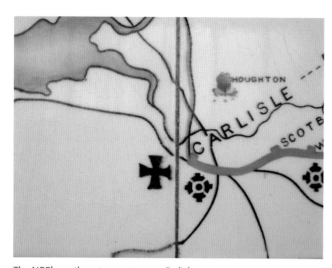

The NER's northwestern outpost at Carlisle.

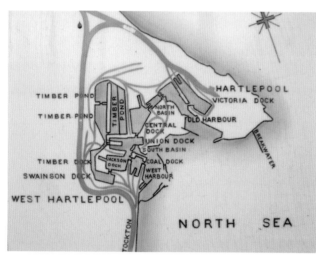

Goods traffic sidings at Hartlepool Docks.

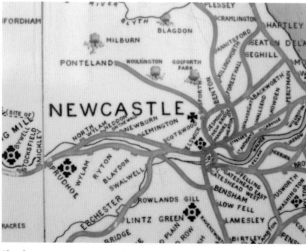

The dense commuter network around Newcastle.

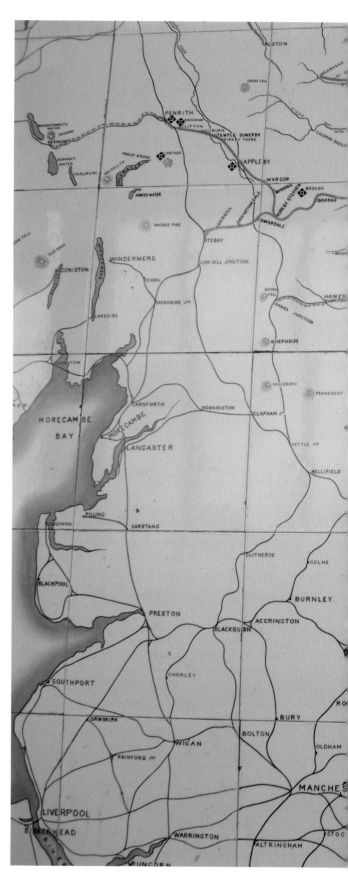

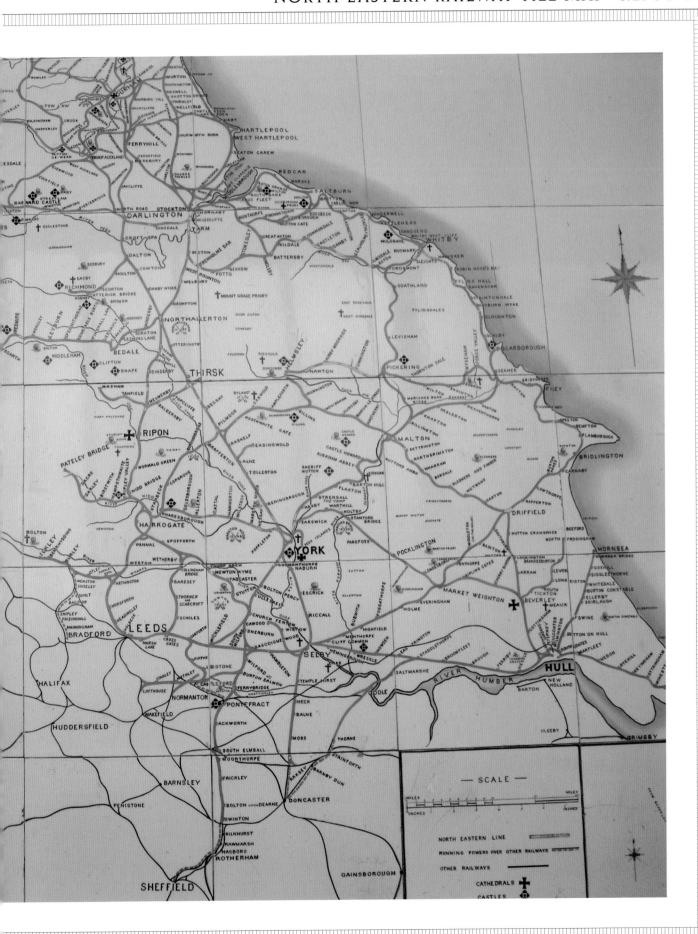

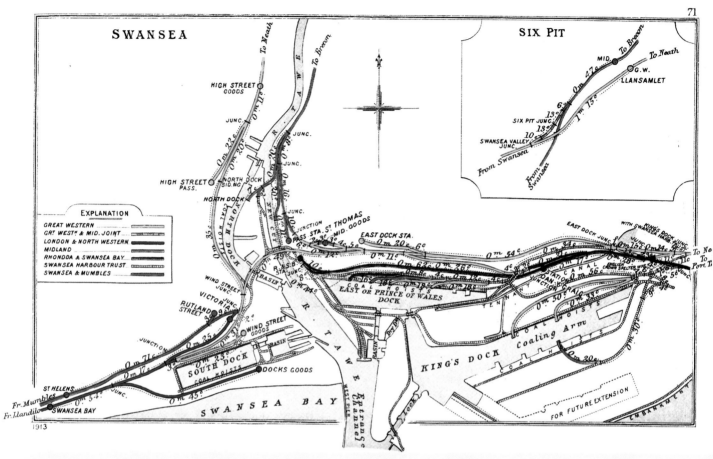

This 1913 Railway Clearing House map of Swansea shows seven different railway companies serving the town and docks.

Coal and steam power were the natural driving forces behind the Industrial Revolution in Britain. By the 18th century the increasing output of coal mines was already being transported on horse-drawn waggonways and tramways to rivers and harbours for onward distribution around Britain by boat – it was not by chance that the world's first railways were built to serve Britain's growing coal industry.

While coal deposits could be found in many parts of Britain, the main concentrations were in central Scotland, Teesside and Tyneside, South Yorkshire, Derbyshire, Nottinghamshire and South Wales and it was in these areas that railway development was the most rapid.

By far the largest coal-producing area in Britain was in South Wales. Its reserves are reckoned to cover around 1,000 square miles with much of it under water – consequently a large proportion has never been exploited. The region was one of the birthplaces of the Industrial Revolution in the late 18th century with a canal and tramway system feeding coal to nearly 100 blast furnaces.

At the height of coal production in the early 20th century nearly 37 million tons of coal were being exported around

the world from ports along the coast of South Wales. At this time a total of 16 railway companies were involved in transporting the coal from the hundreds of mines in the Welsh Valleys down to the mechanical tips at Newport, Cardiff, Barry, Port Talbot, Swansea and Llanelli docks. There was so much coal being mined that the steep-sided valleys often had competing railway lines running along each side – morning, noon and night, they echoed to a continuous procession of loaded coal trains trundling down to the docks and rattling empty trains returning.

Such was the importance of the docks that two of the major railway companies, the Alexandra (Newport & South Wales) and the Barry were originally incorporated primarily as dock companies. Competition between the docks for the lucrative coal traffic was intense with some of them being served by no less than six railway companies – for example, Cardiff Docks was served by the Great Western Railway, London & North Western Railway, Taff Vale Railway, Rhymney Railway, Barry Railway and Cardiff Railway.

By far the most successful of these coal-carrying railway and docks companies was the Barry Docks & Railway Company which was incorporated in 1884 to build 68 miles of railway

Great Western Railway

SWANSEA DOCKS

The Great Western Railway's docks at Swansea once exported vast amounts of Welsh coal to the far-flung corners of the British Empire.

between a new purpose-built 73-acre deep-water dock at Barry and the Rhondda and Aberdare Valleys. Engineered by Henry Marc Brunel (second son of Isambard Kingdom Brunel) and Sir John Wolfe Barry, the railway featured several long tunnels and three massive viaducts. With nearby Cardiff Docks already working to full capacity, the resourceful new railway was an instant success and on the day the line opened in 1889 several thousand invited guests were treated to a grandstand view of newly arrived coal trains discharging their loads into the first ship. With its conveniently located deep-water dock the railway delivered three million tons of coal to 1,700 ships in the first year of its existence and by 1913 was exporting 30 per cent of all of South Wales' coal.

One of the key innovations of the Beeching Report was the introduction of 'merry-go-round' coal trains – so named because the train both loads and unloads its cargo while moving at slow speed. Despite the massive changes in the coal industry since the 1960s, it is still closely linked to the railways, with trains of 1,000 tonnes and more providing a regular supply of coal from Britain's three remaining

deep mines (in Nottinghamshire, the West Midlands and Yorkshire), from open cast sites in south Wales, the north of England and Scotland, and from major coal-importing ports such as Avonmouth, Hunterston and Immingham, to coal-fired power stations in all three countries. Coal remains by far the most important freight commodity on the railways.

One positive outcome of the Beeching Report was the introduction of 'merry-go-round' coal trains such as this one seen at Ratcliffe-on-Soar power station, Nottinghamshire, in 1993.

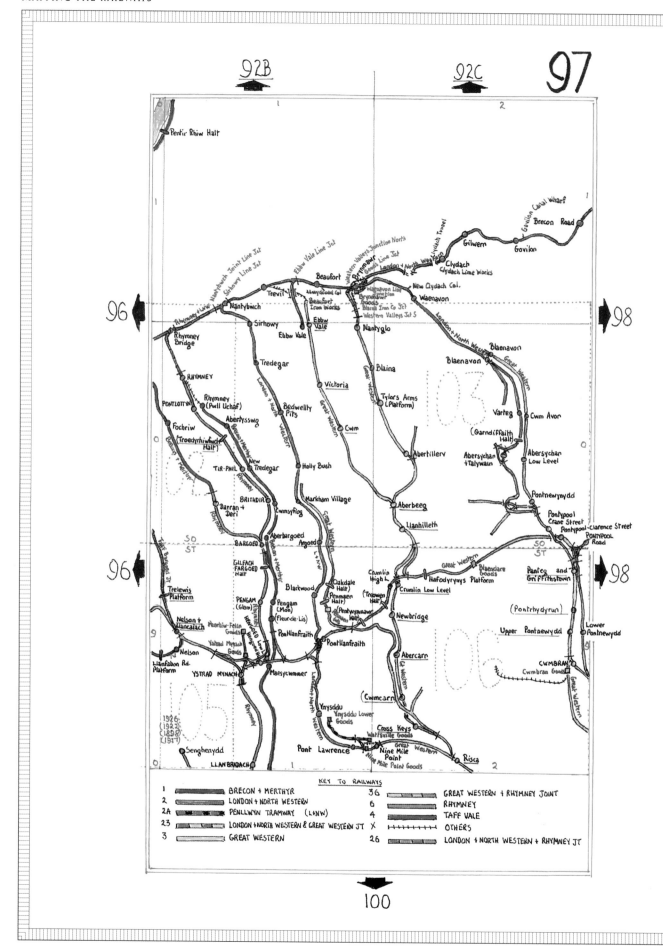

Title	Jowett's Railway Atlas (page 97)
By	Alan Jowett
Publisher	Patrick Stephens Ltd, Cambridge
Date	1989

Jowett's Railway Atlas, published in 1989, is an historical atlas portraying Britain's rail network at or close to its zenith. Produced by the railway author Alan Jowett, the atlas is a meticulously hand drawn and written production. Like the map of the western valleys of South Wales on pages 170–173, Jowett's map of the upper eastern valleys shows the rail network at its peak – the culmination of heroic engineering and intensive competition for the big prize, coal. This sheet – at an original scale of 3 in. to 10 km – focuses on the northeast corner of the South Wales coalfield, where no less than 10 companies or joint lines vied for the potentially lucrative business of shifting the 'black diamonds' to markets near and far, not least the big export business through the docks at Barry, Cardiff and Newport.

The two major rail companies fighting for market share in this part of the valleys were the Great Western Railway (GWR), for which this was core territory, and the London & North Western Railway (LNWR) which had managed to penetrate far from its principal routes between London, Birmingham and northwest England. The GWR struck north from Cardiff,

Newport and its east–west Pontypool–Hengoed–Aberdare route, while the LNWR pushed south from the east–west Abergavenny–Brynmawr–Merthyr Tydfil ('Heads of the Valleys') line. Such was the competition that on two routes, up the Afon Llwyd and Sirhowy valleys through Abersychan and Argoed respectively, both companies even managed to squeeze into the same narrow valley, as did the locally based Rhymney and Brecon & Merthyr railways through Bargoed.

There is stark contrast at the northern end of the map, where the physical barrier of the Brecon Beacons – and the absence of coal – meant that only one railway penetrated north into rural Mid Wales. This was the Brecon & Merthyr, part of whose route just meanders into the northwest corner of the map.

The decline of coal and the rise of road competition have denuded this area of most, but by no means all, of its rail network. Passenger services survive from Cardiff to Rhymney (along the old Rhymney Railway line); through Cwmbran and Pontypool on the inter-city route from Cardiff to Crewe; and on the Newport–Ebbw Vale Parkway line, whose passenger services were reinstated in 2008, following their earlier withdrawal in 1962. Coal traffic from northwest of Ystrad Mynach continues to move down the valley by train, while an isolated preserved line serves the 'Big Pit' colliery heritage site at Blaenavon.

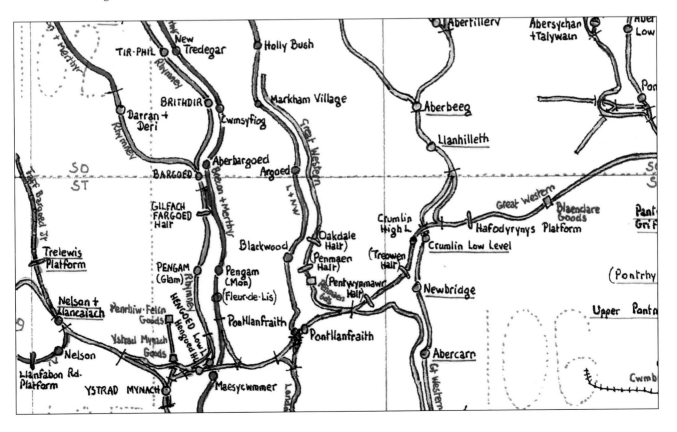

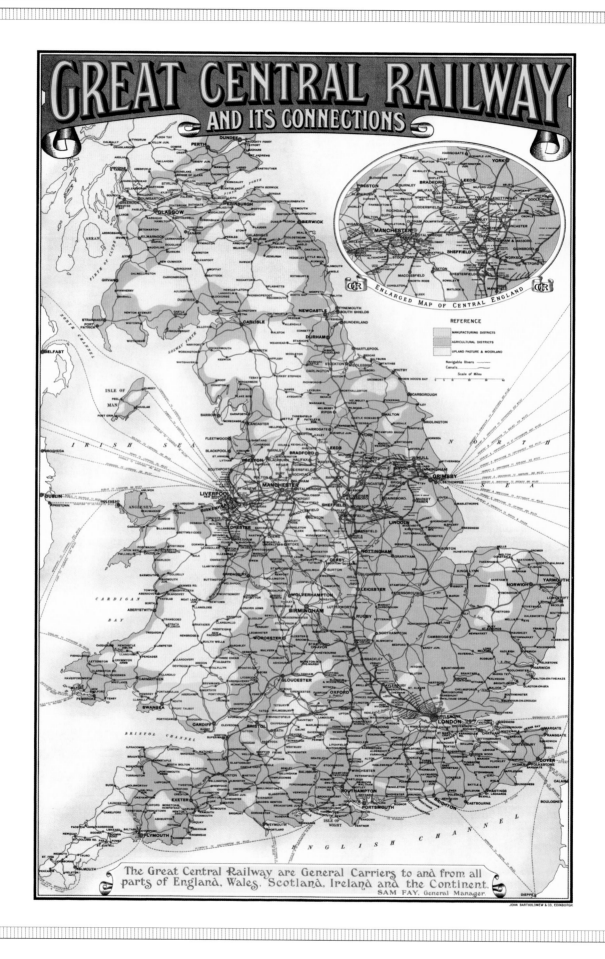

Title	Great Central Railway and its connections
Publisher	Great Central Railway
Mapmaker	J Bartholomew, Edinburgh
Date	1913

Map posters became a key tool of passenger information and railway marketing, with railway stations providing almost countless opportunities to proudly display each company's ability to transport the traveller the length and breadth of the country. A note handwritten in the margin of this poster for the Great Central Railway on 6 March 1913 records '26,550 copies'. The Bartholomew style of 'Great Central Railway and its connections' has close echoes with 'North British Railway and its communications' (see pages 120–123) and 'the L.&N.W.R. and its communications' (see pages 104–107) – all were produced by the Edinburgh mapmaker.

The Great Central, who built the last main line to reach London (in 1899), evidently felt sufficiently confident of its competitive strength not to downplay the extent of its rivals' routes on this map. The entire British rail network, as far as the map's northern limit beyond Central Scotland, is shown as the Great Central's 'connections' – and the Great Central's own lines are represented only marginally bolder than all the other railway companies'. Interestingly, navigable rivers and canals are also shown, while the map key distinguishes the underlying topography of the country as either manufacturing district, agricultural district or upland pasture and moorland.

The enlarged map of 'Central England', as shown in the extract overleaf, does not in fact show an area which would normally be regarded as the central part of England, but rather was central to the Great Central's core operations. Other than its long main line southwards to London, the railway's network was largely concentrated in the Lancashire/Yorkshire corridor from Manchester through Sheffield and Doncaster to Grimsby, with joint ownership and 'running powers' extending its influence beyond, for example west to Merseyside over the Cheshire Lines Committee tracks.

The critical importance of the Great Central's connectivity with the west and east coast shipping hubs at Liverpool and Grimsby respectively is graphically shown by the heavy concentration of shipping routes fanning out from these two ports.

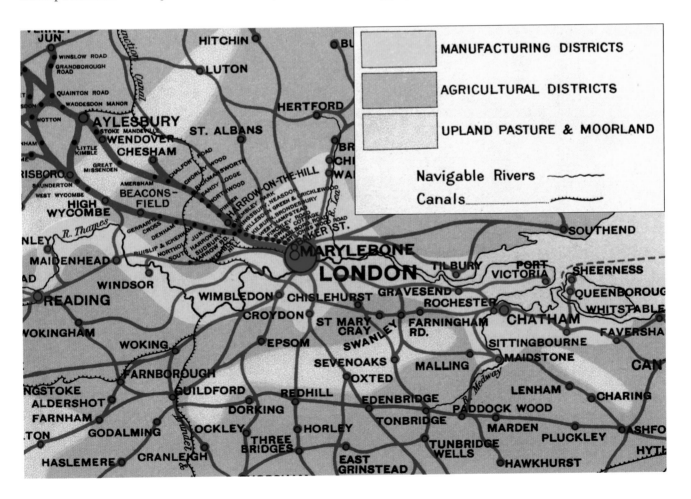

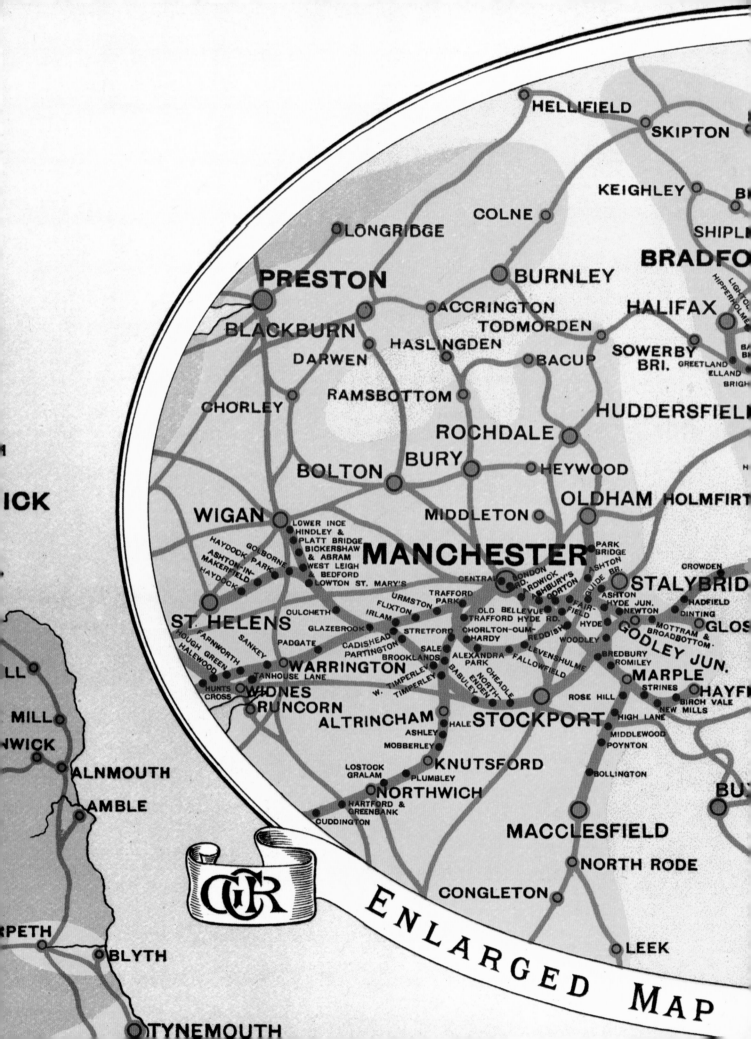

CENTRAL ENGLAND

At the start of the Second World War the GWR carried nearly 70,000 children from Paddington station to safe locations in the countryside. Here a large group of child evacuees has just arrived at Maidenhead station in 1940.

There is no doubt that Britain's railways played a vital role during the two World Wars. Even before the First World War, the London & South Western Railway had played a key part during the Second Boer War when it transported thousands of troops and their equipment from military camps in southern England to the new railway-owned docks at Southampton for embarkation on troopships to South Africa.

During the First World War, Britain's railways came under Government control and, with war raging in France and Belgium, they transported vast numbers of soldiers, their equipment and munitions to ports in southern England for embarkation across the English Channel. In the reverse direction came thousands of injured soldiers who were transported in ambulance trains to hospitals around the country. On the other side of the Channel the overloaded French railway system was soon in disarray so, in 1915, the Railway Operating Division (ROD) of the Royal Engineers

was formed to operate railways in theatres of war. By 1916 the ROD had requisitioned around 600 freight locomotives and thousands of goods wagons from British railway companies for use not only in France but also in Italy, Palestine, the Balkans and Mesopotamia. With the war in northern France virtually at stalemate, the demand for heavy freight locomotives outstripped supply and so the ROD adopted the Great Central Railway's Class '8K' 2-8-0 as its standard freight locomotive. Over 500 of these powerful locomotives were built for service overseas, the majority returning home at the end of the war.

During the Second World War, the railways came under Government control for the second time in 20 years, but their task was made doubly difficult by the conditions under which they had to operate. Despite blackouts, major disruption caused by bombing, lack of maintenance and overworked staff and locomotives they kept on running. In 1939 the railways not only operated over 4,000 special trains carrying nearly 1.5 million passengers away from the capital during the first evacuation of London, but also carried almost 400,000 troops of the British Expeditionary Force (BEF) in over 1,000 trains to Channel ports for embarkation to France. The following May and June around 320,000 troops of the BEF were snatched from the Dunkirk beaches and carried to safety over the Channel in a flotilla of small boats – in a period of a fortnight the railways ran over 600 special trains to carry the traumatized troops away from the south coast ports.

The railways also suffered heavily during the German bombing of London, other cities and key installations – stations, junctions, engine sheds and railway works were all targeted but despite suffering considerable damage the railways kept running. Troop trains, workmen's trains and freight trains all had priority over passenger trains where delays and overcrowding were the norm. The war effort not only depended on the mining and railway distribution of coal, which by 1942 amounted to 160 million tons a year, but also the distribution of other raw materials, war equipment and munitions between rail-connected docks and war factories.

The lead up to the D-Day landings in 1944 saw US Army Transportation Corps locomotives shipped into Britain to assist with the largest mass movement of troops and military equipment in the history of warfare. By 3 June the railways had moved in great secrecy 500,000 British soldiers, 2,000,000 US soldiers and 1,500,000 tons of stores from their concentration areas to their ports of embarkation along the English south coast. The war left a terrible legacy for Britain's railways, their rundown state and lack of investment leading inevitably to nationalization in 1948.

During the Second World War, the railways were a major target for German bombers and were attacked over 10,000 times between 1939 and 1945. However, stations and permanent way damage was cleared up quickly and services resumed.

Title	Jowett's Railway Centres (pages 58, 62 and 63)
By	Alan Jowett
Publisher	Patrick Stephens Ltd, Cambridge
Date	1993

Jowett's Railway Centres, published in 1993, expands the coverage of *Jowett's Railway Atlas* by focusing on various snapshots in time, showing the development and decline of the railway network in key centres over 140 years and more. The same hand-drawn cartographic technique is used, graphically illustrating – with supporting commentary – the significant rail route changes seen over this period of time in a variety of British towns and cities.

The three selected snapshots of central Hull contrast the earliest railways in 1846, the zenith of the local network in 1915, and the truncated system of 1990. Jowett notes in his commentary that, 'Hull, in common with most railway centres, had a unique set of circumstances affecting its growth and

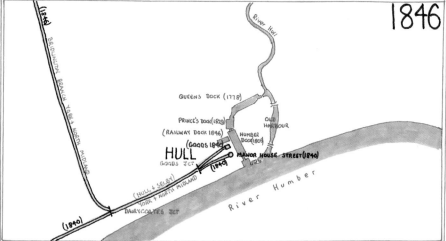

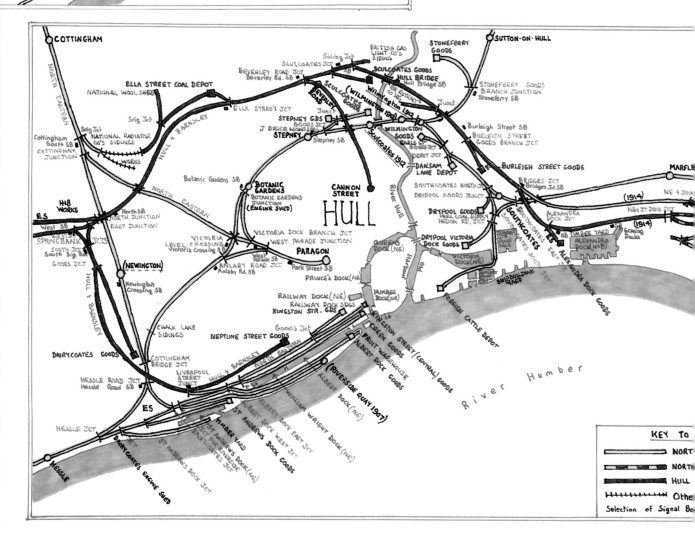

decline'. These were: its position on the Humber, serving important shipping trade routes; the barrier created by the Humber, which has tended to isolate Hull; its mainly agricultural hinterland, leaving the city 'at the end of the line'; and the relative absence of competition, as from the beginning Hull's rail network was effectively under the control of one company, the North Eastern Railway (NER). Jowett also compares and contrasts railway development with dock development:

> *With railways, usually the last railway to open is the first to close and quite often the present-day situation is very similar to that reached around 1850 and in very few places is this better illustrated than at Hull. . . . With dock development, however, exactly the opposite prevails, the first docks opened, being of shallow depth, are usually the first to close and the later deep-water docks that can accommodate the larger vessels at all states of the tide are the ones to remain.*

Following the 1923 Grouping only a small measure of rationalization was possible, closing the Cannon Street passenger terminus of the Hull & Barnsley Railway (HBR), which had been the one serious, but only partially successful, attempt to break the NER's monopoly in Hull.

Extensive rationalization took place following the Beeching Report, with all dock goods traffic concentrated on the former HBR route, sweeping round the north of the city centre on an embankment – and thereby eliminating road congestion in the city caused by the other lines' level crossings. Today the network is virtually identical to that of 1990, with Hull Paragon station handling local trains to York and Scarborough, trans-Pennine expresses to Leeds and beyond, and inter-city services to London. The single-track King George Dock branch line serves coal and steel terminals, and a chemicals plant at Saltend, now the very end of the line in east Yorkshire.

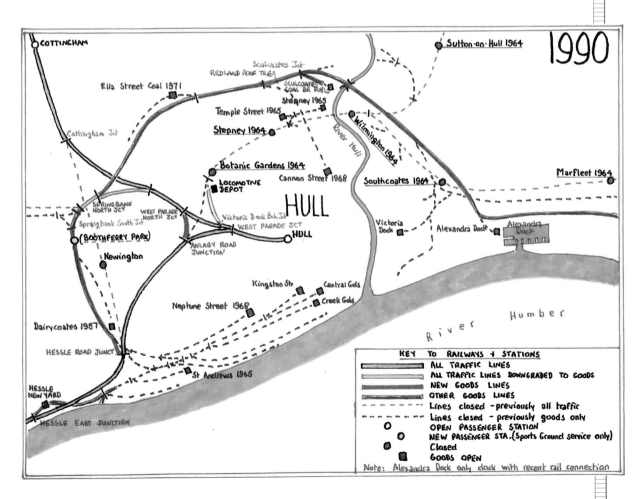

Prior to the Light Railways Act of 1896, all new railway lines in Britain required a specific Act of Parliament before they could be built. This was an expensive and time-consuming affair and the severe economic recession and associated high interest rates of the 1870s and 1880s had brought a halt to many new railway schemes in Britain. With the Light Railways Act in place railway companies could build new railways in sparsely populated regions of the country without requiring a specific Act of Parliament. While cutting out much of the red tape and expensive legislation, it did impose severe limitations including a weight limit of 12 tons per axle and a speed limit of 25 m.p.h. Cost-cutting measures included minimal earthworks, bridges and stations, lightly laid track spiked directly onto sleepers, the absence of level crossing gates, minimal signalling and the operation of 'One Engine in Steam' – i.e. only one locomotive was allowed to work on the line at any given time. Over 30 standard gauge and narrow gauge lines were built under the Act's provisions between 1896 and 1925.

Seeing a potential business opportunity, the arch proponent of light railways in England and Wales was the colourful Colonel H F Stephens who formed the Light Railway Syndicate a year before the Act was passed. By the time of his death in 1931 he had control of an eccentric railway empire of light railways across the land. Using second-hand equipment and with the minimum of maintenance these ranged from narrow gauge enterprises such as the Ffestiniog Railway, the Snailbeach District Railway and the Ashover Light Railway to meandering standard gauge rural lines such as the Kent & East Sussex Railway, the Shropshire & Montgomeryshire Railway and the East Kent Railway. That three of his ramshackle, standard gauge lines survived into British Railways ownership in 1948 can only be described as a miracle!

While the provisions of the Light Railway Act were perfect for the sparsely populated regions of Scotland, there were very few light railways actually built in the country. Of those that saw the light of day were the Dornoch Light Railway and the Leadhills & Wanlockhead Light Railway, both of which opened in 1902, and the Wick & Lybster Railway which opened in 1903. At the southern end of the Kintyre peninsula the narrow gauge Campbeltown & Macrihanish Railway (formerly a canal) was converted from a coal-carrying line to a light railway in 1906. North of Inverness construction of the Cromarty & Dingwall Railway was started but never completed.

By the end of the First World War the building of light railways in Scotland was back on the political agenda and the question of rural transport in Scotland was studied by a Parliamentary Committee which published its findings in

A train waits to depart from Lybster station on the short-lived Wick & Lybster Light Railway in 1928.

1919. In their report the Committee advocated the building of 382 miles of new railway, 85 miles of new road, road improvements and the introduction of new bus and steamer services. Schemes looked at were railways to serve the northwest fishing ports of Ullapool and Lochinver, narrow gauge lines on the islands of Lewis, Skye and Arran, an isolated railway from Dunoon to Strachur and a 28-mile line across the wilds of Galloway linking Dalmellington with the Portpatrick & Wigtownshire Joint Railway at Parton. As all of these proposed schemes would pass through sparsely populated and remote countryside the Committee pressed the point that Government funding would be necessary. Not surprisingly, during this period of austerity and increased competition from road transport none of these lines were built.

Light railway provisions enjoyed a new lease of life from the 1960s, enabling volunteer-run preserved railways to be operated without onerous legislative requirements. In the early years of the 21st century, an eagle-eyed civil servant in the then Scottish Executive spotted that the old legislation would allow a new two-mile branch line to be constructed to a open-cast coal site in East Ayrshire without an Act of Parliament – and so the Greenburn Light Railway (Scotland) Order 2003 came to pass, limiting coal trains to 20 m.p.h. and prohibiting the operation of passenger trains, albeit to an unlikely destination.

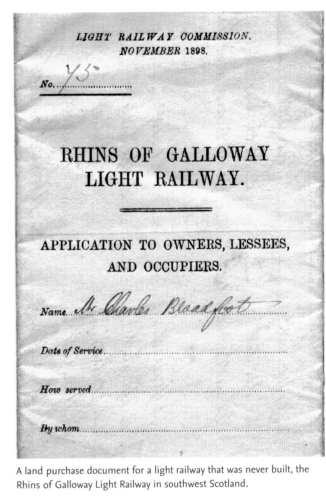

A land purchase document for a light railway that was never built, the Rhins of Galloway Light Railway in southwest Scotland.

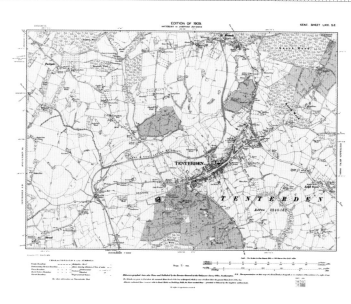

Series	Ordnance Survey Edition of 1909. 6 in. to 1 mile
Sheet	Kent LXXI, S.E.
Date	Surveyed 1870, revised 1906, printed 1909

The Rother Valley Railway, as it was initially known, was the first line to be built under the new Light Railway legislation of 1896. The first section, from the Hastings–London main line at Robertsbridge to Rolvenden, was opened in 1900, followed by a short extension to the present Tenterden Town station in 1903. In 1905 the final section to Headcorn on the Dover–Ashford–London main line was opened, providing a through cross-country route from East Sussex to Kent.

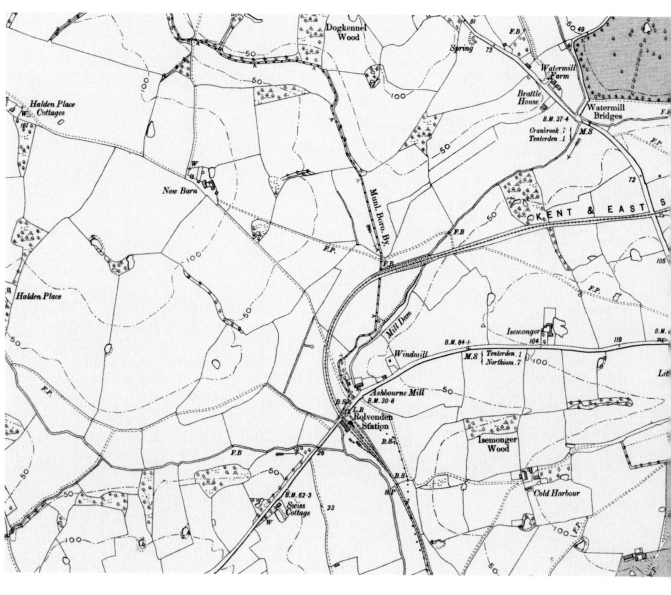

The Kent & East Sussex Railway (KESR), as it eventually became known, was built, owned and managed by Colonel H F Stephens, who went on to run a collection of light railways across England and Wales from his office in Tonbridge. He also managed the narrow gauge Ffestiniog Railway from 1923 until his death in 1931.

The map extract, from an Ordnance Survey 6 in. to 1 mile sheet of 1909, illustrates a number of aspects of the lower-cost engineering of light railways. From Tenterden Town station, despite having a destination to the south, the railway takes a wide sweep to the west, sticking to the contours and avoiding breaching the established fabric of the village.
In a distance of just 1½ miles, the railways makes three level crossings with roads – whereas on lines built to more main-line standards, bridges might well have been constructed.

Unlike most railways, the KESR did not lose its independence at the 'Grouping' in 1923, and it was one of only three independent light railways which survived to be nationalized in 1948. However, growing road competition resulted in the closure of the passenger service in 1954; goods traffic lingered on south of Tenterden, and the occasional passenger train, particularly for hop-pickers and ramblers, operated in the summer; but the line closed completely in 1961. Soon after closure, a society was formed with the object of preserving the line as a volunteer-run steam railway, but it was not until 1974 that trains again ran over the first two miles south from Tenterden. In 2000, 100 years after it originally opened, the KESR finally reached its current terminus at Bodiam – and there are plans to once again make the main line connection at Robertsbridge.

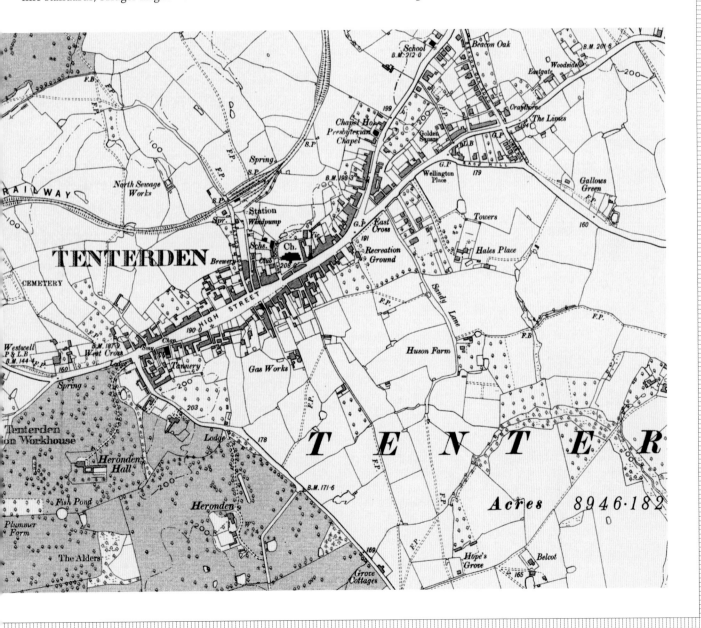

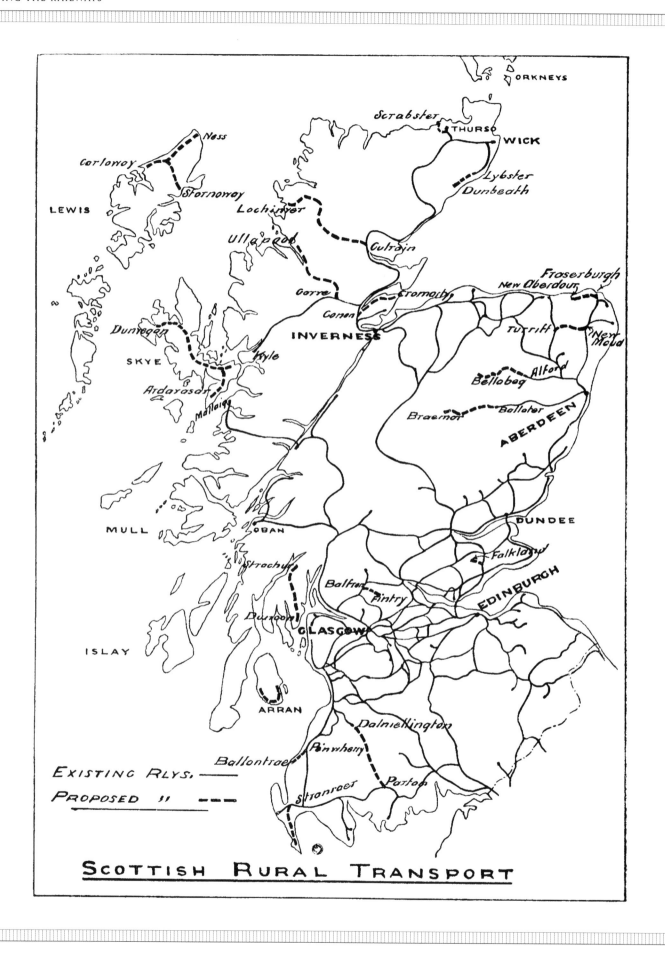

ORKNEYS

Scrabster

THURSO

WICK

Lybster
Dunbeath

Ness

Carloway

Stornoway

LEWIS

Lochinver

Ullapool

Cultain

Fraserburgh

New Oberdour

Garve

Cromarty

Turriff

New Maud

Conon

INVERNESS

Alford

Dunvegan

Bellabeg

SKYE

Kyle

Braemar

Ballater

ABERDEEN

Ardarosan

Mallaig

DUNDEE

MULL

OBAN

Falkland

Strachur

Balfron

EDINBURGH

Fintry

Duroon

GLASGOW

ISLAY

ARRAN

Dalmellington

Pinwherry

Ballontrae

Patron

EXISTING RLYS. ——

PROPOSED ,, ----

Stranraer

SCOTTISH RURAL TRANSPORT

Title	Scottish Rural Transport
Publisher	The Railway Gazette
Date	1919

Light railways were built to lower engineering standards than main lines – with more flexible operating arrangements for signalling, fencing, level crossings, etc., but lower speed limits – in order to open up rural areas at the lowest possible cost. There was great enthusiasm for this concept in the late Victorian and Edwardian era in Scotland, where a Parliamentary Committee in 1919 advocated extensive development of new lines from one end of the country to the other, as illustrated by this map from the *Railway Gazette*.

However, economic constraints – and the rise of the motor car and the lorry after the First World War – meant that not one of the proposed light railways shown here was ever opened. All were in areas of low population and little industrial activity, with particular concentrations in northeast Scotland and the Highlands and Islands. At the opposite end of the country, the suggested link from Stranraer to the isolated village of Drummore in the Rhins of Galloway would undoubtedly have struggled. Not much further north, the proposed route from the Ayr–Stranraer

line to coastal Ballantrae would only have made strategic sense if pushed further south through the hills to Cairnryan (where all ferry services over the North Channel to Northern Ireland are now concentrated), but this would have required very heavy engineering works, well beyond the scope of a light railway. One port where engineering to light railway standards might have worked, and where direct rail–sea connection would have benefited both modes right through to modern times was Scrabster in Caithness, where the Committee proposed a short light-railway link from the Highland Railway terminus at Thurso, but it was not to be.

The *Oxford Companion to British Railway History* advances two reasons for the comparative failure of light railways in Britain:

Firstly, agricultural decline gathered pace in the 1880s, by which time much of the country was well served by a network of railways and branches built to main-line standards, so that the demand for better rural transport came from relatively few areas. Secondly, railway companies and the Board of Trade by then had entrenched ideas about how railways should be built and equipped. Reduced standards were considered to be retrograde. Had light railways developed earlier their history might have been very different.

Opened throughout in 1902 to serve silver and lead mines, the Leadhills & Wanlockhead Railway in southwest Scotland was one of the first light railways built in Britain. A mixed train is seen here at Elvanfoot in 1931, only eight years before the line closed.

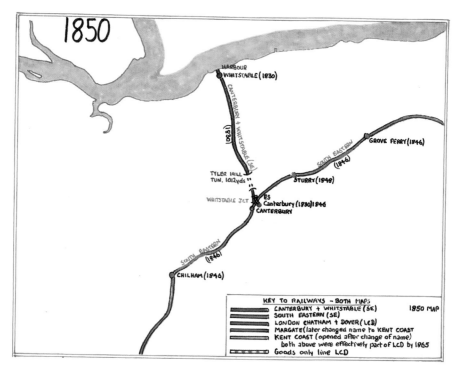

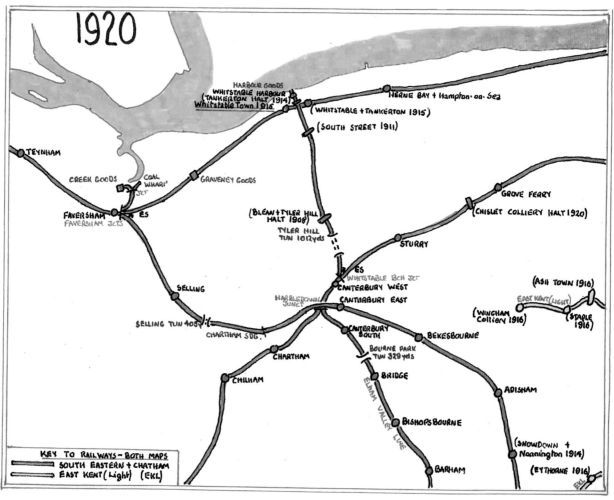

Title	Jowett's Railway Centres (pages 234, 235 and 239)
By	Alan Jowett
Publisher	Patrick Stephens Ltd, Cambridge
Date	1850/1920/1991

These three selected snapshots in time from *Jowett's Railway Centres* – at an original scale of 2 miles to the inch – illustrate the growth and relative decline of the rail network around Canterbury in Kent between 1850, 1920 and 1991. In his commentary, Jowett notes that the rail network in the district has had a number of distinctive features. The first railway to be built in the district, the Canterbury & Whitstable (CWR), offered Britain's first fare-paying passenger service which was also steam-hauled (on 3 May 1830); it was also the first company to issue season tickets, in 1834; and it closed to passengers at an early date, in 1931.

The second route to open, the South Eastern Railway (SER), running southwest to northeast through what is now

Canterbury West station, commenced operations in 1846, followed in 1860 by the London, Chatham & Dover Railway (LCDR), serving Canterbury East. There was no physical connection between the two lines, one crossing the other on a bridge, and Jowett notes that although both lines belonged to a single company by 1900, 'over 90 years later they remain unconnected'.

Railway development in the area was virtually complete by 1863, other than the Elham Valley Railway south to Folkestone via Canterbury South (1889) and, on the fringes of the area, the East Kent Light Railway, which, although largely completed by 1916, did not reach its ultimate terminus at Canterbury Road until 1925. This station had one of the shortest lives of any British railway station, succumbing to road competition just 23 years later. Unusually, all the passenger line closures in this area were implemented *before* the 1963 publication of the Beeching Report, the only casualties thereafter being two small intermediate stations on the former SER route northeast of Canterbury.

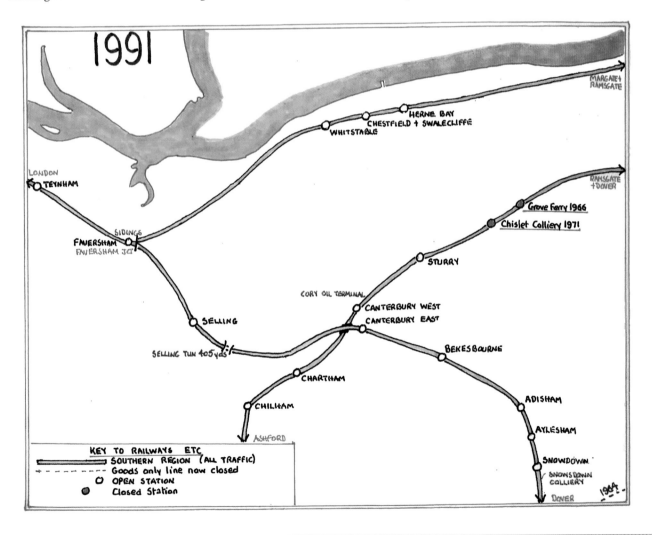

Title	Bartholomew's Half-Inch to Mile Map of England & Wales Sheet 27 Swansea
Mapmaker	J Bartholomew & Son Ltd, Edinburgh
Date	1921

The name of Bartholomew was synonymous with general mapping and with railway mapping from the 1830s to the 1980s. Their use of layer colouring on maps, in which low ground is shown in shades of green and higher ground in shades of brown is demonstrated to great advantage in this 1921 sheet covering Swansea, Cardiff and the Valleys. The widespread use of brown colouring underlines the difficult topography for railways in the north and east of the region – they were forced along narrow valleys in order to reach key sources of coal, and in some cases to penetrate into rural Wales around and beyond the Brecon Beacons.

While the half-inch scale meant that Bartholomew's could not replicate the level of detail of the classic one-inch maps produced by their Ordnance Survey competitors, they did manage to create some distinctive treatments of railways and roads. All railways are shown in black (like the Ordnance Survey representation of multiple-track railways at the time), but station names are shown in full where it is not obvious from the adjacent town or village. In an interesting twist – perhaps reflecting the intended appeal to tourists – there is a different symbol for 'stations with refreshment rooms', although this is so small as to be barely distinguishable.

While these maps were 'reduced [sic] by permission from the Ordnance Survey', the footnotes record that roads were revised by the Cyclists' Touring Club, which explains the quaint reference in the key to 'Indifferent Roads (Passable for Cyclists)'.

The extract overleaf of the area around Swansea – which had six passenger rail termini, more than any other British town outside London – shows the route of the Swansea & Mumbles Railway, originally a horse-drawn waggonway, which survived as an electrified tramway until 1960. Taking a wide sweep to the west and then north is the London & North Western Railway's Central Wales Line to Shrewsbury. The southern section of this route, from Swansea Victoria via Gowerton South to Pontardulais, was axed when the rest of the line was reprieved from the 'Beeching Axe' in 1964. Trains were diverted to run from the former Great Western Railway terminus at Swansea High Street to Llanelli, then reversing to reach the original routing at Pontardulais.

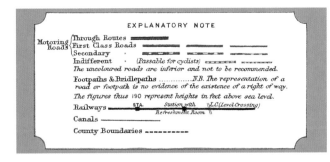

BARTHOLOMEW

The Edinburgh cartographic firm of Bartholomew was founded in 1826 by John Bartholomew (1805–1861). The second John Bartholomew (1831–1893) trained with his father and the eminent German geographer, August Petermann (1822–1878). Under John Junior, the business expanded from contract engraving into lithography and printing, with a particular emphasis on map production. John Junior and his son, John George (1860–1920), introduced the continental technique of layer colouring to Britain in *Baddeley's Guide to the Lake District*. The firm subsequently became synonymous with the renowned series of *Times* atlases.

Bartholomew remained a family business, passing from son to son, until 1980, when the business was sold to Reader's Digest Association, Inc., and then to News International, who later merged it with the Glasgow publisher Collins, as part of HarperCollins Publishers. The Bartholomew Archive – http://digital.nls.uk/bartholomew – is one of the most extensive cartographic archives available for research in a public institution. HarperCollins and John C Bartholomew and family donated the firm's business records, working maps and printing plates to the National Library of Scotland (NLS) between 1983 and 2008. Fittingly, the NLS Map Reading Room lies only a short walk from the site of Bartholomew's former Edinburgh base.

THE 'GROUPING' – AND A QUEST FOR SPEED

After wartime experience of the benefits of unified operation, the Government amalgamated 120 railway companies into just four large groups. The railway system as a whole stagnated, but on the principal main lines a short 'golden era' of ever faster and more luxurious services was launched.

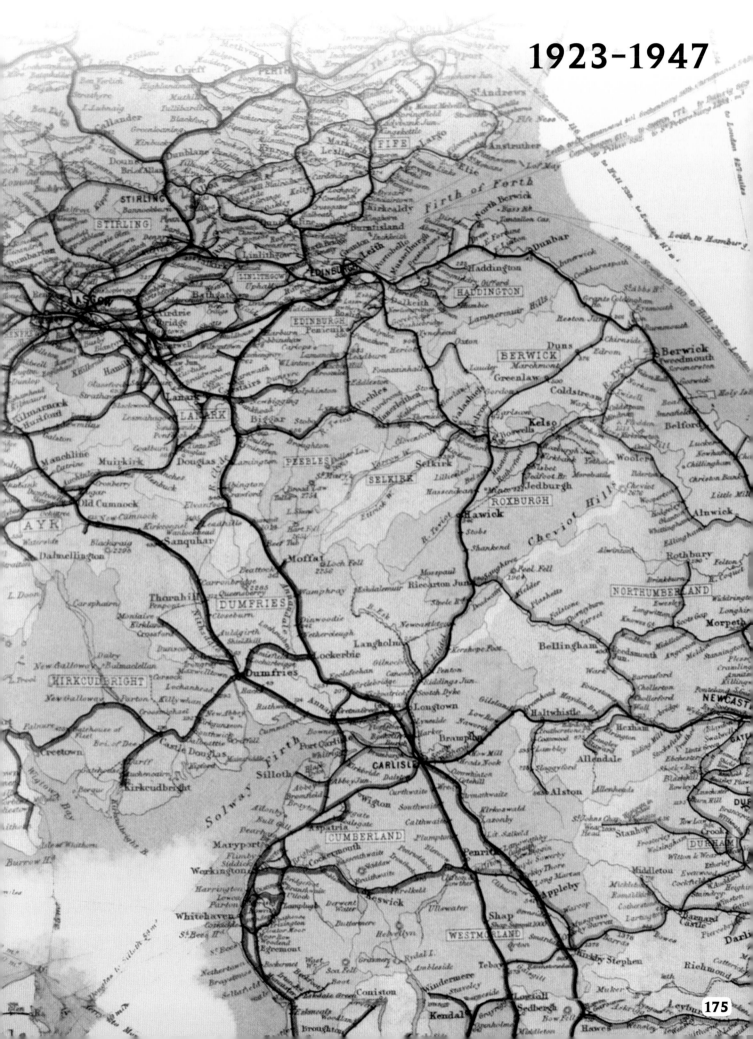

An empty art room at the London & North Western Railway's Mechanics' Institute at Crewe in 1907.

The peace and quiet of England's green and pleasant land was rudely shattered by the coming of the railways in the mid-19th century – what were once just green pastures and sleepy villages were soon to become the throbbing workshops of the early railway companies. The railway town had arrived.

In the south of the country the village of Swindon was initially ignored by Brunel's broad-gauge Great Western Railway (GWR) when it partially opened in 1840 between Paddington and Bristol. This was soon to change when Swindon became the junction for the new railway to Gloucester and Cheltenham and by 1843 the GWR had established their locomotive repair depot on the land between the two railway lines. In the beginning only 200 men were employed here but by 1846 the works had started building new locomotives and within five years the workforce had soared to 2,000. Swindon expanded rapidly and by the early 20th century was home to over 13,000 railway workers plus their families and others employed in their support. The GWR took a paternalistic view of their employees and engendered a great deal of loyalty among them, providing housing, libraries, reading rooms, medical insurance, a hospital, entertainment venues, a sports and social club and annual outings. Swindon's output of steam locomotives was prolific and continued until 1960, when the last steam locomotive built for British Railways, 'Evening Star', emerged from the works. Although the building of

diesels carried on until 1965, the works eventually closed in 1986. The buildings were converted into shops, a railway museum and the headquarters of English Heritage. Despite the loss of its railway works Swindon, with its excellent road and rail connections, has continued to be a boom town in the 21st century.

The opening of the Grand Junction Railway between Birmingham, Liverpool and Manchester in 1837 soon saw that company establishing their railway works on a greenfield site near the small village of Monks Coppenhall. Renamed Crewe after nearby Crewe Hall, the railway town, like Swindon, grew up around an important railway junction and in 1846 became the main locomotive works for the newly formed London & North Western Railway (LNWR). By the beginning of the 20th century the works and its steel-producing plant had a workforce of 8,000 and Crewe had become a railway town of 40,000 people. As with the GWR, the LNWR looked after its employees, providing housing, an educational institution, a hospital, church, school and recreational facilities. At its peak under the London, Midland & Scottish Railway in the 1930s, Crewe Works employed over 20,000 staff and the town's population had grown to around 60,000. It remained the most important railway works in Britain until 1990, by which time over 8,000 steam, diesel and electric locomotives had been built there. While Crewe still remains an important railway centre, with extensive freight and civil engineering

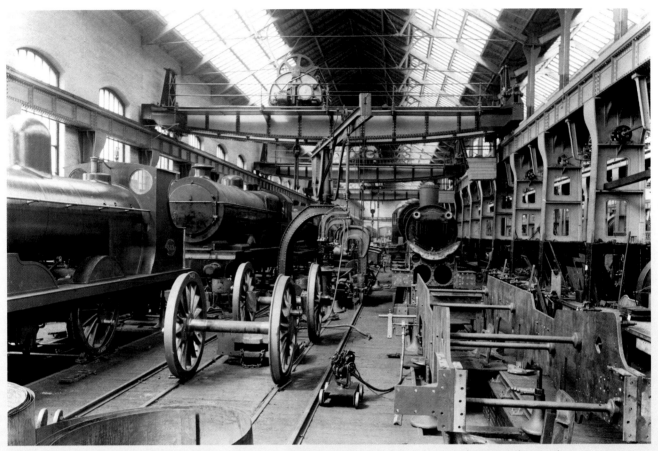

An early 20th-century scene inside the locomotive erecting shop at the Lancashire & Yorkshire Railway's works at Horwich, Lancashire.

yards to the south and west, what little remains of the once extensive railway works is now owned by Bombardier Transportation who carry out train maintenance and inspection.

Around Britain other railway towns also sprung up around locomotive works. Principal among these were the London &

South Western Railway at Eastleigh, the South Eastern & Chatham Railway at Ashford, the Great Northern Railway at Doncaster, the North Eastern Railway at Darlington, the Lancashire & Yorkshire Railway at Horwich and the Glasgow & South Western Railway at Corkerhill. Today most of these railway works have long since disappeared with new locomotives now being imported from North America.

Men from the Horwich Railway Mechanics Institute play at the Lancashire & Yorkshire Railway's cricket ground, c.1892.

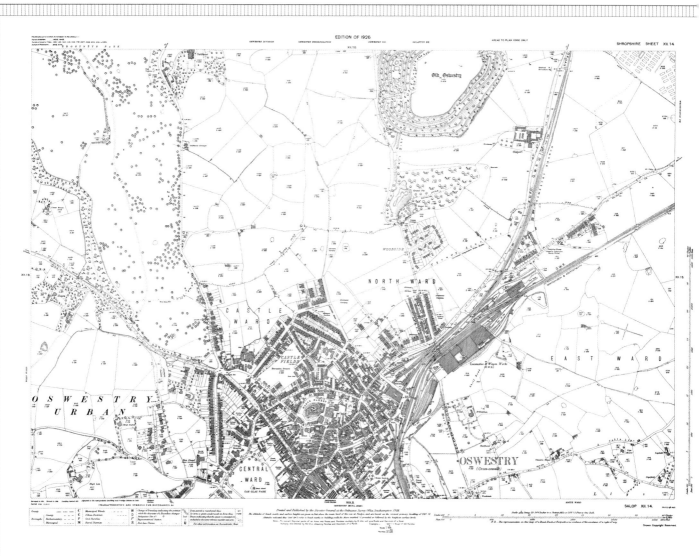

Series	Ordnance Survey 25 in. to 1 mile
Sheet	Shropshire Sheet XII.14 Oswestry
Date	Surveyed 1874, revised 1924, printed and published 1926

The first railway to reach Oswestry was a short branch from Gobowen, opened in January 1849 by the Shrewsbury & Chester Railway, which had bypassed the town to the north and east. Despite their Welsh-sounding names, both towns lie in England, a few miles from the border.

Independent cross-country lines were promoted southwest to Newtown and northeast to Whitchurch, opening in 1861 and 1864 respectively, but Oswestry was far from being a major railway junction. However, its status as a 'railway town' was assured in 1864 by the amalgamation of the Newtown and Whitchurch lines, together with the Newtown & Machynlleth and Llanidloes & Newtown Railways, to form the Cambrian Railway. The new concern decided to site its headquarters in the town, with facilities which included

administrative offices in the substantial station building, a well-equipped locomotive, carriage and wagon works, and a locomotive running shed eventually expanded to six 'roads' (rail tracks).

In a small town whose population barely reached 10,000 even after the development stimulated by the railway, these topographical features of the railway were relatively dominant, as can be seen in the Ordnance Survey map on this page and overleaf, published four years after the Cambrian was absorbed into the Great Western Railway in 1922. The railway was kept on the edge of the town, where it had ample room for expansion as passenger and freight traffic and supporting activities grew. In addition to the works and locomotive ('engine') shed, and the passenger station, the map depicts goods sheds, goods stations, a coal depot, a timber yard and rail-connected cattle pens.

The railway at Oswestry saw little change until British Railways' 1955 Modernisation Plan and the 1963 Beeching Report resulted in not just a rapid decline, but the almost complete removal of the town from the railway map. After withdrawal of the remaining shuttle passenger services to Gobowen in 1966, all that survived were freight trains, latterly serving Blodwel quarry (five miles to the south), for which a single track through the former station sufficed.

This traffic lingered on until 1988, but more recent years have seen a mini railway revival in Oswestry with the establishment of the Cambrian Railways Society, which hopes to develop a heritage railway operation through the town from Gobowen to Blodwel.

Before – still multiple tracks to and through Oswestry just after the 1966 closure of the passenger station.

After – by 1978 only a single track was required through the station for the remaining freight branch line.

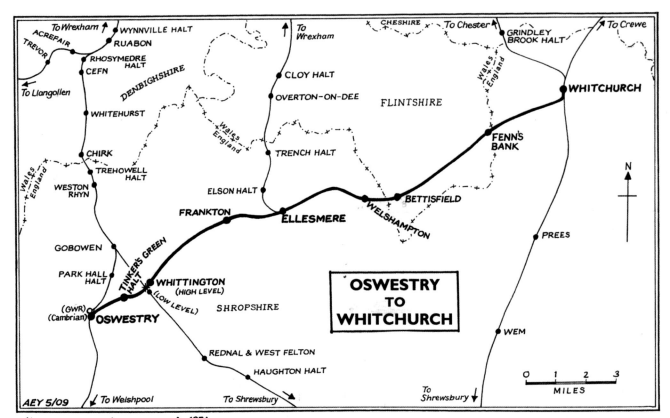

Network and station names as in 1951.

Alan Young's contemporary map shows Oswestry's position in the wider rail network in 1951.

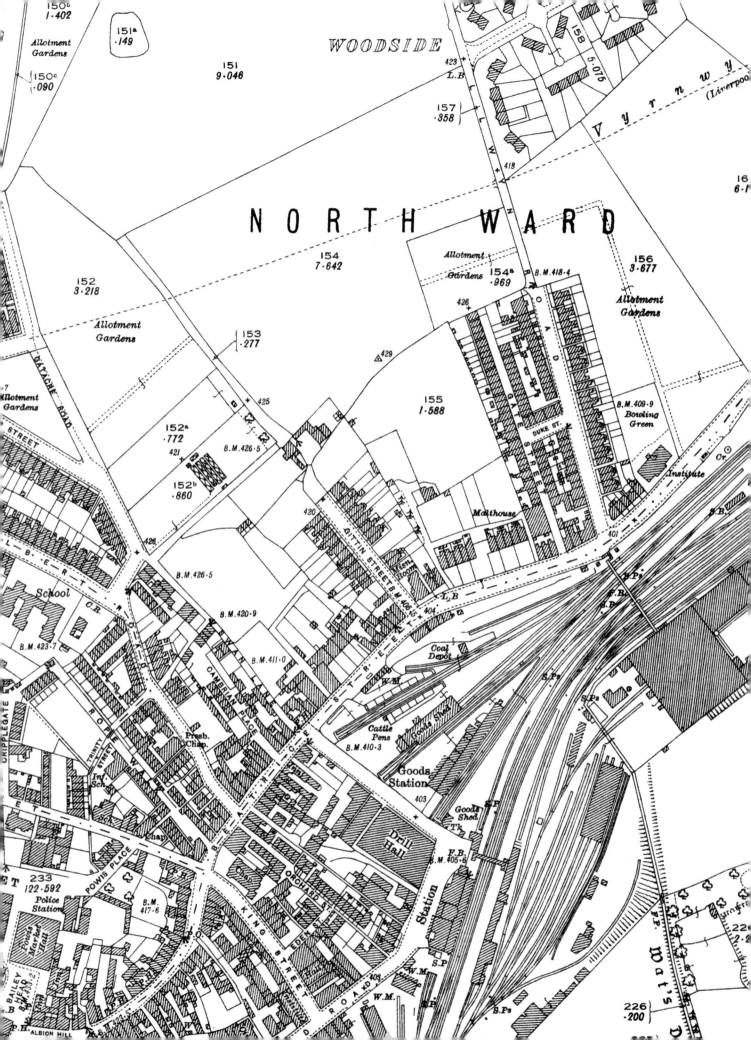

WOODSIDE

N O R T H   W A R D

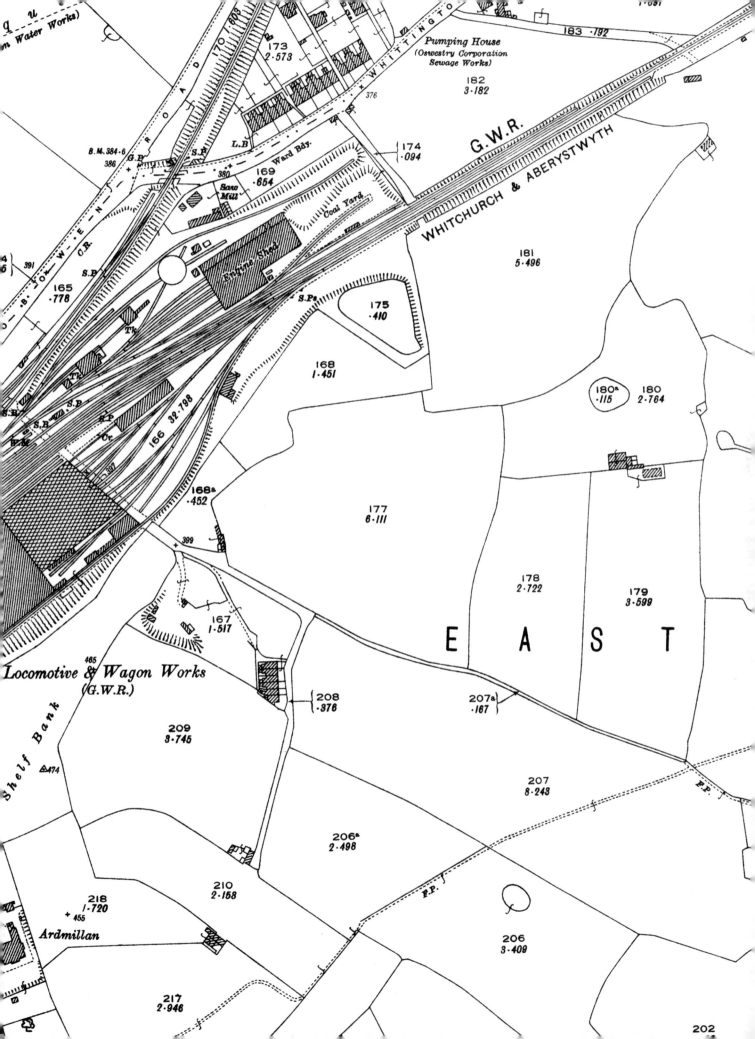

By the end of the First World War, the 120 railway companies operating in Britain were facing a difficult future. Losses were mounting and in 1921 the Government passed the Railways Act which amalgamated these companies into four large regional companies. Commonly known as the Big Four Grouping, this took effect on 1 January 1923. Within a few years these four companies – Great Western Railway (GWR), London, Midland & Scottish Railway (LMS), London & North Eastern Railway (LNER) and Southern Railway (SR) – were getting their act together with the development of more powerful steam locomotives and modern coaching stock. Striving for faster and faster services, the rivalry between these publicity-seeking companies was intense.

Always at the forefront of railway technology, the GWR was first off the starting block with its world-beating 'Cheltenham Flyer'. Hauled by one of Collett's new 'Castle' Class 4-6-0 locomotives, this famous train gained the title 'The World's Fastest Train' in 1932 when 'Tregenna Castle' and its six coaches took just under 57 minutes to travel the

Introduced in 1935, the London & North Eastern Railway's 'Silver Jubilee' express between King's Cross and Newcastle was hauled by Nigel Gresley's streamlined 'A4' Pacific locomotives.

No. 5000 'Launceston Castle' speeds across the Thames at Maidenhead with the world's fastest scheduled train, the 'Cheltenham Flyer', in 1934.

77¼ miles between Swindon and Paddington at an average speed of 81.6 m.p.h. The train was soon rescheduled to take 65 minutes for the journey and became officially the fastest scheduled train service in the world.

Elsewhere in the world the German 'Flying Hamburger' and the American 'Burlington Zephyr' were setting new standards using streamlined high-speed diesels. After visiting Germany, Nigel Gresley, the Chief Mechanical Engineer of the LNER carried out trials with his 'A3' Pacific 'Papyrus', which set a speed record of 108 m.p.h., proving that steam was every bit as good as diesel. This success led to Gresley designing his world-famous 'A4' streamlined Pacifics, the first of which, 'Silver Link', reached a speed of 112.5 m.p.h. while hauling seven streamlined articulated coaches in September 1935. The new A4s were soon in regular service hauling the 'Silver Jubilee' express between King's Cross and Newcastle – the locomotives proved very reliable and were popular with their crews.

Not to be outdone by the LNER's success, the LMS introduced its 'Coronation Scot' streamlined train between Euston and Glasgow in 1937. Motive power was provided by William Stanier's new 'Coronation' Class Pacifics, the first ten members being fitted with streamlined casings, hauling matching coaches. During a test run in June 1937, No. 6220

'Coronation' achieved a speed of 114 m.p.h. just south of Crewe, narrowly avoiding a derailment as it approached the station at an excessive speed.

The competition was hotting up, and back on the LNER new streamlined expresses were soon introduced from King's Cross to Edinburgh and Leeds. However, the best was yet to come when, on 3 July 1938, Gresley's 'A4' Class 'Mallard' achieved a world speed record for steam traction of 126 m.p.h. while hauling a test train down Stoke Bank south of Grantham – this record still stands today.

Sadly, the onset of the Second World War in 1939 put a stop to these high jinks and the post-war austerity years never saw a return to this Golden Age. The LMS 'Coronations' lost their streamlined casings and the LNER 'A4's were shorn of their streamlined side valances, although the 'Elizabethan' non-stop express between King's Cross and Edinburgh provided a little glamour until it was withdrawn in 1961.

Fortunately six members of the 'A4' Class (including 'Mallard') have been preserved, including one each in museums in the USA and Canada. The preserved ex-LMS 'Coronation' Class Pacific 'Duchess of Hamilton' has recently had its streamlined casing reinstated, and the locomotive can be seen in all its glory at the National Railway Museum in York.

Three preserved 'A4' locomotives. In the foreground is 'Mallard' which attained 126 m.p.h. in 1938 – an unbeaten world record for steam locomotives.

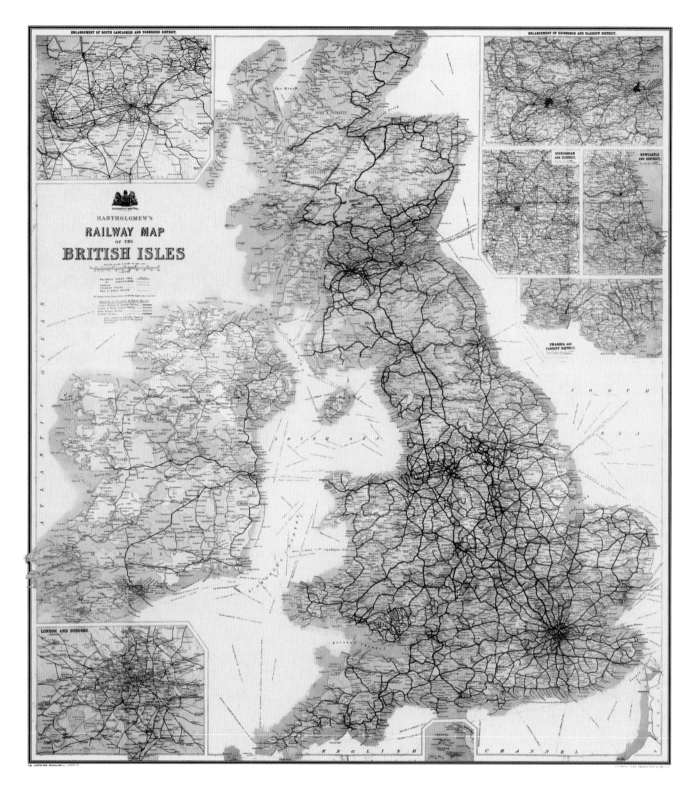

Title	Bartholomew's Railway Map of the British Isles
By	J Bartholomew, Edinburgh
Date	*c.*1923–8

John Bartholomew & Son Ltd, the prestigious Edinburgh mapmaker, produced specialist railway maps not just on commission from the railway companies, but also as their own bespoke sheets showing the complete national network. In this particular case, an earlier map has been overprinted in colour to distinguish the routes of the 'Big Four' companies created by the Government's 1923 Grouping – the Great Western Railway (GWR), London, Midland & Scottish Railway (LMS), London & North Eastern Railway (LNER) and the Southern Railway (SR).

The base map was clearly produced some time before the Grouping, as it depicts a number of routes which had already closed by 1923, such as the Highland Railway's Keith to Buckie branch (closed in 1915), and the 'seventh Anglo-Scottish route' across the Solway Firth Viaduct, west of Port Carlisle (closed in 1922). The original key also has a symbol for 'railways constructing', but only a couple of very minor lines were built after the Grouping.

The overlaid key highlights a very British quirk which continued after the Grouping – 'joint railways', which were lines owned by more than one company. Designed to find a compromise between competing aims, in many ways they were a costly solution. Not only was there the cost of legal requirements to determine working arrangements, but in the case of the bigger joint railways there were separate headquarters and staff to be funded. A more sensible outcome would have been for a single company to take ownership and to charge the other company for train running rights, extending the principle of 'running powers' which was long established and accepted throughout the rail network.

The Grouping did reduce the number of joint lines from over 70 to just 16, perhaps the most famous of which were the Somerset & Dorset and the Midland & Great Northern.

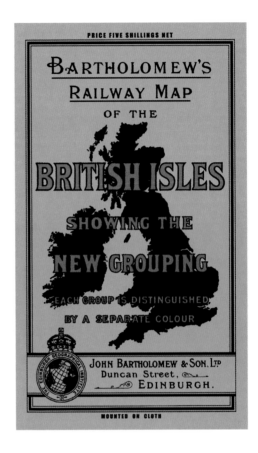

The latter is shown in some detail in the extract on this page from another Bartholomew's map (of 1927), and was the longest of the joint railways, at 183 miles. It penetrated deep into Great Eastern Railway territory, designed to tap the Norfolk coast holiday market and fish traffic to the Midlands. As essentially a duplicate route for longer distance traffic and an early casualty of local road competition, it closed completely in 1959 – other than for a few freight stubs, and the Sheringham–Cromer link, which survives to this day.

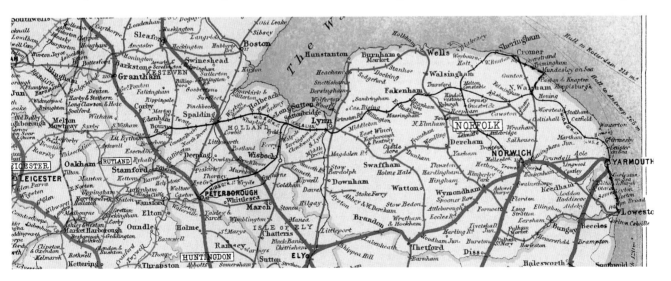

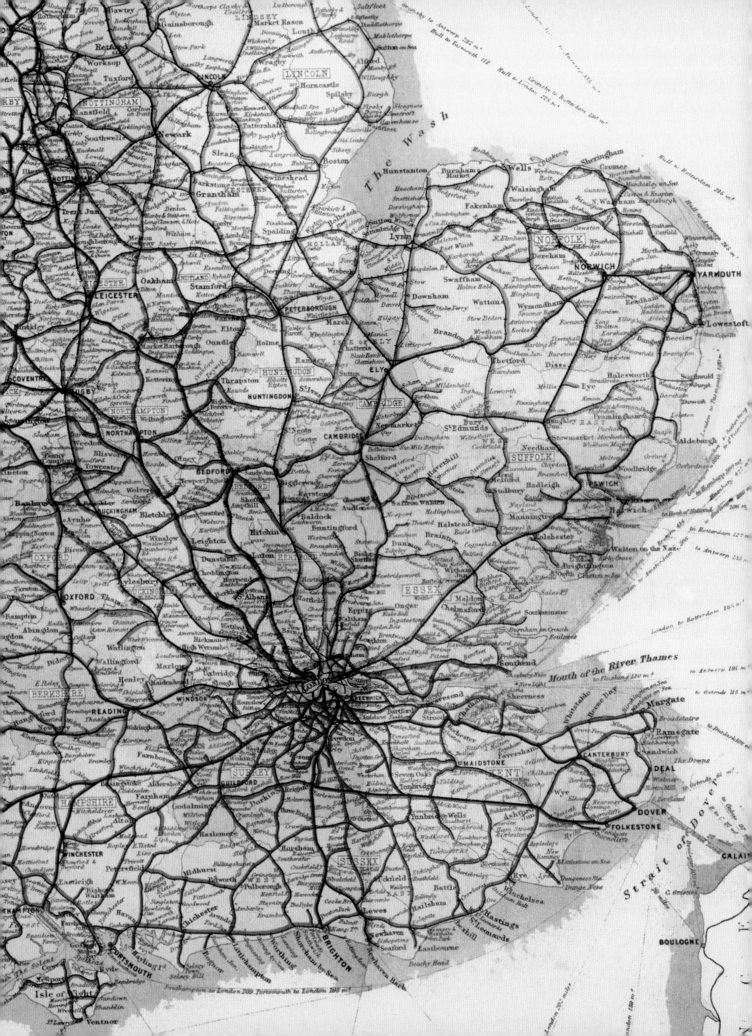

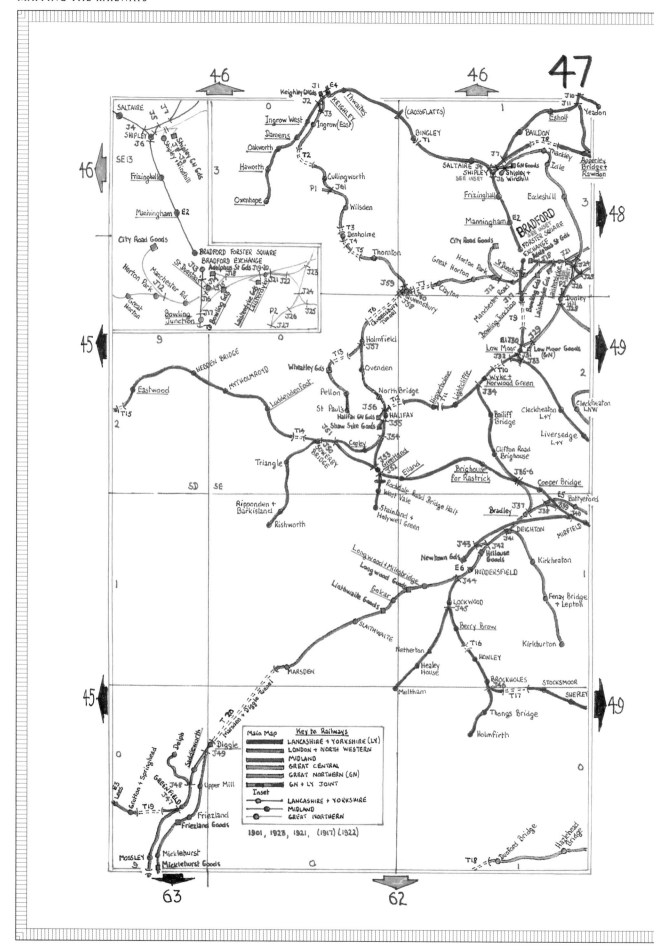

Series	Jowett's Railway Atlas (page 47)
By	Alan Jowett
Publisher	Patrick Stephens Ltd, Cambridge
Date	1989

This map from *Jowett's Railway Atlas* portrays the zenith of the rail network on the West Yorkshire side of the Pennines to the southwest of Bradford. Originally mapped at a scale of 5 miles to the inch, it shows no less than six different railway companies competing for passenger and freight traffic with a dense network of lines in the industrialized and heavily populated valleys around Bradford, Halifax and Huddersfield. Further west, the topography of the Pennines and the relative absence of development thinned out the opportunities for the railways to just three main lines – the Midland Railway (MR) striking northwestwards from Leeds and Bradford through Keighley to Hellifield, then west to Lancaster and north to Carlisle via Settle; the Lancashire & Yorkshire Railway (LYR) through Halifax and Hebden Bridge to Manchester and Preston; and the London & North Western Railway through Huddersfield and the long Marsden and Diggle (Standedge) Tunnel to Manchester.

These three main lines are the principal survivors from that era, serving key inter-city, commuter and freight markets. The route southeastwards from Huddersfield via Stocksmoor to Penistone (and onwards to Barnsley and Sheffield) was reprieved from the 'Beeching Axe', while the previously freight-only lines from Huddersfield and Mirfield to Halifax and Sowerby Bridge via Brighouse re-opened to passenger traffic in 2000. The MR's scenic branch line from Keighley to Oxenhope closed in 1962, but in 1968 re-opened as the volunteer-run Keighley & Worth Valley Railway, famous for its scenes in the classic film *The Railway Children*.

The largest concentration of through routes that closed is the network of former Great Northern Railway lines connecting Bradford, Halifax and Keighley, centred on the triangular junction at Queensbury. This system was fully opened by 1884, both to serve local mill towns and villages and to compete with the MR and LYR. The lines were heavily engineered and steeply graded, with no less than 16 tunnels totalling over four and a half miles in length. Relatively slow through journeys, and intensifying bus competition after the First World War (and car competition after the Second World War), led to the early demise of passenger services in 1955. The last stretches, surviving for freight only, in Bradford (to City Road Goods) and in Halifax (to North Bridge) closed in 1972 and 1974 respectively.

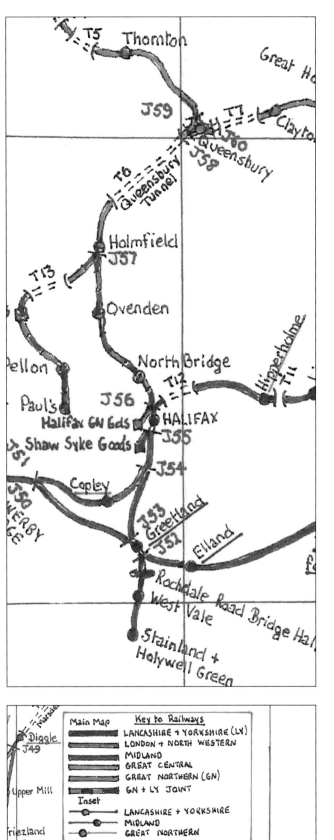

By the beginning of the 20th century Britain's railway companies had discovered the value of marketing their services, routes and destinations to the travelling public. Long before the First World War, railway publicity departments all over the land were extolling their companies' virtues with guidebooks, illustrated route maps, postcards and posters. Of note were the publicity departments of the North British Railway and the London & North Western Railway, but smaller companies such as the North Staffordshire Railway and the Furness Railway also led the way. In addition, the Great Northern Railway was in the forefront of publicity with its 'Skegness is So Bracing' poster – designed by the illustrator John Hassall in 1908, it is probably the most famous railway poster of all time.

However, by far the most prolific publicity department was that of the Great Western Railway (GWR) which, as early as 1903, was promoting its route to the southwest as 'The Holiday Line'. The GWR even commissioned its own film, 'The Story of the Holiday Line', which was first shown at the London Coliseum in 1914. By the 1920s the GWR was promoting the scenic delights of Devon and Cornwall as the 'Cornish Riviera', a marketing slogan which was used to good effect on posters, guide books and even on its premier express to Penzance. In the early 1930s the GWR's 'Cheltenham Flyer' – dubbed the 'World's Fastest Train' – was a tremendous coup for its publicity department, as was the centenary of the company in 1935. Posters by artists such as Murray Secretan, Leonard Richmond and Charles Mayo could be seen adorning stations the length and breadth of the GWR's system. Not content with its abundant output of posters and holiday guides, the GWR also produced over 40 jigsaw puzzles (manufactured by Chad Valley) and a series of books for railway enthusiasts.

Even the luggage labels of the 1930s were stylishly designed.

Written by the prolific author, S P B Mais, the Southern Railway published a series of walking guide books in the 1930s.

The 1930s was the Golden Age of Railways in Britain and the publicity departments of the other three of the 'Big Four' railway companies – the London, Midland & Scottish (LMS), the London & North Eastern (LNER) and the Southern (SR) railways – were also hard at work glamourizing travel on their respective systems. The most prolific poster artist of this period was Norman Wilkinson, who produced a large number of classic large-format posters for both the LMS and the SR and was instrumental in introducing 17 Royal Academicians to work for the LMS publicity department. In addition to its classic holiday destination posters, the SR also produced a series of attractive railway walks books written by the author and broadcaster S P B (Stuart Petre Brodie) Mais.

Introduced in 1937, the London & North Eastern Railway's 'Coronation' express was the first streamlined train between London and Edinburgh.

THE CORONATION SCOT
ASCENDING SHAP FELL
by Norman Wilkinson, P.R.I.

The Coronation Scot, blue and silver express of the L M S Railway, runs each weekday (except Saturdays) between London and Glasgow in 6½ hours, leaving Euston Station and Central Station at 1-30 p.m. The trains consist of nine air-conditioned coaches, internally panelled in decorative woods. The locomotive Coronation Scot (No. 6220) is one of five high-speed streamlined engines designed to maintain high average speeds in all weathers over the famous West Coast Route to Scotland, which includes such difficult ascents as Shap Fell (915 ft.), and Beattock Summit (1,014 ft.). Coronation Scot attained on a test run with the train in 1937 a maximum speed of 114 miles an hour, creating a British railway record.

Painted by Norman Wilkinson, this London Midland & Scottish Railway poster of 1937 depicts the streamlined 'Coronation Scot' express climbing up Shap in 1937.

CORPORATE IDENTITY

The post-war years brought nationalization of Britain's railways and a new period of corporate identity.

A lion (nicknamed the 'Unicycling Lion') was chosen by British Railways (BR) to adorn the sides of locomotives while a 'sausage'-shaped totem was selected to appear on BR publicity material and for station nameboards. With some variations these remained as the BR corporate identity until the introduction of the famous double-arrow logo in 1965 – nicknamed the 'arrow of indecision' at the time, but subsequently proving to be one of the most enduring of logos, still an identifying sign for railway station locations today.

Introduced after nationalization in 1948, the 'Unicycling Lion' device was used to adorn the sides of British Railways' locomotives.

The 'sausage' logo was used by British Railways as their corporate identity on station signs and publicity material.

British Rail's famous double-arrow logo was introduced in 1965 and is still an identifying sign for railway station locations today.

Always ready to capitalize on a publicity coup, the LNER's department had a field day in 1935 when that company introduced Britain's first streamlined high-speed train, the 'Silver Jubilee', between King's Cross and Newcastle. Stylish locomotives and matching coaches ushered in a new age of modern travel, complemented by the company's stylish brochures and posters. By 1937 the LNER's new streamliner, 'Coronation', was competing with the LMS's streamlined 'Coronation Scot' for the important Anglo-Scottish traffic, with both companies vying with each other for the ultimate publicity coup – the LNER was the winner when one of their streamlined locomotives, 'Mallard', achieved a world record for steam traction in 1938. Just over a year later the Second World War broke out, and a new age of austerity descended on the railways.

By the early 1950s the newly formed British Railways (BR) publicity department had got back into full swing after the post-war austerity period and was producing posters, holiday guides, brochures, leaflets and regional timetables all carrying the corporate identity logo. The most famous

Illustrated by 'Michie', this stylish tariff for the 'Cornish Riviera Express' was produced by the Western Region of British Railways in the 1950s.

artist of the BR era was undoubtedly Terence Cuneo, who had started his career as a magazine and book illustrator before he was appointed an official war artist during the Second World War. From 1953, when he was also appointed official artist of Queen Elizabeth II's Coronation, Cuneo was commissioned by BR to produce a large number of oil paintings of the railways, their locomotives and infrastructure. Often putting his own personal safety at risk when sketching on location, Cuneo's masterpieces always included his personal trademark – a small mouse lurking in a corner of each painting. His output continued into the diesel and electric era and, today, his posters are prized and valuable possessions for collectors of railway ephemera.

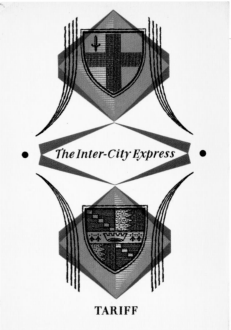

Dating from the late 1950s, this elegant tariff for the Western Region's 'The Inter-City Express' contained a dinner menu and wine list.

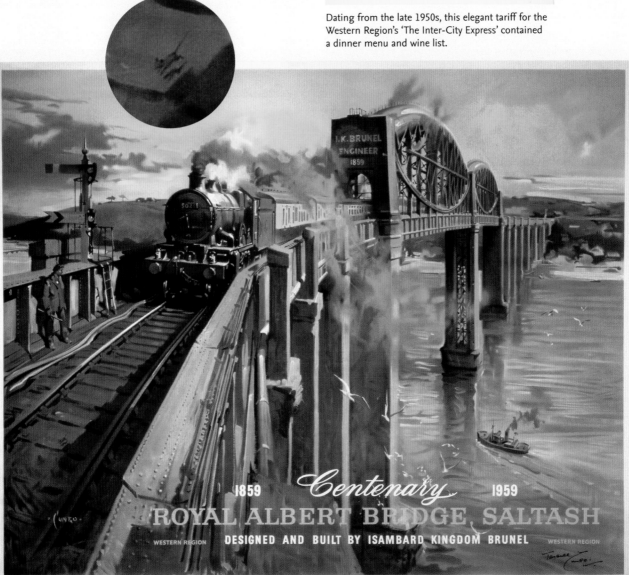

Painted by Terence Cuneo, this BR poster celebrated the centenary of Brunel's Royal Albert Bridge at Saltash, Cornwall, in 1959. Inset: His trademark mouse can be seen in the bottom left of the poster.

As we have seen, simplified strip maps appeared at a relatively early stage of the development of Britain's rail network, but it was not until the early years of the 20th century that truly diagrammatic maps of railways were first produced. Around 1904 both the City & South London Railway and the Great Central Railway introduced maps with railways shown as straight lines with equal spacing between stations – designed to ease passenger understanding of how to use the dense and complex commuter networks which had developed, particularly in London. Over the next 25 years an increasing number of railways – notably the constituent routes of the London Underground – published maps with other essential diagrammatic characteristics such as coloured, vertical, horizontal and 45-degree lines.

However, it was not until George Dow produced his Great Eastern and Great Northern suburban lines maps for the London & North Eastern Railway (LNER) in 1929 that an entire *system* – as opposed to individual lines – was shown fully diagrammatically. Dow was also the first to introduce lines of common angle, and to show other companies' routes as pairs of thin lines – a double line known as 'casing'.

The end product – as seen in the Great Northern route diagram shown below – was two striking maps which in the words of the cartographer Doug Rose, 'straightened out the tangled geographical lines so that users could allow their eyes to flow effortlessly along each route on the map'. As described by George Dow's son, Andrew, in *Telling the Passenger Where to Get Off* (2005):

They were designed specifically to be placed in compartments of passenger stock, and they were therefore sized and proportioned to fit in the standard glazed frames above seatbacks, with the lettering of a size readable from any corner of the compartment.

Dow went on to produce a total of some 15 diagrammatic maps for the LNER, London Midland & Scottish Railway (LMS) and British Railways (BR), including the dramatically distinctive 1935 London Suburban map for the LMS in 1935, and the Tyneside Electric Lines Route Diagram created to coincide with the LNER's electrification of the Newcastle–South Shields line in 1938.

Unlike Harry Beck, the famed designer of the classic London Underground map (see overleaf), George Dow drew maps of a wide range of different rail networks, but as none of these would ever have the massive visitor base of the Underground – which ensured that Beck's design quickly became internationally recognizable – Dow's key role in the history of railway mapping was destined to be neglected for many years. Fortunately that is now being put right.

Title	Great Northern Suburban Lines Route Diagram
Mapmaker	George Dow
Publisher	London & North Eastern Railway
Date	1929

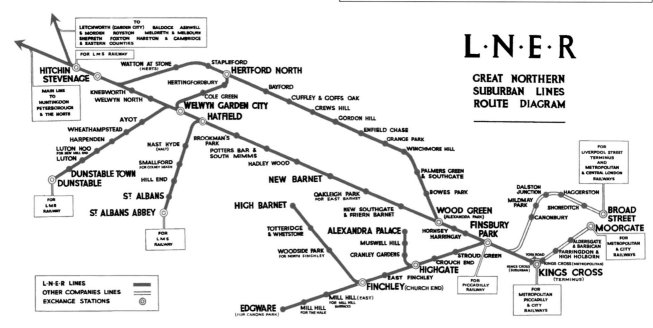

GEORGE DOW

George Dow (born 1907) was a grade five clerk who had worked for the LNER for two years when, in his own time and at his own initiative, he designed and drew the diagrammatic maps for the Great Eastern and Great Northern lines.

Having trained in engineering drawing, he became involved in preparing maps and diagrams for internal railway purposes – from which he extended the principles of simplified mapping to produce diagrams that provided passengers with easily identifiable information while they were *en route* on the train.

As Dow progressed upwards through railway management he inevitably had to withdraw from direct map making, but during his period as Public Relations & Publicity Officer for BR London Midland Region (1949–55) he commissioned award-winning posters, and under his guidance some 25 diagrammatic maps were produced by a member of his staff, Vic Welch.

Dow retired as BR Divisional Manager Stoke-on-Trent in 1968, but went on to have a very productive retirement – lecturing, railway modelling and writing many books on railway subjects, including the classic *Great Central* which includes 27 maps from his own pen. He died in 1987.

Title	LMS London Suburban Electric Lines Route Diagram
Mapmaker	George Dow
Publisher	London Midland & Scottish Railway
Date	1935

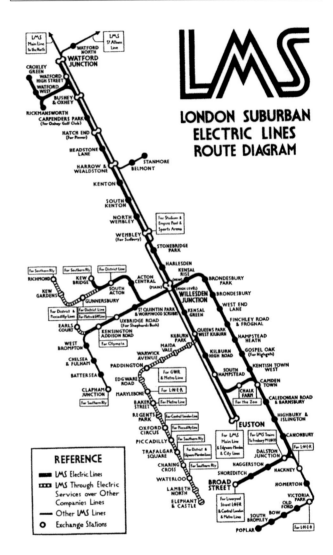

Title	Tyneside Electric Lines Route Diagram
Mapmaker	George Dow
Publisher	London & North Eastern Railway
Date	1938

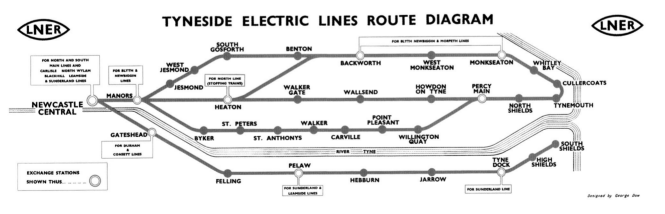

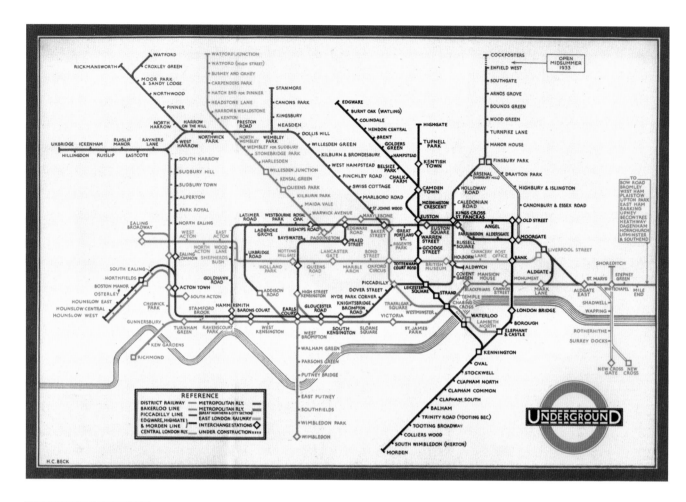

Series	The London Underground Diagram
Mapmaker	Henry C (Harry) Beck
Publisher	The Underground Group
Date	1933

The best known railway map in Britain – and indeed the world – is based on Harry Beck's classic diagrammatic map of the London Underground, first published in 1933, and which quickly became an iconic representation of Britain's capital city. Today's London Underground map is instantly recognizable as a direct descendant of Beck's abstract design of 80 years ago, a map concept which has largely stood the test of time by regular adaptation to changing circumstances. While the current map, as shown overleaf, includes far more information than Beck had to incorporate – inevitably affecting the ease of understanding – the essence of his simplified design, which made it the bench mark for underground system maps worldwide, is still evident.

As we have seen, Beck was far from being the first designer to deploy diagrammatic representation of railways, and as Andrew Dow (George Dow's son) notes in *Telling the Passenger*

Where to Get Off (2005), '...it is clear that most or all of the eight lines that made up the Underground system [by 1933] were already represented in individual diagrammatic route maps'. Beck must have been familiar with at least some of them, and interestingly, as a resident of Highgate on the London & North Eastern Railway's Great Northern suburban system, it seems highly likely that he would have seen George Dow's diagrammatic map (see page 194) on the trains in which he travelled, and would have been influenced by them.

However, Beck's good fortune – although in light of his later dealings with London Transport management, he might not have seen it this way – was to pull together coherently a variety of elements of diagrammatic mapping to create a unique map design for one of the busiest rail networks in the world, increasingly heavily used by visitors, and thereby destined to achieve international recognition. Beck's map can be seen as part of a wider drive to apply consistent design standards across the growing London transport system, much of it led by Frank Pick – as Managing Director of the Underground Group from 1928 and from 1933 of the new London Passenger Transport Board, which managed underground railway, bus and tram transport across London after the system was brought into public ownership.

Beck sketched out his first design concept in 1931, initially rejected by the Underground Group, before they recognized that his schematic representation of reality would transform understanding of the system's links and connections – both for Londoners and its many visitors. The key features of the 1933 map and its modern successors are:

- simplification of the route lines to verticals, horizontals or diagonals;
- enlargement of the central area relative to the suburbs;
- elimination of all surface detail except the River Thames.

Beck had to accommodate many enforced changes in the design – some of them ill-advised management interference – as well as making his own improvements. A regular challenge was the extension and augmentation of existing 'tube' lines from 1933 through to 1948, with just one closure in his time – the withdrawal of the shuttle service from Acton Town to South Acton in 1959.

Early design changes, in 1934, involved a change of colouring for the Central Line – always intended as a strong horizontal base for the map – from orange to red, and for the Bakerloo Line from red to brown. The colour representation of the routes open in 1934 has remained largely unchanged ever since, but there have been a number of important design changes since Beck's first vision – such as the use of rings instead of diamonds to denote interchange stations, and the identification of station names in lower case, with an initial capital, rather than upper case.

Since Beck's last map, many Underground network changes have had to be incorporated into 'the diagram', notably the opening of the Victoria and Jubilee lines, and the closure of the Aldwych

and Epping to Ongar branches. The current version of the diagram shown overleaf has had to accommodate too much additional detail to maintain the essential simplicity of the original concept, notably through the incorporation of the various Docklands Light Railway and 'London Overground' routes. Some modern critics have even suggested that too strict an adherence to Beck's 'rules' – horizontal lines, vertical lines, and diagonal lines at 45 degrees – has inhibited the clarity and utility of the design. However, it seems more likely that these rules have in fact ensured that the essential coherence of the map has been protected from the visual clutter which a large variety of angles would have introduced.

While Beck may have been less of an innovator than typically credited in the last two decades since his 'rediscovery', no doubt the majority of the countless millions of people who have used the Underground map would concur with the sentiments of Ken Garland, in *Mr Beck's Underground Map* (1994), where he concludes that this seminal and enduring map 'achieved both visual distinction and proven usefulness in equal measure'.

HARRY BECK

Henry (Harry) Beck (born 1902) was an out-of-work engineering draughtsman – formerly an employee of the Underground Group – when he first sketched out his design concept in 1931. He returned to the employ of the Group on the eve of the almost immediate success of his first published design in 1933, but amazingly remained a 'temporary' employee until 1937. Being both an employee and a contracted freelance created a status problem for Beck as a designer, and he had an uneasy relationship with management for most of his career. On a number of occasions changes were made to the map design without Beck even being consulted, and 'the diagram' became something of an obsession in his life. As Ken Garland notes, 'he was determined to guard and nurture his creation against all opposition.'

After his 1959 version of the map, other designers were brought in, and increasingly angry exchanges with what was by then London Transport did nothing to improve the relationship. All of Beck's subsequent ideas – including a simpler way of representing the new Victoria Line than that which was adopted – were rejected. He died in 1974, aged 72, a somewhat embittered man, still working on the map design – and it would not be until the 1990s that London Transport fully acknowledged his central role in creating the world's best-known railway map.

Chesham
Chalfont & Latimer
Amersham
Watford
Chorleywood
Croxley
Rickmansworth
Moor Park
West Ruislip
Northwood
Northwood Hills
Hillingdon
Ruislip
Ruislip Manor
Pinner
Uxbridge   Ickenham
Eastcote
North Harrow
Harrow-on-the-Hill
Rayners Lane
West Harrow
Ruislip Gardens
South Harrow
Sudbury Hill
South Ruislip
Northolt
Sudbury Town
Greenford
Alperton
Perivale
Hanger Lane
Park Royal
North Ealing
Ealing Broadway
Ealing Common

Watford Junction
Watford High Street
Bushey
Carpenders Park
Hatch End
Headstone Lane
Harrow & Wealdstone
Kenton
Preston Road
Northwick Park
Wembley Park
South Kenton
North Wembley
Wembley Central
Stonebridge Park
Harlesden
Willesden Junction

Stanmore
Canons Park
Queensbury
Kingsbury
Neasden
Dollis Hill
Willesden Green
Kilburn
Brondesbury Park
Kensal Rise   Brondesbury
Kensal Green
Queen's Park   Kilburn High Road   South Hampstead
Kilburn Park
Maida Vale
Warwick Avenue
Royal Oak
Westbourne Park
Ladbroke Grove
Latimer Road
East Acton   White City   Shepherd's Bush
West Acton   North Acton   Wood Lane
Acton Central
Shepherd's Bush Market
South Acton
Goldhawk Road
Kensington (Olympia)
Barons Court
Hammersmith
Acton Town
South Ealing
Northfields
Boston Manor
Chiswick Park
Turnham Green   Stamford Brook   Ravenscourt Park   West Kensington
Earl's Court
West Brompton
Gunnersbury
Fulham Broadway
Imperial Wharf
Kew Gardens
Parsons Green
Putney Bridge
Richmond
East Putney
Southfields
Wimbledon Park
Wimbledon

Edgware
Burnt Oak
Colindale
Hendon Central
Brent Cross
Golders Green
Hampstead Heath
Hampstead
Finchley Road & Frognal
Belsize Park
Chalk Farm
West Hampstead
Finchley Road
Swiss Cottage
St. John's Wood
Camden
Morning Crescent
Edgware Road   Marylebone
Paddington
Baker Street
Great Portland Street
Euston
Warren Street
Regent's Park
Edgware Road
Bayswater
Notting Hill Gate   Lancaster Gate   Bond Street   Oxford Circus   Goodge Street
Queensway   Marble Arch   Tottenham Court Road
Holland Park
High Street Kensington
Hyde Park Corner
Green Park
Knightsbridge
Piccadilly Circus
Gloucester Road
Sloane Square   St. James's Park
South Kensington   Victoria   Westminster
Pimlico
Waterloo
River Thames
Vauxhall
Clapham Junction
Kennington
Clapham North   Stock
Clapham Common
Clapham South
Balham
Tooting Bec
Tooting Broadway
Colliers Wood
South Wimbledon
Morden

Heathrow Terminals 1, 2, 3
Heathrow Terminal 4
Heathrow Terminal 5
Osterley
Hounslow East
Hounslow Central
Hounslow West
Hatton Cross

Legend:
Bakerloo
Central
Circle
District
District open weekends, public holidays and some Olympia events
Hammersmith & City
Jubilee

Metropolitan
Northern
Piccadilly
Victoria
Waterloo & City
DLR
London Overground
Emirates Air Line

Interchange stations
Step-free access from street to train
Step-free access from street to platform
National Rail
Riverboat services
Tramlink
Airport
Emirates Air Line (opening summer 2012)

MAYOR OF LONDON

Website
tfl.gov.uk

24 hour travel information
0843 222 123-

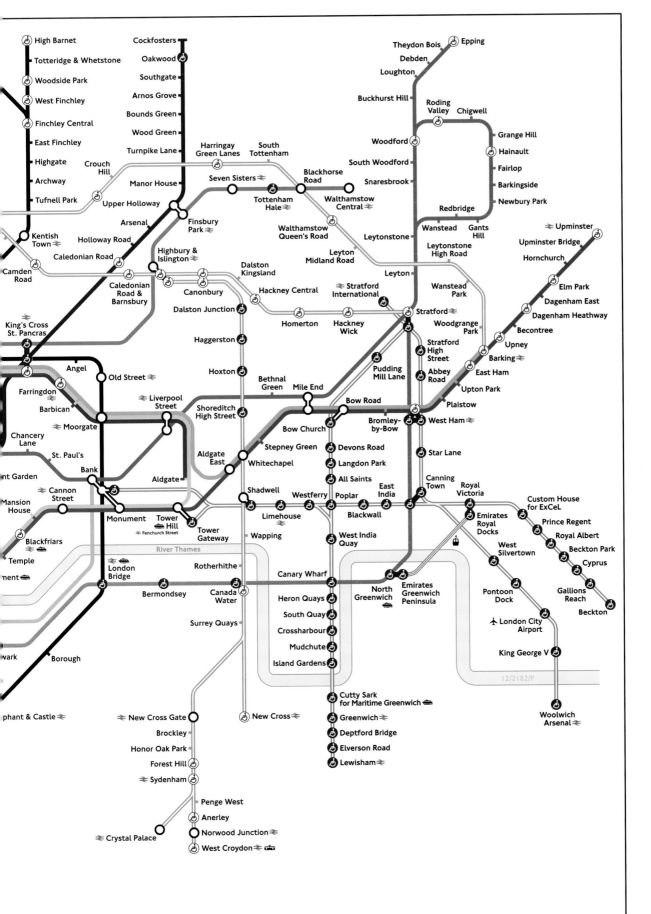

Transport for London UNDERGROUND

Correct at time of going to print

...u pay no more than 5p per minute if calling
...m a BT landline. There may be a connection charge.
...arges from mobiles or other landline providers may vary.

...ourney, please check before you travel

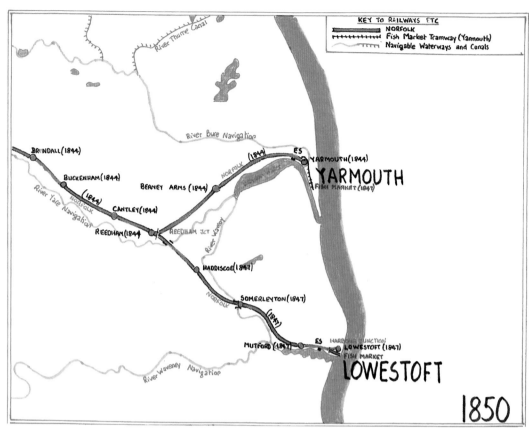

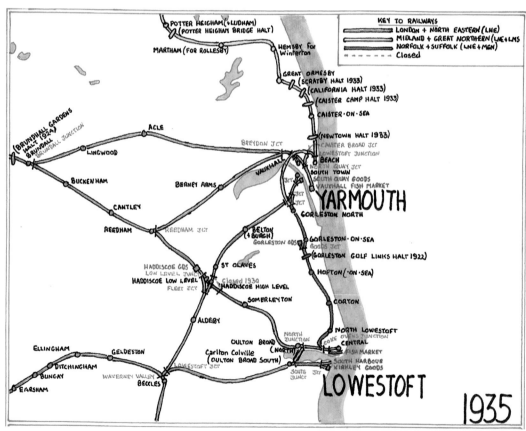

Title	Jowett's Railway Centres (pages 150, 154 and 155)
By	Alan Jowett
Publisher	Patrick Stephens Ltd, Cambridge
Date	1993

These 1850, 1935 and 1990 snapshots of Yarmouth and Lowestoft – at an original scale of 2 miles to the inch – focus on a very short stretch of Norfolk and Suffolk coast which was the object of intensive competition between three railway operators for more than 50 years. The railways opened up this area of East Anglia for two key traffics – holidaymakers and fish – and while the Great Eastern Railway (GER) was pre-eminent for flows from and to London through its core territory to the south, the spoils were shared on the corridor west to the major Midlands markets.

The two competitors for the longer distance traffic were the GER, with routes from Yarmouth and Lowestoft to Norwich then onwards via Thetford and March to Peterborough and the Midlands, and the Midland & Great Northern (joint) Railway (M&GNR) which meandered from Yarmouth through north Norfolk to Wisbech, Spalding and Peterborough. The M&GNR's wish to get to Lowestoft, and competition

for tourist traffic at small coastal resorts, led to the construction of yet another joint line, the Norfolk & Suffolk Joint Railway (NSJR), which was the creation of one joint railway (the M&GNR) and the GER.

The 1935 map shows that both joint railways survived the Grouping of 1923, despite being deep in London & North Eastern Railway (LNER) territory. No less than seven new halts – most of them for coastal holiday traffic – were opened between 1922 and 1933. The M&GNR and the NSJR came entirely under the control of the LNER in 1936, but other than the 1959 loss of the M&GNR north of Yarmouth and the short link south from Yarmouth Beach station over Breydon Water to the Yarmouth–Lowestoft line, everything in the map area survived until the Beeching Report in 1963. By 1977, however, the local rail network had shrunk back to its minimum extent in modern times – with only the East Suffolk line from Lowestoft south to Ipswich surviving the threat of closure.

Berney Arms station, on the more minor of the two routes between Norwich and Yarmouth, has the unusual distinction of being one of just three stations on the national rail network to which there is no road access, the others being Corrour on the West Highland Line, and Dovey Junction on the Cambrian Coast Line.

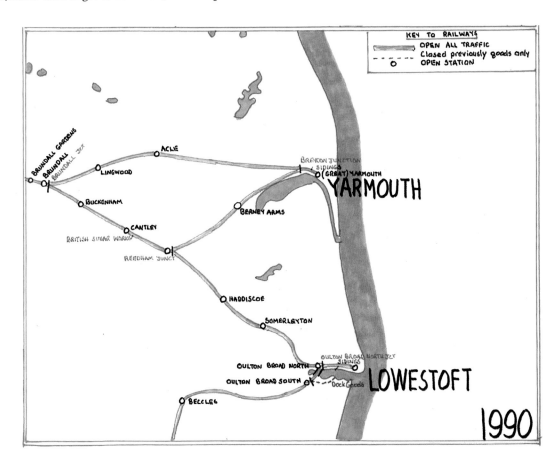

NATIONALIZATION AND MODERNIZATION

Another exhausting war effort was followed by nationalization of the railways under British Railways. The process of upgrading the largely worn-out system culminated in the 1955 Modernisation Plan – which failed to stem the steady tide of traffic losses to fast-growing road competition.

Darlington
Richmond
Eaglescliffe
Picton
Battersby
Grosmont
Whitby
Robin Hood's Bay
Ravenscar
Cloughton
SCARBOROUGH

Bedale
Catterick Bridge
Northallerton
Helmsley
Filey
Speeton

Aysgarth
Leyburn
Thirsk
Pilmoor
Gilling
Pickering
Flamborough Head
Bridlington

Ripon
Alne
Malton
Driffield

Pateley Bridge
Knaresborough
Hornsea

Skipton
Harrogate
Wetherby
YORK
Beverley

Ilkley
Keighley
Arthington
Church Fenton
Market Weighton
HULL

Shipley
LEEDS
Selby
South Howden
Witchernsea

RADFORD
ALIFAX
Dewsbury
Castleford
Goole
New Holland
Spurn Head

acup
ERSFIELD
Wakefield
Normanton
Knottingley
PONTEFRACT
GRIMSBY

Rochdale
Barnsley
Hemsworth
Scunthorpe
Barnetby

MANCHESTER
Penistone
Doncaster
Cleethorpes

Stalybridge
Swinton
Market Rasen
Louth

SHEFFIELD
Rotherham
Gainsborough
Mablethorpe

Stockport
Worksop
Retford
LINCOLN
Horncastle
Sutton-on

cham
Buxton
Miller's Dale
Chesterfield
Tuxford
Willoughby

Macclesfield
Bakewell
Clay Cross
Bardney
Firsby

Congleton
Matlock
Mansfield
Southwell
Woodhall Junc
Skegn

Leek
Matlock Bath
Alfreton
Kirkby-in-Ashfield
Newark
Sleaford
The Wash

STOKE
Ambergate
Ilkeston
NOTTINGHAM
Hunstanton

Ashbourne
Grantham
Boston

Cheadle
DERBY
Trent
Harby and Stathern
Spalding
Wolferton

rayton
Uttoxeter
Kegworth
Castle Bytham
Bourne
King's Lynn

Burton
Repton
Ashby-de-la-Zouch
Loughborough
Oakham
Wisbech

Rugeley
Melton Mowbray
Stamford
Sw

Lichfield
LEICESTER
Syston
Manton
Wansford
Peterborough
March

Walsall
Tamworth
Wigston
Uppingham

ON
Sutton Coldfield
Seaton
Oundle
Holme

Numeaton
Hinckley
Market Harborough

dley

On 1 January 1948, the newly nationalized railways of Britain inherited a vast array of steam engine types, some dating to the 1870s. Despite the introduction of standardized parts such as boilers and driving wheels by G. J. Churchward and Charles Collett of the Great Western Railway (GWR) and their protégé, William Stanier of the London, Midland & Scottish Railway (LMS), many of Britain's steam locomotives belonged to a bygone age.

Diesels were still in their early stages of development and it would be some years before suitable designs could be mass-produced in sufficient numbers to replace the tried and tested steam locomotive. The progress of steam locomotive development by the Big Four companies in the 1930s had been stopped dead in its tracks by the onset of the Second World War, and by 1948 steam motive power and the railway system as a whole were in a very rundown state. Despite this,

some proven and some groundbreaking designs from the Big Four continued to be built into the British Railways' era – notable among the former were Collett's 'Castle' Class 4-6-0s, Stanier's 'go-anywhere' Class '5MT' (Black Five) 4-6-0s and Peppercorn's Class 'A1' 4-6-2s. Of the latter, Oliver Bulleid's highly innovative 'Merchant Navy' and the lighter 'West Country' and 'Battle of Britain' 4-6-2s, and Hawksworth's 'County' Class 4-6-0s, are worthy of mention.

Meanwhile, in 1947, with nationalization looming, the newly formed Railway Executive appointed Robert Riddles as the first Chief Mechanical & Electrical Engineer of British Railways (BR). His job was to introduce a series of new and efficient steam locomotives using interchangeable standardized parts, thus allowing for the wholesale withdrawal of out-of-date steam types and the consequential savings for the British taxpayer. Drawing on his considerable

British Railways Standard 'Britannia' Class 4-6-2 heads a parcels train up Shap on the West Coast Main Line in June 1966.

experience while working under the LMS's William Stanier and for the Ministry of Supply during the war, Riddles went on to design 12 different classes of locomotives ranging from the humble Class '2MT' 2-6-2Ts right through to the powerful '9F' 2-10-0s.

By 1951 Riddles' new standard class locomotives were starting to emerge from the main locomotive works around the country – notable among these were the 'Britannia' Class '7P6F' 4-6-2s which were soon putting in superlative performances on the Great Eastern main line out of Liverpool Street; the Class '4' and Class '5' 4-6-0s; and the Class '4' 2-6-4Ts. By 1954 all of the 12 new classes had been introduced, culminating in the heavy freight Class '9F' 2-10-0s which mark the high-point of British steam locomotive design. However, a year later the writing was on the wall for steam traction with the publication of the British Transport Commission's Modernisation Plan (see Milepost 18) – this ill-conceived and ill-timed document announced the death sentence for steam and the rapid introduction of, at that time, many types of untried main line diesel.

Construction of new steam locomotives continued until 18 March 1960 when the last example (and the 999th Standard

By 1968 thousands of withdrawn steam locomotives had ended their lives awaiting the cutter's torch at scrapyards around the country.

locomotive) to be built by BR, Class '9F' 2-10-0 No. 92220 'Evening Star', emerged from Swindon Works. Just over eight years later the last standard gauge steam locomotives were withdrawn from service on BR – many of Riddles' fine locomotives had had a working life of less than ten years.

The last steam locomotive to be built for British Railways, Standard Class '9F' 2-10-0 'Evening Star', was named at Swindon in 1960.

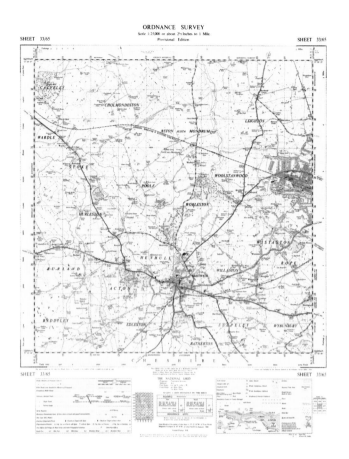

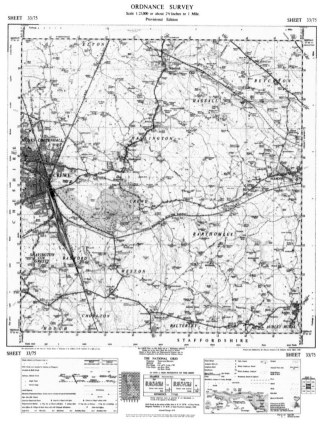

Series	Ordnance Survey 1:25,000
Sheets	33/65 and 33/75
Date	1948

Crewe was a classic railway town, shown in the composite Ordnance Survey map overleaf from the year of nationalization, not long after its heyday. In 1948 all the key components of the railway presence at Crewe were still very much in evidence – a junction of six important lines (as it is to this day), a large works (which, as we have seen in Milepost 9, employed over 20,000 staff during its peak of activity in the 1930s) and extensive freight marshalling yards marked as 'Sorting Sidings'. North and west of the passenger station were the (un-named) steam locomotive running sheds, two belonging to the London, Midland & Scottish Railway (LMS) and a third for the exclusive use of the Great Western Railway, which reached Crewe using running powers over the LMS from nearby Nantwich, and extended onwards to Manchester.

The map demonstrates that despite being a railway town, Crewe's substantial station was by 1948 some distance away from the geographical centre of the town, with two of the rail routes effectively acting as barriers to development to the

east. Virtually all the built-up area remained west of the line running northeast to Manchester and north of the line running southwest to Shrewsbury.

Crewe would later benefit directly from the 1955 British Railways Modernisation Plan, with the first stages of overhead electrification of the West Coast Main Line (WCML) concentrated on Crewe. The initial phase to Manchester was electrified in 1960, to Liverpool in 1962, to Euston in 1966 and finally to Birmingham in 1967. Although the completion of the WCML electrification in 1974 – from Weaver Junction, 17 miles to the north, to Glasgow – did not impact on the railway infrastructure at Crewe, there was some consequent downgrading of its passenger interchange function, with fewer Glasgow–London trains calling at Crewe and the principal cross-country 'hub' role shifting to Birmingham's grimly modernized New Street station.

Crewe remains an important railway centre today, with diesel and electric locomotive depots active beside the station; a continuing works presence under the ownership of Bombardier Transportation; and Freightliner container trains re-marshalled day and night at Basford Hall sidings to the south – many of these trains still using the freight-only lines which tunnel under Crewe station.

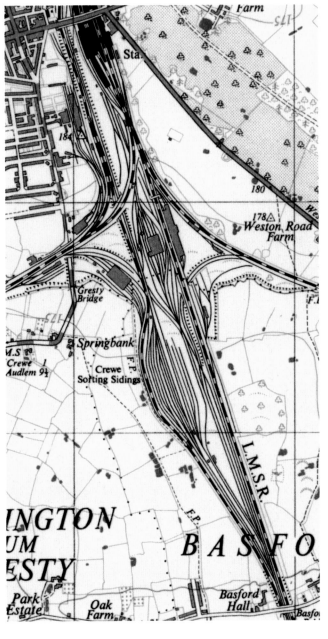

CREW JUNCTION

Until 1965, there was another Crewe which served as a British railway junction. The Caledonian Railway's branches from Granton and Leith joined at Crewe Toll in northwest Edinburgh, and to avoid confusion with its much bigger namesake, the location was described as 'Crew Junction', as shown in this photo taken a few months after closure.

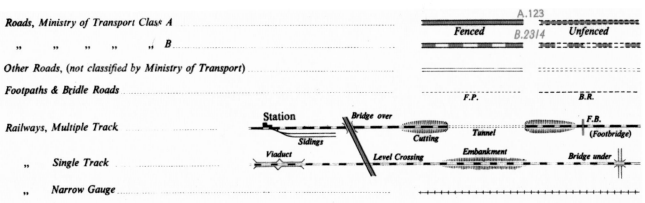

Roads, Ministry of Transport Class A		A.123
„ „ „ „ „ B	Fenced	B.2314 Unfenced
Other Roads, (not classified by Ministry of Transport)		
Footpaths & Bridle Roads	F.P.	B.R.
Railways, Multiple Track	Station Bridge over Cutting Tunnel	F.B. (Footbridge)
„ Single Track	Viaduct Sidings Level Crossing Embankment	Bridge under
„ Narrow Gauge		

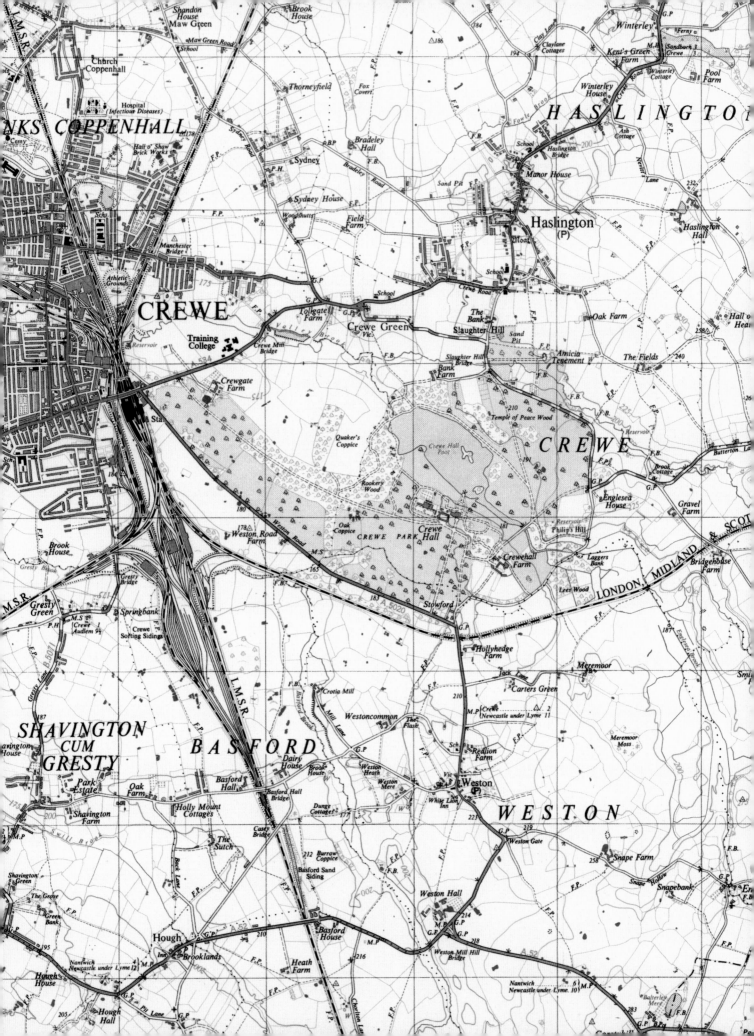

Title	A Map of Yorkshire
Mapmaker	Estra Clark
Publisher	British Railways North Eastern Region
Date	1949

Pictorial maps – where drawings or paintings are used to illustrate locations within the map – represent a distinctive sub-genre of railway mapping, often associated with tourist or leisure markets, and in the more modern era typically designed in a more stylized way than conventional topographical or rail network mapping.

This map – the original of which measures some 50 in. by 40 in. – was created by Estra Clark for British Railways in the early period of nationalization for display on station poster boards. It very effectively combines a slightly simplified geographic representation of all the principal rail routes, at a relatively small scale, with charming painted illustrations of more than a hundred locations throughout Yorkshire – on a backcloth of layered colouring to depict lowland and upland, with important land and sea features also marked and named.

This is not a stereotypical tourist map, in that major industries and services are proudly illustrated beside the towns with which they were associated. The map extract opposite features town sketches extolling Bradford wool, Halifax carpet making and the 'fine worsted fabrics, chemicals & dyestuffs' of Huddersfield – whose past sporting glories are evoked by the illustration of a footballer in the distinctive blue and white stripes of Huddersfield Town AFC. However, it was the Yorkshire Dales, the North Sea coast, and towns like Skipton, Scarborough and Whitby which continued to draw tourists by train in Yorkshire, as they had done since Victorian times.

At its full size, this map poster is a feast of revelations about the settlements, landscape features, history and folk tales that make up Yorkshire – as well as providing an attractive picture of just how much of the county was accessible by rail in 1949.

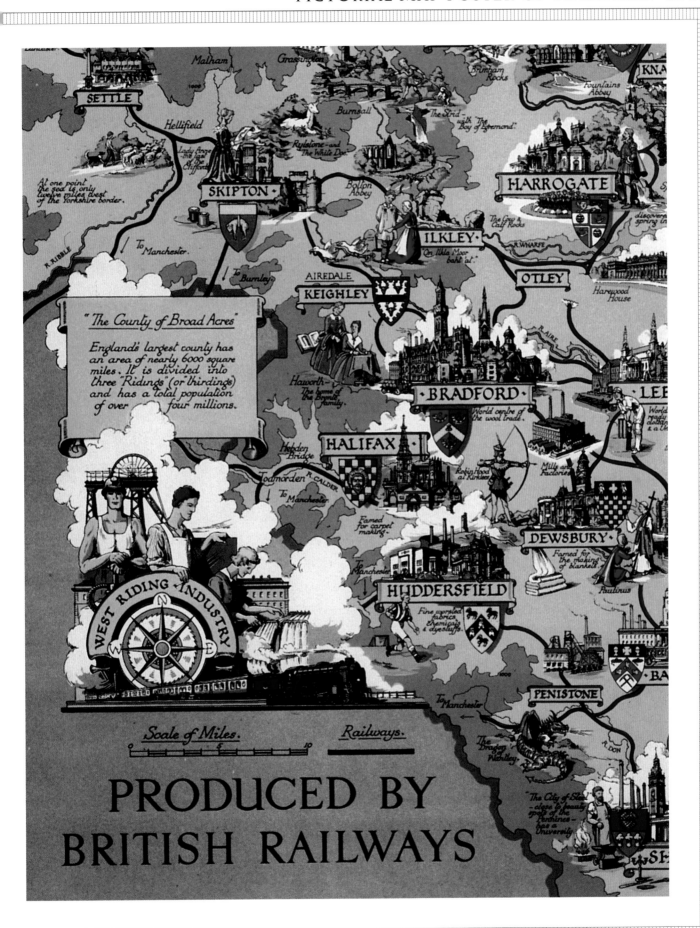

As events in the last two decades at Ladbroke Grove, Hatfield and Potters Bar have shown, railway safety continues to be a major issue in the modern era of the high-speed train. However, compared to other forms of land transport the railways are by far the safest way to travel. Since the early days of the railways many lessons have been learnt and put into practice, with new safety technology continually evolving.

The first known railway accident to a passenger occurred on 15 September 1830 when the unfortunate politician, William Huskisson, was run over by George Stephenson's 'Rocket' at Parkside station during the opening ceremony of the Liverpool & Manchester Railway – he later died in hospital from his injuries. Safety on these early railways was either non-existent or at best extremely basic with collisions, runaway trains, mechanical failure, excessive speed, derailments and human error all common events. The first attempts at early signalling – a vital ingredient in railway safety – were rudimentary to say the least, with signalmen holding flags or lamps positioned along the line. The introduction of the electric telegraph in 1848, the token system for single line railways – to avoid head-on collisions only one driver was allowed to be in possession of the metal token that was issued for each stretch of track between passing stations – and John Saxby's invention of interlocking signals and points in 1856 were all key aspects in railway safety. The gradual

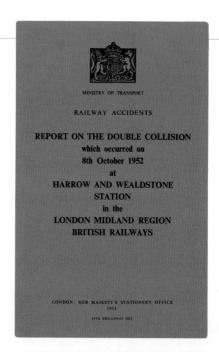

MINISTRY OF TRANSPORT

RAILWAY ACCIDENTS

REPORT ON THE DOUBLE COLLISION
which occurred on
8th October 1952
at
**HARROW AND WEALDSTONE
STATION**
in the
**LONDON MIDLAND REGION
BRITISH RAILWAYS**

LONDON: HER MAJESTY'S STATIONERY OFFICE
1953
FIVE SHILLINGS NET

introduction in the 1850s and 1860s of block signalling – this ensured that trains travelling in the same direction on double-tracked railway lines were kept far enough apart to avoid collisions – was a major step forward, and became mandatory in 1889 following the Armagh disaster in Ireland when a runaway train killed 78 passengers.

Britain's worst railway disaster occurred during the First World War at Quintinshill, ten miles north of Carlisle, when correct signalling practice was not followed. On 22 May

The triple train crash at Harrow & Wealdstone station in 1952, when 112 people died, was Britain's worst peacetime rail disaster.

1915, a speeding southbound troop train collided head-on with a stationary local train. The wooden carriages of the troop train, lit by acetylene gas, completely disintegrated but worse was to follow when a northbound express not only ploughed into the wreckage but also hit a stationary goods train in the adjoining loop. Hot cinders from the derailed locomotives ignited the acetylene gas and an inferno ensued – 227 people were killed including 215 soldiers from the Royal Scots Regiment. Because the accident happened during the war it was not publicized, but the two signalmen on duty were found guilty of gross neglect and culpable homicide.

Britain's worst peacetime railway disaster occurred at Harrow & Wealdstone station on 8 October 1952, when a stationary local train was hit in the rear by a southbound Perth to Euston sleeping car train. Seconds after the crash a northbound express hit the wreckage – 112 people were killed and 340 injured.

The second worst peacetime railway disaster happened in thick fog at St John's, Lewisham, on 4 December 1957, when a suburban electric train was hit in the rear by a steam-hauled Cannon Street to Ramsgate express – 90 people were killed and 173 injured. Driver error (the steam locomotive driver had passed a red signal) and the lack of an Automatic Warning System in the steam locomotive were to blame.

In more recent times the head-on crash between a High Speed Train (InterCity 125) express and a diesel multiple unit at Ladbroke Grove outside Paddington on 5 October 1999 killed 31 people and injured 523. The accident occurred after the driver of the diesel multiple unit had passed a red signal – poorly positioned signals, poor driver training procedures and driver error were all to blame.

Since Ladbroke Grove, Hatfield and Potters Bar, safety on Britain's railways has seen a marked improvement. In the most recent statistics (2009/10) there were no fatalities for either passengers or workforce in train accidents while only five passengers died in accidents at stations and there were only three workforce fatalities. However, by far the most dangerous place on the railways is at level crossings where the number of deaths to pedestrians and motorists has been rising steadily since 2003 – in 2009/10 there were 12 public fatalities while in the first four months of 2011 alone a similar number had already been killed in this way. Of course, the vast majority of level crossing accidents are caused by road users disobeying the rules. Sadly the highest mortality rate on the railways are suicides or suspected suicides with a staggering 236 being recorded in 2009/10.

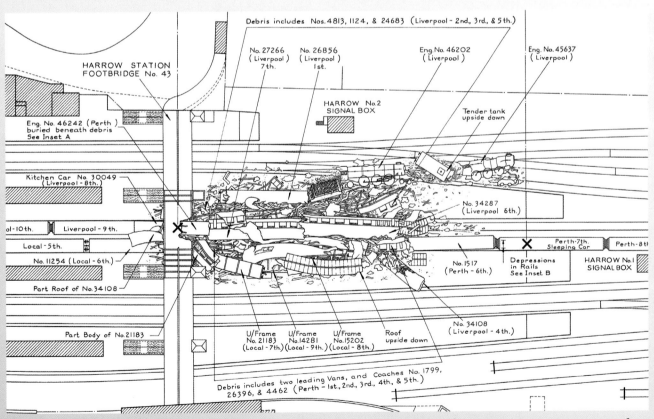

The official report into the appalling 1952 Harrow & Wealdstone crash blamed driver error and the lack of an Automatic Warning System on one of the locomotives.

Title	British Railways – travel by train: Passenger facilities and Map
Publisher	The Railway Executive
Date	1951

While rail closures – due to both road competition and industrial change – had become a growing phenomenon from the 1920s onwards, a very substantial rail network remained in 1951 throughout rural and urban Britain. But the newly nationalized railway was generally in poor shape after a massive war effort, and the big investment of the 1955 Modernisation Plan had yet to come. Many lines were in their last years – unbeknown to staff or passengers.

Every part of Britain suffered from the closure of rail routes after 1951, and the pain was not spread evenly. A striking feature of this map and its extract, is the extent to which the Home Counties north of London lost so many cross-country routes which could have been playing a crucial role in today's transport system. These generally more affluent areas were among the first to benefit from the 'never had it so good' era of growing household incomes – and rising car ownership – which sealed the fate of so many railway routes. The irony is that 30 years later – when the routes of most closed lines had been breached by roads, industry and housing development – road congestion was becoming a big problem which cross-country railways could have alleviated, but it was generally too late to retrieve the situation.

As comparison with page 240 demonstrates, many routes in the 'commuter belt' north of London had succumbed *before* the Beeching Report. Very few were terminating branch lines, and most provided lateral connections between the many main routes radiating out of London to the rest of the country. A notable pre-Beeching loss was the Northampton–Bedford line which could have formed part of an important east–west cross-country route, but the key cut came with a route which even the Beeching Report had not proposed for closure – the Oxford–Cambridge line, built by the London & North Western Railway. During the Second World War, the Government chose Bletchley Park as the location for its crucial base for monitoring German military signals, in part because Bletchley station was virtually equidistant between the two university centres of intellectual excellence.

Other than the reprieved Bletchley–Bedford section, all passenger services between Oxford and Cambridge were withdrawn in 1968 by a Labour Government which had opposed most of Beeching's cuts while in opposition. Freight services survived on the western section only, and passenger trains were reinstated by British Rail between Oxford and Bicester in 1987. Local authorities and development agencies have been campaigning for complete reinstatement of the 'East West Rail' route, initially between Bletchley and Bicester, so that at long last travellers who wish to make direct journeys across England north of London and south of Birmingham can once again do so by rail. To the delight of campaigners, in late 2011 the Chancellor of the Exchequer announced that the western section of the projected route would now be part of the National Infrastructure Plan – re-establishing a strategic railway linking Oxford, Reading and Aylesbury with Milton Keynes and Bedford.

The map was to remain as the standard design of British Railways' network map until 1967. The version shown overleaf has been enhanced to show the boundaries of the new British Railways' regions.

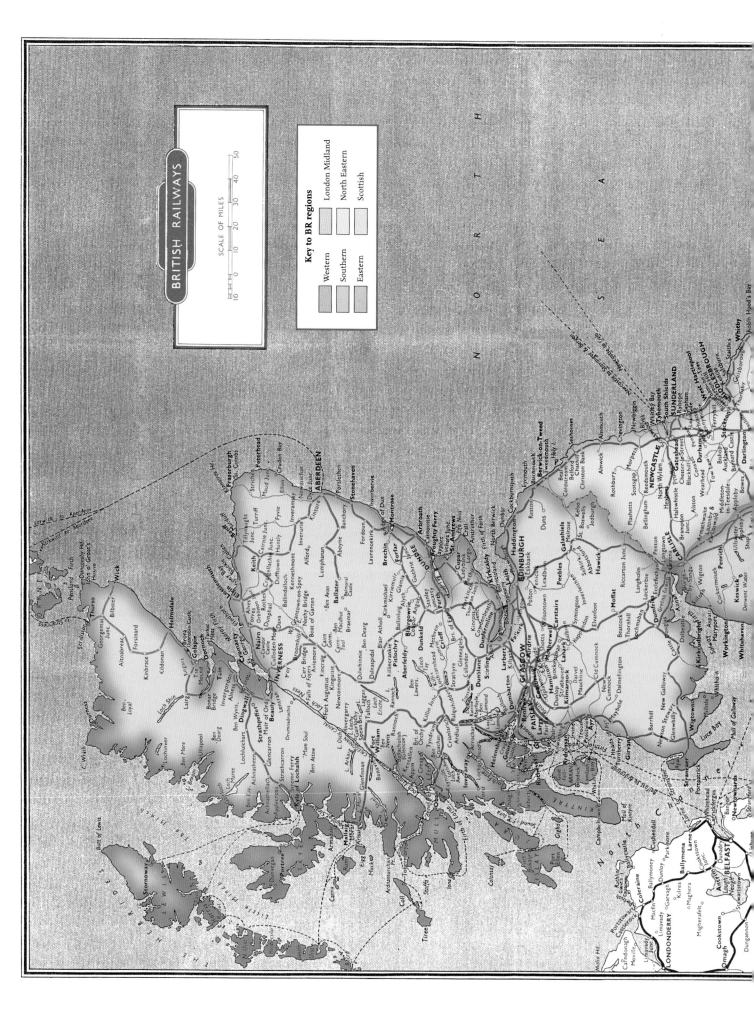

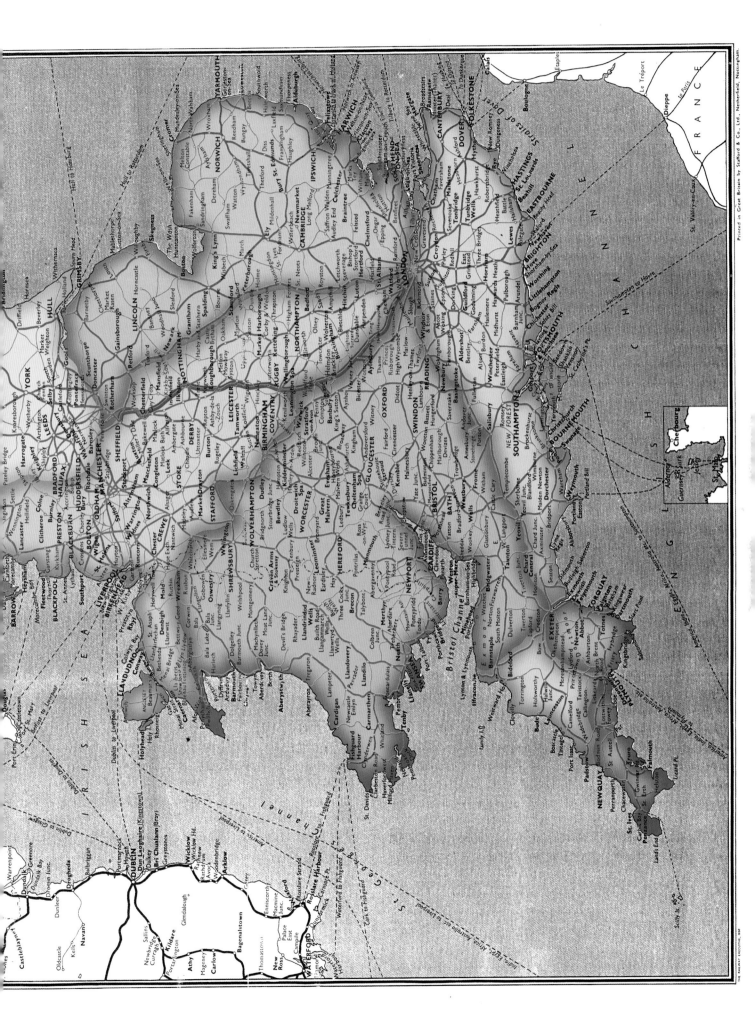

Printed in Great Britain by Stafford & Co., Ltd., Netherfield, Nottingham.

The Ffestiniog (FR) was a railway of firsts – the first British narrow gauge line (using horse power for its first 27 years), the first successful application of the double Fairlie-type articulated steam locomotives (1870), and the first British railway to use bogie carriages (1873). Narrow gauge – in this case, just 1 ft 11½ in. between the rails – was much better suited to the difficult mountain terrain, using much sharper curves than was possible with standard (4 ft 8½ in.) gauge, and allowing construction at much lower capital cost.

Although built for slate traffic, the FR ran passenger trains from 1864 until 1939, the outbreak of war in that year curtailing the tourist traffic which had by then become its mainstay. By the time the Ordnance Survey (OS) produced the 1953 1 in. map, from which an extract is reproduced overleaf, the FR had lain dormant for seven years. The OS used a barely discernible 'ladder' representation for narrow gauge railways from the 1930s onwards – and this hardly does justice to the prodigious efforts made by the railway, over the 110 years from 1836, in moving slate from the Blaenau quarries down to the harbour at Porthmadog for export (133,000 tons moved by rail in the peak year of 1894). One needs to go to more detailed maps to appreciate the scale of the undertaking involved.

At the 6 in. scale shown overleaf, the above-ground impact of the slate industry around Blaenau Ffestiniog can be clearly seen, not least in the extensive spoil heaps which (still) so dominate the landscape there. Also evident are the standard gauge lines which reached the town from Llandudno Junction (to the north) and Bala Junction (to the south), in 1879 and 1883 respectively – thereby ending the FR's monopoly of the slate traffic. Down at Porthmadog (then anglicized as Portmadoc), the extract opposite of the 1909 25 in. OS map shows in great detail the rail-served wharves on each bank of the river, at a time when slate production was still near its peak volume, albeit shortly to go into long-term decline.

Following complete closure in 1946, the line was saved for preservation and a modest tourist service started across the Cob causeway between Porthmadog and Boston Lodge in 1955, later extended to allow direct connections from British Railways' Cambrian Coast Line trains at Minffordd. Since that time the railway has gone from strength to strength, with re-opening through to Blaenau Ffestiniog – and direct connection with BR services north to Llandudno Junction – taking place in 1982.

Ordnance Survey 1909 (Carnarvonshire) – see extract opposite

Ordnance Survey 1953 (Caernarvonshire) – see extract overleaf

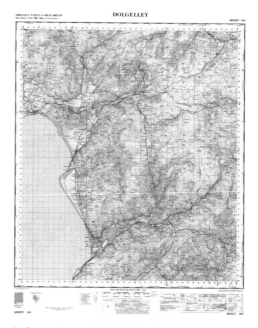

Ordnance Survey 1953 (Dolgelley) – see extract overleaf

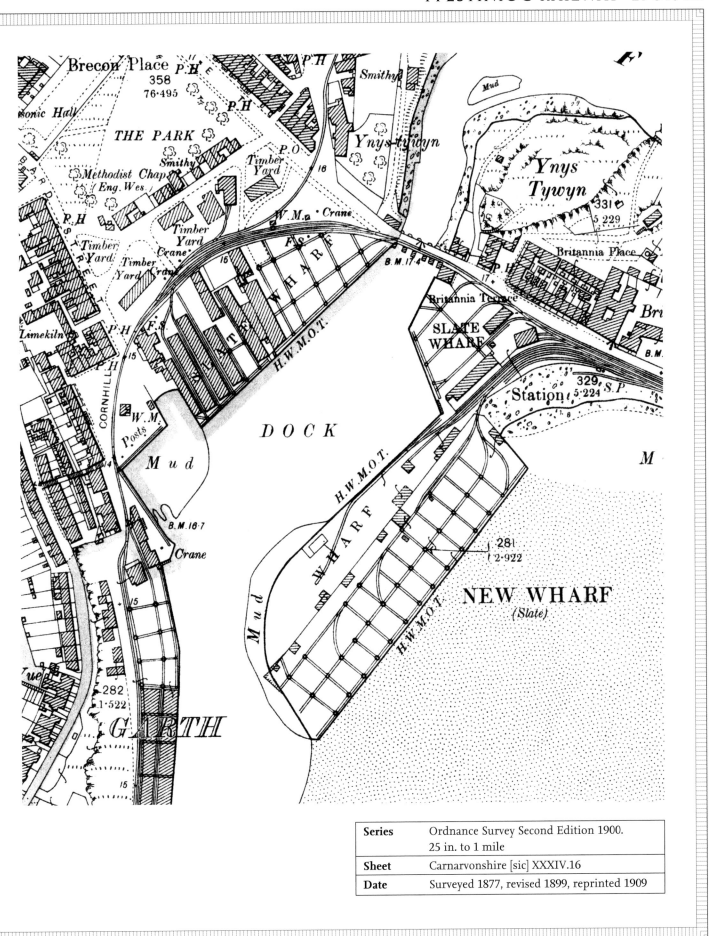

Series	Ordnance Survey Second Edition 1900. 25 in. to 1 mile
Sheet	Carnarvonshire [sic] XXXIV.16
Date	Surveyed 1877, revised 1899, reprinted 1909

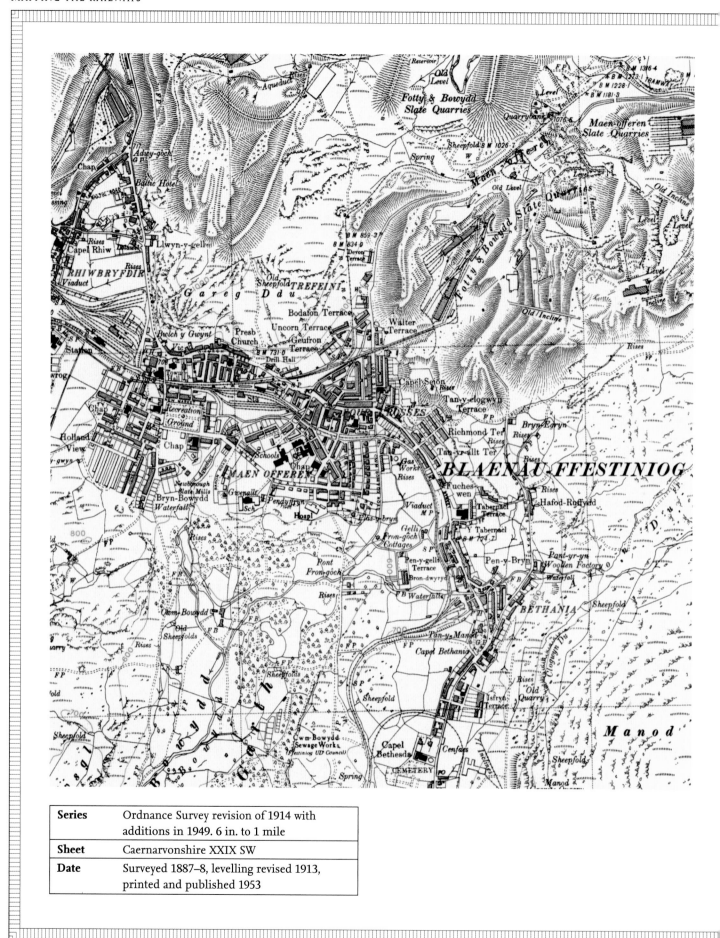

Series	Ordnance Survey revision of 1914 with additions in 1949. 6 in. to 1 mile
Sheet	Caernarvonshire XXIX SW
Date	Surveyed 1887–8, levelling revised 1913, printed and published 1953

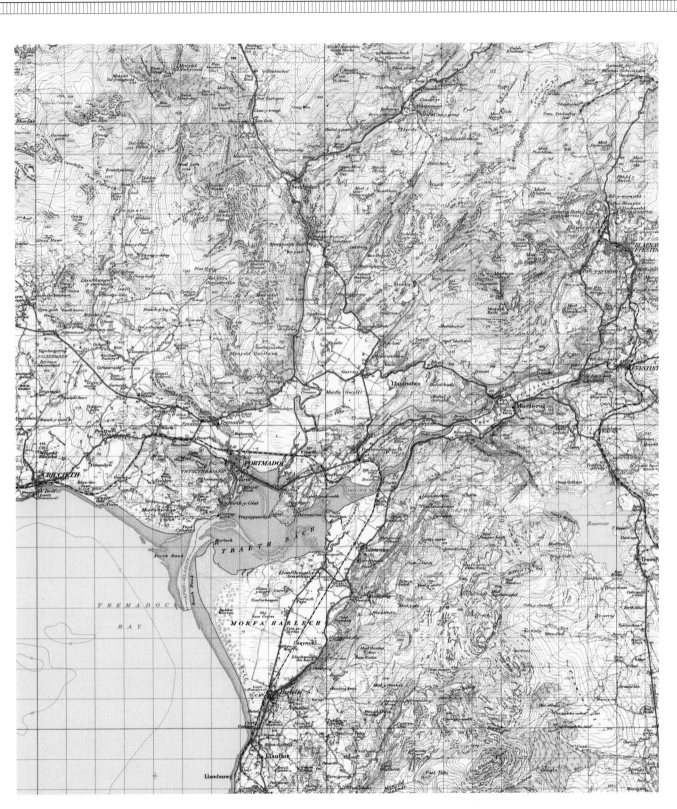

Series	Ordnance Survey Seventh Series. 1 in. to 1 mile
Sheet	116 Dolgelley
Date	1953

Apart from the London suburban and Brighton line electrification on the Southern Railway (SR), a few diesel shunters, some Great Western Railway railcars and two main line diesel prototypes being developed by the London, Midlands & Scottish Railway (LMS) and the SR, the railway scene in Britain on 1 January 1948 was 100 per cent steam powered. Lagging behind the USA by at least a decade, the advent of diesel haulage on British Railways was slow in coming and, when it did, was ill-conceived and poorly implemented.

The war and its aftermath had killed off any hopes of main-line electrification and, apart from the ex-London & North Eastern Railway's Woodhead route across the Pennines which was 'switched on' in 1954, steam power continued to rule the rails. This was soon to change.

Published on 24 January 1955, the British Transport Commission's *Modernisation and Re-Equipment of British Railways*, a 35-page 'blueprint' document, recommended a £1.24 billion (£24.8 billion at today's prices) investment over a period of 15 years to modernize and re-equip British Railways. The document outlined five key areas for modernization, including £345 million for replacement of steam locomotives by diesel and electric traction.

Of these two types of traction, diesel won the day, as the cost of implementing widespread electrification was enormous. While diesels were more expensive to build than steam locomotives, their benefits compared to steam were obvious – they were cleaner, their running costs were lower and their range was much greater.

This was all well intentioned – albeit involving vast amounts of taxpayers' money – but the authors of the Modernisation Plan had failed not only to take into account the almost complete lack of expertise in building diesel locomotives in Britain, but also the selfish and autonomous aspirations of some regions of British Railways – in fact they were still being run more-or-less on the same lines as the old Big Four prior to nationalization.

While Ivatt's two ex-LMS prototype mainline diesel-electrics, Nos. 10000 and 10001, and Bulleid's three examples, Nos 10201–10203, belched their fumes up and down the West Coast Main Line (WCML), the drawing offices in Britain's railway industry were working overtime to design some of the biggest calamities ever to run on Britain's railways. Despite the lessons to be learnt from steam locomotive design, standardization was never part of the master plan and within a few years perfectly good and, in many cases, nearly new steam locomotives were being sent to the scrapyard to make way for a motley crew of first generation diesel-hydraulic and diesel-electric locomotives. These locomotives

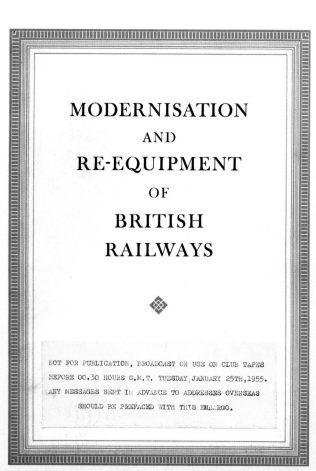

MODERNISATION
AND
RE-EQUIPMENT
OF
BRITISH
RAILWAYS

NOT FOR PUBLICATION, BROADCAST OR USE ON CLUB TAPES BEFORE 00.30 HOURS G.M.T. TUESDAY, JANUARY 25TH, 1955. ANY MESSAGES SENT IN ADVANCE TO ADDRESSES OVERSEAS SHOULD BE PREFACED WITH THIS EMBARGO.

The 1955 Modernisation Plan for British Railways recommended the replacement of steam locomotives by diesel and electric traction.

were categorized according to power output, with Type 1 the least powerful and Type 5 the most powerful.

By far the biggest culprit was the Western Region which decided to opt for lightweight diesel-hydraulic transmission based on a successful German design. But there the similarity ended, as the early British examples (Type 4 'Warships' and Type 2 'Baby Warships'), built by the North British Locomotive Company in Glasgow and by BR at Swindon, were unreliable, expensive to maintain and of a non-standard design. Introduced in 1961, the Beyer-Peacock Type 3 'Hymeks' were a vast improvement but they and the more powerful 'Westerns' had a short working life, with the last being withdrawn in 1977.

Opting for heavier diesel-electric transmission, other regions had more success than Swindon with the London Midland Region's (LMR) Sulzer-engined Type 4 'Peaks' and the Eastern Region's (ER) English Electric Types 1 and 4 and Brush Type 2s being reasonably successful (the latter when re-engined), and some of which still survive today. Introduced in 1961, the Type 5 'Deltics' were impressive machines which transformed East Coast Main Line services, but even they only had a working life of 20 years. Probably the most successful design was the humble diesel shunter (now classified 08) which was introduced in 1953 and is still a familiar sight the length and breadth of the network.

To be fair to Swindon, other regions also had their spectacular failures, notable among them being the Scottish Region's Type 2s whose chronic unreliability brought about the collapse of their builders, the world-renowned North British Locomotive Company; the same region's Clayton Type 1s; the LMR's Metrovick Type 2s; and the ER's English Electric Type 2 'Baby Deltics'. All in all, this was a sad story.

Fortunately BR eventually got it right with many of their second-generation diesels, some of which, such as the English-Electric Type 3s (or Class 37s in current parlance) and Brush Type 4s (Class 47s) can still be seen in service today, but by the late 1980s the writing was on the wall for British diesel locomotive manufacturers. Now Britain buys its locomotives from the North American companies of General Electric and General Motors.

The introduction of modern electric services was much slower despite the obvious benefits such as energy efficiency, absence of pollution, unlimited range and rapid acceleration. Unfortunately the Government of the day was not prepared to invest in the initial high cost of widespread electrification of BR and because of this only a limited, but successful, programme was embarked upon, with new 25 kV schemes for the WCML and suburban lines out of Liverpool Street being some of the earliest. Starting in 1959, electrification of the WCML was not completed through from Euston to Glasgow until 1974, while full electrification of the former Great Eastern main line from Liverpool Street to Norwich was completed in 1987. Elsewhere in the country the Glasgow electric suburban 'Blue Trains' were 'switched on' between 1960 and 1967 and the Southern Region third-rail system was extended to Bournemouth in 1967. Electrification of the East Coast Main Line was completed in 1991, but only a few short 'infill' schemes have been undertaken since then – other than in Scotland where re-opened lines to Larkhall (2005) and from Airdrie to Bathgate (2010) have been electric since services resumed.

Built by the North British Locomotive Company, the short-lived 'Warship' diesel-hydraulic locomotives were introduced on the Western Region in 1958.

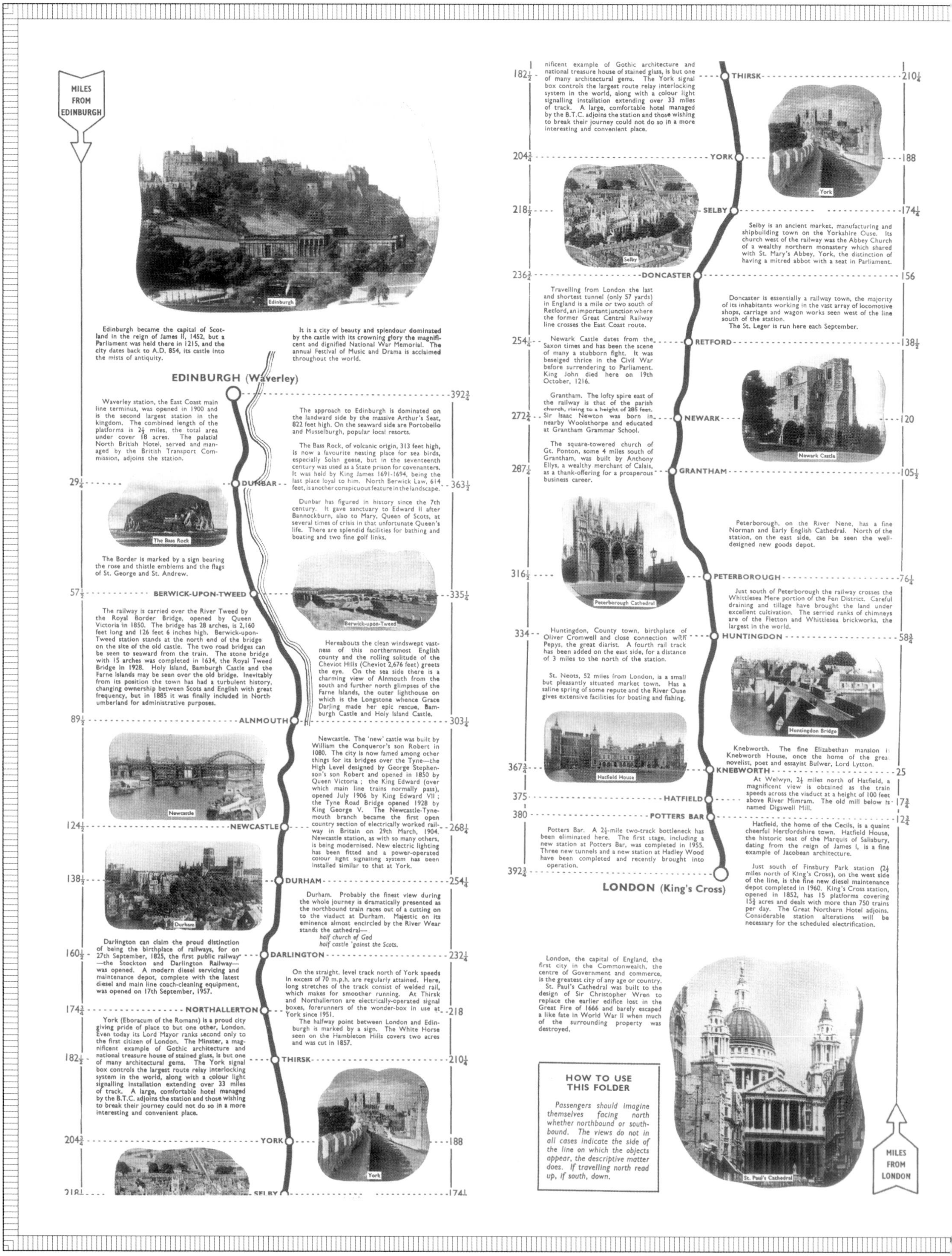
MILES FROM EDINBURGH
Edinburgh
Edinburgh became the capital of Scotland in the reign of James II, 1452, but a Parliament was held there in 1215, and the city dates back to A.D. 854, its castle into the mists of antiquity.
It is a city of beauty and splendour dominated by the castle with its crowning glory the magnificent and dignified National War Memorial. The annual Festival of Music and Drama is acclaimed throughout the world.
EDINBURGH (Waverley)
392¾
Waverley station, the East Coast main line terminus, was opened in 1900 and is the second largest station in the kingdom. The combined length of the platforms is 2¼ miles, the total area under cover 18 acres. The palatial North British Hotel, served and managed by the British Transport Commission, adjoins the station.
The approach to Edinburgh is dominated on the landward side by the massive Arthur's Seat, 822 feet high. On the seaward side are Portobello and Musselburgh, popular local resorts.
The Bass Rock, of volcanic origin, 313 feet high, is now a favourite nesting place for sea birds, especially Solan geese, but in the seventeenth century was used as a State prison for covenanters. It was held by King James 1691-1694, being the last place loyal to him. North Berwick Law, 614 feet, is another conspicuous feature in the landscape.
29¼ DUNBAR 363½
The Bass Rock
Dunbar has figured in history since the 7th century. It gave sanctuary to Edward II after Bannockburn, also to Mary, Queen of Scots, at several times of crisis in that unfortunate Queen's life. There are splendid facilities for bathing and boating and two fine golf links.
The Border is marked by a sign bearing the rose and thistle emblems and the flags of St. George and St. Andrew.
57½ BERWICK-UPON-TWEED 335¼
Berwick-upon-Tweed
The railway is carried over the River Tweed by the Royal Border Bridge, opened by Queen Victoria in 1850. The bridge has 28 arches, is 2,160 feet long and 126 feet 6 inches high. Berwick-upon-Tweed station stands at the north end of the bridge on the site of the old castle. The two road bridges can be seen to seaward from the train. The stone bridge with 15 arches was completed in 1634, the Royal Tweed Bridge in 1928. Holy Island, Bamburgh Castle and the Farne Islands may be seen over the old bridge. Inevitably from its position the town has had a turbulent history, changing ownership between Scots and English with great frequency, but in 1885 it was finally included in Northumberland for administrative purposes.
Hereabouts the clean windswept vastness of this northernmost English county and the rolling solitude of the Cheviot Hills (Cheviot 2,676 feet) greets the eye. On the sea side there is a charming view of Alnmouth from the south and further north glimpses of the Farne Islands, the outer lighthouse on which is the Longstone whence Grace Darling made her epic rescue, Bamburgh Castle and Holy Island Castle.
89½ ALNMOUTH 303¼
Newcastle
Newcastle. The 'new' castle was built by William the Conqueror's son Robert in 1080. The city is now famed among other things for its bridges over the Tyne—the High Level designed by George Stephenson's son Robert and opened in 1850 by Queen Victoria ; the King Edward (over which main line trains normally pass), opened July 1906 by King Edward VII ; the Tyne Road Bridge opened 1928 by King George V. The Newcastle-Tynemouth branch became the first open country section of electrically worked railway in Britain on 29th March, 1904. Newcastle station, as with so many others, is being modernised. New electric lighting has been fitted and a power-operated colour light signalling system has been installed similar to that at York.
124½ NEWCASTLE 268¼
Durham
138½ DURHAM 254¼
Durham. Probably the finest view during the whole journey is dramatically presented as the northbound train races out of a cutting on to the viaduct at Durham. Majestic on its eminence almost encircled by the River Wear stands the cathedral— half church of God half castle 'gainst the Scots.
Darlington can claim the proud distinction of being the birthplace of railways, for on 27th September, 1825, the first public railway —the Stockton and Darlington Railway— was opened. A modern diesel servicing and maintenance depot, complete with the latest diesel and main line coach-cleaning equipment, was opened on 17th September, 1957.
160½ DARLINGTON 232¼
On the straight, level track north of York speeds in excess of 70 m.p.h. are regularly attained. Here, long stretches of the track consist of welded rail, which makes for smoother running. At Thirsk and Northallerton are electrically-operated signal boxes, forerunners of the wonder-box in use at York since 1951.
The halfway point between London and Edinburgh is marked by a sign. The White Horse seen on the Hambleton Hills covers two acres and was cut in 1857.
174¾ NORTHALLERTON 218
York (Eboracum of the Romans) is a proud city giving pride of place to but one other, London. Even today its Lord Mayor ranks second only to the first citizen of London. The Minster, a magnificent example of Gothic architecture and national treasure house of stained glass, is but one of many architectural gems. The York signal box controls the largest route relay interlocking system in the world, along with a colour light signalling installation extending over 33 miles of track. A large, comfortable hotel managed by the B.T.C. adjoins the station and those wishing to break their journey could not do so in a more interesting and convenient place.
182½ THIRSK 210¼
York
204¾ YORK 188
218½ SELBY 174¼
nificent example of Gothic architecture and national treasure house of stained glass, is but one of many architectural gems. The York signal box controls the largest route relay interlocking system in the world, along with a colour light signalling installation extending over 33 miles of track. A large, comfortable hotel managed by the B.T.C. adjoins the station and those wishing to break their journey could not do so in a more interesting and convenient place.
182½ THIRSK 210¼
York
204¾ YORK 188
Selby
218½ SELBY 174¼
Selby is an ancient market, manufacturing and shipbuilding town on the Yorkshire Ouse. Its church west of the railway was the Abbey Church of a wealthy northern monastery which shared with St. Mary's Abbey, York, the distinction of having a mitred abbot with a seat in Parliament.
236¾ DONCASTER 156
Travelling from London the last and shortest tunnel (only 57 yards) in England is a mile or two south of Retford, an important junction where the former Great Central Railway line crosses the East Coast route.
Doncaster is essentially a railway town, the majority of its inhabitants working in the vast array of locomotive shops, carriage and wagon works seen west of the line south of the station.
The St. Leger is run here each September.
254¼ RETFORD 138½
Newark Castle dates from the Saxon times and has been the scene of many a stubborn fight. It was beseiged thrice in the Civil War before surrendering to Parliament. King John died here on 19th October, 1216.
Grantham. The lofty spire east of the railway is that of the parish church, rising to a height of 285 feet. Sir Isaac Newton was born in nearby Woolsthorpe and educated at Grantham Grammar School.
272¾ NEWARK 120
Newark Castle
The square-towered church of Gt. Ponton, some 4 miles south of Grantham, was built by Anthony Ellys, a wealthy merchant of Calais, as a thank-offering for a prosperous business career.
287¼ GRANTHAM 105½
Peterborough, on the River Nene, has a fine Norman and Early English Cathedral. North of the station, on the east side, can be seen the well-designed new goods depot.
Peterborough Cathedral
316½ PETERBOROUGH 76¼
Just south of Peterborough the railway crosses the Whittlesea Mere portion of the Fen District. Careful draining and tillage have brought the land under excellent cultivation. The serried ranks of chimneys are of the Fletton and Whittlesea brickworks, the largest in the world.
334 HUNTINGDON 58¾
Huntingdon, County town, birthplace of Oliver Cromwell and close connection with Pepys, the great diarist. A fourth rail track has been added on the east side, for a distance of 3 miles to the north of the station.
St. Neots, 52 miles from London, is a small but pleasantly situated market town. Has a saline spring of some repute and the River Ouse gives extensive facilities for boating and fishing.
Huntingdon Bridge
Hatfield House
Knebworth. The fine Elizabethan mansion is Knebworth House, once the home of the great novelist, poet and essayist Bulwer, Lord Lytton.
367¾ KNEBWORTH 25
At Welwyn, 2½ miles north of Hatfield, a magnificent view is obtained as the train speeds across the viaduct at a height of 100 feet above River Mimram. The old mill below is named Digswell Mill.
375 HATFIELD 17¾
380 POTTERS BAR 12¾
Potters Bar. A 2½-mile two-track bottleneck has been eliminated here. The first stage, including a new station at Potters Bar, was completed in 1955. Three new tunnels and a new station at Hadley Wood have been completed and recently brought into operation.
Hatfield, the home of the Cecils, is a quaint cheerful Hertfordshire town. Hatfield House, the historic seat of the Marquis of Salisbury, dating from the reign of James I, is a fine example of Jacobean architecture.
392¾
LONDON (King's Cross)
Just south of Finsbury Park station (2½ miles north of King's Cross), on the west side of the line, is the fine new diesel maintenance depot completed in 1960. King's Cross station, opened in 1852, has 15 platforms covering 15¾ acres and deals with more than 750 trains per day. The Great Northern Hotel adjoins. Considerable station alterations will be necessary for the scheduled electrification.
London, the capital of England, the first city in the Commonwealth, the centre of Government and commerce, is the greatest city of any age or country.
St. Paul's Cathedral was built to the design of Sir Christopher Wren to replace the earlier edifice lost in the Great Fire of 1666 and barely escaped a like fate in World War II when much of the surrounding property was destroyed.
HOW TO USE THIS FOLDER
Passengers should imagine themselves facing north whether northbound or southbound. The views do not in all cases indicate the side of the line on which the objects appear, the descriptive matter does. If travelling north read up, if south, down.
St. Paul's Cathedral
MILES FROM LONDON

Title	Named Trains on the East Coast Main Line
Publisher	British Railways (North Eastern Region)
Date	1961

As we have seen on pages 48–51, the concept of strip maps – diagrammatically transforming the representation of rail routes into roughly straight lines, and thereby facilitating reproduction in booklet or leaflet form – has a long tradition on Britain's railways. So, 112 years after the *Reid's Railway Ride* map illustrated the route for travellers at a time when the East Coast Main Line (ECML) had still not been completed south of York, British Railways (BR) published this 1961 map with commentaries on the towns and landscape en route, accompanied by black and white photographs.

On the reverse of the map is a timetable for all 11 'named' trains operating on the East Coast Main Line north of York on weekdays during the period 12 June to 9 September 1961. This was an epochal period for the ECML, with the steady replacement of the former LNER A1, A3 and streamlined A4 Pacific steam locomotives by diesels – in particular BR's iconic Type 5 'Deltics', which cut typical end-to-end journey times from seven to six hours.

The named trains conjure up nostalgic memories of a golden era of rail travel – of particular note are 'The Elizabethan', the non-stop Edinburgh–London train (which only out-lasted

steam haulage by one year, as the ability to change drivers comfortably and safely en route without stopping depended on the through corridor connections incorporated in the A4 locomotive design), and 'The Queen of Scots', an all-'Pullman' luxury train, which left the ECML at Northallerton to travel over the now closed line through Ripon to Harrogate, then onwards via Leeds to rejoin the traditional route to London at Doncaster.

The commentary notes that, 'On the straight track north of York speeds in excess of 70 m.p.h. are regularly attained' – a reference to the disappearing steam era, as the new Deltic diesels would regularly attain their maximum 100 m.p.h. speed on this section and on many other stretches of the ECML. An interesting feature of the timetable is the reference, *'The figures shown in italics, e.g. 1 34½, indicate passing times and that the train does not call'* – allowing attentive passengers to assess whether or not their train was on time.

At the time of writing, only one of these named trains is still so named – the world-renowned 'The Flying Scotsman', which, in its modern incarnation, departs from Edinburgh at 05.40 and arrives at King's Cross at 09.40, a far cry from the 7 hours 5 minutes of summer 1961.

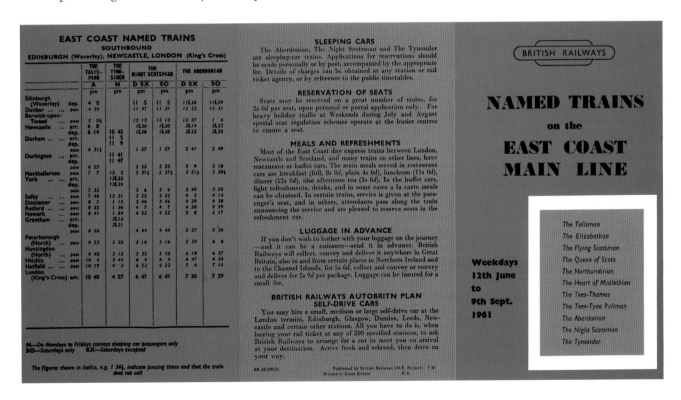

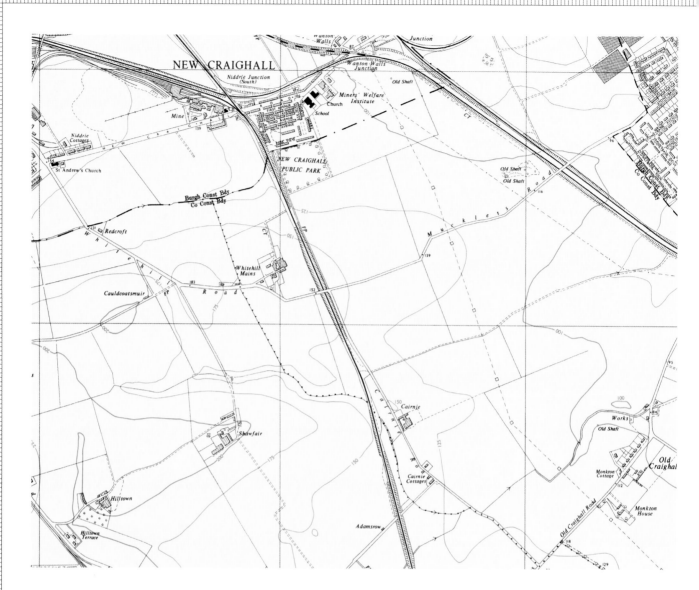

Series	Ordnance Survey 6 in. to 1 mile
Sheets	NT 37 SW (extracts, reduced)
Dates	1958 and 1966

Marshalling yards were developed at an early stage of the growth of the rail network, allowing individual freight wagons from a local catchment area to be sorted and re-marshalled into longer distance trains destined for yards closer to the wagons' ultimate destination.

In response to the operational inefficiencies of much freight traffic being handled at a multiplicity of smaller yards of pre-Grouping origin, the 1955 British Railways Modernisation Plan had allocated £85 million for the construction of between 20 and 30 large mechanized marshalling yards. The yards which were built incorporated: shunting over a hump from which wagons gravitated into the appropriate siding to

form a train; remote-controlled points; and power-operated retarders decelerating wagons descending from the hump.

While Edinburgh in the 1950s was a relatively modest industrial centre, it did have extensive local goods traffic from breweries, collieries, and the docks in Granton and Leith, as well as long distance traffic in transit between the east of Scotland and eastern England. This traffic was handled at six unmechanized yards scattered throughout the eastern outskirts of the capital – an inefficient operation, which the new yard on a green field site at Millerhill, astride the Waverley Route to Carlisle via Hawick, was designed to largely replace.

However, by 1960 some senior railway managers were beginning to doubt the rationale for many of these expensive new yards – arguing that the future largely lay in cost-effective full trainloads running direct from A to B, and in

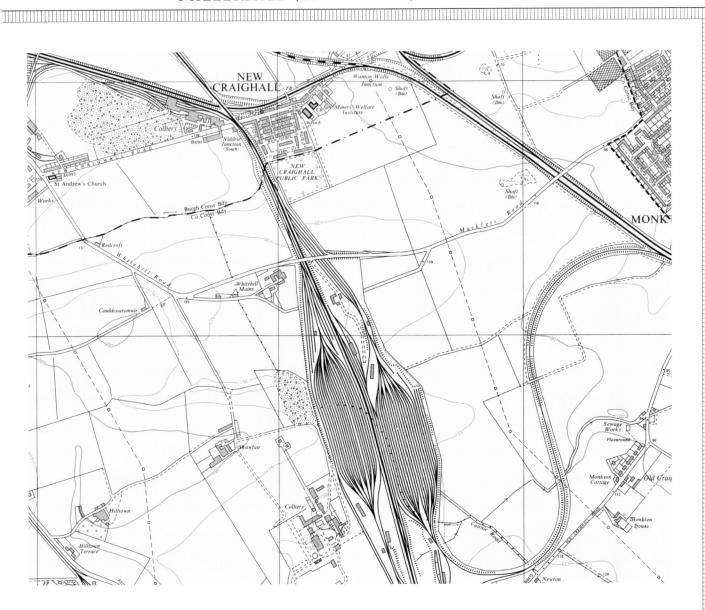

containerization. But it was too late to stop the Edinburgh scheme, which was already under construction, transforming the landscape of the Millerhill area, as shown in the contrast between these 1958 and 1966 Ordnance Survey map extracts. When fully completed in 1963, Millerhill's 100 sorting sidings had the capacity to handle up to 5,000 wagons daily, and to optimize its 'hub' role a new connecting line was built on a sweeping reverse curve to the East Coast Main Line. A further change in the landscape was the construction of the Monktonhall deep coal mine immediately west of the yard, with its own rail sidings. This colliery would generate substantial freight movements for the railway over the next three decades, but ironically most of it would be in full trainloads which had no need for Millerhill's wagonload sorting facilities.

By the end of the 1960s the marshalling yard had suffered from the continuing nationwide decline in wagonload rail freight traffic – through increased road competition, industrial change, and BR's ongoing switch of remaining traffic to trainload operation. The complete closure of the Waverley Route in 1969 led to significant rationalization at Millerhill, and with further traffic decline the entire 'Down Yard' – the fan of sidings between the old Waverley Route and Monktonhall colliery – was closed completely in 1983. The loop line running through the yard from the East Coast Main Line was, however, electrified in 1991; a new passenger station opened at Newcraighall in 2002; and in recent years aggregates and open cast coal have been loaded to rail at sidings within the remaining shrunken Millerhill complex. Advance works for the planned re-opening of the Borders Railway to Galashiels and Tweedbank in 2014 have been undertaken at the north end of the old Down Yard, now a forest of birch trees, but which has been proposed as the site for a new rail-connected waste transfer station.

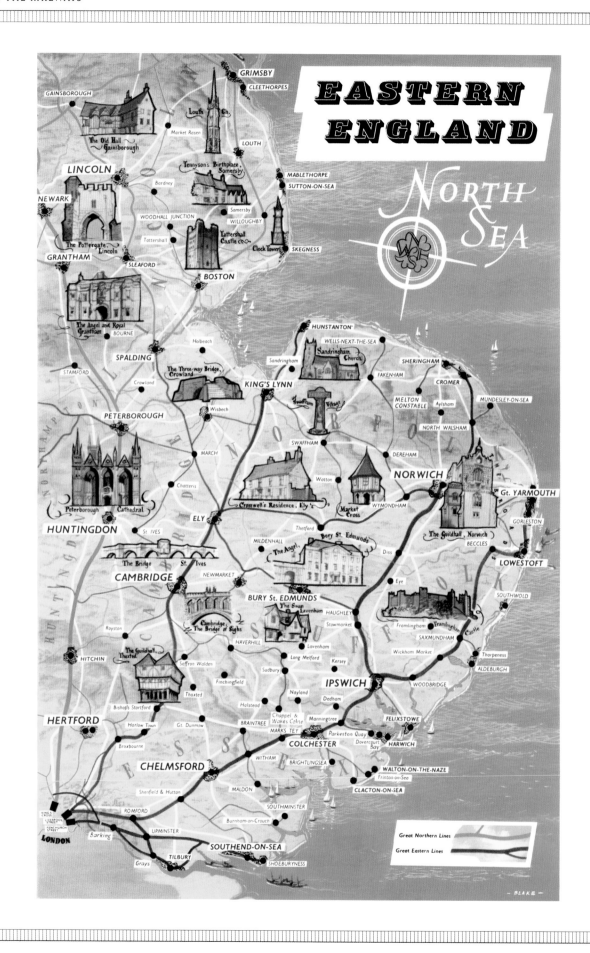

Title	Eastern England
Publisher	British Railways (Eastern Region)
Date	1963

This map brochure captures the last year in which travellers could use the rail network to reach almost every significant holiday destination in a wide swathe of eastern England from Lincolnshire through Norfolk and Suffolk to the borders of Essex and London. The text notes that, 'fast and comfortable trains serve most of the places mentioned in this folder', and – in an evocation of a service concept soon to disappear from the railways – reminds readers that:

> Luggage can be sent in advance – it can be collected from your home and delivered to the holiday address for 5/6 or, for 2/9, it can be collected from your home and delivered to your holiday station; alternatively you can hand it in at your local station and have it delivered to your holiday address for 2/9.

Although this is a pictorial map, it does not have the accomplished art work and attention to detail of the Yorkshire map on pages 210–11, published just 14 years previously by British Railways. The small paintings of buildings and monuments of note are rather two-dimensional, and collectively over-dominate the map – however, as an illustration for a brochure, rather than a large poster for display, it serves its purpose. The charming postcard-style snapshot photos certainly underline the sheer range of different types of towns and villages which the holidaymaker could still visit by rail in 1963.

The brochure – timed to promote the 1963 holiday season – must have been published within months, if not weeks, of the 27 March publication of the Beeching Report which was to seal the fate of so many of the routes on the map. By the end of that year, the branch line from Fakenham to the charmingly named Wells-next-the-Sea had gone, to be followed in 1964 by Fakenham's own connection to the rest of the network at Dereham; branch lines to Maldon, Melton Constable, and Mundesley-on-Sea; and minor through routes from Swaffham to Thetford and through Saffron Walden.

Other communities put up stiffer opposition to the closure programme, and it was not until 1967 that the Sudbury–Haverhill–Cambridge cross-country line succumbed – deemed to be just too uneconomic to be salvageable by the innovative 'Basic Railway' and 'Paytrain' concepts, which as described in Milepost 20 saved the nearby Ipswich–Lowestoft 'East Suffolk Line'. Much of the rail network in east and south Lincolnshire finally succumbed under Dr Beeching's prescription in 1970, but perhaps the most draconian cuts came in north Cambridgeshire and northwest Norfolk between the late 1960s and early 1980s – as we shall see on pages 248–9.

MABLETHORPE

With its neighbour, Sutton-on-Sea, has been at pains to preserve the natural charm of the sandy coastline.

HUNSTANTON

An East coast resort that faces West! Famed golden sands, championship golf course, tennis, bathing, boating etc.

CROMER

Popular holiday resort for over 150 years. Splendid golf course, tennis, sands, and safe bathing.

SKEGNESS

One of Britain's premier holiday resorts, with accommodation for 80,000 staying visitors. Every possible amenity is to be found here.

WELLS-NEXT-THE-SEA

Slowly being deserted by the sea. Quaint houses cluster round the quayside and there is good bathing and boating.

GREAT YARMOUTH

With Gorleston, a magnificent holiday resort. Six miles of promenade and golden sands; golf, tennis, skating, horse and greyhound racing, boating, bathing, fishing.

DR BEECHING'S PRESCRIPTION

Rising railway deficits led to a drastic re-appraisal of the network, with extensive closure of branch lines, cross-country routes and even some main lines. While these cuts made relatively little impression on overall railway finances, some of Beeching's innovations on the freight railway had a lasting and positive impact on the rail system.

1963-1970

NEWCASTLE

MIDDLESBROUGH

SCARBOROUGH

YORK

LEEDS

HULL

GRIMSBY

MANCHESTER

SHEFFIELD

LINCOLN

DERBY

STAFFORD

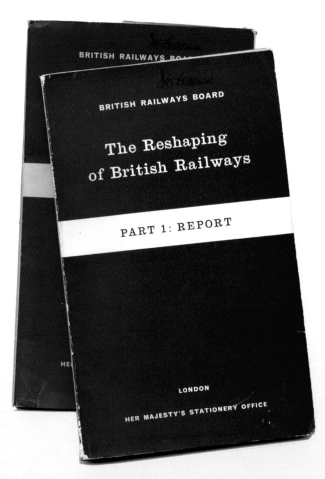

Dr Richard Beeching holds a copy of his infamous report, *The Reshaping of British Railways*, at a press conference on 27 March 1963.

Price one shilling the Beeching Report was published in two parts – the second part consisting of 13 maps showing traffic flows, proposed closures and new liner-train routes.

While closure of unprofitable railway lines had been a small part of the railway scene until the Second World War, the austerity years that followed were a prelude to the biggest shake-up of Britain's railways ever witnessed. In the immediate years after the war the railways were in a run-down, lamentable state, and nationalization seemed the only answer. So, in 1948, the Labour Government did nationalize the railways at the same time as the canals, road haulage, bus services and airlines. The newly formed British Railways (BR) was faced with the enormous task of modernizing its vast network while turning it into a profitable concern. Modernization plans were slow to evolve (see Milepost 19), but cost-cutting, in the shape of line closures, was fairly rapid, and by the beginning of the 1960s about 3,300 miles of uneconomic lines had already disappeared. Probably the most famous of these was the Midland & Great Northern Joint Railway's network of lines in East Anglia which closed in 1959 – a leftover from the Victorian age, its duplication of other lines in this rural area being its final undoing.

Despite these closures and the implementation of the 1955 £1.24 billion Modernisation Plan, BR was continuing to lose

taxpayers' money hand over fist – drastic action needed to be taken to counter ever-increasing competition from road transport, out-of-date working practices and mainly 19th-century technology.

Harold Macmillan's Conservative Government soon turned its attention to the near-bankrupt railways which by 1960 were losing £67.7 million a year (£1.15 billion at today's prices). In March of that year Macmillan had given this message in the House of Commons:

> *First the industry must be of a size and pattern suited to modern conditions and prospects. In particular, the railway system must be remodelled to meet current needs, and the Modernisation Plan must be adapted to this new shape.*

With this ringing in his ears and rail losses escalating, the Transport Minister, Ernest Marples, set up in 1960 an advisory group, known as the Stedeford Committee, to report on the state of the railways, and to come up with some solutions. One of the committee's members was Dr Richard Beeching who was then the Technical Director

Withdrawal of railway passenger services

Western Region

British Railways Board

Transport Act 1962

The Minister of Transport has given his consent to the Board's proposal to withdraw all local passenger railway services between BRISTOL (Temple Meads), GLOUCESTER (Eastgate) and WORCESTER (Shrub Hill) and discontinue all passenger railway services from the following stations:-

YATE	STONEHOUSE (Bristol Road)
WICKWAR	HARESFIELD
CHARFIELD	BREDON
BERKELEY ROAD	ECKINGTON
COALEY	DEFFORD
	WADBOROUGH

The terms of the Minister's consent can be inspected at local booking offices

The services will be withdrawn on and from Monday, 4th January, 1965.

Notices such as this one announcing withdrawal of stopping trains between Bristol, Gloucester and Worcester were soon appearing at railway stations all over Britain.

of ICI, renowned for his analytical mind and undoubted skill in solving business problems. Beeching suggested that the railways should not provide a public service at any cost, and should instead be run as a profitable concern. While Beeching's ideas were not initially implemented, they certainly were noted by Marples, who appointed him as Chairman of the British Transport Commission (BTC) from June 1961, and then as Chairman of the British Railways Board which replaced the BTC in late 1962.

A pre-Beeching initiative to undertake detailed surveys of both passenger and freight traffic on British Railways was implemented over the week 17-23 April 1961 inclusive; this was then followed – after Beeching had taken over as BTC Chairman – by further detailed traffic studies which were undertaken in July 1961. In his eventual report, *The Reshaping of British Railways*, Beeching and his team acknowledged that 'it was impossible to continue the massive recording effort involved for a longer period.' Even the most loyal of his lieutenants admitted to doubts about the way they went about their analysis and decision-making on lines to be put up for closure. In his 1989 biography, *Beeching: Champion of*

the Railway?, former senior BR manager R H N Hardy conceded that:

> . . . there were innumerable critics who said, not without some justification, that our figures were suspect, that we based everything on one single week's traffic – which was true – that we closed on crude statistics – they had a point – and that both our staff and the public were bulldozed into submission.

Nearly two years then elapsed before the publication of his 'notorious' report on 27 March 1963. Priced one shilling and available from Her Majesty's Stationery Office, *The Reshaping of British Railways* was a two-volume collection of graphs, statistics, analysis and maps that became commonly known as the 'Beeching Report'. Part 1 consisted of 148 pages of statistics and their analysis, the majority of which were effectively a death sentence for around 5,000 route miles of railway and the closure of over a third of the country's stations. With the 41-page Appendix 2 to the Report listing lines and stations throughout England, Scotland and Wales proposed for closure, there was little room for optimism.

According to the report one third of the route mileage carried only 1 per cent of the total passenger miles and 1 per cent of freight ton miles on BR – but of course, a similar analysis of Britain's road network would have produced much the same picture. Beeching was in fact commissioned by the 1964 Labour Government to produce such a study, examining the co-ordination of passenger and freight transport by road and rail – but the Prime Minister, Harold Wilson, under pressure from road haulage interests, soon concluded that Beeching was too pro-rail and too anti-road! He decided that Beeching must have 'assessors' imposed on him, but Beeching was unwilling to be shackled, declined the consultancy, and left BR to return to ICI earlier than expected, in May 1965.

An important flaw in Beeching's approach was identified by the charismatic and controversial General Manager of BR Eastern Region, Gerry Fiennes, who demonstrated one of the key omissions of the Report by showing that 'Paytrains' and 'Basic Railways' could cut costs dramatically on loss-making lines, while still retaining and even increasing patronage. Paytrains operated like buses where passengers paid their fare to a conductor on board. Basic railways had unstaffed stations so doing away with booking offices, etc. In this way the whole line could be run with a minimum of staff and facilities, thus reducing costs. In his 1967 book, *I Tried to Run a Railway* he commented that:

> [the Marples/Beeching axis] took no account of the new techniques; either coming into operation like diesel traction;

or just round the corner like automatic level crossings, mechanized track maintenance, tokenless block signalling, and 'bus stop' operation which can cut the cost of rural railways by more than a half. . . . They laid it down in general that rural railways did not pay, which was true; and could never pay, which was false.

Part 2 of the Beeching Report consisted of 13 large fold-out maps that had been produced to illustrate graphically the statistical information gathered for Part 1. Ranging from 'Density of passenger traffic' and 'Density of freight traffic' to 'Proposed withdrawal of passenger services' and 'Proposed modification of passenger train services', they nearly all gave bad news for the railway industry. However, the map of 'Liner train routes and terminals under consideration' was an important pointer to one of the positive outcomes of the report – and the Freightliner train service (using rail for the trunk haul and road for local collection and delivery) is today the market leader for movement of export and import containers to and from England's big five Deep Sea ports. Another positive legacy of Beeching was the widespread introduction of merry-go-round trains – so called because they load and unload coal while still moving – from collieries to power stations, a practice which continues to this day.

Protesters against the proposed Beeching cuts parade through the streets of Manchester in 1963.

As a fig leaf for the proposed passenger service closures the final route map in Part 2 showed 'Bus Services in Britain'.

Dubbed the 'Beeching Axe' by the press, the report's predominantly negative conclusions sparked a nationwide outcry, especially from the rural communities who were most at risk. Despite this, Beeching's report claimed to have all the answers – 'most areas of the country are already served by a network of buses' and that 'it appears that hardship will arise on only a very limited scale.' The consideration of hardship was the special responsibility of Transport Users' Consultative Committees where objections to closures could be lodged. If no bus service already existed then, in some cases, replacement bus services had to be laid on. At the end of the day it was for the Government – having also consulted its regional economic planning councils – to decide whether a line closed or not.

Beeching did not altogether get his own way, although over the next ten years 4,065 route miles succumbed to closure. While strong public and political pressure saved the Scottish lines from Inverness to Wick and Thurso and to Kyle of Lochalsh and in the southwest from Ayr to Stranraer, the closure of the Waverley Route between Edinburgh and Carlisle in January 1969 left the Borders region as by far the largest population grouping in Britain with no accessible railway services (although it is now planned to reopen the northern third of the line, to Edinburgh, in 2014). Conversely, its English equivalent, the Settle to Carlisle line, was reprieved as late as 1989 and is now an important freight route and alternative to the West Coast Main Line. Poor roads and the lack of bus services (but above all the fact that it passed through a number of marginal parliamentary constituencies) saved the Central Wales line, along with several Cornish branch lines, while in East Anglia the East Suffolk line from Ipswich to Lowestoft benefited from clever cost cutting, inspired by Gerry Fiennes. Despite the latter success story, other lines in East Anglia were not so lucky, including several that had not originally been listed for closure by Beeching, around King's Lynn and Peterborough. Ironically it was the 1964–70 Labour Government which wielded the axe more swingeingly than any other administration, despite their criticism of Beeching while in opposition.

In retrospect, many of the Beeching closures were very short-sighted – closing a third of the network brought savings of only £30 million, and the railways continued to run at an enormous loss. Cutting off the branches only starved the main lines of feeder traffic, causing an even greater downward spiral for rail finances. Fortunately a second Beeching report published in 1965, *The Development of the Major Railway Trunk Routes*, was not implemented – otherwise Britain's rail network would have shrunk even further.

Protesters halted the passage of the last train on the Waverley Route at Newcastleton on the night of 5–6 January 1969.

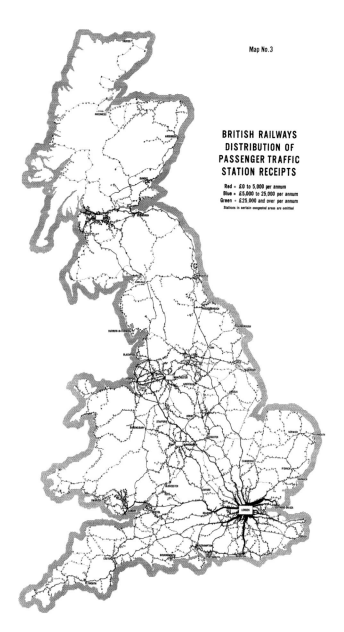

Map No.3

**BRITISH RAILWAYS
DISTRIBUTION OF
PASSENGER TRAFFIC
STATION RECEIPTS**

Red • £0 to 5,000 per annum
Blue • £5,000 to 25,000 per annum
Green • £25,000 and over per annum
Stations in certain congested areas are omitted

Title	Map No.3 – British Railways: distribution of passenger traffic station receipts
From	*The Reshaping of British Railways* (Part 2: Maps)
Publisher	British Railways Board, London
Date	1963

With its breathtaking plan for swingeing line closures the length and breadth of Britain, the Beeching Report did not hide its light under a bushel. Some critics felt that Dr Beeching was naïve in not foreseeing the political storm that such a transparent announcement of drastic surgery would cause. Part of that transparency came in Part 2 of the report – in a fascinating portfolio of 13 detailed maps showing line traffic densities, station receipts, services proposed for closure, and other aspects of the programme for reshaping the rail system. Beeching's Map 3 of passenger traffic station receipts in theory shows every passenger station still operational at the time of the report's research, other than those in the congested conurbations, but in practice some routes – such as March–Spalding–Lincoln – were completely omitted, demonstrating that mapmakers also make mistakes.

Stations were allocated to three categories – those earning up to £5,000 per annum; those between £5,000 and £25,000, and those of £25,000 and over – marked by coloured 'blobs' (solid circles). By far the most striking feature of the map (shown in detail overleaf) is its demonstration that the overwhelming majority of Britain's stations fell into the lowest revenue category, thereby visually underpinning the finding of Part 1 of the report that one third of the railway route mileage carried just 1 per cent of the total passenger miles.

A comparison of the station receipts map with Beeching's Map 9 of lines proposed for passenger service withdrawal (see pages 240–43) shows that very few stations in the highest revenue category were threatened with closure – but there were notable exceptions in East Anglia and Scotland. North of the Border, Stranraer and Thurso – at the southwestern and northern extremities respectively of the Scottish network – faced closure, as did Galashiels and Hawick on the Waverley Route from Edinburgh to Carlisle through the Scottish Borders, perhaps the most controversial of all Beeching's line closure proposals. In East Anglia, the planned closure of the East Suffolk line from Ipswich to Lowestoft would remove rail services from two stations which fell into the highest revenue category – Beccles and Saxmundham.

Following strong local protests, the East Suffolk line was saved, while in Scotland the Far North Line to Thurso (and the Kyle of Lochalsh line) benefited from the vociferous 'MacPuff' campaign which traded on political sensitivities about Highland depopulation. The line to Stranraer was reprieved in order to maintain the rail–ferry connection from Scotland to Northern Ireland, but the entire Waverley Route was closed by a Labour Government in 1969.

The contrast with rural mid-Wales was stark, as illustrated in the map extract. The Central Wales line service from

Shrewsbury to Swansea served more than 30 intermediate
stations, none of which fell into Beeching's highest revenue
category, and just three of which (at the southern end) earned
between £5,000 and £25,000 annually. While the provision of
replacement bus services was undoubtedly problematic, the
line served a small declining population – but crucially it
passed through three marginal constituencies, and as a result
was reprieved twice, in 1964 and again in 1969. By contrast,
the Waverley Route corridor had no key marginals, and the
Borders lacked the political resonance of mid-Wales or the
Highlands; its 98-mile railway closed on 6 January 1969,
leaving the region it served as by far the largest population
grouping in Britain with no accessible rail services. Such was
the rough justice of British railway closures in the 1960s.

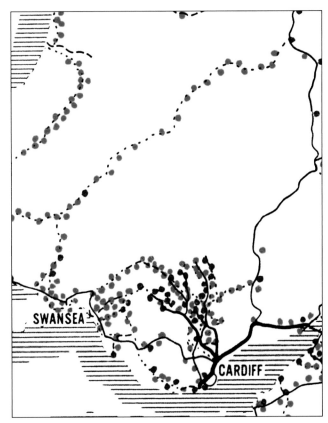

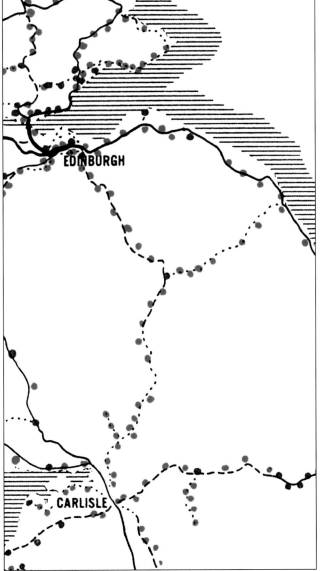

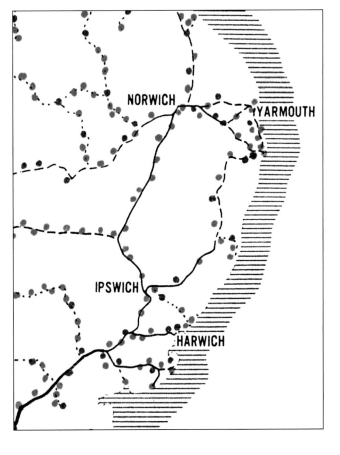

Map No.3

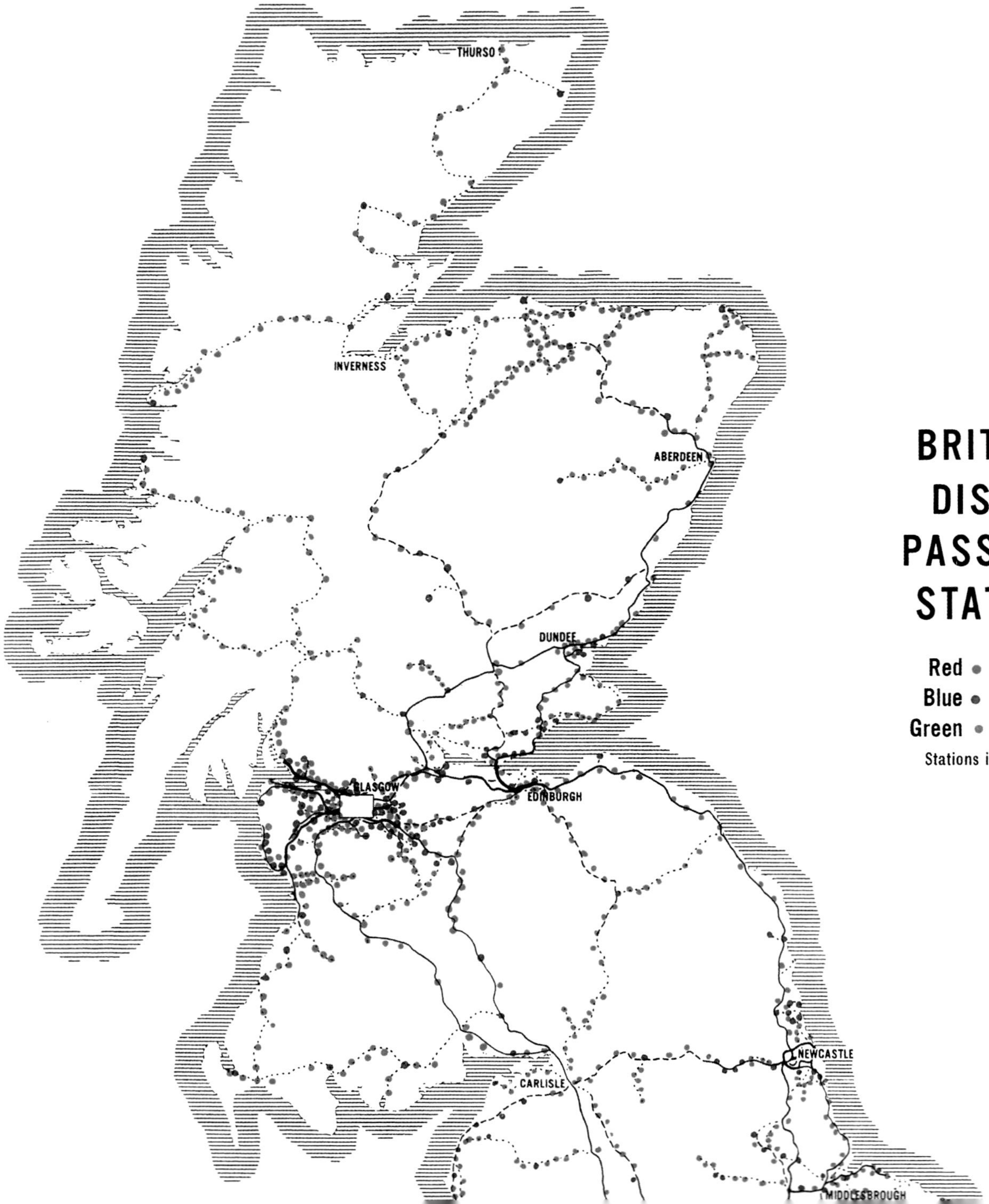

BRITISH RAILWAYS
DISTRIBUTION OF
PASSENGER TRAFFIC
STATION RECEIPTS

Red ● £0 to 5,000 per annum
Blue ● £5,000 to 25,000 per annum
Green ● £25,000 and over per annum

Stations in certain congested areas are omitted

THURSO

INVERNESS

ABERDEEN

DUNDEE

EDINBURGH

GLASGOW

CARLISLE

NEWCASTLE

MIDDLESBROUGH

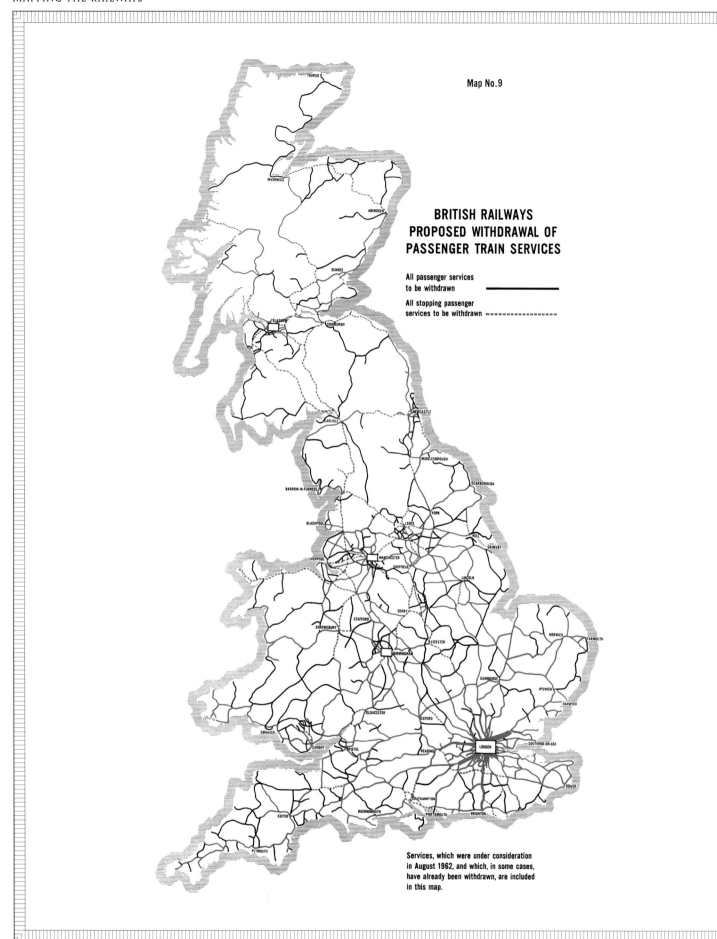

Map No.9

**BRITISH RAILWAYS
PROPOSED WITHDRAWAL OF
PASSENGER TRAIN SERVICES**

All passenger services
to be withdrawn ————————

All stopping passenger
services to be withdrawn ------------------------

Services, which were under consideration
in August 1962, and which, in some cases,
have already been withdrawn, are included
in this map.

Title	Map No.9 – British Railways: proposed withdrawal of passenger train services. Map No.9a – British Railways: proposed withdrawal of passenger train services London area.
From	*The Reshaping of British Railways* (Part 2: Maps)
Publisher	British Railways Board, London
Date	1963

For most readers of the Beeching Report, the nub of its message lay in Maps 9 and 9a which set out the routes over which passenger services were proposed for withdrawal, and the surviving routes over which all local stopping passenger services were to suffer a similar fate. Every region of the country was faced with the consequences of closing 5,000 route miles of railway nationwide, the only exception being the majority of Kent – admittedly part of the London-focused commuter network, but very much unscathed compared to other parts of the Home Counties rail system.

In practice, due to the vagaries of politics, only a relatively few areas experienced the full implementation of Beeching's line closure proposals – northeast Scotland, Fife, the Scottish Borders, the West Midlands, north Cornwall, north Devon, Somerset, Dorset and the threatened branches of the 'outer suburban' commuter network west and southwest of London.

As noted earlier, London's passenger rail network survived Beeching almost untouched. The only inner London line to succumb was the Palace Gates branch, while in the suburbs just the short Belmont branch from Harrow & Wealdstone, and the Uxbridge and Staines branches from West Drayton, were closed. The threatened branches from Watford Junction to Croxley Green and St Albans City, and from Woodside to Sanderstead in south London, were all reprieved.

We explore the lines which were reprieved nationwide on pages 248–249 – but which were the worst Beeching passenger closures? The longest route to be closed was the Great Central Railway (GCR) from Aylesbury, north of London, through the East Midlands to Sheffield, a total route length of 126 miles. The GCR was unquestionably a main line of strategic value, not least through its continental 'loading gauge' for freight traffic, which nowadays could have been playing a key role in intermodal transport of the modern generation of tall containers. The Great Central was also a major loss in terms of cross-country connectivity, but the small towns which lost their train service were virtually all left within 10 miles of the nearest surviving railheads. The closure of the 86 miles of the 'Somerset & Dorset' network removed train services from a number of significant towns –

including Glastonbury – and although all were within 20 miles of the nearest stations on the continuing 'main line' network, it left an area of fast growing population completely dependent on road transport.

Of all the areas that lost their rail services, in terms of population or distance from the surviving rail network the most drastic cuts came in Scotland. The northeast fishing towns of Fraserburgh (population 11,000) and Peterhead (17,000) were left just over 40 miles and 30 miles respectively from the rail network. The severity of loss was even greater in the Scottish Borders served by the Waverley Route, with Galashiels (population 13,000) left 33 miles from the nearest railhead and Hawick (16,000) 45 miles. The closure of the East Lincolnshire Line from Spalding to Grimsby left one town of comparable size to Galashiels or Hawick – Louth – cut off from the rail network, but by less than 20 miles.

It is clear that while a substantial proportion of Beeching's closure proposals may have made sense in an era of growing car ownership, a more strategic vision of Britain's transport future would have spared some very significant routes from the fate of crude closure.

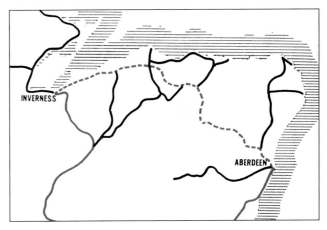

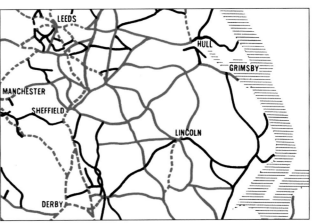

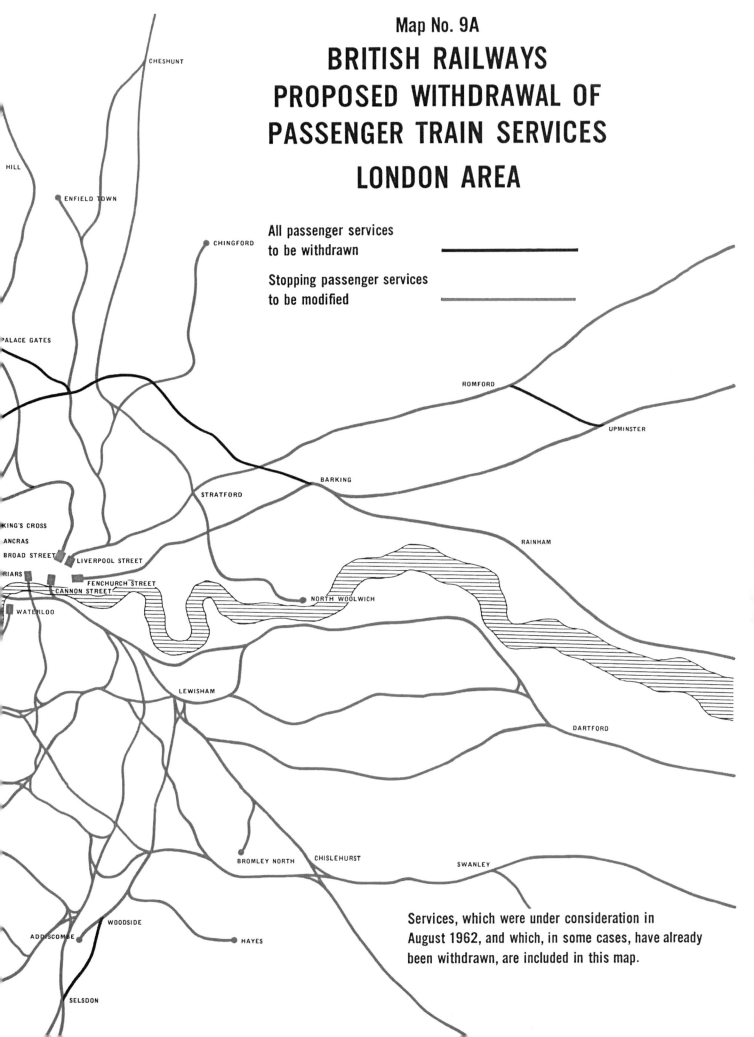

Map No. 9A
BRITISH RAILWAYS
PROPOSED WITHDRAWAL OF
PASSENGER TRAIN SERVICES
LONDON AREA

All passenger services
to be withdrawn

Stopping passenger services
to be modified

Services, which were under consideration in
August 1962, and which, in some cases, have already
been withdrawn, are included in this map.

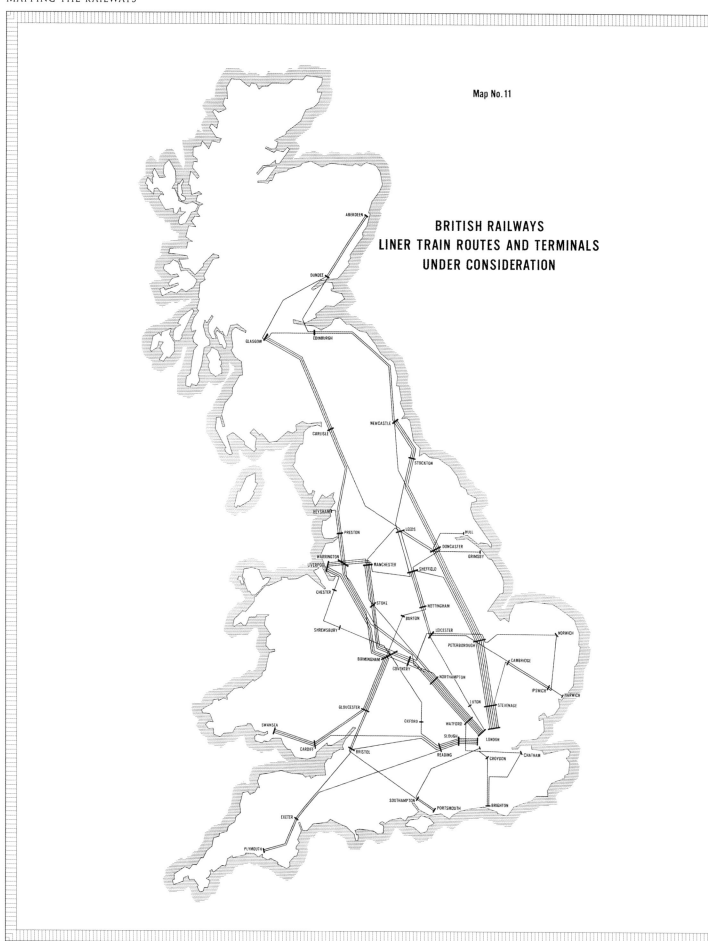

Map No. 11

BRITISH RAILWAYS
LINER TRAIN ROUTES AND TERMINALS
UNDER CONSIDERATION

Title	Map No.11 – British Railways: liner train routes and terminals under consideration
From	*The Reshaping of British Railways* (Part 2: Maps)
Publisher	British Railways Board, London
Date	1963

The wholesale closure programme which was the centrepiece of *The Reshaping of British Railways* – and the controversy which it provoked – have ensured that the name 'Beeching' will always have negative connotations. As Christian Wolmar concludes in *Fire & Steam* (2007), it was not all Beeching's fault, however:

> *His terms of reference had been too narrow: he was only supposed to find a way of returning the industry to profitability as soon as possible rather than consider the social and economic value of the railway or examine the economics of other modes of transport.*

The widespread condemnation of Beeching has tended to obscure the positive aspects of the report, where his fiercely intellectual analysis of problems yielded solutions from which the rail system has benefited right through to the present day. This was particularly the case in terms of the freight market – which inevitably was of less interest to the media, politicians or the public. Here Beeching came up with innovative ideas to equip the railway to do what it was inherently best at, in competition with a road haulage industry which was making major inroads into rail traffic, on the back of the expanding motorway network and bigger and faster lorries.

The biggest challenge was in the non-bulk market where the flexibility of the lorry – and its door-to-door capability – was causing a haemorrhaging of wagonload freight from rail to road. Part 1 of the report set out the thinking behind 'liner' trains as the key future method of moving 'general merchandise' traffic by rail:

> *The basic [intermodal] idea is to combine road and rail movement in such a way as to take advantage of the low cost of fast through-train movement as the means of providing trunk haulage over medium to long distances, for flows of traffic which, though dense are composed of consignments too small in themselves to justify through-train operation, and to do so without the disadvantages of the costly assembly of trains by wagon-load movements on rail, or costly transfer of merchandise between road and rail vehicles.*

Based on the intermodal concept – using high-capacity

containers – being cheaper door-to-door than road haulage for distances of 100 miles or more, Beeching envisaged about 55 terminals being required. In practice, the relative economics of road haulage improved dramatically, pushing the 'break-even' point between road and rail to ever higher distances, which effectively shrunk the profitable market available to rail. More than half of the terminals 'under consideration' in this map were never built, but the new Freightliner division of British Rail (BR) did play a pioneering global role in containerization, in parallel with the American shipping company Sealand. It was the presence of a BR official at a 1966 conference in Moscow which ensured that the future international ('ISO') standard for containerization would be based on an 8 ft cross-section – if the agreed height had been any greater the restricted 'loading gauge' on most of Britain's rail routes would have severely diminished Freightliner's future ability to serve the maritime market at major ports.

Freightliner was eventually privatized with the rest of BR's freight businesses, and today continues to be the market leader for overland movement of containers to Britain's big Deep Sea ports at Felixstowe, Liverpool, Southampton, Thamesport and Tilbury. Lord Beeching (who died in 1985, aged 71) would have been proud of that legacy.

The Freightliner network in 2011, focused on Britain's big Deep Sea ports.

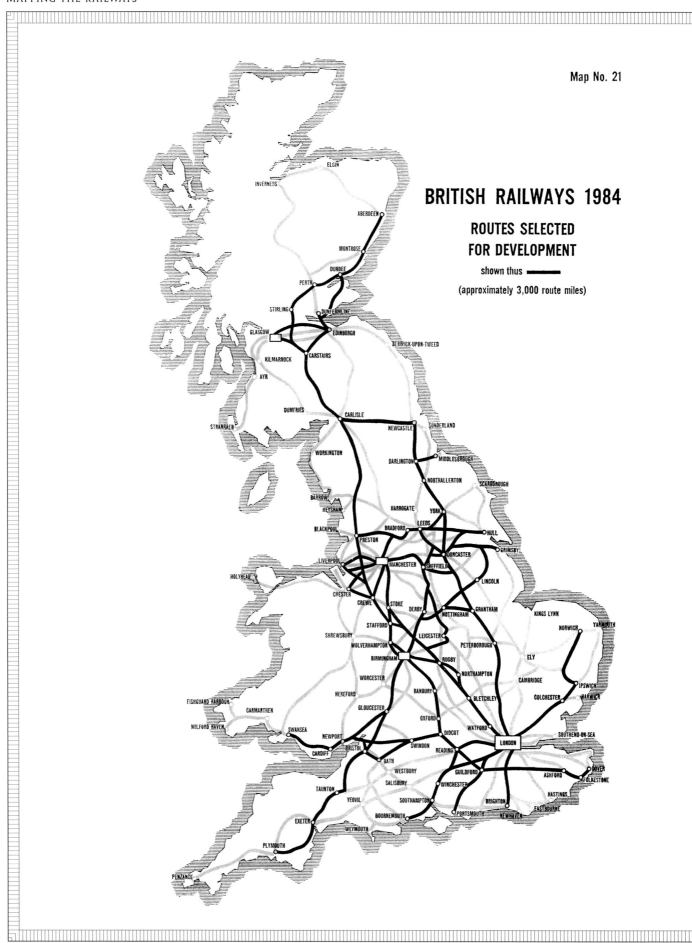

Map No. 21

BRITISH RAILWAYS 1984

ROUTES SELECTED
FOR DEVELOPMENT

shown thus ▄▄▄▄▄

(approximately 3,000 route miles)

Title	Map No. 21 – British Railways 1984: routes selected for development
From	*The development of the major railway trunk routes*
Publisher	British Railways Board, London
Date	1965

Dr Beeching's final major report for British Railways (BR) before he returned to ICI was *The development of the major railway trunk routes*, published in February 1965. This report focused on trunk routes as the key element of that part of the rail system, 'which is clearly sound now, and potentially sound under any foreseeable future conditions', with the crucial caveat that, 'Not all existing trunk routes can be included, however, because of the duplication which has resulted from the competitive building of the past.'

The report examined the pattern of traffic between main centres at that time, likely changes in the economy over the next 20 years, and forecasts of the pattern of transport demand between main centres in 1984, illustrated by no less than 27 maps. It concluded that:

The railways must reshape and redeploy their assets and service, so as to concentrate on cheap bulk movement, if the decline [in railway traffic] is to be arrested and reversed.

The network of through routes was underutilized, resulting in higher than necessary costs of track and signalling per unit of traffic, and to get these costs down to about half their then level it was:

demonstrably practical to channel the through movement over a reduced network of lines amounting to some 3,000 route miles rather than the 7,500 miles provided today.

It was argued that once the lines most likely to form the trunk rail network during the next 20 years had been determined, it would be possible to concentrate investment on the selected routes in the confidence that the essential dense flows of traffic would be maintained. As one would expect from Beeching, this was in many ways a logical argument – playing to the railways' strengths rather than weaknesses – but to the average passenger Map 21 implied, almost incredibly, a much greater threat to the network than even the 1963 report. To name but a few of the shocks, the 'routes selected for development' penetrated no further than Swansea in Wales, only the London–Norwich route would be developed in East Anglia, and Scotland faced the prospect of just one Anglo-Scottish line securing significant investment – echoing the 1839 Royal Commission, which believed that the traffic could support only one route, and Gladstone's

1889 comment to the House of Commons that 'as late as 1842, it was firmly believed to be absolutely impossible that there should ever be more than one railway to Scotland.'

The report's clarification that:

non-selection of lines for intensive development does not necessarily mean that they will be abandoned in the foreseeable future, nor even that money will not be spent upon some of them to improve their suitability for their continuing purpose

would provide little comfort for most readers. But Beeching left BR just three months later; in three years' time a radical Transport Act introduced specific line-by-line grants in belated recognition of the railways' wider social value; and BR steadily developed their world-leading InterCity brand across a far wider range of routes than the shrunken network for development envisaged by Beeching.

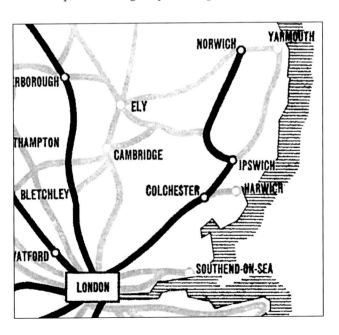

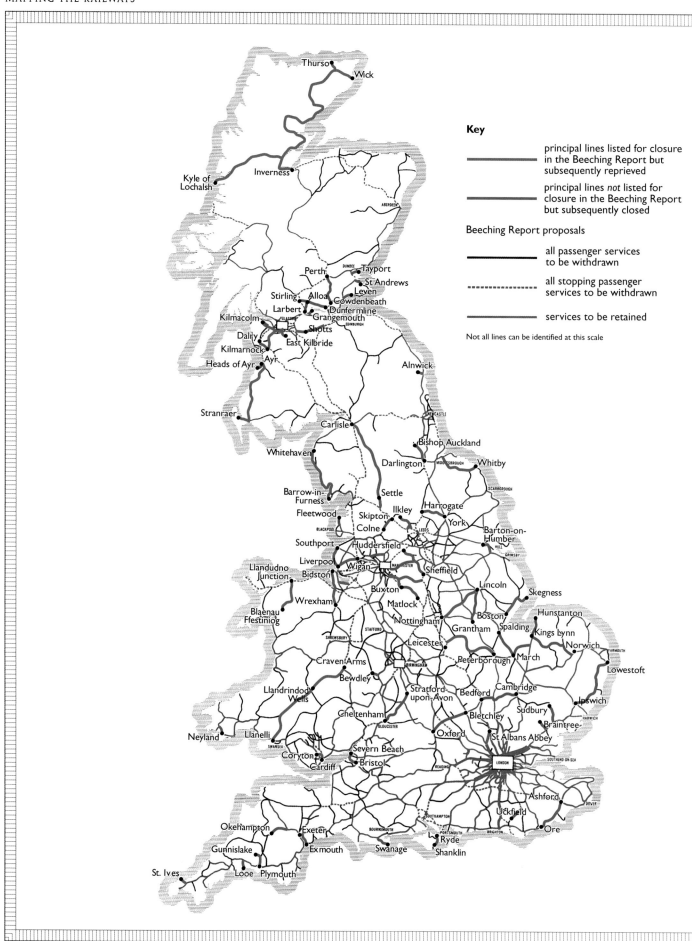

Key

principal lines listed for closure in the Beeching Report but subsequently reprieved

principal lines *not* listed for closure in the Beeching Report but subsequently closed

Beeching Report proposals

all passenger services to be withdrawn

all stopping passenger services to be withdrawn

services to be retained

Not all lines can be identified at this scale

Title	Map of (a) principal lines listed for closure in the Beeching Report but subsequently reprieved, and (b) principal lines *not* listed for closure in the Beeching Report but subsequently closed.
By	Collins Bartholomew (using data compiled by David Spaven)
Date	2011

Strong local campaigns and party political factors ensured that a significant number of routes threatened by the 'Beeching Axe' won reprieves from Ministers of Transport, the ultimate arbiters of what did and did not close. Because local issues were paramount, it is difficult to identify common underlying factors across the wide variety of services saved – from the 4-mile St Ives branch in Cornwall to the 168 miles of the Far North line from Inverness to Wick and Thurso. The latter was easily the longest route reprieved, but other lengthy loss-making lines also survived, including the 88-mile Central Wales line, and the 73 miles of the magnificent Settle & Carlisle line – saved by dogged campaigning and inventive promotion in the face of closure threats and a management run-down which began with Beeching and were not finally lifted until 1989.

The biggest geographical concentrations of reprieves – most of which were given between 1964 and 1970, while Labour was in power – were in the Highlands (always sensitive political territory), west Central Scotland, Merseyside, Yorkshire, Cornwall and eastern East Anglia. The 44-mile East Suffolk line from Ipswich to Lowestoft is an interesting case study. Following strong public protests – there were 1,916 written objections to the Transport Users' Consultative Committee which considered the hardship implications of all closure proposals – the railway secured a Ministerial reprieve. Its costs of operation were then transformed through the application of emerging new methods of operation, in the 'Basic Railway' concept pioneered by BR Eastern Region General Manager, Gerry Fiennes – with tickets sold on board trains ('Paytrains'); destaffing of stations; singling of sections of double track; radio signalling; automatic level crossings; and mechanized track maintenance.

The map also illustrates a little-appreciated story – the surprisingly large number of lines which the report had *not* proposed for closure, but which were in practice axed by the Labour Governments of 1964–70, concerned about railway finances continuing to deteriorate despite the implement-ation of much of the Beeching closure programme. As the map demonstrates, the pattern of post-Beeching closures was far from evenly spread across the country.

The loss of most of the important cross-country line from Oxford to Cambridge was explored on page 214; not much further north, the late 1960s saw the axing of a collection of routes well beyond the surgery originally proposed by Beeching. The cross-country lines from March and Dereham to King's Lynn lost their passenger services in 1968, while 1969 saw the loss of the King's Lynn–Hunstanton branch (immortalized in a classic TV documentary by the Poet Laureate, John Betjeman) and Dereham's last rail link, to Wymondham. Fortunately the latter has survived as a preserved line, the Mid Norfolk Railway. In a strange sequence of events, Spalding lost its trains to Peterborough and Boston in 1970 as part of the Beeching plan, but then saw the service to Peterborough reinstated less than a year later; to add a further negative twist to the story, the line from March to Spalding was closed as late as 1982.

The other notable concentration of post-Beeching closures was in Fife and along the Forth Estuary. Most of the scenic Fife Coast line was lost in 1965, with the remaining short stub lines to Tayport, St Andrews and Leven not originally proposed for closure – but by the end of 1969 all three had gone. Further up the estuary, Alloa lost all three of its remaining passenger rail routes in 1968 – but happily regained a passenger service to Stirling in 2008, quickly proving to be one of the most successful rail re-openings of modern times. Grangemouth, just across the Forth, lost its passenger train service in 1968, while the last and most serious closure in this part of the world came in 1970 when the direct Edinburgh to Perth main line via Kinross was closed by the London-based Ministry of Transport, to make way for the construction of the M90 motorway by the Edinburgh-based Scottish Office!

BR management's theory was that most passengers from closed branch lines would jump into a car or hop on a bus to the nearest station and continue their journey by train, with BR retaining most of the revenue but ridding itself of many of the costs. In practice, given the lack of integrated timetables and tickets, many passengers simply switched to car or bus for the whole journey.

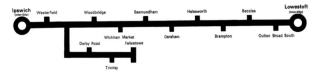

East Suffolk line pocket timetable and map.

Title	Gradient Profiles E1 (part) and M1
From	BR Main Line Gradient Profiles
Publisher	Ian Allan Publishing Ltd
Date	2003 impression of 1966 publication

Gradient profiles have long been used by rail staff and railway enthusiasts to understand the challenge posed to train operation by the vertical topography of specific stretches of route. Unlike the typical map, gradient profiles do not offer a 'bird's eye view' of the horizontal disposition of railways in the landscape, but rather a cross-section along the route of railway, with mileages and gradients numbered beside. Signal boxes traditionally had gradient diagrams for the stretches of track they controlled. These two extracts come from a volume which brought together on a route-by-route basis the gradient profiles of all the main lines and many cross-country routes as they were in 1966, not long before the end of steam traction.

The two profiles here provide an insight to the contrasting challenges posed to locomotive drivers and train service planners by two stretches of the East and West Coast Main Lines (ECML and WCML), both of similar length and at similar latitude, but featuring very different gradients.

These routes were host to the famous – but short-lived – 'railway races' of 1888 and 1895. Prior to 1888 the East Coast route from London to Edinburgh (operated by the Great Northern and North Eastern companies) was much faster than the West Coast route (operated by the London & North Western and Caledonian) – nine hours against ten. The 1887 decision by the East Coast companies to permit 3rd class passengers on the 10 a.m. departure from King's Cross led to a drastic loss of traffic for the West Coast companies. They responded at the start of the 1888 tourist season in early June by matching the East Coast timing with the 10 a.m. departure from Euston. Schedules got faster and faster over the next two months, until the East Coast train did the journey in just 7 hours 27 minutes on 13 August. The next day both sets of companies agreed to minimum train times, and the races stopped.

By 1895, the focus had moved further north with the opening of the Forth Bridge, and Aberdeen was the goal. The mid-

LONDON – NEWCASTLE – EDINBURGH (Continued)   E1

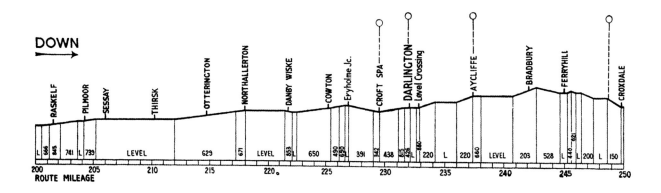

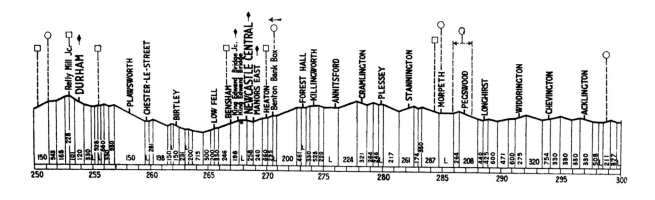

summer races were precipitated by the West Coast companies' concern that the arrival time of the overnight train from Euston did not give enough leeway for the important connection to the Deeside line and the consequent acceleration of their train by 10 minutes. This led to conflicts with the North British at Kinnaber Junction near Montrose, where the two routes converged, and the overnight trains from King's Cross and Euston were now due to pass within five minutes of each other. This started a tit-for-tat slashing of the timings (as in 1888) but their value probably lay more in the resulting publicity than any benefit for passengers, who ended up being deposited in Aberdeen at an unearthly hour in the morning.

The gradient profiles demonstrate just how much more steeply inclined is the WCML, in particular with its four-mile northbound climb at 1 in 75 to Shap summit (and the 10-mile climb to Beattock summit north of Carlisle). On the ECML, much of the route between York and Newcastle is at or near level, with nothing more severe than a very short stretch of 1 in 101 just south of Durham. Throughout its

existence, rail companies have responded to the WCML challenge in a variety of ways – by providing 'banking' engines at the rear of trains; double-heading; and latterly with the completion of electrification in 1974. When British Rail completed ECML electrification in 1991, the fastest timing from Edinburgh to London was 3 hours 59 minutes, but the Glasgow to London service was taking over 5 hours. Now the fastest East Coast journey is 4 hours, but the West Coast has seen a radical speed-up – to as little as 4 hours 8 minutes for the 8-mile longer journey – with the introduction of tilting Pendolino trains, designed to overcome the WCML's additional challenge of generally more severe curvature than the ECML.

KEY

♦	SPEED RESTRICTION	– SEVERE (30 M.P.H. OR LESS)	
⚑	,,	,,	– MODERATE (35-55 M.P.H.)
⚐	,,	,,	– SLIGHT (60 M.P.H. OR OVER)

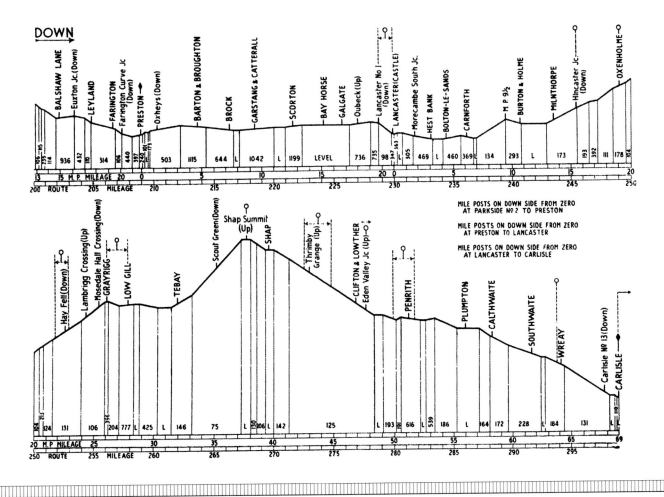

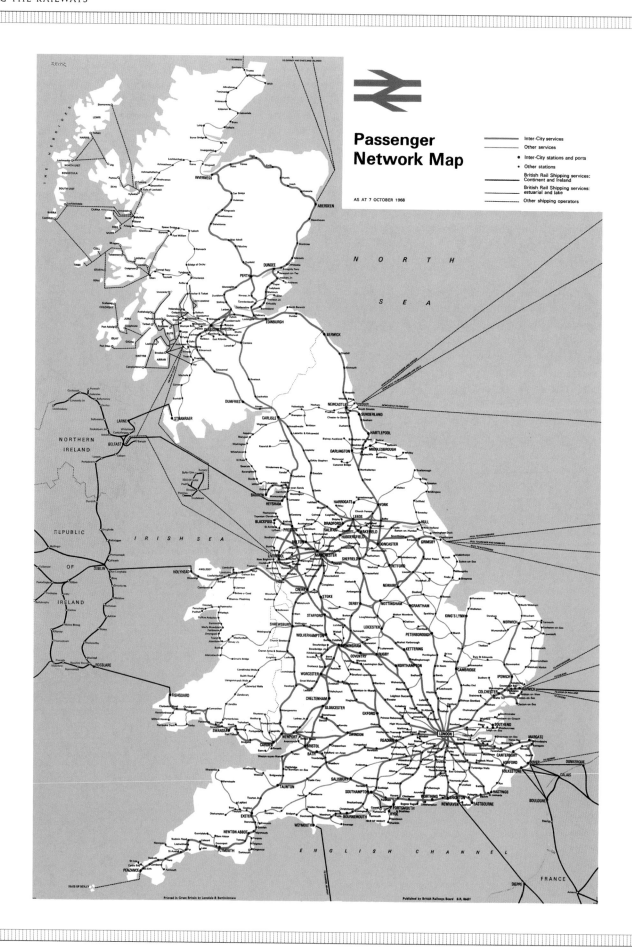

Title	Passenger Network Map
Publisher	British Railways Board
Date	1968

By the time British Rail published this map in October 1968 (issued with its Western Region timetable), the vast majority of passenger services threatened by Beeching and subsequently withdrawn or reprieved had met their fate. However, the Waverley Route from Edinburgh to Carlisle through the Borders still had three months to run before closure – but the mapmakers had clearly decided that no last-minute campaign would save it, and the line was excised from timetable geography before the trains stopped running.

Route-specific problems with adequate replacement bus services and/or road improvements briefly delayed the end for a few more cross-country routes and branch lines proposed for closure in the 1963 Beeching Report, notably in east Lincolnshire. The map also shows two main lines which had still to close, neither of which were Beeching proposals: the direct Edinburgh–Perth route via Kinross, and the Manchester–Woodhead–Sheffield route. The latter had only been electrified in 1954 but lost its passenger service in 1970 as part of an initiative to eliminate passenger rail route 'duplication' between the two cities, leaving the Woodhead line to concentrate on its core coal traffic – ironically, this eventually went into severe decline, and with its non-standard overhead electrification equipment facing renewal, the line closed completely in 1981.

The reverse of the timetable map is an area map of Western Region (extract shown overleaf) with the appropriate table numbers listed beside each line. The southwest had still to feel the full pain of closures, with the Bridport, Ilfracombe and Minehead branch lines lingering on. The Okehampton branch was a 'post-Beeching' closure in 1972, but remained open for freight and ultimately saw the seasonal reinstatement of passenger services. Most of the Minehead branch was revived as a volunteer-led 'preserved railway', while the Paignton–Kingswear branch moved seamlessly from British Rail control to private ownership at the turn of 1972/1973.

The extracts from the Western Region map on this page show the local routes which survived in the Bristol and Cardiff areas in late 1968. Bristol originally had a reasonable suburban rail network, but, with Temple Meads station some distance from the city centre, it lost the route south through the Mendips to Frome before Beeching; the branch to Portbury on the Bristol Channel opposite Avonmouth during the Beeching period; and the first stretch of the former Midland Railway main line northeast from Temple Meads after the publication of this map. The Severn Beach branch was the only Beeching line reprieve in the Bristol area.

All the Beeching-proposed line closures in the South Wales Valleys were implemented except Cardiff–Coryton, although Bridgend to Treherbert did not succumb until 1970 – subsequently to re-open between Bridgend and Maesteg in 1993, accompanied by other pre-devolution re-openings over the Cardiff 'City' line in 1985 and the Aberdare–Abercynon link in 1988. The Welsh Assembly Government subsequently helped to secure the re-opening of the Barry–Bridgend 'Vale of Glamorgan' line in 2005 and the Cardiff–Ebbw Vale Parkway branch in 2008. All have been successful additions to the rail network.

This national map design had just superseded the early British Railways map style, as illustrated on pages 214–217, but it maintains the latter's twin route categories, in this case distinguishing between 'Inter-City and 'other' services. The number of station types represented has dropped from three in the dense network map of the early British Railways period to just two in 1968 – 'Inter-City stations' and 'other stations'. Given that only selected stations are shown – the complete inventory of Western Region stations is marked on the map on the reverse – the overall impact is a clear and pleasing representation of the national network (plus connecting shipping services) in a familiar geographic style.

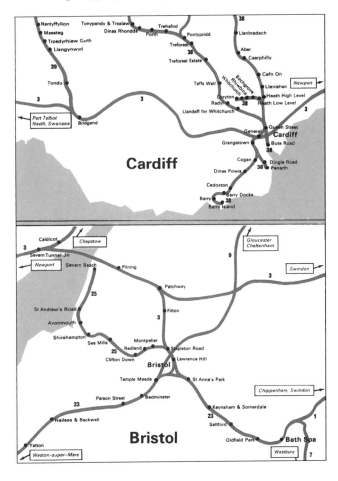

THE REVIVAL OF THE PASSENGER RAILWAY

With growing concerns about the environment and oil security – and line closures largely a thing of the past – British Rail continued the development of a rail system geared up to fight road and air competition. The national network of InterCity services became a successful world-leading brand.

Greencliff Rd.
Abbotsham Richards Court
Combe Walter
Greencliff
Babbacombe
Portledge
Chiddlecombe
Gilscott
Hortway
Alwington
Goldworthy
Hobwell
Horns Cross
Bocombe
Parkham
Herdland
Bableigh
Melbury
Melbury Hill
Melbury Resr.
Winslade
Fowler's Piece
Vennmills
Twitchen
Goutsland
Bilsford
Craneham
Laidland Water
Eckworthy
Tythecott
Milford
Collingsdown
tford
Galsworthy
Mambury
Venn
Bounts Thorne
Hankford
Haytown
Bulkworthy
holladon
Downmoor Venn
Binworthy
Abbots Bickington
Eastbridge
Worden
Woodford Br.
Whitebear
green
Milton Damerel
Gratton
Crawley
Bagbear
S. Wonford
Wonford
Thorne
Woodacott
Windy Cross
Lashbrook
nglefield
Halsdon Barton
Cookbury
Upcott
Dunsland Ho.
Cookbury Wick
Anvil Corner
Stapleton
Dunsland Cross
Eastcombe
Hayne
Tredown
G. Claw Moor
Higher Whitleigh

Bideford
East-the-Water
Abbotsham
Moreton
Upcott
Caddsdown
Jennets Resr.
Ford Ho.
The Barton
Ashridge
Littleham Court
Hallsannery
Pillmouth
Oldiscleave
Landcross
Huxwill
L. Netherdowns
Fairy Cross
Winscott
Ford
Yeo Vale
Rollston
Littleham
R. Yeo
Annery Ho.
Saltrens Cottage
The Hill
Park
Southcott
Weare Gifford
Bulland
Orleigh Court
Upcott
Petticombe
Downes
Beam Mansion
Furze
Furzebeam Hill
Stone
Burrow
Buckland Brewer
Monkleigh
Culleigh
Priory
Frithelstock
Horwood Barton
Frithelstock Stone
Ash
Preston
Priestacott
Stretchacott
Cleave
Tuddiport
Great Torrington
Rosemoor
Smithacott
Knaworthy
Bowden
Watergate Br.
Little Torrington
Hembury Castle
Ashbury
Vielstone
Hollamoor
Southcott
Beadslake
Smytham
Cholash
Bibbear
Holwell
Budal
Langtree Week
Bagbear
Hunshaw
Thorn Moor
Stowford
Eastacott
Bower
Withacott
Langtree
Collacott
Stibb Cross
Burstone
Browns
Rivaton
Suddon
Berry Cross
Track of Old Railway
Yard
Peters Marland
Willeswell
Woollaton
Twigbear
Week
Stapleton
Darpley
Durpley Castle
Badworthy
Moortown
Rowden
Alscott
Stone
Allisland
Newton St. Petrock
Holwill
Ladford
Padlon
Galmington
Awsland
Heaton Barton
Forestreet
Shop
Suddon
Vaddicott
Caute
Pennicknold
Grascott
West Heanton
Netheron
North Town
Oxenpark
Ruxhill
Berry
Pithridge
College
Buckland Filleigh
Chapel Gidott
Shebbear
Dumpinghill
Upcott
Hartleigh
Ash Moor
Thornbury
Henscott
Highworthy
Buvacott Wood
Swardicott
Westacott
Hallwood
Bason
Backway
South Hill
Bradford
Worden
Holroyd Ho.
Libbear Barton
Gortleigh
Sheepwash
Totleigh Barton
Crocker's Hele
Priestcott
Dippermill
Middlecott
Brandsworthy
Cohan
Barton
Black Torrington
Longwood
Highstead
Lana
Ley
Hayne
Blackley
Butterbear
Upcott
East Pulworthy
West
Venton
Stadson
Bovacott
Highampton
Flares
Brandis Corner
Stadson Br.
Northcott
Weekpark
Graddon
Graddon Moor
Odham
Fraunch
Lewmoor
Chilla
Birchen
Holepark
Stewdon Moor

Newton Tracey
Southcott
Woodtown
Webbery
Bulworthy
Gammaton
Alverdiscott
Alverdiscott Barton
Woodland
Langley
Northcote
Yarnscombe
Garnacott
Nethercott
Delley
Cogworthy
Court Barton
Chapple
Huntshaw
Huntshaw Cross
Wiggaton
Darracott
Darracott Moor Resr.
Ward
Cranford
Way Barton
High Bullen
Moortown
Sherwood Green
Pengham Barton
Stevenstone Ho.
Dodscott
St. Giles in the Wood
Beara Moor
Ley
Winscott Barton
Ebberley Ho.
Combe Barton
N. Healand
Wansley Barton
Homer
Long Wood
Whitsleigh
S. Healand
Woodland
Castle Hill
Woolleigh Barton
Ramscliffe
Kiverley
Pearson
Higher Upcott
Abbot's Hill
Beaford
Harepath
Warham
Gt. Potheridge
Speccott Barton
Lit. Potheridge
Whiteland Head
Aswell Venton
Iddlexo
Dunsbear
Dunsbear Halt
Moorhill
Brick Wks.
Merton
Merton Mill
Greatwood
Ford
Halston Ho.
Winscott
Lit. Marland
Rosehill
Heanton Satchville
Huish
Langham
Chapple
Bury
Burstone
Broadmead
Lowistone
Tockley
Newcourt Barton
Petrockstow
Stockleigh Barton
Stone Bramblecombe
Cross
Brake
Westpark
Meeth
Stockey
Woolladon
Ash
Bridge Town
Nethercott Ho.
Hele
R. Torridge
Hele Br.
Fishleigh
Lewer
Holms
Sticklepath
Littlewood
Hatherleigh
Hatherleigh Moor
Venton
Lydacott
Coombe
Stewdon
Passaford
Hamaborough
Cleave
Esseworthy
Westdown

257

The term 'Inter-City' was first used by the Western Region of British Railways in the early 1950s when it gave the name to an express train that ran between London Paddington, Birmingham (Snow Hill) and Wolverhampton (Low Level). Leaving Paddington at 9 a.m. on weekdays and returning from Snow Hill at 5 p.m., it provided a fast two-hour journey between Britain's two largest cities. The train was discontinued in 1967 when the newly electrified West Coast Main Line between Euston and Birmingham (New Street) began to provide a faster service between the two cities.

With steam on the way out British Railways made an effort to change its outdated image. Preceded by the experimental XP64 livery, the standardized livery colour of 'Rail Blue' was introduced in 1965 (along with the shortened name of British Rail) while the brand name of 'Inter-City' was first introduced in 1966 for its long-distance expresses – coaches on these routes were given a new livery of two-tone blue and pale grey with 'Inter-City' picked out in white.

The introduction of Inter-City 125 High Speed Train (HST) sets on the Western Region main line from Paddington to Bristol, Cardiff and Swansea in 1976 was a great success. With a maximum speed of 125 m.p.h. (compared to earlier diesels' 100 m.p.h. limit) and vastly improved passenger comfort, they were soon attracting passengers back to Britain's much-maligned railways – helped along the way by innovative marketing such as the famous TV advert exhortation to 'let the train take the strain'. Within a few years the HSTs were also operating on the East Coast Main Line from King's Cross, to Edinburgh, Aberdeen and Inverness; the Midland main line out of St Pancras; as far west as Swansea and Carmarthen; and to the southwestern tip of England at Penzance. The completion of West Coast Main Line electrification in 1974 also saw vastly improved services on this vital Anglo-Scottish railway artery.

In 1986, British Rail was divided up into different business sectors, with 'InterCity' (rather than 'Inter-City') as the flagship business. The livery for InterCity coaches and locomotives was changed to dark grey on the upper parts, light grey on the lower, separated by red and white stripes (the famous 'Swallow' logo was added in 1989). The new InterCity sector was divided into seven operating divisions: East Coast; West Coast; Midland; Great Western; Great Eastern; Cross-Country; and Gatwick Express. The sector was also responsible for sleeping car and Motorail car-carrying services. It was a very successful and profitable formula and within a few years British Rail was running more 100 m.p.h. services each day than any other country in the world.

Following the completion of East Coast Main Line electrification in June 1991, locomotive-hauled electric InterCity 225 trains entered service between King's Cross and Edinburgh – their brand name refers to their potential top speed of 225 km/h so it is rather misleading! In fact they 'only' operate up to a maximum speed up 125 m.p.h.

The success of the rebranding of Britain's InterCity network was not lost on others, with the brand name being launched

'Castle' Class No. 5053 'Earl Cairns' heads 'The Inter City Express' into Birmingham Snow Hill in the 1950s.

in West Germany in 1971 to replace the former Trans Europe Express trains – Deutsche Bundesbahn even paid a royalty for using the name to British Rail for many years. Introduced in 1991, Intercity-Express (ICE) high-speed trains now operate throughout Germany while the EuroCity brand name is used by international train services within Europe. InterCity is also the brand name used by Iarnród Eireann for its principal services in the Republic of Ireland.

In Britain the Railways Act 1993 heralded the privatization of Britain's railways. Taking effect on 1 April 1994, British Rail was fragmented into numerous companies, with many of the new train operators taking on franchises not dissimilar to the old InterCity sector operating divisions. Following privatization the term 'InterCity' soon fell into disuse, and is no longer used by train operating companies, reflecting the absence of a single centrally branded network of main line services.

Sporting the InterCity 'Swallow' logo a Class 90 electric locomotive pauses at Crewe with the 'Sussex Scot' in September 1989.

Poster produced for British Rail advertising the new HST 125 Inter-City expresses from Paddington to Bristol and South Wales in 1977.

This 1970s BR poster depicts the ill-fated tilting Inter-City Advanced Passenger-Train at speed between Euston and Glasgow.

In 1956, in response to criticism that new post-nationalization railway rolling stock looked out of date, the British Transport Commission (of which British Railways was part) set up its own Design Panel to produce a co-ordinated design policy. While locomotives and passenger coaches were the primary focus of its initial work, eventually every important aspect of the railway business, its operations and supporting activities came within the sphere of design policy – and this had an impact far beyond Britain. Writing in *British Rail Design* (1986), the Director of Design at Danish State Railways commented:

> *The impact of British Rail Design was immediate, and an encouragement to all those in the international railway community who wanted to improve their ware. British Rail became the leader of a new wave in public design. During the following decade it hit first The Netherlands, then Denmark, Austria, France, Federal Germany, Norway and Switzerland where the national railways followed the British example. All the way, British Rail was the guiding spirit and midwife in the creation of better design standards in public service.*

British Rail's enviable corporate identity incorporated, after 1965, a single new font ('Rail Alphabet') and standardized layouts for posters, leaflets, pocket timetables and maps. In *British Rail 1948–83: A Journey by Design* (1983), Brian Haresnape reflects that, 'this simplicity and constancy provides a strong visual contact with the user amidst the general clamour and confusion created by the surrounding commercial advertising.'

The 1971 Inter-City Sleeper network map comes from an information leaflet for the internal Scottish service from Glasgow and Edinburgh (combined at Perth) to Inverness, which ceased operation in 1990. This is an interesting example of a map produced in a clearly 'geographic' style, but using 'diagrammatic' elements to allow the reader to understand the starting point, main intermediate calls, and destination of individual sleeper services. The accompanying text explaining the amenities on sleeping cars has a delightfully old-fashioned service touch – 'Hot-water bottles are supplied on request.'

As a result of increased day-time train speeds, competition from low-priced airlines, and rail privatization, today's sleeper network is much reduced from the wide spread of towns and cities served in 1971, with just two core routes left – from London to Scotland (Aberdeen, Edinburgh, Fort William, Glasgow and Inverness) and from London to Penzance.

By 1985 the branding had changed from Inter-City to InterCity, and the map of (day time) InterCity Routes is far more diagrammatic, with distances distorted to simplify

the presentation, and the British coastline no longer shown. This is certainly an easy map to understand – and does show key connecting cross-country routes – but unlike the 1971 map does not provide information on which towns and cities are directly linked by through train services.

Title	Your journey by Inter-City Sleeper
Publisher	British Railways Board
Date	1971

Your journey by Inter-City Sleeper
Glasgow/Edinburgh – Inverness

Title	InterCity Routes
Publisher	British Railways Board
Date	1985

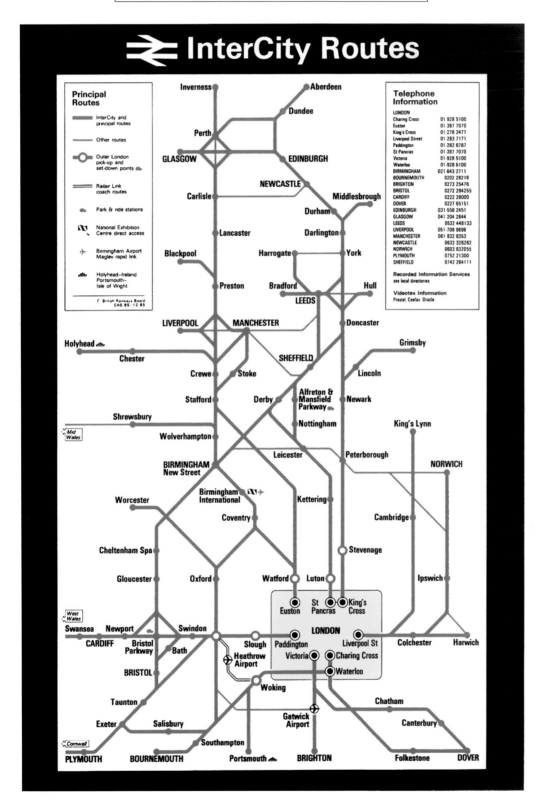

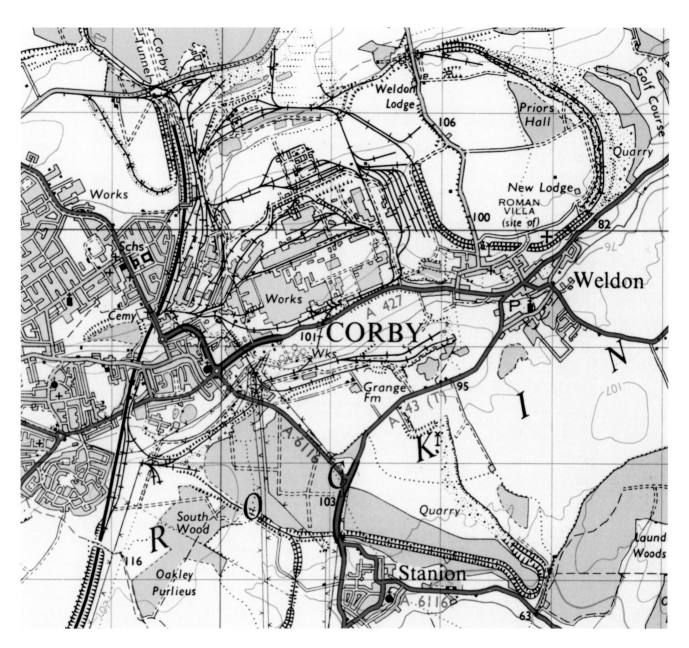

Series	Ordnance Survey 1:50,000 First Series
Sheet	141 (Kettering & Corby) (enlarged)
Date	1974

The principal theme of this map extract is the proximity of a major industry to its source of raw materials, a model that was the norm before the era of globalization.

Local supplies of iron ore – part of a band of ironstone stretching from Lincolnshire to Oxfordshire – led to the transformation of the Northamptonshire village of Corby into one of Britain's major centres of steel production. The Corby blast furnaces, built between 1910 and 1917, were

acquired in 1920 by the Glasgow steel manufacturer Stewarts & Lloyds which began construction of a new iron, steel and tube-making plant on the site in 1933. This became the most advanced integrated steel production plant in England, attracting a huge influx of unemployed men and their families to the town, not least from the Glasgow and Lanarkshire areas, where the steel industry was undergoing a downturn. At one point, it was estimated that over 70 per cent of the population of Corby were of Scottish descent, and it is still known as 'Little Scotland'.

As recently as 1959, new railway lines were being built to access ore pits southeast (the quarry shown north of Stanion) and southwest of the steel works, to complement nine

RAILWAYS ON ORDNANCE SURVEY MAPS

From their earliest years, railways have been an important and distinctive feature of Ordnance Survey maps, not least in the popular 1 in. to 1 mile series, which was ultimately replaced by the metric 1:50,000 scale maps from 1974 onwards. The first 1 in. map was published in 1801 and in the next 70 years the series was extended to cover the whole country. At the start of the 20th century colour was introduced, and the 1 in. map reached its final form in the Seventh Series published from 1952.

The Corby map extract is an example of the First Series of the 1:50,000, produced by photographic enlargement of the existing 1 inch map. The new sheets incorporated a number of design and colour changes – for example motorways were coloured blue instead of red, with B roads changing from brown to orange – but the representation of railways was left entirely untouched. However, the subsequent continuing growth of the road system at the expense of the railways ultimately led to changes in rail feature representation, as shown in the contrasting key extracts of the 1974 Corby map and the current edition.

Where a distinction was once made between single track and multiple track rail routes, there is now just one category. A single-track railway takes up a substantially narrower land corridor than a single-carriageway road, but this is not evident from the OS map – neither of the line symbols for road or rail is strictly to scale. Cutting and embankment symbols for rail (and road) remain unchanged, while level crossings are now marked 'LC' rather than by a narrowing of the road line.

In a reflection of rail development nationally, the distinctive ticked line for freight sidings is now used instead for 'light rapid transit system, narrow gauge or tramway', and the hard-to-identify 'ladder' symbol for narrow gauge lines has been dropped. A further sign of rail expansion is the new pecked line symbol for 'track under construction'. The white circle symbol for 'station closed to passengers' – crucial in the immediate post-Beeching era – became superfluous and was eventually dropped, but a new yellow circle symbol has appeared more recently to identify 'light rapid transit system station'. In many ways, the Ordnance Survey has successfully reflected the changing nature and importance of railways in the landscape in the early 21st century – and doubtless there will be further changes to come.

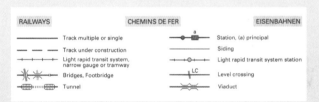

Ordnance Survey railway symbols, 1974

Ordnance Survey railway symbols, 2004

existing short branch lines to the east, northeast and northwest. The map captures the steel works and nearby iron ore workings just a year before the Government agreed a programme that would lead to the phasing-out of steel making at Corby, in favour of plants supplied with higher grade imported ore. The last load of home-produced ore was despatched to the Corby steel works in 1980, although tube manufacturing continued on site, supplied with steel by rail from the remaining plants.

The map shows sidings leading to every part of the works, reflecting the strong hold rail still had on the movement inwards of raw materials and fuel and outwards of finished products and by-products. The internal sidings were controlled by the British Steel Corporation, which operated its own shunting locomotives and wagons to handle the short hauls of iron ore and other traffic movements within the site – 'external' traffic being received from or passed on to British Rail at exchange sidings to the west of the works. The cross-country railway from Kettering on the Midland Main Line through Corby to Oakham and Leicester had lost its passenger services in 1959, and so all railways shown on the map were at the time freight-only.

An experimental Corby–Kettering rail passenger service began in 1987, but suffered from an irregular timetable and unreliable older rolling stock, and was withdrawn in 1990. However, a new station with a bus and taxi interchange opened in 2009, adjacent to the site of the old station, and enjoys an hourly service to Kettering and London. Steel still arrives at the tube works (now owned by Tata Steel) by rail from the Margam plant in South Wales, while the railway has also benefited from Corby's relatively central position in Britain with the establishment of a rail-connected distribution hub on former industrial land to the south of the tube works.

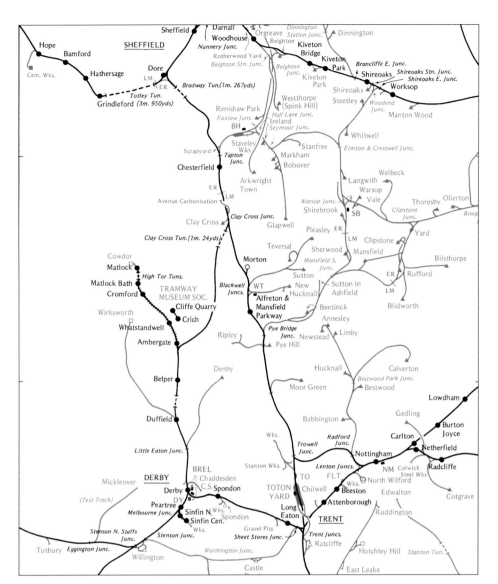

Extract	Page 47
From	
Rail Atlas Great Britain and Ireland – 1st Edition	
Author	S K Baker
Publisher	
Oxford Publishing Company	
Date	1977

These maps, from the popular 'Baker atlas' used extensively by railway professionals and enthusiasts, illustrate the enormity of change in the Nottinghamshire rail network – and the associated coal industry – between 1977 and 2010. This regional change is a microcosm of the national switch from a freight-led railway system to a passenger-led one.

The most striking feature of the 1977 map is the 43 collieries shown, the majority served by an intricate network of freight-only branch lines over a swathe of country bounded by the Midland Main Line through Alfreton & Mansfield Parkway and the cross-country passenger routes linking Nottingham and Sheffield with Lincoln. The coal mined by the National Coal Board was primarily destined for power stations (four of which are marked on the map), and also supplied to industrial and domestic markets in full trainloads, as well as traditional wagonload traffic on local 'trip' trains which

Beeching had identified as a key loss maker – but which survived until shortly before the 1984–5 miners' strike. Many other rail freight terminals and private sidings are shown on the map, including cement works, steel works and a Freightliner terminal ('FLT') west of Nottingham.

By 2010 an extraordinary transformation had taken place. The enormous contraction of the coal industry is immediately apparent, with only four collieries or opencast coal loading points marked – although by 2011 just one of Britain's last three deep mines was actually operational in Nottinghamshire, at Thoresby. Rail freight's fortunes have closely mirrored the coal industry, with the closure or mothballing of many of the freight-only branches. Nottingham Freightliner terminal had also gone, axed as part of a nationwide rationalization of the container-carrying network in 1987.

Extract	Page 53
From	*Rail Atlas Great Britain and Ireland – 12th Edition*
Author	S K Baker
Publisher	Oxford Publishing Company
Date	2010

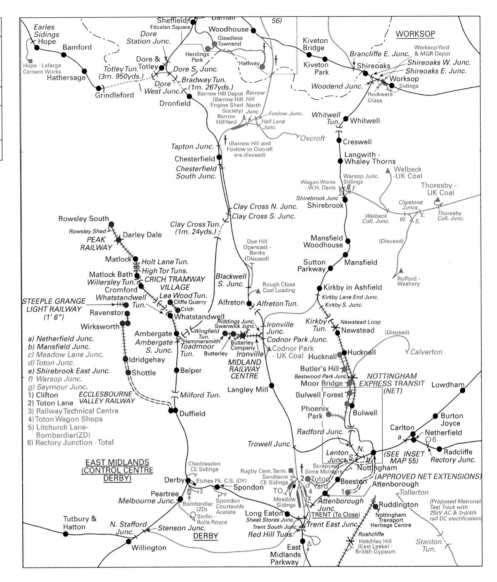

More positively, two of the longest freight routes had been incorporated into the new passenger service on the 'Robin Hood' line from Nottingham to Worksop, which was opened in stages between 1993 and 1998. This heavily populated area, including large towns such as Mansfield, had lost the last of its passenger trains in 1964, and the reinstated service has proved to be very popular. At 29 miles in length, it is by far the longest passenger route re-opening of modern times in Britain.

The Robin Hood line has interchanges with another rail development illustrated on the map – the new Nottingham Express Transit tram system. In the far north can also be seen the southern arms of one more new tram network – the Sheffield-focused South Yorkshire Supertram. A final noteworthy contrast between the 1977 and 2010 maps is the latter's profusion of preserved railways, with no less than six such operations in a relatively small area.

		Surface	Tunnel		
Passenger Rail Network (With gauge where other than standard gauge: i.e. 4' 8½" Britain/5' 3" Ireland)	Multiple Track			**Advertised Passenger Station:** Saltburn	**Power Station**
	Single Track				**Oil Terminal**
Preserved & Minor Passenger Railways (With name, and gauge where other than standard gauge)	Multiple Track			**Crossing Loop at Passenger Station:** Newtown	**Quarry**
	Single Track				**Proposed Railway**
Freight only lines	No Single/ Multiple Distinction			**Crossing Loop on Single Line:** Kincraig	**Colliery** (incl. Washery & Opencast site)- UK Coal unless otherwise specified
					Freight line used for passenger diversions and with regular timetabled services.

There is a very long tradition of railway companies producing descriptive line leaflets, brochures and booklets for rail passengers – particularly leisure travellers and tourists – and these have typically been accompanied by maps. From Victorian times, such maps have simplified and/or straightened the representation of rail routes in order to ease understanding and fit a convenient printed format for use on trains.

Over its nearly 50-year life, British Rail produced many maps of holiday and scenic routes throughout England, Scotland and Wales – with the apotheosis of this genre perhaps being in the Scottish Highlands, with so many outstanding routes through dramatic 'unspoilt' landscapes.

The three map leaflets here come from a 15–year period and show different styles of simplification designed to suit the fashion or purpose of the time. The 1970 leaflet shown on these pages was produced before the Inverness–Kyle of Lochalsh line faced its second threat of closure – it was first reprieved in 1964 – and its illustration is predominantly abstract. The text evokes traditional attractions for the tourist – scenery, history and folk tales – but also draws the reader's attention to the role of the railway in modern times, including the Ness Viaduct which 'carried the tremendous military traffic of two world wars to the major military installations at Invergordon and to Scapa Flow – a vast achievement for a single-track line.'

By 1972, the Government was planning to withdraw grant aid from the Kyle passenger service – parallel roads had been improved, and the line faced losing most of its freight traffic when the Stornoway ferry switched from Kyle to Ullapool. This time British Rail did not have to face accusations of a run-down – a number of its managers based in Glasgow, shocked by the Ministerial consent to close the Waverley Route through the Borders and the direct Edinburgh–Perth line, were determined to do what they could to help ensure that no more major line closures would take place in Scotland. Rail supporters were surprised by the publication of the 1972 promotional leaflet (shown overleaf), coming in the midst of a campaign to save the railway, and enthusiastically assisted British Rail in its distribution to potential rail users at hotels and guest houses in Inverness and Dingwall. The text of the leaflet unapologetically concludes with reference to the *realpolitik* of the planned fate of this grant-dependent railway:

> *The grants are to be discontinued and as a result the British Railways Board has no alternative but to close the line. The closure will not take place before the end of 1973.*

In practice, a determined campaign of opposition – and the prospects of increased freight traffic from siting an oil production platform yard near the railway – led to a second reprieve, and the Kyle line has gone on to be a major summer attraction for tourists, not just in timetabled

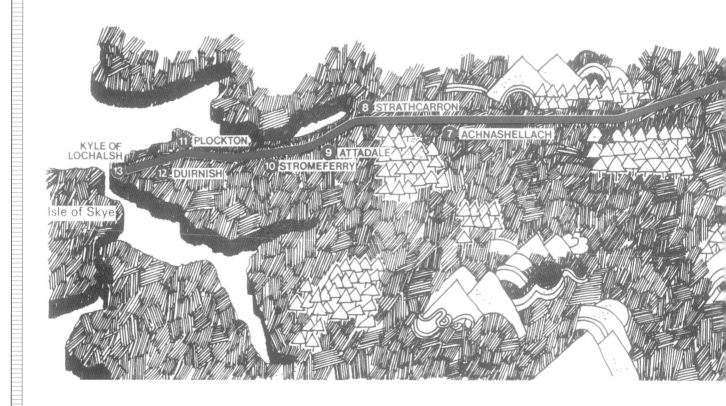

trains but also in charter services from as far away as the south of England.

The 1985 brochure shown overleaf was part of a joint promotion by British Rail and the Government agency, the Highlands and Islands Development Board, which comprised a folder of four different line guides under the branding 'Great Railway Explorations of the Scottish Highlands'. With a lengthy pictorial-style map and a detailed text, it extols the attractions of the Far North line to Wick and Thurso, delves into railway history, and also gives a nod to the modern world served by the railway:

> *Formerly a naval base – and centre of a notorious mutiny in 1931 – Invergordon has a fine harbour, facing Udale Bay and Cromarty Bay on the Black Isle. As you leave Invergordon, the distillery emerges on your left, along with the now closed aluminium factory. To the right lies Saltburn and Nigg Bay, the cradle of vast North Sea oil rigs, and site of the British National Oil Corporation's Beatrice Terminal, where some of Britain's oil comes ashore.*

Rail route.Inverness|Kyle of Lochalsh

Title	Rail route. Inverness/Kyle of Lochalsh
Publisher	British Rail
Date	1970

Title	Inverness–Kyle of Lochalsh
Publisher	British Railways Board
Date	1972

Inverness Kyle of Lochalsh

RONA

RASSAY

SCALPAY

SKYE

Kyleakin

Applecross

Toscaig

Duirinish

Kyle of Lochalsh

Plockton

Loch Carron

Strome Ferry

Strathcarron

Attad[

Achn[

Title	
Great Railway Explorations of the Scottish Highlands – Inverness to Wick and Thurso	
Publisher	
Highlands and Islands Development Board/ British Rail	
Date	1985

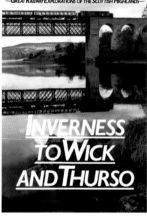

GREAT RAILWAY EXPLORATIONS OF THE SCOTTISH HIGHLANDS

INVERNESS TO WICK AND THURSO

INVERNESS has its roots deep in ancient times, and it provides a splendid starting point for today's Highland journey.

About 563 AD, Inverness was the headquarters of King Brude, monarch of the Picts, the ancient people of Scotland. Local history has it that Brude was converted to Christianity by followers of Saint Columba, on top of Craig Phadraig, a hill overlooking Inverness. Craig Phadraig is a remarkable example of a vitrified fort, and it offers superb views.

In modern Inverness you'll find a wealth of shops, bars, hotels and guest houses. You can stroll along the banks of the Ness. Visit Eden Court Theatre. Take a trip to historic Culloden Moor, to such lovely glens as Affric and Moriston, and to Loch Ness with its elusive monster. Shortly after pulling out of Inverness, you'll cross the Ness Viaduct, built in 1862. To your right lies the harbour. To your left stands Tomnahurich Hill, shaped like an upturned boat with trees on top. Known as the hill of the yew trees, or even Fairy Hill, Tomnahurich is the local cemetery.

View from Inverness Castle, with the River Ness sparkling below.

THE TRAIN SLOWS TO CROSS THE SWING BRIDGE OVER THE CALEDONIAN CANAL.

The Canal is a splendid affair, completed in 1822 by one of Britain's greatest engineers, Thomas Telford. Telford's creation links the North Sea with the Atlantic, joining Inverness to Fort William via Lochs Ness, Oich and Lochy. If you enjoy cruising and sailing through spectacular scenery, this Canal is made for you. The £160,000 lavished on it by Telford was money well spent.

On through Clachnaharry – originally 'Clachnathaire', it means Stone of Watching, a lookout point. Glance left up to the rocks. A statue used to stand on the pedestal there, commemorating a clan battle of 1454, fought between the Munros and the McIntoshes. Some say that a Grey Lady has haunted the pedestal since the statue was blown down in a storm a few years ago.

To your right the Kessock Bridge sweeps in spectacular style over the firth to the Black Isle – which is neither black nor an island.

The Black Isle is a peninsula, and a fair, green country of woods, meadows and cornfields, with friendly, pretty villages. The name may derive from the area's lack of snow in winter (it lies low and near the sea). Or it may be because until the 18th century it was uncultivated 'black' moorland.

Dingwall originally was called Inverpeffer, but when the Vikings occupied these lands, the name became 'Thing Vollr', the Valley of the Court.

True to its past, Dingwall remains the administrative centre of the area. You're in a town with a Royal Charter, which was granted by King Alexander II in 1226, when the Vikings were driven out.

Gaze to your left and you'll see a monument to Sir Hector MacDonald. A local crofter's son, he fought in Britain's South African Wars, and rose from the rank of private to general.

Northwards out of Dingwall. On the left look for the castle which is more

Six miles along the firth you'll see to your right two castles close to each other. The nearer, now a ruin, is Redcastle, built in 1179 by King William the Lion. Beyond is the 16th century Kilcoy Castle. For hundreds of years both were occupied by the MacKenzies of Kintail.

Groam Farm, one of the largest farms in the area, goes by on the left before you go through Clunes.

Watch for Wardlaw Church, for many years the repository of the famous Wardlaw Manuscripts, which record the history of the Clan Fraser from 916 to 1674. You can see the Manuscripts in Inverness Museum.

Approaching Beauly, look right. The ruins of Beauly Priory, founded by John Bisset Lord Lovat, have stood there since 1230.

Over the River Beauly. On your left is Beaufort Castle, seat of the Clan Fraser. The castle was built on the site of the old Castle Downie, which was destroyed by the Duke of Cumberland after the Battle of Culloden in 1746. Culloden was the last pitched battle fought in Britain, and marked the end of the Stuart family's claim to the Crown.

Now you reach your first stop. Some 80 years ago Muir of Ord was the cattle centre of the north of Scotland, and its name derives from 'Moor of the Hammer' – the hammer being the cattle auctioneer's gavel. You'll journey over a golf course which was the site of the cattle market. On your left stood Carn nan Chlarsair, 'the Cairn of the Harper' where Lord MacDonald of the Isles was killed by an Irish harper centuries ago.

AS YOU LEAVE MUIR OF ORD, BEN WYVIS LOOMS UP. FROM ITS SUMMIT, 3,433 FEET UP, YOU CAN ENJOY MAGNIFICENT VIEWS OF THE HIGHLANDS. MIND YOU, IT'S A LONG WALK WHICH CAN TAKE ALL DAY.

Don't be tricked by the rounded bulk of Ben Wyvis – it's one of the highest mountains in Easter Ross. This is rewarding country for walkers, birdwatchers – and anyone who loves exploring.

Conon Bridge goes past. Once renowned for the colour and variety of its cottage gardens, the village is on the River Conon, said to have been the haunt of the dog otter.

After Maryburgh comes Dingwall. The line forks. The Kyle Line wanders left toward mountainous Wester Ross and ends in Kyle of Lochalsh, in the shadow of the Isle of Skye.

Rosemarkie Beach on the Black Isle.

like a house surrounded by a wall. It's said to have been built on the site of – and with stone from – an even older castle, which was the stronghold of the Mormaers, or Great Men, who ruled the area.

FINLAEC, FATHER OF MACBETH, WHO INSPIRED SHAKESPEARE'S PLAY, IS SAID TO HAVE BEEN A MORMAER. AND MACBETH HIMSELF WAS BORN IN THE CASTLE.

(The Highlands and Islands are studded with an abundance of castles – you could easily spend a whole holiday castle hunting.)

Along the shores of the Cromarty Firth. Salmon and sea trout can be caught by fly in the River Conon at low tide, so shallow are the waters.

Soon you see the causeway which carries the road across the firth.

Foulis Castle passes on your left. The 18th century seat of the Clan Munro, it was designed in Dutch courtyard style, and replaced an earlier building which had burnt down.

In the background you can still see Ben Wyvis. The ruins of Castle Craig, once home of the Bishops of Ross, are on your right on the foreshore of the Black Isle.

Past Evanton on the Allt Grand River. It used to be known as Novar, after a local estate.

On the left, look out for one of the most unusual monuments in the Highlands. Crowning Fyrish Hill is a copy of the Gate of Negropatam, a reminder of Britain's days in India.

This exotic creation was commissioned in the 18th century by General Sir Hector Munro, to relieve local unemployment.

Watch for whisky distilleries on your right as you reach Alness. The Teaninich and Dalmore distilleries are two of many in the Highlands and Islands. While all of

Reminder of distant days: The Gate of Negropatam.

them jealously [...] many will welc[...] local Tourist Inf[...]

The villag[...] should its housin[...] ever meet at Ros[...] come true. You [...] the train pulls a[...] INVERGORL[...] GENTLEMA[...] GIVEN A BA[...] CELEBRATE[...] HIMSELF.

Formerly [...] centre of a noto[...] Invergordon has [...] Udale Bay and C[...] Black Isle. As yo[...] the distillery em[...] along with the r[...] factory. To your [...] Nigg Bay, the cr[...] oil rigs, and site [...] Oil Corporation's [...] where some of B[...]

Further in[...] Black Isle seapo[...] geography and g[...] Hugh Miller's C[...] remarkable of p[...] with Balnagow[...]

restored market [...] red sandstone T[...] TAIN HAD ON[...] CHURCHES D[...] PILGRIMS CA[...] BUT NOW TH[...] IN RUINS.

On the oth[...] Dornoch. Once th[...] welcomes many [...] have the chance, [...] recent British Op[...] he described it as [...]

Dornoch's [...] many as 16 Earls [...] hallowed note, D[...] Janet Horne, Sco[...] in 1722.

Inverness–Kyle of Lochalsh

---

*...of 'the water of life',
...tours – ask at the
...etails.
...coming a town, and
...f nearby Invergordon
...prophecy will have
...your left, just before*

**...MES FROM A
...LLIAM GORDON.
..., HE
...E TOWN AFTER**

Hugh Miller's Cottage, Cromarty.

*...ore.
...romarty, the small
...ou're interested in
...the little museum at
...Past Kildary now,
...n Fearn, and fertile
...hich was moved there
...om Edderton in 1338.
...h Eye, one of the few
...lochs around here,
gleams on the
right.
North-west
to Tain, ancient
Royal Burgh on
the Dornoch
Firth. Near the*

**...r IMPORTANT
...ND MANY
... KING JAMES IV,
...AINT DUTHUS IS**

*...another Royal Burgh,
...utherland, Dornoch
...golfers. If you ever
...och course – one
...ed his round so much
...ever had playing golf.'
...und there. On a less
...one' marks where
...was burned to death*

A mile north of Tain, look left to see Morangie
Distillery. The track skirts the shore of the firth. You pass
Meikle Ferry, where at one time you could have a boatman
ferry you to Dornoch.

In years to come a bridge may vault the firth, making
it even easier to explore the constant delights of this
winding coastline.

On through Edderton, with Balblair Distillery on
your left. On your right, on a clear day, you'll see Skibo
Castle, former home of the late Andrew Carnegie, the Scot
who became a millionaire in the United States.

Further on and to the right is the ruin of
Spinningdale's old mill. To the left of
the mill is a large, bungalow-style
house, once home of the film star
James Robertson Justice.

The forested slopes of Struie
Hill gather above you. You go by the old
parish kirk of Kincardine. Ardgay arrives.

**THE DISTINCTIVE WHITE
KINCARDINE STONE, A FOCAL
POINT OF THE WINTER
MARKET, STANDS IN THE
SQUARE.**

To the west, Strath Carron runs deep into glorious
mountain scenery. The roads twist off towards the rugged
west coast, some 40 miles distant as the eagle flies.
One day you might tour over the high passes to the
beaches, lochs, sea-angling harbours and islands. For the
moment, though, you head north.

The road bridge crossing the channel on the right
goes to Bonar Bridge. The channel links the Dornoch Firth
with the Kyle of Sutherland.

Over the Carron River you go, to Culrain, the halt
for Carbisdale Castle. Now a Youth Hostel,
Carbisdale is the only Scottish castle
built this century. Beyond is
Lamentation Hill, scene of a
fierce battle in 1650 between
the Marquis of Montrose and
the Covenanters, who were
fighting to establish their
own kind of religious
freedom.

Invershin's request stop goes by. Rocky cuttings
interrupt your view. On the left, on a good clear day, you can
see all the way to north-west Sutherland, where the
mountains cut a ragged edge along the sky.

You veer right and you're in Lairg. Set at the
southernmost tip of long, fish-filled Loch Shin, Lairg is the
hub of the scattered communities of the north and west.
On sheep days Lairg is thronged and noisy and a most
enjoyable place indeed. The local buses serve such
far-flung romantically named destinations as
Lochinver, Elphin, Kinlochbervie and Inchnadamph.

A steep climb heralds Lairg Summit, then it's
downhill through Strath Fleet to Rogart. On the way
Tressady Lodge appears on the left, to be followed by a

stone cairn raised in memory of the
Canadian Prime Minister MacDonald,
who was a Sutherland man.

Rogart, another important
sheep-market centre, precedes The
Mound. From here a railway used to
run to Dornoch. On you go along the
shores of Loch Fleet.

Beinn a Bhragaidh rises on
your left. On its top is an unmissable
statue, of the first Duke of Sutherland.
Golspie is next, a busy fishing town and holiday
resort. The town provides all the modern services required
by the farming and crofting communities which are
sprinkled around Sutherland's immense reaches of
mountains, glens, lochs, and moors. There's a stone on the
old bridge in Golspie, which in chiselled Gaelic, provides
the rallying focus for the Clan Sutherland.

Dunrobin Bank means a steep clamber for the train.
On the right the North Sea spreads out. Clear days bring
views of the mountains of distant Banffshire, down
towards Aberdeen.

Straight out of a fairytale, Dunrobin Castle appears
on the right, amid its great park. For centuries the seat of
the chiefs of the Clan Sutherland, turreted Dunrobin
commands superb sea views, and welcomes visitors in
the summer.

Finance for the line actually petered out when it
reached Golspie. Then the Duke
of Sutherland stepped in

Dunrobin Castle, Sutherland

with generous capital and
the vision of a privately-owned line serving the
flourishing villages on his coast. The section
between Golspie and Helmsdale was
opened on 19th June 1871.

Soon you're in Brora. There's plenty
to do – bathe from the fine sands, enjoy
excellent fishing, play golf, and tour the
mountains and moors inland. Brora boasted the
only coal mine in the north of Scotland at one time. It
was opened in 1598 but is now closed.

Clynelish Distillery is on your left as you depart
Brora. Within minutes Loth goes by, where Scotland's last
wolf was killed in 1700.

You curve and wind along to Helmsdale, a fishing
village nestling between high moorland ridges. Note the
new road which runs near the mouth of the river. It sweeps
over the site of a castle where the Earl and Countess of
Sutherland were poisoned by Isabel Sinclair – just one of
the deep and dark incidents which cast shadows upon the
realm of Mary Queen of Scots. On a more appetising note,
the river is also known for salmon fishing.

You veer from the sea and follow the River
Helmsdale up through the Strath of Kildonan. This strath
is visited by Prince Charles for fishing and hunting. Beinn
Dubhain towers above you.

Kildonan village arrives, Scotland's Klondyke.
This was the scene of a gold rush in 1868, when prospectors
came from far and near to pan for gold in the Kildonan and
Suisgill streams.

The golden dream came to an
end in 1911 when an expert pronounced
the dust too fine for commercial
purposes. Mind you, people still pan
the streams . . .

The north of Scotland is rich in
prehistoric remains, and you'll find
strange, parallel rows of stones around
Kildonan, particularly on Leivable Hill.

On past Kildonan Lodge and
Suisgill Lodge on your right, then
Borrobol Estate House and the River Frithe on your left.
Watch for the snow fences on either side of the line.
Winters here can bring unbelievably deep drifts.

Beinn Griam Mhor and Beinn Griam Bheag emerge
on the left, after the Kinbrace request stop. Loch an
Ruathair and Loch Lucy are next, Lucy with the little island
at its heart. Between Strath Halladale and Achentoul Forest
lies Forsinard. The hotel is popular with fishermen, and no
wonder – they have eight lochs to choose from, and the
River Halladale.

Slethill Hill is to the left, as you leave Forsinard.
You're climbing now, up on to wild, open moorland beneath
a big sky. Caithness is wide and flat and enchanting. The air
is astonishingly clear up here.

Altnabreac punctuates the wilderness. (All around
is peat – the Hydro Electricity Board experimented with the
idea of using milled peat for the generation of electricity.)
Loch Dhu House, belonging to
Lord Thurso, is nearby.

Scotscalder approaches. Loch Calder glints over to
the left. Close-boarded fences are close to the line, so
that the wind deflects snow away from the track.
They're known as 'blowers'.

On your right, the River Thurso courses through the
landscape, then under the line just before Halkirk.
Every July Halkirk has a Highland Games, one of the finest
anywhere. And fishermen speak highly of Halkirk's trout
and salmon too. More snow fences edge the rails as you
come into Georgemas Junction. Here, the Thurso and Wick
sections of the train part company.

Seven miles north, Thurso is Britain's most northerly
mainland town, and it dates back to Viking times.
(The Viking legacy is everywhere in Caithness, especially
in place names such as Wick, Staxigoe, Watten
and Freswick.)

Thurso's wide streets and bustling shopping area,
and its full range of accommodation, help make it an ideal
touring centre. You'll also discover indoor swimming, golf,
parks, the excellent Folk Museum and refreshing walks
along the river and the coast. One of the town's
most famous sons was Sir William Smith, founder of the
Boys' Brigade.

Thurso needn't
be the end of your
journey. Modern
ferries ply daily out
of nearby Scrabster to
the Orkney Isles. The
cliffscapes and
beaches are rich in

Old Man O'Wick Castle, Caithness

seabirds and seals. You can go sea angling out of Thurso,
into record-breaking waters. Take a walk around Holborn
Head and Dunnet Head, for the views over the Pentland
Firth. Try surfing – the waves can be world class!

**THE ALTERNATIVE FORK IN THE LINE TAKES
YOU TO WICK, THROUGH SCENERY WHICH
BECOMES LESS AND LESS HIGHLAND.**

Notice the way the fields are divided, with great
slabs of slate, unlike the drystone dykes of Sutherland and
Easter Ross.

The rewarding fishing waters of Loch Scarmclett
appear on the left. Loch Watten and Wick Water follow on
the right. Around here a battle was
fought over the Earldom of
Caithness, between Lord
Breadalbane and Sinclair of
Keiss. Wick rolls in. King James
VI made Wick a Royal Burgh in 1589,
and it was at one time county
town of Caithness.
Pay a visit to the
Heritage Museum,
and the old
Sinclair Aisle
in the parish
church, which
is the burial
place of the
Earls of Caithness.

Your exploration
of Wick should include
the castles of Old
Wick to the south
and Sinclair and
Girnigoe to the
north. Take a look
at the quaint Town Hall with
its cupola, and wander
around the suburb
of Pultneytown,
founded by the British
Fishing Society early
last century.

A little to the north,
of course, is the best known of
all Caithness towns –
John O' Groats, last
village on mainland
Britain.

You have travelled
Britain's most northerly railway,
and have travelled through
an area which is unique
in all Europe – the
landscapes are
unspoiled, the wildlife is
teeming and the long summer
days give you time to fully enjoy yourself.
Let your railway exploration be just a beginning.

This pair of Bartholomew maps, separated by 50 years, illustrates how the rail network was decimated across north Devon. The largest town in the area, Barnstaple, had been second only to Exeter and Plymouth as a West Country focus for competition between the Great Western Railway (GWR) and the London & South Western Railway (LSWR). The GWR provided the most direct route from the rest of the country, over the east–west line from Taunton to its Victoria Road station, but the LSWR ran from the main regional centre at Exeter, and also had north Devon branches from Barnstaple Junction through Barnstaple Town to the coastal resort of Ilfracombe, and eastwards to Bideford on a meandering cross-country route to Okehampton, and to Wadebridge and Padstow in distant north Cornwall. The north Devon network was completed by the independently owned narrow-gauge Lynton & Barnstaple Railway, but this had a short life, closing to passengers (as part of the Southern Railway) in the year of publication of the 1935 map.

Some of Bartholomew's charming idiosyncrasies of description of road and rail features – as seen on the 1921 map of the Swansea area on pages 170–173 – had disappeared by 1935, with station refreshment rooms no longer identified, but the distinctive layer colouring is again seen to advantage in this region of steeply undulating hills and the wide expanse of Exmoor. The map extract overleaf shows the separate company stations in Barnstaple, including the GWR's Victoria Road, with the other stations being part of – post Grouping – a distant outlier of the Southern Railway. Victoria Road closed in 1960, with trains diverted to Barnstaple Junction, but this was to prove to be a very minor cut compared to the surgery which was soon to follow.

The Beeching Report made grim reading for north Devon, and for adjoining west Somerset and north Cornwall – everything was to close, other than Exeter to Barnstaple Junction station (on the southwest side of the town) and the Newquay branch in Cornwall. Despite widespread objections, there was to be no reprieve for any line in north Devon. The line west to Bideford and beyond was the first to lose its passenger services, in 1965, followed by the Taunton route in 1966; the Ilfracombe branch (and Barnstaple Town station) finally closed in 1970, the cost of maintaining the bridge over the River Taw being cited as justification for closure of the more centrally located station. A long freight branch to Meeth, south of Bideford survived, carrying milk and china clay traffic until the early 1980s, after which its route was converted into a recreational path and cycleway.

The track of the old line through Bideford is marked correctly on the 1985 1:100,000 map, but strangely the railway from Barnstaple Junction to Barnstaple Town is still shown as being open, despite having closed in 1970. Perhaps this – and the compromising of the layer colouring principle by the introduction of a separate bright green colouring for 'woods' – was a sign that Bartholomew's was losing its way in the face of intense competition from the Ordnance Survey and specialist mapping companies. Just two years later, this series of maps ceased production.

The one surviving railway in north Devon, from Exeter to Barnstaple, is a shadow of its former self, but has enjoyed something of a revival in the last decade, with a local 'community rail partnership' promoting the route as the 'Tarka Line', named after the animal hero in Henry Williamson's book *Tarka the Otter*.

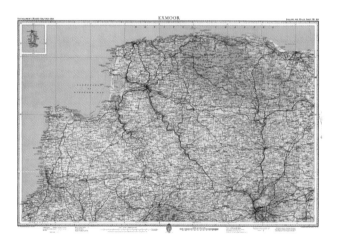

Title	Bartholomew's England & Wales Sheet 35 Exmoor
Mapmaker	J Bartholomew, Edinburgh
Date	1935

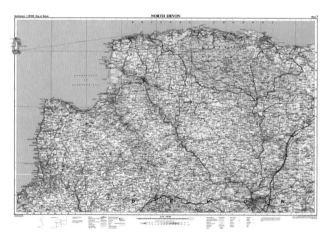

Title	Bartholomew's National Map Series Sheet 3 North Devon
Mapmaker	J Bartholomew, Edinburgh
Date	1985

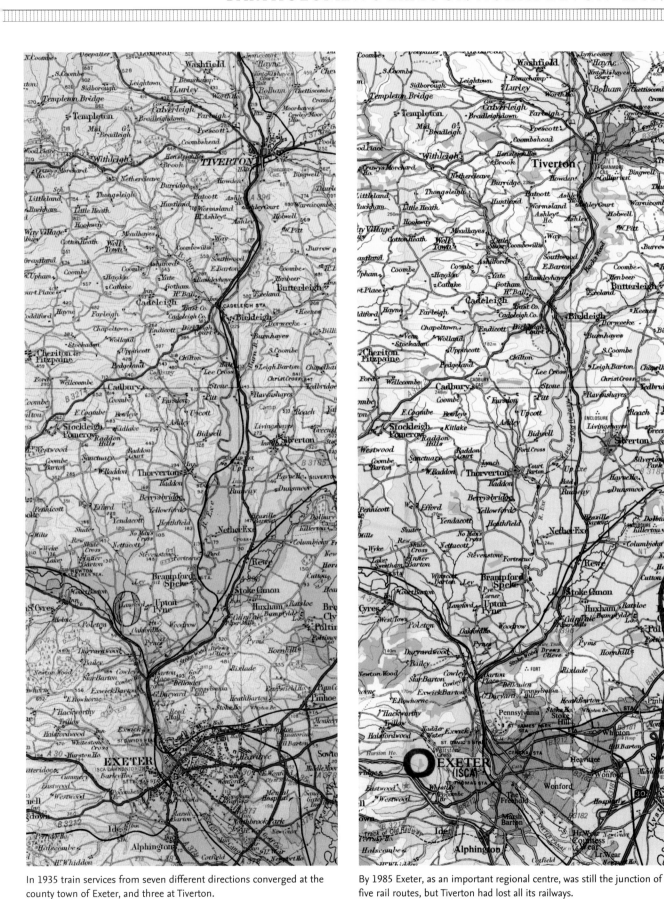

In 1935 train services from seven different directions converged at the county town of Exeter, and three at Tiverton.

By 1985 Exeter, as an important regional centre, was still the junction of five rail routes, but Tiverton had lost all its railways.

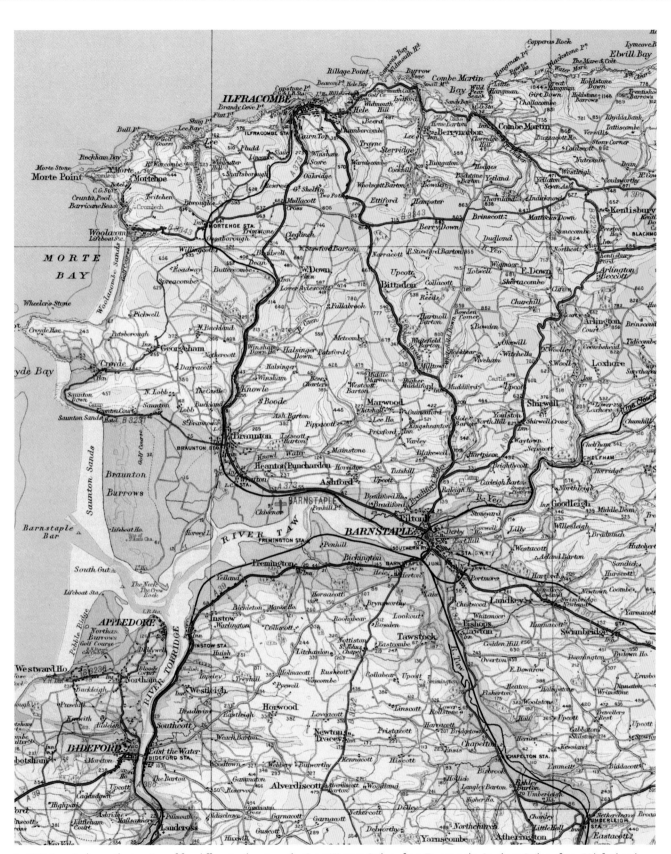

In 1935 Barnstaple was the junction of five different rail routes – the Great Western Railway from Taunton; the Southern Railway from Bideford and beyond, from Exeter and from Ilfracombe, and the formerly independent narrow-gauge line from Lynton.

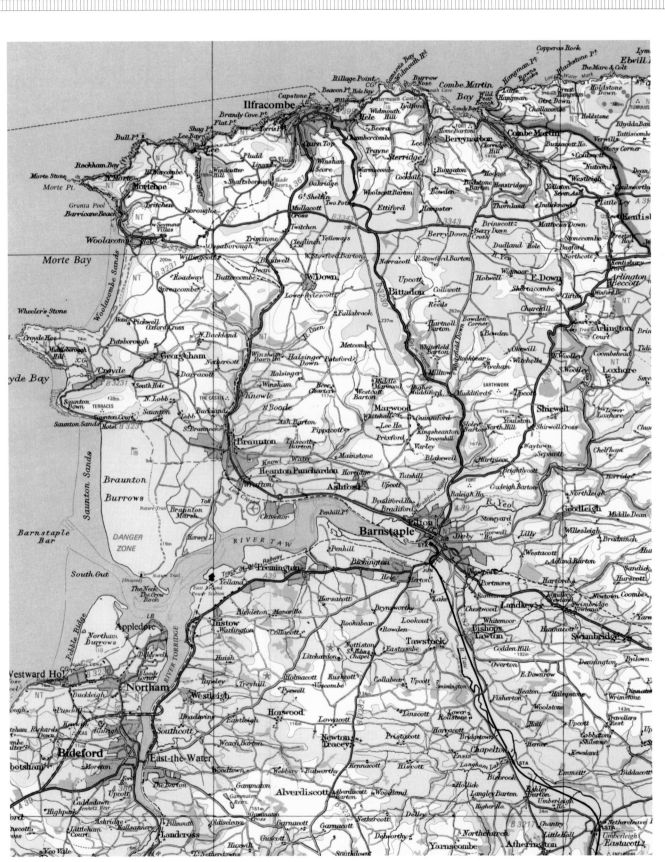

By 1985, the north Devon rail network had shrunk back to a single route, from Barnstaple Junction (by then described as just 'Barnstaple' by British Rail) to Exeter. The map incorrectly shows Barnstaple Town station as still being open, despite having closed 15 years earlier.

Until the opening of the Forth Railway Bridge in 1890, both rail passengers and freight heading north for Perth, Dundee and Aberdeen were forced to break their journey and make the five-mile ferry crossing of the Firth of Forth between Granton, north of Edinburgh, and Burntisland, in Fife. Designed to carry goods wagons on rails, Britain's first train ferry, the 'Leviathan', was introduced on this route by the Edinburgh & Northern Railway in 1850. Another train ferry was introduced across the Firth of Tay a year later. These ferries were meant to be a stop-gap measure but stayed in service for up to 40 years due to delays caused by the Tay Bridge disaster, its subsequent rebuilding and the building of the Forth Bridge.

In the south of England the London, Brighton & South Coast Railway introduced a short-lived train ferry – a converted cargo ship – in the 1880s to carry goods wagons between Langstone Harbour, near Hayling Island, and Bembridge on the Isle of Wight. The ferry service proved unprofitable and ceased running in 1898.

However, as an island nation, Britain depended entirely on sea trade and, by the beginning of the 20th century, the main railway companies all had large vested interests in docks and freight-handling facilities. As we have already seen, carrying goods wagon on rails attached to ships was nothing new, but in 1917 three purpose-built train ferries were introduced to transport war material and munitions to our armies fighting in Belgium and northern France. Running between Richborough Military Port in Kent and Dunkirk the ferries became redundant at the end of the war.

Seeing a golden opportunity for cross-channel rail traffic, the newly formed London & North Eastern Railway and a Belgian company refitted the three ferries and commenced operating a goods-only train ferry service between Harwich

and Zeebrugge in 1924. Cross-Channel freight-carrying train ferry services, albeit with newer purpose-built ships, continued operating until the opening of the Channel Tunnel in 1994.

The first passenger train ferry was introduced between Dover and Dunkirk by the Southern Railway and the French national railways (SNCF) in 1936. Operating as the 'Night Ferry' it carried *wagons-lits* (sleeping cars) and baggage vans specially built for the smaller British loading gauge. The overnight train carried passengers in comfort between London's Victoria station and the Gare du Nord in Paris and, later, also to Brussels. Apart from the Second World War years, the train continued in service until 1980.

Plans to build a tunnel under the English Channel go back to the beginning of the 19th century, but the strained relationships between France and Britain put a stop to all of

This 1953 British Railways poster advertises the overnight 'Night Ferry' sleeping car service between London Victoria and Paris Nord.

Produced for a London & North Eastern Railway poster, Frank Mason's painting shows the Zeebrugge train ferry on its way across the North Sea in the 1930s.

Terence Cuneo's painting of Eurotunnel's 'Le Shuttle' car and lorry carrying train was commissioned for the opening of the Channel Tunnel in 1994. His trademark mice are seen holding the French and British flags in the foreground.

these proposals. Later in the century Sir William Watkin, the enterprising chairman of the Manchester, Sheffield & Lincolnshire Railway, planned a grand continental railway linking northern England to mainland Europe via a Channel Tunnel. Despite exploratory work on both sides of the Channel the tunnel project was abandoned in 1882, although Watkin's Great Central 'London Extension' from the north to Marylebone, which opened in 1899, was still built to the continental loading gauge.

Further proposals for a Channel Tunnel were abandoned after the First World War, and even a 1975 UK–France Government-backed scheme was cancelled (by the British) shortly after tunnelling operations had begun. Finally a privately funded scheme was given the green light at the Treaty of Canterbury in 1986. Responsibility for the scheme was split between British Channel Tunnel Group (two British banks and five construction companies) and the French 'France-Manche (three French banks and five construction companies) and the £2.6 billion raised by private finance was unprecedented for such a project at that time. Tunnelling began in 1988 and was completed, with a cost over-run of 80 per cent, in 1994. The tunnel is used by shuttle trains that carry road vehicles between terminals at Cheriton, near Folkestone, and Coquelles, near Calais; Eurostar services between Paris, Brussels and London; and through international freight services. From 2007 the Eurostar services were rerouted from their previous London terminus of Waterloo International and now travel over the High Speed 1 line to St Pancras International.

A Eurostar passenger train speeds along the new HS1 rail link in Kent. This is the longest new main line to be built in Britain since 1899.

PRIVATIZATION AND BEYOND

The unified railway was split into more than a hundred private companies in an attempt to stimulate competition, improve service and increase efficiency. A number of important new routes opened for passenger and freight business, but the system as a whole now costs the taxpayer far more than when under public ownership.

Although selling off nationalized industries into private ownership had been an important part of Margaret Thatcher's policies during the 1980s the privatization of railways was then considered a step too far. Despite the relatively minor sell-offs of British Transport Hotels, Sealink and the railway engineering works, along with the restructuring of railway operations into business sectors such as Railfreight and InterCity, it took until 1993 (during John Major's term as Prime Minister) and the passing of the Railways Act before the 45-year-old state industry was eventually hived off. As with their opposition to the Beeching rail closures 30 years before, the Labour party was against privatization and pledged to overturn it if they came to power – but in practice did not do so.

Under the controversial Act, British Rail was broken up into over 100 separate companies. The Office of the Rail Regulator was set up to regulate all of the main elements of the industry with the Director of Passenger Rail Franchising responsible for the awarding of franchises to 25 passenger train operators. The track, signalling and stations were taken over by Railtrack who, in turn, let out most of the stations to the newly franchised passenger train operators, and contracted out the maintenance and renewal of the infrastructure. Freight services were sold off to two Freight Operating Companies while three Rolling Stock Leasing Companies (ROSCOs) purchased British Rail's locomotives, multiple units and coaches.

The 25 Train Operating Companies were awarded fixed term leases to run services on specific routes – they owned virtually nothing, hiring both locomotives and rolling stock from the ROSCOs, paying Railtrack for the use of the track and infrastructure and contracting out train maintenance and on-board catering.

Stobart Rail's 'Tesco Express' from Grangemouth to Inverness speeds along the Highland Main Line near Druimuachdar Summit in 2010.

While privatization of Britain's railways officially came into being on 1 April, 1994 the full effects took some years to filter through. There were also further changes on the way – under a new Labour Government the Transport Act 2000 established the Strategic Rail Authority, a non-departmental public body designed to provide strategic direction for the privatized rail industry. Following the passing of the Railways Act 2005 the SRA was wound up in December 2006 with its duties being split between the Government's Department for Transport, Network Rail (the successor to Railtrack) and the Office of Rail Regulation. Some powers were also devolved to the then Scottish Executive, the Welsh Assembly and the Greater London Authority – and the Scottish Government now has almost complete (non-regulatory) control of the internal Scottish rail network, as well as the power to award the ScotRail passenger train franchise.

By far the most controversial element of the original Act, the story of Railtrack was one of the saddest affairs of the rail privatization saga. Following the Ladbroke Grove accident in 1999, where 31 people were killed and 523 injured, the company was severely criticized for its maintenance of the railway infrastructure and its safety record. With the relationship between Railtrack and the Rail Regulator falling apart, the next major accident, at Hatfield in 2000, was the final straw for the company. Repairs and compensation for the accident coupled with out-of-control costs for rebuilding the West Coast Main Line led the company to go cap in hand to the Government. Some of the tax-payer bail-out was then used to pay a £137 million dividend to its shareholders! Not surprisingly Railtrack was declared bankrupt in 2001 and while it was in administration the Government was forced to plough in a further £3.5 billion in order to keep the railways running. The end of this particular story came in October 2002 when the newly formed 'not for profit' government-

The contrasting liveries of two Train Operating Companies – Virgin and Central – are very apparent in this photo taken at Birmingham New Street in 2004.

created company of Network Rail bought the assets of Railtrack. Today Network Rail has a workforce of 35,000 and a revenue from the passenger and freight train operating companies of £6 billion.

There has been a great deal of debate about the overall impact of rail privatization. Supporters argue that customer service has improved, while opponents respond that quality remains patchy across the network. Many more cheap advance fares are now available, but standard fares are amongst the highest in Europe. Passenger traffic has certainly grown substantially, but sceptics attribute this as much to a period of predominantly good economic fortune and to growing road congestion.

Rail freight was fortunate in being privatized in a much simpler way, with no franchises, and has grown significantly. Rail freight revenues have also benefited from a buoyant economy and from the demise of most of Britain's deep coal mines, which were typically close to key power stations –

with the switch to imported coal often resulting in rail movements over hundreds rather than scores of miles.

Reaching an overall verdict on privatization can therefore be difficult, but as Christian Wolmar notes in *Fire and Steam: A New History of the Railways in Britain* (2007):

> *The biggest irony, and indeed failure, of privatization was that far from reducing the cost of the railway to taxpayers, it soared to unprecedented heights. Privatization also brought with it a lack of transparency about the financial affairs of the railways, making comparisons difficult, but a reasonable estimate of the cost to taxpayers since the creation of Network Rail stands at around £5 bn annually.*

As noted in 2011 by Roger Ford, the Industry & Technology Editor of *Modern Railways* magazine, 'By the first decade of the 21st century the privatized railway was costing the taxpayer five times, in real terms, what it cost under BR in 1989/90, and it is still now between four and five times that cost'.

MODERN NETWORK MAPS

Three contrasting styles of modern company network maps are shown here. CrossCountry Trains use a geographic design to show which parts of Britain are served by their trains; East Coast introduces some geographic elements to an essentially diagrammatic design, while Virgin Trains deploy a fully diagrammatic approach, showing which locations are directly linked by their train services. Of these three maps, only Cross Country's shows routes over which the company does not itself operate trains.

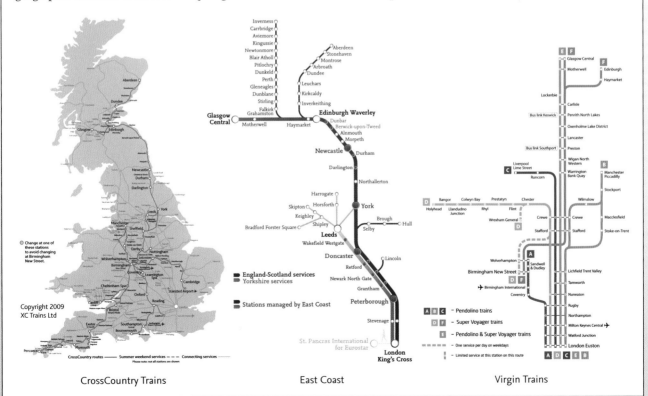

CrossCountry Trains   East Coast   Virgin Trains

As we saw in Milepost 10, the modern docks built in Southampton by the London & South Western Railway (LSWR) were of vital strategic importance during both World Wars. After the Second World War, continental and global shipping services for passengers and freight continued to thrive, but by the time the 1964 map was published transatlantic passenger liners were becoming increasingly unprofitable in the face of air competition – and just four years later the Cunard Line withdrew its year-round service from Southampton to New York.

The 1964 map extract of Southampton Eastern Docks shows freight access lines running to warehouses and transit sheds on every quay, with adjacent access roads evocatively named – Brazil Road, Empress Road and Ocean Road, to name just three. These docks also had their own passenger station – 'Terminus Station', appropriately near the junction of

Terminus Terrace and Platform Road. This was the original Southampton terminus of the LSWR, built in 1839, and later replaced as the main passenger terminus for the city by Southampton Central (named Southampton West until 1935) on the through line to Bournemouth. Many of the RMS *Titanic*'s wealthy First Class passengers stayed in the South Western Hotel next to Southampton Terminus before they boarded the ship for their fateful journey in 1912. The station closed to passengers in 1966, prior to rail electrification between Waterloo, Southampton Central and Bournemouth, but the building and the adjacent hotel (now apartments and a casino) have survived.

The original passenger service to Southampton Terminus was later extended into the Ocean Dock Terminal to allow direct 'boat trains' from London Waterloo to terminate at the quayside. Amongst the most famous of these trains was 'The

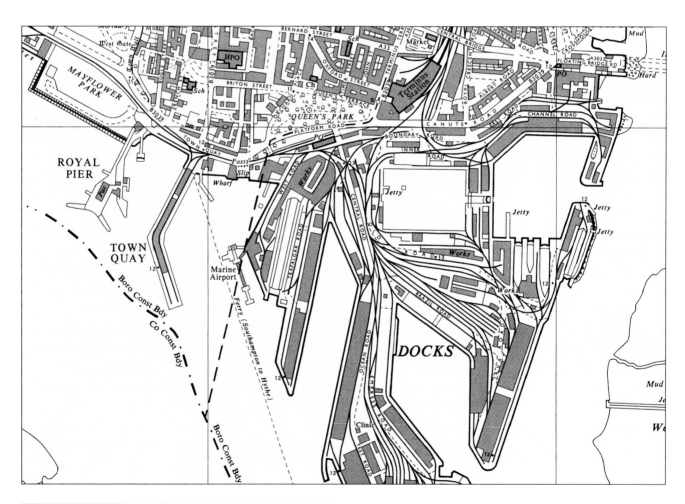

Series	Ordnance Survey 6 in. to 1 mile
Sheet	SU 41 SW (extract)
Date	1964

'Cunarder' connecting with the RMS *Queen Mary* and RMS *Queen Elizabeth* transatlantic services to New York. Traditional boat trains ceased operation when liner services finished, but in recent years there has been a revival of chartered trains running from Edinburgh, Glasgow and north of England cities direct to Southampton Western and Eastern Docks, to connect with cruise liners.

Today, as shown in the 1997 Ordnance Survey 1:50,000 sheet extract, rail sidings penetrate the dock complex primarily for freight traffic – notably Britain's second largest container shipping terminal (after Felixstowe). Rail has played a key role in the container revolution since the 1960s, and Southampton has two Freightliner terminals – 'Maritime' in the container terminal itself, and 'Millbrook' just outside the dock boundary – with train services conveying imports and exports to and from inland terminals in Birmingham,

Cardiff, Coatbridge, Liverpool, Leeds and Manchester. The map illustrates just how few buildings are involved in modern dock handling – large expanses of open ground are the key requirement for container storage and movement, and in a map of this scale even the mammoth travelling ship-to-shore cranes are not shown.

Directly opposite the Port of Southampton is Marchwood Military Port, built in 1943 to support the D-Day assault on Normandy in 1944, and since used during the Falklands War and other military ventures. The port has its own extensive internal rail system connected to Network Rail's freight-only branch line from Totton to the Fawley oil refinery on the south side of Southampton Water.

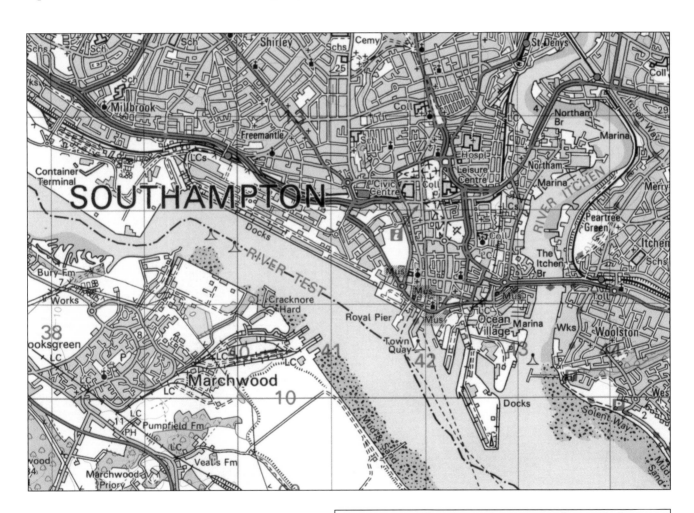

Series	Ordnance Survey 1:50,000 Landranger Series
Sheet	196 (The Solent & Isle of Wight) (extract, enlarged)
Date	1997

Thousands of miles of loss-making railways had already been closed in Britain long before Dr Beeching arrived on the scene. By the outbreak of the Second World War in 1939, over 1,000 route miles had already been closed, not only by the Big Four railway companies but also by many independent companies whose narrow gauge lines had fallen prey to increased competition from road transport.

Following the nationalization of Britain's railways in 1948, the British Transport Commission lost no time in wielding the axe to more loss-making railways. By 1951 the Commission's Branch Line Committee had drawn up a list of a further 3,300 route miles recommended for closure and within 12 years these had been ruthlessly implemented. But worse was to follow.

Enter Conservative Transport Minister, Ernest Marples, and Chairman of British Railways, Dr Richard Beeching. Between them, and also under the following Labour administration, another 4,000 miles of route closures (and 2,000 Beeching-inspired station closures) were implemented, as we saw in Milepost 20. Closures continued until the early 1970s by which time many rural parts of Britain had no rail services at all.

Since then, in what is surely a British phenomenon, the vast network of closed railways across the landscape has seen a new lease of life not only as heritage lines but also as footpaths and cycleways, collectively making a major contribution to the country's tourist industry. To take just one example, the Severn Valley Railway brings in over 200,000 additional visitors to the local economy every year.

While the railway preservation scene took some years to build up steam, the idea of using closed railway lines for recreational purposes goes back to 1937 when the London, Midland & Scottish Railway gave the eight-mile trackbed of the then recently closed Leek & Manifold Valley Light Railway to Staffordshire County Council for use as a footpath and bridleway. Known as the Manifold Way, it is now enjoyed by thousands of visitors each year, contributing much to the local economy. Nearly 50 years later a Bristol-based group of environmentalists, Sustrans, opened its first traffic-free railway path between Bath and Bristol. Today, Sustrans' National Cycle Network extends to 10,000 miles across the length and breadth of Britain; many of their routes incorporate closed railway lines that run through some of the country's most beautiful scenery.

While most of these footpaths and cycleways can be found in the countryside, a few have also found favour with city-dwellers. Notable among these is the Deeside Way on the western outskirts of Aberdeen, the Bristol and Bath Railway Path and the 4½-mile Parkland Walk between Finsbury Park, Highgate and Alexandra Palace in north London. The latter railway was closed in stages between 1954 and 1972 before the trackbed fell into disuse for another 12 years. Reopened as an urban green walkway in 1984, the Parkland Walk is now very popular with weekend strollers, joggers and dog-walkers – unusually, cyclists are banned from using it.

The railway preservation scene had its beginnings in 1951 when a group of enthusiasts led by the writer Tom Rolt saved the narrow gauge Talyllyn Railway in west Wales from closure – the first railway preservation scheme in the world – while in Sussex the Bluebell Railway became the first preserved standard gauge steam-operated passenger railway in the world when it opened in 1960. From these early beginnings over 50 years ago, the preservation movement has grown from strength to strength with currently around 130 heritage railways and museums dotted around Britain. Ranging from major players such as the West Somerset Railway and the North Yorkshire Moors Railway to fledgling projects such as the Aln Valley Railway in Northumberland

A Highgate to Alexandra Palace branch line train disappears away from Cranley Gardens station, shortly before closure in 1954.

The trackbed of the former Alexandra Palace line is now a popular traffic-free route for walkers and joggers in north London.

The narrow gauge Talyllyn Railway in west Wales became the world's first preserved railway when it was saved from closure in 1951.

While eventually scrapping 84 of these locomotives at his Barry scrapyard, he concentrated on the easier task of dismantling enormous numbers of withdrawn wooden freight wagons. This stay of execution for the rusting hulks at Barry gave time for the growing railway preservation movement to start a rescue operation – between September 1968 and October 1987 213 of these locomotives were bought by preservationists for use on the growing number of preserved lines across the country. After years of painstaking restoration, many of these steam locomotives can now be seen at work not only on heritage railways but also on a growing number of main-line charter operations.

and the Eden Valley Railway in Cumbria, they all depend for their survival upon an enormous amount of freely given labour by bands of volunteers.

The railway preservation movement was also greatly assisted by a Welsh scrap merchant, Dai Woodham, who, during the 1960s, bought a total of 297 withdrawn steam locomotives.

The culmination of the steam preservation movement in Britain came in 2008 when the brand-new 'A1' Class 4-6-2 No. 60163 'Tornado' emerged from Darlington Locomotive Works. A culmination of 18 years work at a cost of £3 million, this superb machine has not only put in many fine performances on the main line but also draws enormous crowds wherever it appears. Other new-build locomotives of classes not saved from the scrapheap are currently in the pipeline.

The Bluebell Railway in Sussex became the world's first preserved standard gauge railway to operate a public service when it reopened in 1960.

Series	Ordnance Survey 1:50,000 Landranger Series
Sheet	200 (Newquay & Bodmin) (enlarged)
Date	1997

This 1997 sheet of the Ordnance Survey 1:50,000 series illustrates three very different uses of long established railway routes – a main line; a preserved (or 'heritage') railway; and a cycleway and footpath using the solum (trackbed) of an abandoned rail route.

The first line to be opened (as early as 1834) was the Bodmin & Wadebridge Railway – the route entering the map extract from the west – which extended as far as a terminus (later known as Bodmin North) on the north side of the town centre. Parts of its route can be traced from the pecked line running eastwards from Boscarne Junction, the western terminus of the current railway. This was the first steam-worked railway in Cornwall, and one of the first in Britain to carry passengers.

The London & South Western Railway (LSWR) purchased the Bodmin & Wadebridge Railway in 1846, but it was not until 1895 that this isolated branch connected with the rest of its empire fanning out across southwest England from London's Waterloo station. The LSWR's great rival, the Great Western Railway (GWR) opened a branch line from its Plymouth to Penzance main line (at 'Bodmin Road' station, now called Bodmin Parkway) to Bodmin General station in 1887, and a year later opened a connecting line from Bodmin General to Boscarne Junction (the railway running west from the Bodmin terminus on the current map). In 1923, the LSWR lines became part of the Southern Railway and the rivalry with the GWR continued. Particularly in wartime, the local lines formed part of a diversionary route for main-line

traffic around Plymouth. In 1944, Field Marshal Montgomery and General Eisenhower arrived at Bodmin by train when visiting the nearby Duke of Cornwall's Light Infantry barracks.

Following the Beeching Report, both branch lines lost their passenger services in 1967, replaced by a bus link to Bodmin Road station. China clay traffic continued thereafter via Bodmin and the Boscarne Junction to Wenfordbridge branch line until 1983, when a need to invest in new track forced closure of the line – its former route can be traced on the eastern bank of the River Camel north of Dunmere.

During the 1980s North Cornwall District Council converted the solum of the former Bodmin & Wadebridge Railway into a cycle- and footpath from Padstow, skirting the western outskirts of Bodmin, to Wenfordbridge – and the picturesque 18-mile length of the 'Camel Trail' now attracts 400,000 visitors a year. The volunteer-led Bodmin & Wenford Railway opened between Bodmin Parkway and Bodmin General in 1990, and was extended to Boscarne Junction in 1996.

In the late 1990s it was proposed to re-open the Boscarne Junction to Wenfordbridge section as a freight railway conveying china clay from the Wenford works by train instead of lorry. More recently there has been a proposal to extend the Bodmin & Wenford Railway westwards to Wadebridge, but objections have stopped both schemes, reflecting the high popularity and economic benefits of the Camel Trail – and the fact that railways are not necessarily seen as environmentally friendly in people's own backyards.

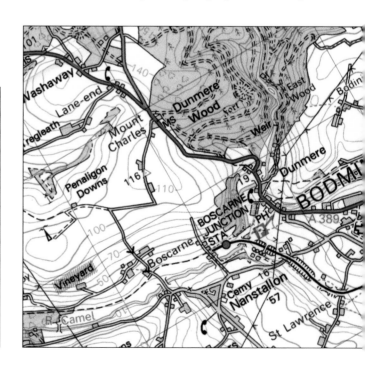

RAILWAYS

────────	Track multiple or single
·+·+·+·+·+·+·	Track narrow gauge
─╫╫╳╫─╫─	Bridges, Footbridge
═▨▨▨═════▨▨▨═	Tunnel
~~▱▱▱~~	Viaduct
──┼──┼──┼──	Freight line, siding or tramway
●──■──○ a b	Station (a) principal (b) closed to passengers
──────╫╫──── LC	Level crossing
▪▪▪▪▪▪▪▪▪▪▪	Embankment
═▨▨▨▨▨▨▨▨═	Cutting

Hauled by preserved Beattie Well Tank No. 30587, a demonstration freight train of vintage china clay wagons heads along the Bodmin & Wenford Railway near Boscarne Junction in Cornwall.

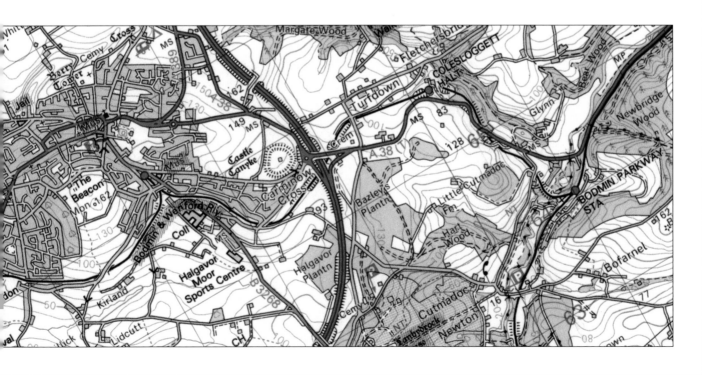

Railway track diagrams have a long history. In *The Railways of Britain: An Unstudied Map Corpus* (2009), the cartographic and railway historians David Challis and Andy Rush record that as the Victorian railway infrastructure became more complicated:

> *Staff needed to know what was where for operational purposes, but they did not require the full topographical layout shown on large, unwieldy regulatory plans, only specific details derived from it. . . . In general terms, operational plans were used for the day-to-day operation of the system and engineering work. Given the linear nature of a railway as well as the nature of the information required, an economical and simple presentation was called for, and increasingly a diagrammatic format was adopted.*

The classic modern inheritor of that tradition has been 'the Quail' – industry shorthand for the *Track Diagrams* – first published in 1998 when career railwayman Gerald Jacobs joined forces with John Yonge of the Quail Map Company as cartographer and publisher, to produce what has now become the standard reference work for infrastructure managers, train planners, transport consultants, railway enthusiasts and modellers alike. In 2004 Mike Bridge at TRACKmaps took over publication of the five volumes covering Britain (based on the old British Rail regions), and subsequently digitized and updated the information.

One of the most dramatic of over 200 pages of diagrams in the Quail series is that showing London's Victoria and Waterloo stations and their approaches. Waterloo, on the south bank of the Thames, is by far the busiest railway station in Britain in terms of passenger throughput, with 86 million passengers a year. It currently has 20 operational terminus platforms – similar to nearby Victoria – the four former Eurostar platforms being out of use since international train services switched to St Pancras in 2007. The station (as well as the track infrastructure) is managed by Network Rail, and all normal train services are operated by South West Trains over an inner and outer suburban network to Berkshire, Hampshire and Surrey, as well as longer distance services to Bournemouth, Exeter, Portsmouth and Southampton.

The rail route approaches to Waterloo are intertwined with the infrastructure of nearby Victoria station, on the north bank of the Thames – the second busiest station in Britain after Waterloo, with 70 million passengers annually. Victoria has 19 platforms, and is managed by Network Rail – with timetabled train services operated by the Gatwick Express, Southern and Southeastern train operating companies to Kent, Surrey and Sussex. The complexity of railway engineering and train operations can be appreciated by studying the large number of 'crossovers' (from one track to another), route junctions, fly-overs and fly-unders in the area bounded by the two termini and the Stewart's Lane traction and rolling stock maintenance depot.

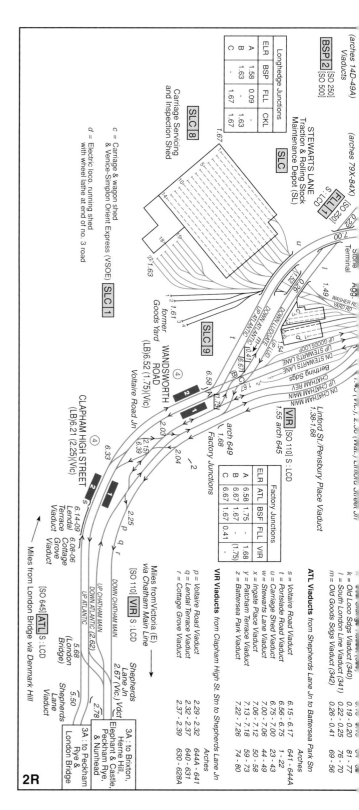

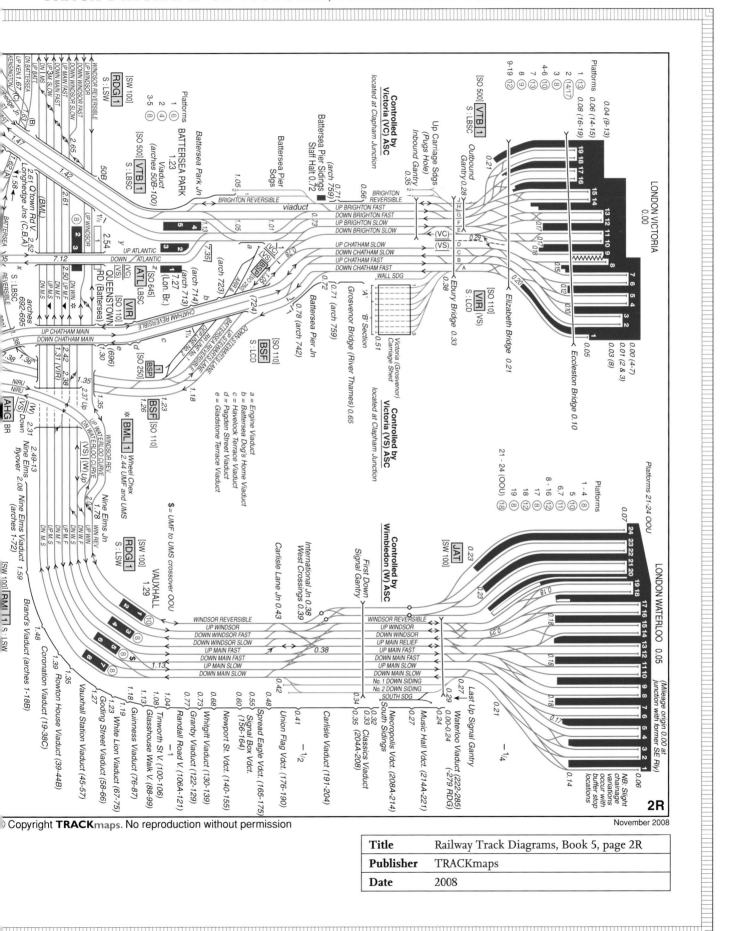

November 2008

Title	Railway Track Diagrams, Book 5, page 2R
Publisher	TRACKmaps
Date	2008

2R

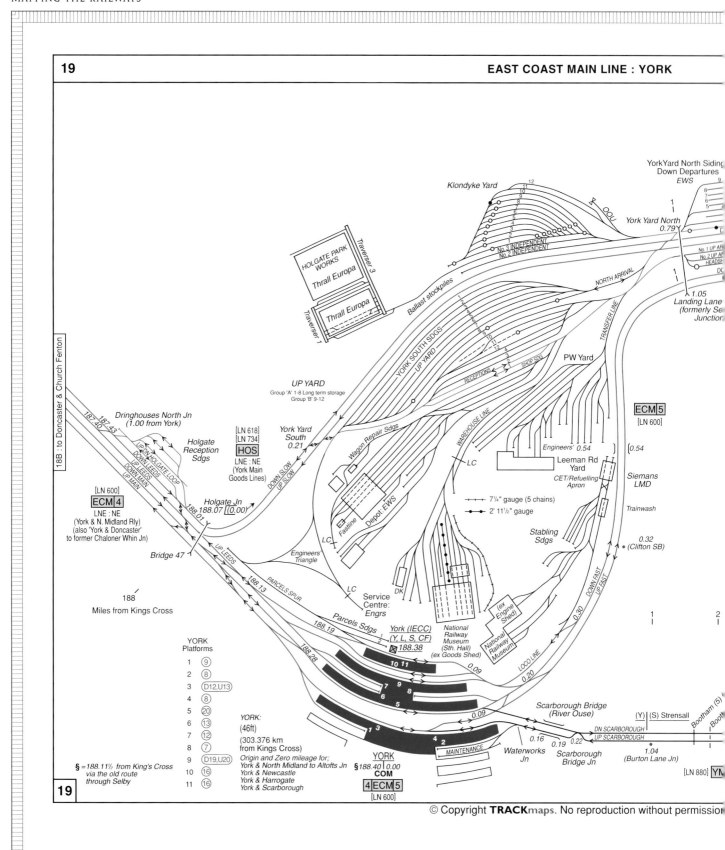

YORK
Platforms

1	⑨
2	⑧
3	D12,U13
4	⑧
5	⑳
6	⑬
7	⑫
8	⑦
9	D19,U20
10	⑯
11	⑯

YORK:
(46ft)
(303.376 km
from Kings Cross)

Origin and Zero mileage for;
York & North Midland to Altofts Jn
York & Newcastle
York & Harrogate
York & Scarborough

§ = 188.11½ from King's Cross
via the old route
through Selby

YORK
COM
§188.40 | 0.00
4 ECM 5
[LN 600]

188
Miles from Kings Cross

Title	Railway Track Diagrams, Book 2, page 19
Publisher	TRACKmaps
Date	2006

The track diagram of York illustrates a very different kind of layout at this important through station on the East Coast Main Line. York has been a major railway centre since Victorian times, and is still a key junction for routes to Edinburgh, Harrogate, Leeds, London and Scarborough. The station is operated by East Coast on behalf of Network Rail and provides a wide range of regional and longer distance services operated by no less than six different train operating companies. Adjacent to the station is the rail-connected National Railway Museum, while the wider railway complex includes freight sidings, engineers' yards and maintenance depots. An unusual feature is the 'Engineers' Triangle' near the station, where track maintenance machines – and steam locomotives – can be turned.

The tracks shown in red are those which have overhead electrified wires – provided as part of the East Coast Main Line electrification completed in 1991 – while only diesel services can operate over the non-electrified lines shown in black. York's signalling centre – shown in green adjacent to Platform 11 – controls all train operations not just in York but also as far away as Northallerton, the fringes of Doncaster and the Leeds area. The track layout at York is still relatively complex, but is much simplified from what it used to be, following a rationalization and resignalling scheme in the late 1980s – one example being the restricted access to the Scarborough line east of the station. In contrast, the infrastructure around Victoria and Waterloo reflects fewer changes in travel and train service patterns over the years.

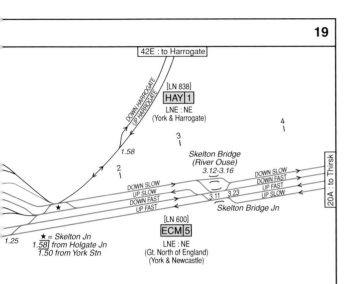

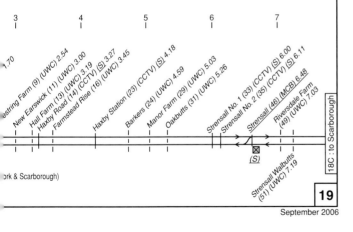

September 2006

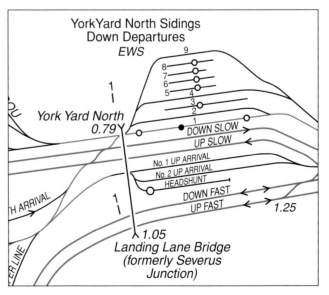

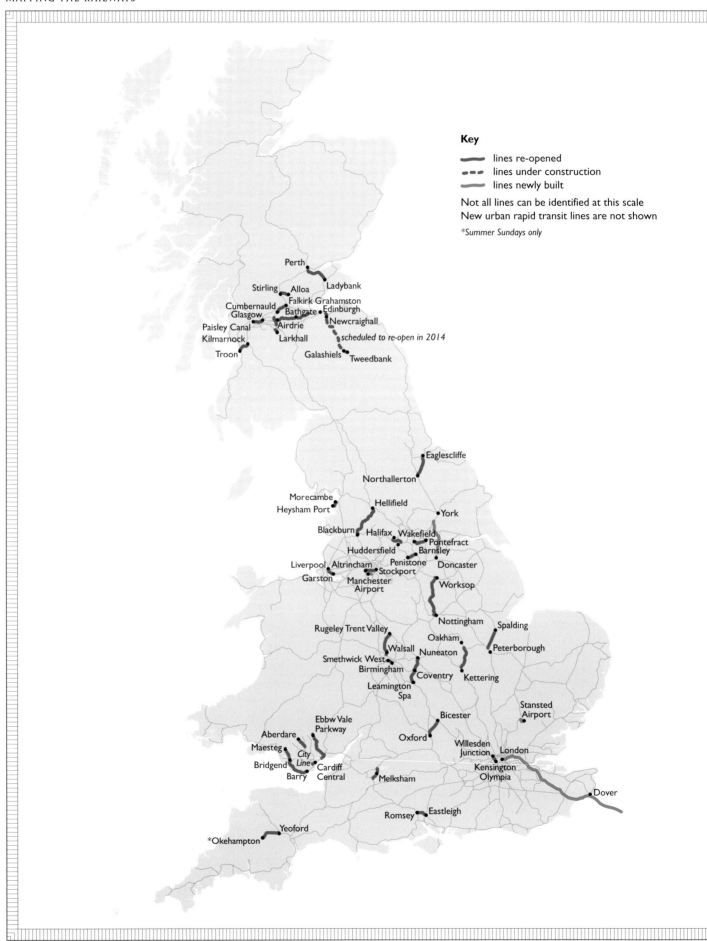

Key

lines re-opened
lines under construction
lines newly built

Not all lines can be identified at this scale
New urban rapid transit lines are not shown

Summer Sundays only

Perth

Stirling Alloa Ladybank
Falkirk Grahamston
Cumbernauld Bathgate Edinburgh
Glasgow Newcraighall
Paisley Canal Airdrie
Kilmarnock Larkhall *scheduled to re-open in 2014*
Troon Galashiels Tweedbank

Eaglescliffe

Northallerton

Morecambe Hellifield
Heysham Port York

Blackburn Halifax Wakefield
Huddersfield Pontefract
Barnsley
Liverpool Altrincham Penistone Doncaster
Garston Stockport
Manchester Worksop
Airport

Nottingham Spalding

Rugeley Trent Valley Oakham Peterborough
Walsall Nuneaton
Smethwick West Kettering
Birmingham Coventry
Leamington
Spa Stansted
Airport
Bicester
Ebbw Vale Oxford
Parkway Willesden
Aberdare Junction London
Maesteg *City* Kensington
Bridgend *Line* Cardiff Olympia
Barry Central Melksham
Dover
Romsey Eastleigh

*Okehampton Yeoford

Title	Rail route re-openings since 1969
By	Collins Bartholomew (using data published by Railfuture in 2010)
Date	2011

After the retrenchment of the Beeching Era, it was some time before the concept of re-opening stations or building new stations became a priority for the railways. However, by the late 1970s, concerns about the environment, road congestion, and changing patterns of urban development were such that a growing number of new names began to appear on the rail network map. This has been a gradual and uncoordinated process, but with a very significant cumulative impact – over 350 new stations and more than 500 miles of new passenger routes opened since 1960 – *Britain's Growing Railway* by Railfuture (2010) noting that:

> There has been no central government or rail industry plan to achieve this but progress has come usually as a result of local or regional initiatives by rail managers, local authorities and rail campaigners.

One of the first routes to re-open came in response to the suggestion of a campaigning group, when passenger services were reinstated over the freight line between Perth and Ladybank (15 miles) in 1975 – this followed the closure of the direct line from Perth to Edinburgh via Kinross in 1970 and the consequent lengthy detour via Stirling.

Most station re-openings have been intermediate stops on lines which still had a passenger service – so, typically, no new track or no new trains would be required, just the station itself – but by the late 1980s a growing number of

routes which were freight-only, or had been completely abandoned, were being brought back into passenger service.

The peak year for route re-openings was 1987 (seven routes) and 1988 for station re-openings (26 locations) – both under devolved British Rail management – but after a hiatus caused by rail privatization it has increasingly been longer routes which have returned to the passenger network, including Barry to Bridgend (19 miles) and Cardiff to Ebbw Vale Parkway (18 miles of re-opened route), both in South Wales. As noted in *Britain's Growing Railway*, analysis of the re-opened station locations shows:

> that since 2000, most of the new or reopened stations are either in Scotland or South Wales, where the new national governments have taken a much more determined, pro-active and independent transport role.

The greatest concentration of re-opened lines has been in Central Scotland, where no less than 15 sections of route have seen the re-introduction of passenger services, latterly funded by the Scottish Government, under which three completely abandoned railways have been re-opened to passenger traffic – Hamilton to Larkhall, Stirling to Alloa and Drumgelloch (Airdrie) to Bathgate.

As well as re-openings, some very significant stretches of entirely new passenger railway have been built in modern times – notably the 12-mile 'Selby diversion' of the East Coast Main Line in 1983 (to avoid future mining subsidence); links to Heathrow, Stansted and Manchester airports; and the 102 miles of the Channel Tunnel and associated 'HS1' rail route from Folkestone to London St Pancras, finally completed in 2007.

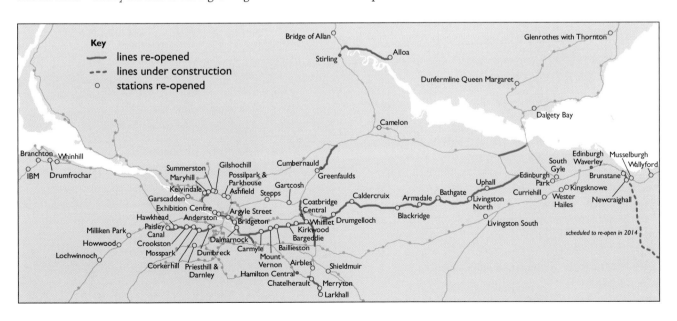

Rail companies have produced or commissioned maps of their networks since the earliest days of the railway. Once the entire British network came into public ownership in 1948, British Railways developed an initial style which lasted until 1967, as illustrated on pages 214–217. In its fresh identity as British Rail a new design was created, as shown on pages 252–255, and elements of this have survived to the present day. Railtrack took over responsibility for the entire infrastructure (the track, as opposed to the trains) from British Rail, and after Railtrack went into administration, control was vested with Network Rail – officially a private-sector organization, but with its debts underwritten by the UK Government, and partial funding of its investment programme by the UK Government, Scottish Government and Welsh Assembly Government.

In its capacity as guardian of the network, Network Rail publishes a geographic network map to illustrate the on-line national timetable which it produces twice a year. Its web site also presents a diagrammatic network map by 'National Rail' – which is not a company, but effectively a brand promoted by the Association of Train Operating Companies (ATOC) – and a 'National Rail Network Diagram', which is an amalgam of both styles, produced by an independent company called Project Mapping. All three are shown in this feature.

Network Rail's map opposite has the merit of showing the recognizable shape of Britain's land mass, together with an essentially geographic representation of every railway line (with adjacent table number) – and every station is named, except in the conurbations where detailed insert maps are shown separately to a different scale. Selected bus and ferry links are also shown, the former including some routes which were 1960s' replacements for rail closures – such as those through the Scottish Borders, between Oxford and Cambridge, and in north Cornwall. The map is a recognizable descendant of the 1968 British Rail map on page 252, with twin categorization of stations – in this case 'principal places' and 'other places' – and use of a similar upper case font for the names of principal places. However, while accommodating a large amount of detail for a national map, the 'hierarchy' of information is not well developed – all lines are of an equal width. The principle of showing every station results in one's eye being drawn to the corridors with greater density of marking, such as rural routes with very frequent stops – as along the Cambrian Coast and the Cumbrian Coast – rather than other rural routes with fewer intermediate stations, like that from Ayr to Stranraer.

The ATOC map overleaf is unashamedly diagrammatic and, interestingly, follows the 'Beck rules' dating back to his 1933 London Underground map – only horizontal, vertical or 45 degree angle lines being used. To provide a clear overview of the main national network, two categories of route are presented – identified by distinctly different line widths – but inevitably the map's simplification prevents every station being shown, even in rural areas. Britain's familiar coastline is understandably omitted, as it would have an uneasy fit with a diagrammatic map, and distances are in some cases very distorted to accommodate to the simplified design – for example, the 60-mile Carlisle–Newcastle line appears to be four times the length of the 59-mile Ayr–Stranraer line. All names (except London) are tilted, when it might have been visually easier to re-orientate the whole map and have horizontal station names.

The Project Mapping design overleaf seeks a compromise between the geographic and diagrammatic approaches, its designer Andrew Smithers endeavouring, 'to show the individuality and personality of the network being depicted, rather than force it to follow traditional abstract rules'. The coastline is shown – albeit in very abstract form in places – and there is a useful hierarchy of visual distinction between four types of route: principal, regional, local and 'limited service'.

In some parts of the country – such as Devon and Cornwall – using only straight lines allows clarity of presentation within a recognizable regional geography. However, in other areas, such as the Cumbrian Coast and northeast Scotland, gently curving lines are introduced, Smithers commenting that this, 'has become an important aspect of the map's design, with softer curves leading to a more pleasing appearance'. Of course, beauty is in the eye of the beholder, railway author and mapmaker Alan Young arguing that the juxtaposition 'creates an unsettling tension between straight lines and self-conscious curves that don't really reflect the true shape of the network'. A large variety of angles are used in the Project Mapping design, with no Beck-type rules to simplify the visual impact, and some distances are severely distorted – with the five-mile Edinburgh–Newcraighall line shown as of equal length to the 59-mile Ayr–Stranraer line. Certain parts of the rail network seem fated to be minimized in importance in modern mapping, irrespective of the technique used.

Map design is of course a matter of personal taste, as well as utility, and it is difficult to achieve comprehensive coverage and ease of understanding in a single design. However, it can be argued that while the novel Project Mapping approach may show the network more clearly than its two contemporaries, the classic 1968 British Rail design succeeded in achieving a pleasing clarity and appropriate hierarchy of information without losing familiar geography – in a way which its modern counterparts have not emulated.

National Rail Timetable Map 2011

National Rail
Britain's train companies working together

Title	National Rail Timetable Map 2011
Publisher	Network Rail
Date	2011

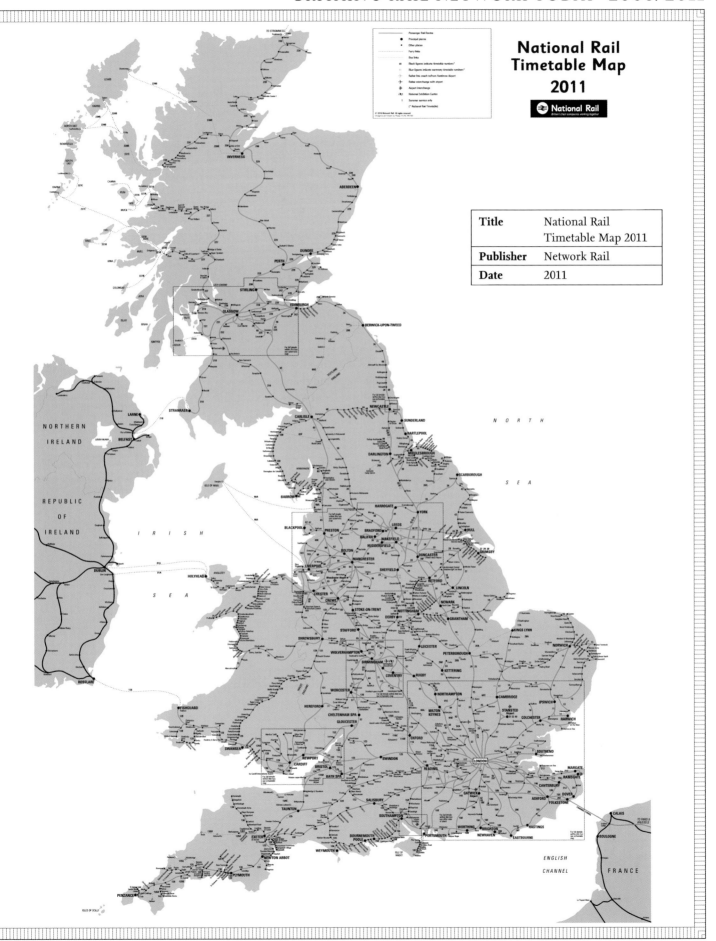

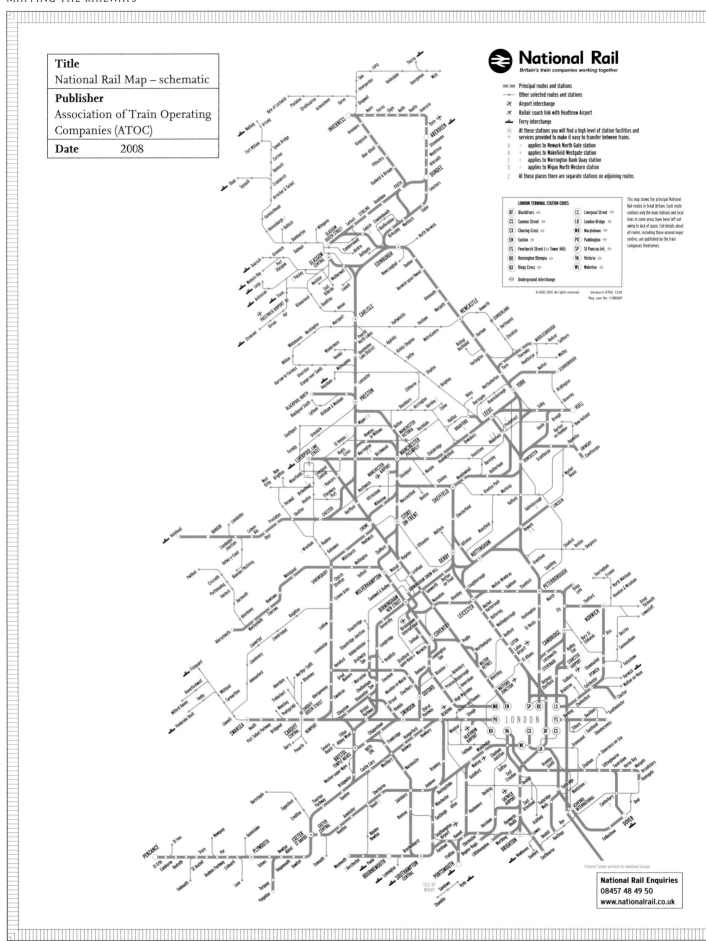

Title	National Rail Network Diagram
Publisher	Project Mapping
Date	2011

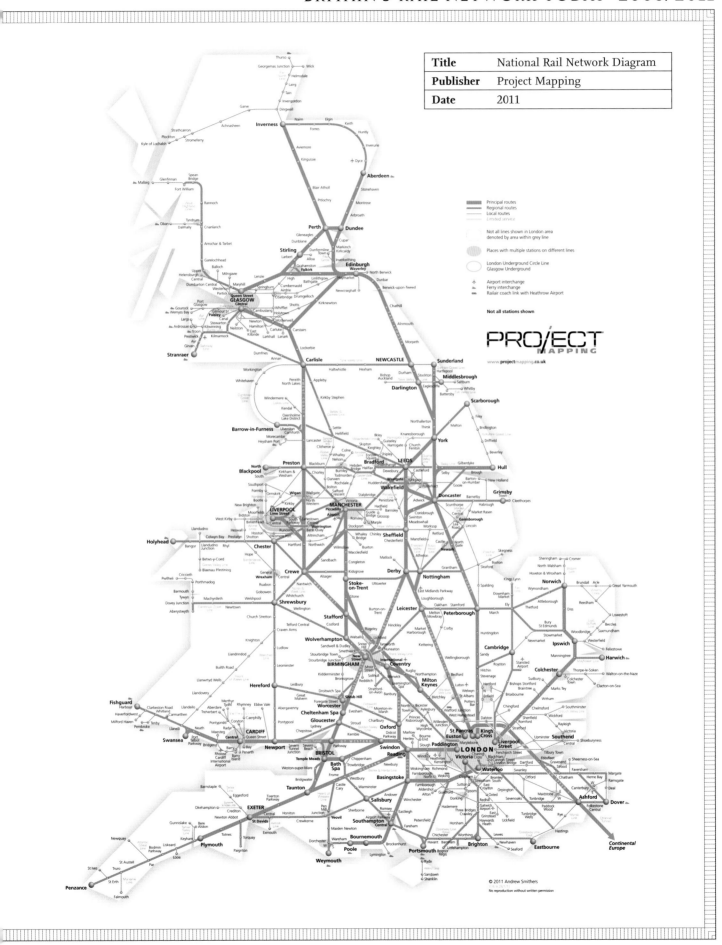

Title	A high-speed rail strategy for Britain
Publisher	Greengauge21
Date	2010

Encouraged by the success of new high speed railways in mainland Europe and the completion of the Channel Tunnel Rail Link (now known as HS1) in 2007, the case for building additional high-speed lines in Britain has gathered pace in

recent years. In early 2012, the UK Government confirmed its 'in principle' support for a new ('HS2') route from London to Birmingham, potentially extended to the north of England and central Scotland, while the lobby group Greengauge21 – which published the map on this page – argues the case for a comprehensive British network on the grounds that, 'high-speed rail is an essential part of our national infrastructure and will be needed to accommodate the growth that will come with economic recovery'.

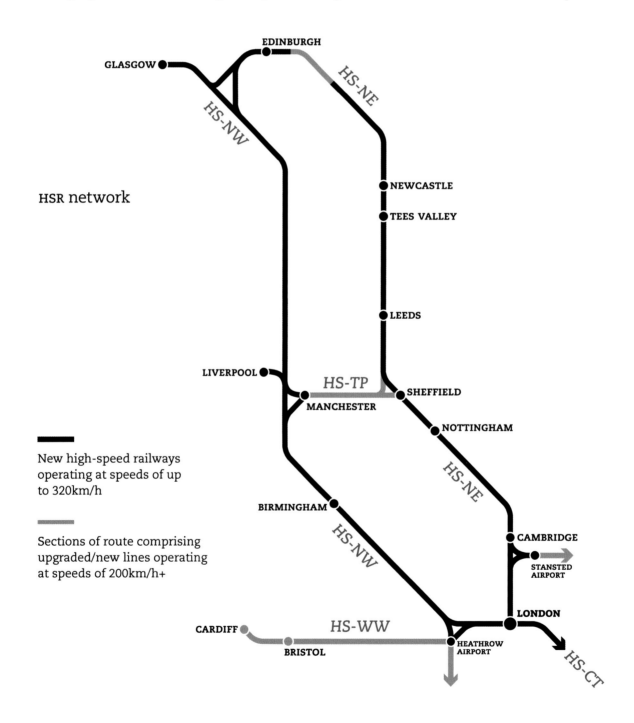

A classic view of Chilterns countryside in the Misbourne Valley between Great Missenden and Wendover – if the HS2 high speed rail route from London to Birmingham is built, it will pass through the middle of this scene.

Not surprisingly, the prospect of noise and visual intrusion from a new 250 m.p.h. railway – with up to 14 trains an hour in each direction – has not been well received along the planned corridor between London and Birmingham. Objectors along the route, which would cut through some beautiful countryside and many affluent communities, have formed an opposition group, StopHS2, whose stance is that:

> We oppose the HS2 High Speed Rail link, because the business case is based on unrealistic assumptions, the environmental impact has not been assessed, it is not green, the strategic benefits are questionable, and the money could be better spent on other things.

Supporters of the new line, including the Department for Transport, argue that the impact on the landscape and the local environment would be minimized, for example, by following 'existing rail or road transport corridors, using deep cuttings and tunnels, and avoiding sensitive sites wherever possible'. Wider environmental benefits are claimed by Greengauge21 which has stated that, 'high speed rail is the most sustainable of transport investments', with a projected saving of a million tonnes of carbon annually by 2055. Sceptics point out that Network Rail's 2009 report on an Anglo-Scottish High Speed Railway (HSR) forecast that just 6 per cent of HSR passengers would switch from air transport and 9 per cent from cars, with the vast majority generating additional carbon – the 53 per cent switching from more energy-efficient conventional rail services, and the 32 per cent who would be making entirely new trips.

Arguments for HSR do not, however, rest just on speed –

the case is also based on a big release of capacity on existing main lines that, in turn, would allow an expansion of commuter services and freight on rail. Critics have responded that more can be done to accommodate extra traffic on the current network – for example by lengthening existing trains, and reducing the number of intermediate calls on long-distance trains – while an alternative proposal has been for a freight-prioritized rail route from the Channel Tunnel to Scotland, predominantly using existing rail lines and closed track beds, with just four miles of entirely new construction.

HSR would be expensive – Greengauge21 has estimated a full network cost of £69 billion – and critics have argued that it would choke off quicker investment in the existing network, such as more electrification and new trains. In contrast, HSR would involve a long lead time, and its justification depends on difficult assumptions about the state of our economy and environment 40 and more years ahead.

It has also been pointed out that the successful high-speed rail corridors at the heart of mainland Europe have typically involved new sections which secured very dramatic improvements in journey times through by-passing relatively slow conventional routes along river valleys like the Rhine or across significant mountain regions. The geography of Britain's trunk rail routes is very different, and we do not have the same pattern of heavily populated metropolitan regions separated by very long HSR-suited distances. Ultimately, in an age of financial austerity, a national High Speed Rail network – whatever its merits and demerits – may prove to be an idea that came just too late to Britain.

In 1819, in the very first map of this journey through the history and geography of Britain's railways, the engineer Robert Stevenson was uncertain whether he would be building a canal or railway. Our exploration has illustrated how quickly and overwhelmingly railways became *the* dominant mode of transport across the country, remaining so until well after the middle of the 20th century. We have also seen how the railways recovered from the massive retrenchment of the 1960s – caused by car, bus and lorry competition – to carve out a continuing and expanding role in Britain's transport system. New routes and stations have opened in almost every part of the country, and more are due to arrive – including the return of train services to the Scottish Borders in 2014, after an absence of 45 years, and London's new Crossrail route in 2018.

Not only has the density and pattern of the rail network across Britain changed enormously over nearly two centuries, so too have styles of mapping. Where double-pecked lines were good enough to show waggonways in the county maps of 1820, during much of the 20th century the Ordnance Survey used no less than four line symbols to distinguish different types of rail route. As a whole, railways are now a far less dominant part of the transport system, but their character and role have also changed, and new map symbols have been designed to reflect this. Yet, while the technology and techniques for mapping railways have been transformed, there are some reassuring constancies – the black lines and red circles denoting rail routes and stations respectively in *Reid's Railway Rides* of 1847 are still to be seen in the latest Ordnance Survey Landranger maps.

All the best explorations lead to new understanding and appreciation of the country travelled. While hopefully every reader will have learnt something new about railways and maps, each is likely to have taken something different from the history, the geography and the cartography. For the authors, a particular fascination has been the research and analysis which underpins the specially commissioned maps of Beeching reprieves, post-Beeching closures, and railway re-openings since 1969 – seeing these patterns on maps for the first time raises new questions about the politics and economics of railways. Other maps from the most modern era illustrate how local circumstances can change the conventional view of railways as 'environmentally friendly' to an altogether less benign perspective – a standpoint which, as we have seen, can be traced back to the late Victorian era in London.

As we have noted earlier, maps are not just a matter of utility – they also have the capacity to please and delight. The age, background, education and motivation of the reader will to some extent determine his or her view as to whether they are looking at a 'good map' or a 'bad map', irrespective of its theoretical technical merit. Our selection has allowed a very wide variety of maps to be showcased, and different readers will have different views of the most attractive, the most unusual and the most useful.

A recurrent theme of this book has been change, and today we live in an era of constant adjustment to new technology and new fashions stimulated by a highly competitive market place. This produces both opportunities and threats for the

The distinctive 'Double Arrow' platform brickwork logo of the re-opened Robin Hood Line is in evidence at Bulwell train/tram interchange in Nottinghamshire, as an NET tram pulls away.

Right: Nottingham area extract from the 'Baker atlas' – see page 265.

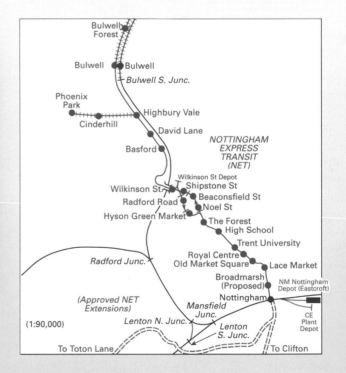

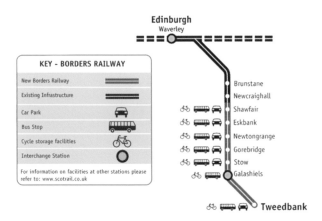

A map of the new Borders Railway by Transport Scotland, the Scottish Government agency which is delivering the project in partnership with local authorities and the rail industry.

Advance engineering works on the new Borders Railway in 2011 – the first stretch of track approaches the main line connection at Millerhill, southeast of Edinburgh.

mapping of railways. So, for example, interactive maps on mobile phones may effectively change what some of us understand by the term 'map', while fast-changing design trends (and the lack of a unified national system of rail services) mean that we are never again likely to see a consistent method of representing railways on publicity maps in the way that British Rail achieved from the 1950s to the 1990s.

Mapping the Railways has inevitably displayed only a very small sample from nearly 200 years of mapping railways in Britain. Beyond this material, which is largely in the public domain, a large corpus of unsung and unstudied private maps of the railways has survived, but as the cartographic

and railway historians Challis and Rush have noted, these:

> *were produced by the railway companies for internal or business use and were regarded as private documents from the outset. The vast majority of these remain the preserve of the companies' modern institutional successors. Unsurprisingly these private maps tend to be less, if at all, available.*

It is hoped that this introduction to the story of railways and mapping will stimulate further interest in a neglected aspect of our history and geography, and will encourage the rail industry to make more of its map legacy available to the public for exploration, analysis – and sheer enjoyment.

INDEX

ACKNOWLEDGEMENTS

t = top; b = bottom; r = right; l = left; m = middle

Maps and additional material courtesy of:
Ian Allan Publishing Ltd: 250–251, 264–265, 298br
ATOC: 276–277, 294
BRB (Residuary) Ltd: 228–231, 236–244, 246, 247, 249, 252–255, 260, 261,
    266–269
© Collins Bartholomew: 248, 290–291
Andrew Dow: 194–195
East Coast Main Line Company Ltd: 279bm
Freightliner Ltd: 245
© Greengauge 21: 296
Julian Holland collection: 80t, 150t, 166, 202–203, 214–217
Bill Jamieson collection: 252–255
Alan Jowett: 152–153, 160–161, 168–169, 188–189, 200–201
Mapseeker: 4–5, 10–11, 23t, 36–39, 56–59, 64–65, 72–79, 82–85, 110–113,
    118–119, 130–131, 136–143, 174–175, 184, 185tr, 186–187, front cover,
    back cover
Bruce McCartney collection: 185b
National Library of Scotland: endpapers, 9br, 14–19, 22, 23b, 24–25, 28–33,
    40–41, 44–55, 60–63, 68–71, 86–99, 102–109, 120–123, 128–129, 134–135,
    144–145, 154–157, 164–165, 170–173, 178, 180–181, 206, 207tl, 207b,
    208–209, 218–221, 226–227, 256–257, 262, 270–273, 280–281, 284–285
National Railway Museum / Science & Society Picture Library: 210–211
Network Rail: 293
Ordnance Survey ® map data licensed with the permission of the Controller
    of Her Majesty's Stationery Office. © Crown copyright. Licence number
    100018598: 227, 262–263, 280–281, 284–285
Andrew Smithers: 295
David Spaven collection: 114–117, 224–225, 228–231, 236–244, 246–247, 249br,
    260–261, 266–269
© TfL from the London Transport Museum collection: 196t, 197bl
TRACKmaps, reproduced by kind permission: 286–289
Transport for London: 198–199
Transport Scotland, © Crown copyright: 299tl
Virgin Trains: 279br
XC Trains Ltd: 279bl
Alan Young: 179b

Photo credits:
Ben Ashworth: 233tl
Henry Casserley: 162/163b, 167b, 212b, 282bl
Colour-Rail: 179tl, 192ml, 258b, 259tr, 278bl, 299b
Paul Francis: 297t
John Goss: 283b, 285t
Julian Holland: 163tr, 190ml, 190bl, 190br, 191tr, 192br, 193tr, 212tr, 213b,
    222tr, 232tr, 278tr, 282br, 283tl
M C Kemp: 204
Bruce McCartney: 235t, 235b
Gavin Morrison: 6/7b
National Railway Museum / Science & Society Picture Library: 12b, 13tl, 13b,
    20tl, 20b, 21bl, 26t, 27tr, 27b, 34b, 35tr, 35bl, 42tl, 42b, 43bl, 66/67b, 67t,
    80bl, 81b, 100t, 101tr, 101b, 124t, 125tr, 125b, 132t, 133t, 133br, 151t, 158t,
    159b, 176t, 177t, 177b, 182tr, 182b, 183b, 191b, 192tl, 193b, 205tr, 205b,
    223b, 232tl, 234bl, 259bl, 259br, 274bl, 274br, 275t
© railphotolibrary.com: 8/9t, 151br, 192bl, 275br, 298bl
Bill Roberton: 299tr
Gordon Sharp: 146, 147tr, 147mr, 147br, 148tl, 148ml, 148bl, 148–149
David Spaven: 119br
Frank Spaven: 207mr
Alan Young: 179tr

Cover image:
Now a listed structure and nominated as a UNESCO World Heritage Site,
the iconic Forth Railway Bridge across the Firth of Forth near Edinburgh
was opened in 1890 and has the second-longest single cantilever bridge span
in the world. © Anna Kucherova/Shutterstock.com.

With thanks for research assistance/advice to:
Andrew Dow, Chris Fleet, Roger Ford, Michael Jowett, Neil MacDonald,
Allan McLean, David Prescott, Doug Rose, Gordon Sharp, John Yellowlees,
Alan Young.

With special thanks to Bill Jamieson for historical and mapping research.

BIBLIOGRAPHY

Alycidon Rail http://www.alycidon.com – the official website of Roger Ford's *Informed Sources*
Beeching: Champion of the Railway? RHN Hardy, Ian Allan Ltd 1989
Britain's Growing Railway, Railfuture (the Railway Development Society Ltd) 2010
British Rail Design, James Cousins, Danish Design Council 1986
British Rail 1948-83: A Journey by Design, Brian Haresnape, Ian Allan Ltd 1983
English Maps: A History, Catherine Delano-Smith and Roger JP Kain, The British Library 1999
Fire & Steam: A New History of the Railways in Britain, Christian Wolmar, Atlantic Books 2007
Henry Beck invented what? http://www.dougrose.co.uk/index_henry_beck.htm
I Tried to Run a Railway, GF Fiennes, Ian Allan Ltd 1967
Maps and Plans for the Local Historian and Collector, David Smith, Batsford Books 1988
Maps for Local History, Brian Hindle, Batsford Books 1988
Mr Beck's Underground Map, Ken Garland, Capital Press 1994
New ideas in the interpretation of complex rail networks, Andrew Smithers in 'The Bulletin of the Society of Cartographers', Vol 43, Issues 1&2, SoC 2009
The Oxford Companion to British Railway History, edited by Jack Simmons & Gordon Biddle, Oxford University Press 1999
The Railways of Britain: An Unstudied Map Corpus, David Millbank Challis and Andy Rush, in 'Imago Mundi' (the international journal for the history of cartography)
    Vol. 61, Part 2, Informa Ltd 2009
Telling the Passenger Where to Get Off: George Dow and the Development of the Diagrammatic Railway Map, Andrew Dow, Fastline Books 2005.